MINNESOTA NORTH STARS

HISTORY AND MEMORIES WITH LOU NANNE

BOB SHOWERS

Beaver's Pond Press

From Al Shaver's Foreword on pages 1, 2 & 3:
"You Keep Coming Back To Me Like A Song" by Irving Berlin
© Copyright 1943 by Irving Berlin
© Copyright Renewed
International Copyright Secured   All Rights Reserved   Reprinted by Permission

ISBN 13: 978-1-59298-197-7
ISBN 10: 1-59298-197-6

Library of Congress Catalog Number: 2007934396

Book design and typesetting: Rick Korab, Punch Design, Inc.
Printed in Canada

First Printing: September 2007

11   10   09   08   07 5   4   3   2   1

Beaver's Pond Press

7104 Ohms Lane, Suite 216
Edina, Minnesota 55439 USA
(952) 829-8818
www.BeaversPondPress.com

To order, visit www.BookHouseFulfillment.com or call
1-800-901-3480. Reseller and special sales discounts available

TABLE OF CONTENTS

DEDICATIONS

LOU NANNE

I want to dedicate this book to my wife Francine and our children Michelle, Michael, Marc and Marty, and their spouses, Tino, Sheila, Lisa and Patti, for their love, support and sacrifice through all the years that I spent playing, working and traveling with hockey.

To George and Gordon Gund, Walter Bush Jr., the late Gordon Ritz and Bob McNulty, John Driscoll, Wheelock Whitney, Harry McNeely Jr., Bill Rasmussen, John Ordway Jr. and Robert Ridder, the owners who gave me the opportunity to be a part of the North Stars.

To all my former teammates, players, coaches, scouts, staff and people in the North Stars organization who were part of my professional life.

To my fellow general managers. We all wanted to win on the ice, but we had a camaraderie that made a tough job enjoyable and a genuine concern for one another's success and well-being.

To those in the National Hockey League, USA Hockey, Hockey Canada, and the IIHF with whom I interacted over the years.

To Bob Naegele, Jac Sperling and Doug Risebrough for bringing the NHL back where it belongs.
No one in this area ever did a better marketing job with a sports team.

To the fans of hockey in the state of Minnesota for their undying support of the game at all levels. They are the reason that this is the State of Hockey.

BOB SHOWERS

This book is dedicated to my wife Donna and our daughters, Jenny and Audrey.

To all of the former North Star players who made the Met Center such a special place.

Finally, to Minnesota North Star fans who will always love and miss their team.

Acknowledgements

This book was completed with the help of many individuals.

First and foremost, I am grateful to the Dallas Stars organization for their approval of this project. Team President Jim Lites and P.R. Director Rob Schicili were extremely cooperative in allowing me access to the North Stars archives that were moved to Texas. Special thanks go to Stars' P.R. executive Jason Rademan for his ongoing assistance and support.

Thanks go to the contributing photographers for their fine work and generosity:

- Billy Robin McFarland, professional photographer from South St. Paul, photographed the North Stars in the late '80s and early '90s. His work appeared in North Stars media guides, game programs and marketing materials. He specializes in sports and commercial photography. (www.billyrobin.com)
- Rick Kolodziej, professional photographer from Minneapolis, photographed the North Stars in the '80s. His work appeared in North Stars media guides, game programs and marketing materials. He specializes in sports photography. (rickk@visi.com)
- Larry Grace, professional photographer from Bloomington, photographed the North Stars during their final two seasons in Minnesota. His work appeared in publications for USA Hockey as well as numerous regional hockey publications. He specializes in sports photography. (www.larrygrace.com)
- Jim Gallop, of Gallop Studio, Minneapolis, photographed unique images that became the North Stars' team posters in the late '80s and early '90s. Gallop Studio specializes in advertising photography. (www.gallop.com)
- Larry Granger, North Star fan and hockey dad from Bloomington, photographed the North Stars in the early '70s, most notably their practices at the Bloomington Ice Garden. His photos are from the archive of the Bloomington Historical Society.
- Irv Norling, freelance photographer from Bloomington, captured a wide range of Bloomington images from the 1950's to the 1980's. His collection of photographs is property of the Bloomington Historical Society. (www.bloomingtonhistoricalsociety.org)
- Bill Wippert is a professional photographer from Buffalo, New York.
- Glen James is a professional photographer from Dallas, Texas.

North Stars archive photographers:

- John Croft was a photographer for the *Minneapolis Star Tribune*. Aside from his work with the newspaper, John took many action shots and publicity photos on behalf of the North Stars. His work appeared in North Star publications from the 1970's through the mid '80s.
- Spence Hollstadt was a photographer for the *St. Paul Pioneer Press*. Aside from his work with the newspaper, Spence took many action shots and publicity photos on behalf of the North Stars. His work appeared in North Star publications from the late 1960's through the '70s.
- Joe Black was a professional photographer. His work appeared in North Star publications during the team's early years.
- Sonny John was from the east side of St. Paul. As a freelance photographer, he spent many nights at the Met Center capturing images of the North Stars.

ACKNOWLEDGEMENTS

Newspapers:

Minneapolis Star Tribune
Bob Jansen, Photo Librarian
Peter Koeleman, Director of Photography
St. Paul Pioneer Press
Pat Thraen, Library Researcher
Kay Ritchie, Call Center Manager

Former North Stars Players and Staff:

Walter Bush Jr.
Gordon Gund
Joe Janasz
Frank Jirik
Jack Larson
Dan Mandich
Cesare Maniago
Bob Paradise
J.P. Parise
Bill Peters
Patty Connolly Reid
Tom Reid
Al Shaver
Glen Sonmor
Joanie Preston St. Peter
Mary Ann Wadsworth

National Hockey League:

Wayne Gretzky
Bobby Orr
Glen Sather
Bill Wirtz
Boston Bruins
Buffalo Sabres
Calgary Flames
Chicago Blackhawks
Montreal Canadiens
New Jersey Devils
New York Rangers
Philadelphia Flyers
San Jose Sharks
Washington Capitals

Others:

USA Hockey
University of Minnesota
Let's Play Hockey magazine
KARE-TV
WCCO Radio
Pabst Brewing Company
Jim Martin, Gopher State Litho
Vonda Kelly, Bloomington Historical Society
David W. Koehser, Attorney at Law, Minneapolis
Vince Casaregola

Voyageur Asset Management:

Mike Lee
Terry Magnuson
John Taft

Production:

Thanks to Barbara Ketter of Edina, who handled the transcription of Lou's stories, as well as word processing, proofreading and editing. Her expertise and support are greatly appreciated.

Story Editing:
Patrick Reusse, *Minneapolis Star Tribune*

Digital Photo Scanning:
Fast Foto & Digital, Edina
Brad Fox, Owner
Sandy Magdziarz-Rainey
April Bezdichek
(www.ffdigital.biz)

Book / Cover Design:
Rick Korab, Punch Design, Inc.
(www.punch-design.com)

Thanks again to everyone, especially Beaver's Pond Press — Bob Showers

FOREWORD

by Al Shaver

Hall of Fame broadcaster and radio voice for all 26 years of North Stars hockey

"You keep coming back like a song,
A song that keeps saying "Remember"

Those are words from a beautiful old ballad, sung with warmth and feeling by the late Dinah Shore in my teen years of the 1940s. It's a song about an old flame from a long-ago love affair whose memory keeps haunting the singer. The Minnesota North Stars affect me the same way. It was a 26-year love affair that began on an October night in St. Louis, 1967, and ended abruptly on an April evening in 1993 when my love left me and moved to Dallas.

Breaking up is hard to do after 26 years. I still have thoughts about my lost love, like the other night when I panicked and broke into a cold sweat. It was a dream in which I was standing outside of a large and unfamiliar building, about 100 yards away. I could see a man in front of the building. He was doing some kind of strange dance, standing on one leg with his other leg raised and bent so his foot dangled in the air. One of his arms hung at a right angle with his hand closed in a fist, and he was pumping the arm back and forth in a punching motion. His other arm was extended towards me, beckoning me to approach. As I got closer, I recognized the symbol on the front of his green shirt. It was the letter "N" with a star above it surrounded by a circle — the original logo of "Les etoiles du nord."

I was finally close enough to see the man's face — Goldy! It was Bill Goldsworthy, one of the original Minnesota North Stars who once held the club record of 48 goals in a single season. "Goldy!" I screamed, "Great to see the old shuffle again, but what the heck are you doing here?"

No reply. Instead, he took me by the arm and led me through a huge glass door that put us inside the big building. We walked down a long corridor between walls of concrete blocks and came to a door marked MEDIA ROOM. Goldy opened the door and signaled for me to enter. The door closed behind me, and suddenly Goldy was gone. The room offered a most tantalizing and familiar aroma — pizza. It was Little Caesars pizza. I immediately knew where I was: Detroit's Joe Louis Arena, in the Red Wings' press lounge. The owner of the Red Wings also owns Little Caesars, and they always serve slices of the popular product to the media to appease pre-game appetites.

I looked around the room filled with big round tables, occupied by people with notebooks, laptops, and tape recorders. There, over in a far corner, sat Maroosh — John Mariucci — flanked on one side by Lou Nanne and on the other by Herb Brooks. In Maroosh's hand was a generous slab of pizza, slathered with great gobs of cheese, onions, black olives and pepperoni. But he wasn't eating. Instead, he was singing, trying to teach Louie and Herbie the words to "Danny Boy." (It always amazed me how a man like Mariucci, whose face had his entire life engraved upon it, could sing like an angel. Then again, it was probably a rehearsal for his present occupation.)

Back to the dream.

My watch tells me it's 7:30. Gotta go … almost air time … face-off in five minutes … can't be late or else I'll lose my job … can't find the broadcast booth … I'm lost and I need help.

From deep inside the building comes the sound of an organ, then a strong voice singing the words, "Oh say can you see …." I know that voice. It's Jimmy Bowers. They'll be dropping the puck as soon as he finishes. The anthem ends and there's a brief pause as I continue my search in the grip of panic. Then, another voice echoes from within the arena: "And now, LET'S — PLAY — HOCKEY!" Uh-oh, that's Bob Utecht.

The game is starting. Now I'm really stressed out. I'm running as fast as I can but I'm not going anywhere or seeing what I'm looking for. I hear the thunderous roar of thousands of people chanting "Booooooood," then "Moooooose," followed by "Loooooou" and "Marooooook."

I'm a goner. Where the heck is the darned broadcast booth? A big fellow is standing in front of me, maybe he can help. "Excuse me, sir, can you help me find the North Stars' broadcast booth?" The guy turns around and I can't believe my eyes. It's Moose Vasko. "Moose, you old scoundrel, help me out big fella. I thought I knew the location of the press box in Joe Louis Arena, but I can't seem to find it." The Moose glares at me and says: "What are you, some kind of idiot? There are no North Stars anymore and you're not in Joe Louis Arena. This is the American Airlines Center. You're in Dallas, and you don't need to worry about broadcasting the game. You're unemployed, moron." The dream ends and I wake up. It's a tough life not having a job.

The morning of August 31, 2006 was sunny and warm in Qualicam Beach, British Columbia. A light, cooling breeze off the water caressed my face as I strolled along the sea wall of the Georgia Strait, an arm of the Pacific Ocean that separates Vancouver Island from the mainland. As I sauntered along without a care in the world, it occurred to me that summer was almost gone. The town would soon be back to normal after the departure of summer tourists, and in a couple of weeks NHL training camps would open. I began to wonder how the Wild would do this season. I figured my old flame in Dallas should be strong again. Why couldn't they have won that big Cup a couple of years sooner when I was still employed?

I completed my walk and headed home for lunch. As I entered our condo, I heard my wife Shirley chatting on the phone. Then she said: "Hang on a minute, Al must be home, I think I heard the door close …. Al, it's Bob Showers calling from Minnesota." Bob Showers — a name from the past — a member of the North Stars Sales & Marketing Department. I took the phone and we began a conversation that continued for the better part of an hour.

Bob revealed that he and Lou Nanne were going to publish a book on the history of the North Stars. You, dear reader, are now in possession of that book, and I hope you enjoy reliving the memories of Minnesota's original NHL gladiators. Bob asked if I would write the foreword to the book, to which I replied: "Sounds good to me, it's about time the story was told. I will be honored to make a little contribution, a welcome project for an old radio guy with plenty of time to spare."

Sing some more, Dinah …

"FROM OUT OF THE PAST
WHERE FORGOTTEN THINGS BELONG
YOU KEEP COMING BACK LIKE A SONG"

It's a project of noble stature for Bob and Louie, bringing back wonderful memories to thousands of former fans, making them once again hear the sound of steel blades biting into the frozen water; of pucks clanging off goal posts and Plexiglas or thudding off wooden boards and blocker pads; of shrill ref whistles, grunts and groans from crunching body checks, and sticks banging the boards to celebrate a goal.

There was much good, bad and ugly that transpired during the 26 years the North Stars dwelt in Minnesota. Good things, like two appearances in the Stanley Cup Finals, where they lost in five games to the Islanders in '81 and in six games to big Mario and the Penguins in '91; the night in Madison Square Garden when Tim Young scored five goals on five shots against Eddie Giacomin and the Rangers; the 1980 playoffs when they eliminated the great Montreal Canadiens in seven games to become the first expansion team from '67 to win a playoff series against one of the Original Six NHL clubs. And of course, the spring of '68 when the North Stars came within one victory of advancing to the Stanley Cup Finals in their first season.

Then there was the bad: a terrible Saturday night in January of 1968, when tragedy struck at the Met. In the third period against the Seals,

North Star Bill Masterton fell heavily, hitting the back of his helmet-less head on the rock-hard ice. As trainer Stan Waylett rushed to Bill's aid, a pool of blood spread around the injured player. Out came the stretcher, and Masterton was carried to the dressing room and then to the hospital, all the while unconscious. He was dead less than 48 hours later. The ugliness occurred in '81, in the old, rat-infested Boston Garden.

The North Stars and Bruins set an NHL record that still stands: The teams took a combined total of 406 penalty minutes. Minnesota was assessed 18 minor penalties, 13 majors for fighting, four 10-minute misconducts, and seven game misconducts. The North Stars finished the game with only 13 of their 20 starters still eligible.

Robert and Luigi, challenge the North Star fans to connect the real names of the players, coaches and trainers to the multitude of nicknames they were tagged with. Everything from "A" for Axe to "Z" for Zoo, including Bat … Bazz … BeeBee … Big Bird … The Bird … Blah … Bood … Bomber … Brots … Butts … Cat … Cully … Cyclops … Doc … Eaver … Frankie … Gags … Gator … Gibby … Gilly (two of them) … Hartsy … Hexy … Jeep … Jughead … Kraut … Lots … Mandy … Maxie (two of them) … Millie … Modo … Muzz … O'Bee … Oly … Pee Wee … Pengy … Potsy … Rosie … Rosko … Sarge … Scoop … Sharps … Slats … Slick … Smitty (three of them) … Spud … Stork … Swoop … Tin Man … Tuna … Woody … Woyto. There were many more.

Bring back those golden memories, and wrap them all up in Green & Gold. Forget the black, it was added to the uniform later on. Black is for funerals, and a book about the North Stars should be no funeral. The old Stars live on in our minds, so celebrate the many nights we spent together at Met Center. They may be in the past, but they certainly are not forgotten. And as Dinah says, they "keep coming back like a song."

—*Al Shaver,* *Qualicum Beach, British Columbia*

[Note: The player identities for Al's nicknames can be found on page 187.]

Al, Met Center press box, November 1979

John Croft / Minneapolis Star Tribune

Met Center,
Inaugural Season

North Stars archives

North Stars archives

TEAM HISTORY

The Original North Stars

1967 Expansion Draft

The 1967 NHL Expansion Draft took

place on June 6ᵗʰ in Montreal. Each of the

six new teams selected 20 players from the

rosters of the Original Six franchises.

Goaltenders were chosen first, followed

by skaters. The following are the original

members of the Minnesota North Stars

and the teams from which they were chosen.

	PLAYER	GAMES PLAYED FIRST SEASON
1.	Cesare Maniago, New York	52
2.	Gary Bauman, Montreal	26
3.	Dave Balon, Montreal	73
4.	Ray Cullen, Detroit	67
5.	Bob Woytowich, Boston	66
6.	Jean-Guy Talbot, Montreal	4
7.	Wayne Connelly, Boston	74
8.	Ted Taylor, Detroit	31
9.	Pete Goegan, Detroit	45
10.	Len Lunde, Chicago	7
11.	Bill Goldsworthy, Boston	68
12.	Andre Pronovost, Detroit	8
13.	Elmer Vasko, Chicago	70
14.	Murray Hall, Chicago	17
15.	Bryan Watson, Detroit	0
16.	Bill Collins, New York	71
17.	Sandy Fitzpatrick, New York	18
18.	Parker MacDonald, Detroit	69
19.	Billy Taylor, Chicago	0
20.	Dave Richardson, Chicago	0

Maniago

Bauman

T. Taylor

Cullen

Vasko

Talbot

Masterton

Wetzel

—*Bill Masterton and Carl Wetzel signed with the North Stars on June 14, 1967.*

—*Bryan Watson was traded to Montreal in exchange for Bill Plager, Leo Thiffault and Barrie Meissner.*

—*Billy Taylor spent the '67-68 season with the North Stars' farm team, the Memphis South Stars.*

—*Dave Richardson was traded to Detroit in exchange for Duke Harris and Bob McCord.*

Connelly

Balon

Goegan

Lunde

Goldsworthy

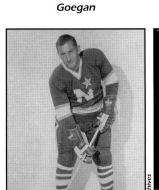

Woytowich

MacDonald

Hall

Collins

Fitzpatrick

Pronovost

Dick Dillman, 1976

Dick Dillman's Early Team History

Dick Dillman was the Public Relations Director for the Minnesota North Stars from the inaugural season in 1967 until his death in 1988.

Dick was a meticulous caretaker of the team's statistics and photo archives. The media guides, game programs and other North Star publications produced by Dick's office were always informative, entertaining and a feast for the eye. The exceptional quality of his work, combined with his good nature and genuine warmth, made "Dilly" an immensely popular figure throughout the National Hockey League.

Each year, the Professional Hockey Writer's Association presents an award to the NHL team with the most outstanding public relations department. The award is called "The Dick Dillman Press Box Award."

MINNESOTA NORTH STARS HOCKEY HISTORY

The following release, from the office of Dick Dillman in 1972, describes the formative years of the North Stars:

The story of how the National Hockey League came to Minnesota boils down to this basic fact — a group of Twin Cities men were determined to bring the fastest, most exciting sport in the world to this state.

This means that the announcement by National Hockey League President Clarence Campbell on March 11, 1965 that the then-six team circuit would expand was a signal for action for first eight, then nine Twin Cities figures.

It took a bit of doing.

First, a syndicate of eight men (later enlarged to nine) was formed to pursue the object of landing a franchise.

That partnership was revealed on June 19, 1965. Some eight months later – with thousands of hours of work behind them – the Minnesotans learned on February 9, 1966 that they would become one of the six new teams in the NHL's West Division.

They had a franchise. All they needed now was a building, a general manager, a coach, a team and customers.

First and foremost, the building problem loomed ahead of them. Time was of the essence. But plans were made as swiftly as possible and ground was broken for a $7 million Metropolitan Sports Center on October 3, 1966. In a remarkable job of construction, the structure was erected in just over 12 months, in time for the North Stars' maiden season in the league.

A general manager? Wren Blair was the choice. The former Boston farm boss came to the North Stars on May 25, 1966, with impeccable credentials, then proceeded to prove the truth of those notices by conducting a talent search that didn't overlook a single hockey player worth mention in North America.

That search paid dividends on June 6, 1967 — the day after the North Stars gave the NHL a $2 million check for the price of membership and the right to draft 20 players. Blair, who later decided to take the coaching reigns, drew a lavish helping of praise for the manner in which he chose Minnesota's top 20.

Over the six seasons that the North Stars have played in the NHL, they have attracted more than three million customers to Met Sports Center. During the past two years, the average crowd has been in excess of 15,000 per game.

The team also earned a measure of success on the ice. The 1967-68 squad finished fourth in the West, only four points from first and went on to win the West semifinal and go to seven games before losing the West final in the Stanley Cup playoffs. In 1968-69, the North Stars got off to a slow start, then made a gallant run before missing the playoffs and finishing in a tie for fifth. The North Stars' furious finish in 1969-70 brought them from far back in the final month to third place and a spot in the playoffs.

Jack Gordon took over the Minnesota coaching reins at the start of the 1970-71 season and led the team to two highly-successful seasons. The North Stars finished fourth in the West in 1970-71, eliminated St. Louis in the first round of the playoffs and became the first West (expansion) team to ever win a playoff game from the East (Original Six) before

MINNESOTA NORTH STARS

Metropolitan Sports Center
7901 Cedar Avenue South
Bloomington, Minn. 55420
(612) 854-4411

MINNESOTA NORTH STARS HOCKEY HISTORY

The story of how the National Hockey League came to Minnesota boils down to this basic fact - a group of Twin Cities men were determined to bring the fastest, most exciting sport in the world to this state.

This means that the announcement by National Hockey League President Clarence Campbell on March 11, 1965 that the then-six team circuit would expand was a signal for action for first eight, then nine Twin Cities figures.

It took a bit of doing.

First, a syndicate of eight men (later enlarged to nine) was formed to pursue the object of landing a franchise.

That partnership was revealed on June 19, 1965. Some eight months later - with thousands of hours of work behind them - the Minnesotans learned on February 9, 1966 that they would become one of the six new teams in the NHL's West Division.

They had a franchise. All they needed now was a building, a general manager, a coach, a team and customers.

First and foremost, the building problem loomed ahead of them. Time was of the essence. But plans were made as swiftly as possible and ground was broken for a $7 million Metropolitan Sports Center on October 3, 1966. In a remarkable job of construction, the structure was erected in just over 12 months, in time for the North Stars' maiden season in the league.

A general manager? Wren Blair was the choice. The former Boston farm boss came to the North Stars on May 25, 1966, with impeccable credentials, then proceeded to prove the truth of those notices by conducting a talent search that didn't overlook a single hockey player worth mention in North America.

That search paid dividends on June 6, 1967 - the day after the North Stars gave the NHL a $2 million check for the price of membership and the right to draft 20 players. Blair, who later decided to take the coaching reins, drew a lavish helping of praise for the manner in which he chose Minnesota's top 20.

Over the six seasons that the North Stars have played in the NHL, they have attracted more than three million customers to Met Sports Center. During the past two years, the average crowd has been in excess of 15,000 per game.

The team also earned a measure of success on the ice. The 1967-68 squad finished fourth in the West, only four points from first and went on to win the West semifinal and go to seven games before losing the West final in the Stanley Cup playoffs. In 1968-69, the North Stars got off to a slow start, then made a gallant run before missing the playoffs and finishing in a tie for fifth. The North Stars' furious finish in 1969-70 brought them from far back in the final month to third place and a spot in the playoffs.

Jack Gordon took over the Minnesota coaching reins at the start of the 1970-71 season and led the team to two highly-successful seasons. The North Stars finished fourth in the West in 1970-71, eliminated St. Louis in the first round of the playoffs and became the first West team ever to win a playoff game from the East before bowing, four games to two in a thrilling semifinal against Montreal. Minnesota won more games, lost less games and attained more points than ever before when the North Stars finished second in the West in 1971-72 before losing a seven-game series to St. Louis in the playoffs.

All this success can be credited to many people, but most of all to the nine Minnesotans who brought the NHL to this state---President Walter Bush, Jr.; W. John Driscoll; Harry McNeely, Jr.; Robert McNulty; John Ordway, Jr.; William Rasmussen; Robert Ridder; Gordon Ritz, and Wheelock Whitney.

bowing four games to two in a thrilling semifinal against Montreal. Minnesota won more games, lost less games, and attained more points than ever before when the North Stars finished second in the West in 1971-72 before losing a seven-game series to St. Louis in the playoffs.

All this success can be credited to many people, but most of all to the nine Minnesotans who brought the NHL to this state – President Walter Bush Jr.; W. John Driscoll; Harry McNeely Jr.; Robert McNulty; John Ordway Jr.; William Rasmussen; Robert Ridder; Gordon Ritz; and Wheelock Whitney.

CHRONOLOGY OF THE NORTH STARS

Pre-1966 Group headed by Walter Bush Jr., Gordon Ritz and Bob McNulty begins effort to bring an NHL franchise to Minnesota.

Feb. 9, 1966 NHL awards expansion franchises to California (Oakland), Los Angeles, Philadelphia, Pittsburgh, St. Louis and Minnesota. Nine-member board led by Chairman John Driscoll and President Walter Bush Jr., takes control of the team. Other board members: Harry McNeely Jr., Robert McNulty, John Ordway Jr., William Rasmussen, Robert Ridder, Gordon Ritz and Wheelock Whitney.

May 25, 1966 Wren Blair is named general manager and later becomes the first head coach in team history.

May 25, 1966 Following a public contest, "North Stars" is selected as the name for Minnesota's first NHL team.

Oct. 3, 1966 Ground is broken in Bloomington to begin construction of the Metropolitan Sports Center, future home of the North Stars.

June 6, 1967 The North Stars select 20 players in the NHL Expansion Draft. The first player chosen by Minnesota is Cesare Maniago.

Oct. 11, 1967 Minnesota's first National Hockey League game is played in St. Louis. Bill Masterton scores the first goal in franchise history at 15:20 of the second period. The North Stars and Blues skate to a 2-2 tie.

Oct. 21, 1967 Minnesota's first NHL home game is played in the new Met Center against the California Seals. Bill Goldsworthy scores the first goal in Met history at 8:23 of the second period, and the North Stars go on to beat the Seals 3-1. (The California Seals would change their name to the Oakland Seals in December, 1967).

Jan. 13, 1968 In a game against the Oakland Seals at Met Center, North Star forward Bill Masterton is seriously injured after hitting his head on the ice.

Jan. 15, 1968 Bill Masterton dies as a result of head injuries suffered on Jan. 13th. He is the first player in NHL history to die from injuries sustained in a game. No other North Star player ever wears his jersey No. 19. The jersey is officially retired in 1987.

June 1968 The NHL names Claude Provost of Montreal as the first recipient of the Bill Masterton Memorial Trophy. The annual award is presented to the NHL player who best exemplifies the qualities of sportsmanship, perseverance and dedication to hockey.

Nov. 4, 1968 Wren Blair resigns as coach and is replaced by John Muckler.

Jan. 19, 1969 Muckler is fired and Blair resumes coaching duties.

June 1969 Danny Grant receives the Calder Memorial Trophy as NHL Rookie of the Year.

Dec. 28, 1969 Blair resigns as coach and is replaced by Charlie Burns.

April 1970 Jack Gordon replaces Burns as head coach.

Jan. 25, 1972 Minnesota is host to the 25th Annual NHL All-Star Game. Representing the North Stars at Met Center: Gump Worsley, Doug Mohns, Ted Harris and Bill Goldsworthy.

June 1973 Walter Bush Jr. receives the NHL's Lester Patrick Trophy for outstanding service to hockey in the United States.

Dec. 20, 1973 Parker McDonald replaces Gordon as coach.

Apr. 19, 1974 Wren Blair is fired as general manager.

Apr. 24, 1974 Jack Gordon takes over as general manager.

Apr. 29, 1974 Gordon replaces MacDonald as coach.

Jan. 5, 1975 Charlie Burns replaces Gordon as coach.

April 1975 Ted Harris takes over head coaching position.

June 14, 1976 Walter Bush resigns as club president to become chairman of the board, replacing John Driscoll. Gordon Ritz is named president.

June 1977 John Mariucci receives the NHL's Lester Patrick Trophy for outstanding service to hockey in the United States.

Nov. 24, 1977 Harris is fired as coach and replaced by Andre Beaulieu.

Feb. 10, 1978 Lou Nanne is named GM/coach, replacing Gordon and Beaulieu.

June 14, 1978 North Stars merger with the Cleveland Barons is announced. George and Gordon Gund assume ownership of the North Stars, and John Karr replaces Gordon Ritz as president.

July 5, 1978 Nanne turns over coaching duties to Harry Howell.

Nov. 11, 1978 Howell resigns due to health reasons and is replaced by Glen Sonmor.

June 1979 Bobby Smith receives the Calder Memorial Trophy as NHL Rookie of the Year.

June 1980 Al MacAdam receives the NHL's Bill Masterton Memorial Trophy for sportsmanship, perseverance and dedication to hockey.

May 12, 1981 North Stars advance to the Stanley Cup Finals for the first time in team history, facing the New York Islanders. The Islanders take the series, 4 games to 1.

June 3, 1983 Glen Sonmor is replaced by Bill Mahoney.

Nov. 8, 1984 Mahoney is replaced by Sonmor.

June 21, 1985 Sonmor is replaced by Lorne Henning.

Mar. 26, 1986 Neal Broten becomes the NHL's first American-born player to achieve 100 points in a season, collecting two assists in a 6-1 win over Toronto at Maple Leaf Gardens.

Mar. 31, 1987 Henning is fired. Sonmor coaches on interim basis until end of season.

Apr. 23, 1987 Herb Brooks is named head coach.

Feb. 1988 Lou Nanne resigns as GM, but agrees to remain until a new GM is named.

Mar. 9, 1988 Lou Nanne becomes president of the North Stars and Met Center.

June 14, 1988 Jack Ferreira is appointed GM.

July 6, 1988 Pierre Page replaces Brooks as head coach.

June 1989 Lou Nanne receives the NHL's Lester Patrick Trophy for outstanding service to hockey in the United States.

1967-92 DRAFT CHOICES

Year	POS	RD	OV	FROM
1992				
Jarkko Varvio	RW	2	34	HPK
Jeff Bes	C	3	58	Guelph
Jere Lehtinen	RW	4	88	Espoo, Finland
Michael Johnson	D	6	130	Ottawa
Kyle Peterson	C	7	154	Thunder Bay
Juha Lind	C	8	178	Jokerit, Finland
Lars Edstrom	LW	9	202	Lulea, Sweden
Jeff Romfo	C	10	226	Blaine HS
Jeffrey Moen	G	11	250	Roseville
1991				
Richard Matvichuk	D	1	8	Saskatoon
Mike Torchia	G	4	74	Kitchener
Mike Kennedy	LW	5	97	Univ. of B.C.
Mark Lawrence	RW	6	118	Detroit Amb.
Geoff Finch	G	7	137	Brown Univ.
Michael Burkett	LW	8	159	Michigan State
Derek Herlofsky	G	9	184	St. Paul Jr. A
Tom Nemeth	LW	10	206	Cornwall
Shayne Green	RW	11	228	Kamloops
Jukka Suomalainen	D	12	250	Grifka
1990				
Derian Hatcher	D	1	8	North Bay
Laurie Billeck	D	3	50	Prince Albert
Cal McGowan	C	4	70	Kamloops
Frank Kovacs	LW	4	71	Regina Pats
Enrico Ciccone	D	5	92	Trois-Rivers
Roman Turek	G	6	115	Czech. Nat. Jr.
Jeff Levy	G	7	134	Rochester
Doug Barrault	RW	8	155	Lethbridge
Joe Biondi	C	9	176	U. of MN-Duluth
Troy Binnie	RW	10	197	Ottawa
Ole Dahlstrom	C	11	218	Furuset
John McKenzie	G	12	239	W. Madison HS
1989				
Doug Zmolek	D	1	7	Rochester J.M.
Mike Craig	RW	2	28	Oshawa 67's
Murray Garbutt	C	3	60	Medicine Hat
Pat MacLeod	D	5	87	Kamloops
Bryan Schoen	G	5	91	Minnesota HS
Rhys Hollyman	D	6	112	Kanata BCJHL
Scott Cashman	G	6	133	Pingree Prep
Jonathan Pratt	C	8	154	Pingree Prep
Ken Blum	C	9	175	St. Joseph's HS
Artur Irbe	G	10	196	Dynamo Riga
Tom Pederson	D	11	217	Univ. of Minn.
Helmut Balderis	RW	12	238	Did not play
1988				
Mike Modano	C	1	1	Prince Albert
Link Gaetz	D	2	40	Spokane
Shaun Kane	D	3	43	Springfield Jr. B
Jeffrey Stolp	G	4	64	Greenway HS
Ken MacArthur	D	9	148	Univ. of Denver
Travis Richards	D	9	169	Armstrong HS
Ari Matilainen	RW	10	190	Assat Pori (Fin.)
Grant Bischoff	LW	11	211	Univ. of Minn.
Trent Andison	RW	12	232	Cornell Univ.
Helmut Balderis	RW	12	238	Did not play
1987				
Dave Archibald	C	1	6	Portland
Scott McCrady	D	2	35	Medicine Hat
John Weisbrod	C	4	73	Choate (Prep)
Teppo Kivela	C	5	88	Jokerit Finland
Darcy Norton	LW	6	109	Kamloops
Timo Kulonen	D	7	130	Kalpa Finland
Don Schmidt	D	8	151	Kamloops
Jarmo Myllys	G	9	172	Lukko Finland
Larry Olimb	D	10	193	Warroad (MN)
Marc Felicio	C	11	214	Northwood Prep
Dave Shields	C	12	235	Univ. of Denver
1986				
Warren Babe	LW	1	12	Lethbridge
Neil Wilkinson	D	2	30	Selkirk (MJHL)
Dean Kolstad	D	2	33	Prince Albert
Eric Bennett	RW	3	54	Wilbraham Prep
Rob Zettler	D	3	55	Sault Ste. Marie
Brad Turner	D	3	58	Calgary (Midget)
Kirk Tomlinson	C	4	75	Hamilton
Jari Gronstand	D	5	96	Tappara Finland
Scott Mathias	C	6	159	Univ. of Denver
Lance Pitlick	D	9	180	Cooper HS
Dan Keczmer	D	10	201	Detroit
Garth Joy	D	11	222	Hamilton
Kurt Stahura	LW	12	243	Williston
1985				
Stephane Roy	C	3	51	Granby Bisons
Mike Berger	D	4	69	Lethbridge
Dwight Mullins	C	5	90	Lethbridge
Mike Mullowney	D	6	111	Deerfield Acad.
Mike Kelfer	C	7	132	St. John's Prep
Ross Johnson	D	8	153	Rochester Mayo
Tim Helmer	C	9	174	Ottawa 67's
Gordon Ernst	C	10	195	Cranston E. HS
Ladislav Lubina	LW	11	216	Pardubice, Czech.
Tommy Sjodin	D	12	237	Timar, Sweden
1984				
David Quinn	D	1	13	Kent HS
Ken Hodge	C	2	46	St. John's Prep
Miroslav Maly	D	4	76	Bayreuth, W. Ger.
Jiri Poner	RW	5	89	Landshut, W. Ger.
Jali Takko	C	6	97	Finnish Olyp. Trn.
Gary McColgan	C	7	118	Oshawa
Vladimir Kyhos	D	7	139	Litinov, Czech.
Darin MacInnis	D	8	160	Kent HS
Duane Wahlin	RW	9	181	Johnson HS
Mike Orn	C	10	201	Stillwater HS
Tom Terwilliger	D	11	222	Edina HS
Mike Nightengale	D	12	242	Simloy HS
1983				
Brian Lawton	C	1	1	Mt. St. Charles
Malcolm Parks	RW	2	36	St. Albert Tier II
Frantisek Musil	D	2	38	Czech. Nat.
Mitch Messier	C	3	56	Notre Dama
Brian Durand	C	4	76	Cloquet HS
Rich Geist	C	5	97	St. Paul Acad.
Tom McComb	D	6	116	Mt. St. Charles
Sean Toomey	C	7	136	Cretin HS
Don Biggs	C	8	156	Oshawa
Paul Pulis	RW	9	176	Hibbing HS
Milos Riha	LW	10	196	Czech.
Oldrich Valek	RW	11	212	Czech. Nat.
Paul Roff	RW	12	236	Edina HS
1982				
Brian Bellows	RW	1	2	Kitchener
Wally Chapman	C	3	59	Edina HS
Bob Rouse	D	4	80	Billings
Dusan Pasek	C	4	81	Slovan Czech
Marty Wiitala	C	5	101	Superior HS
Todd Carlile	D	6	122	North St. Paul
Jali Wahlsten	C	7	143	CSKA Moscow
Paul Miller	D	8	164	Crookston HS
Pat Micheletti	C	9	185	Hibbing HS
Arnold Kadlec	D	10	206	CHZ Lit. Czech.
Scott Knutson	D	11	227	Warroad HS
1981				
Ron Meighan	D	1	13	Niagara Falls
Dave Donnelly	C	2	27	St. Albert, Alta.
Mike Sands	G	3	48	Sudbury
Tom Hirsch	D	4	69	Patrick Henry HS
Dave Preuss	RW	5	90	St. Thomas Acad.
Jim Malwitz	C	6	111	Grand Rapids
Kelly Hubbard	D	7	132	Portland
Paul Guay	RW	8	153	Mt. St. Charles
Jim Archibald	RW	9	174	Moose Jaw
Kari Kanervo	C	10	160	TPS Finland
Scott Bjugstad	C	11	181	Univ. of Minn.
Steve Kudebeh	G	12	202	Breck HS

Jan. 30, 1990 George and Gordon Gund request $15 million from the Met Sports Commission for improvements to Met Center. The request is denied.

May 2, 1990 The Gunds agree to sell the North Stars to a group of investors led by former Hartford Whalers owner Howard Baldwin. The Gunds will be awarded an expansion franchise for the San Francisco Bay Area.

May 4, 1990 Page resigns to become GM of the Quebec Nordiques.

May 9, 1990 NHL approves sale of North Stars from the Gunds to Howard Baldwin and Morris Belzberg. The Gunds are awarded an expansion franchise that will consist of players from the North Stars system. The San Jose Sharks will begin play at the start of the '91-92 season.

June 6, 1990 Former Calgary Flames co-owner Norman Green purchases controlling interest of the North Stars franchise. Baldwin and Belzberg remain as shareholders. Baldwin is named President and Chief Operating Officer.

June 8, 1990 Former Philadelphia Flyers GM Bob Clarke is named North Stars GM, replacing Jack Ferreira. Ferreira had previously been named GM of the San Jose Sharks expansion team.

June 19, 1990 Former Montreal Canadiens center Bob Gainey is named North Stars head coach.

July 25, 1990 Green takes over as North Stars President with Baldwin's resignation.

Aug. 24, 1990 Baldwin sells his share of the North Stars to Green and leaves the franchise.

Oct. 22, 1990 Belzberg sells his share of the North Stars to Green and leaves the franchise. Green is sole owner of the North Stars.

Apr. 3, 1991 Lou Nanne resigns from the North Stars after 23 years with the franchise, but agrees to stay until the conclusion of the Stanley Cup playoffs.

May 15, 1991 North Stars advance to the Stanley Cup Finals for the second time in team history, facing the Pittsburgh Penguins. The Penguins take the series, 4 games to 2.

May 30, 1991 Player Dispersal Draft is held between the North Stars and San Jose Sharks, thus completing the sale of the North Stars from the Gund brothers to Green.

Nov. 30, 1991 Bobby Smith becomes the 32nd player in NHL history to record 1,000 points in his career. Smith scores the North Stars' first goal in a 4-3 win over Toronto at Maple Leaf Gardens.

Jan. 4, 1992 Bobby Smith plays in his 1,000 NHL game, a 4-3 win over Vancouver at Met Center.

Feb. 15, 1992 Bill Goldsworthy's jersey No. 8 is retired.

Oct. 6, 1992 The North Stars open their 26th and final season with a 6-4 loss at St. Louis.

Oct. 8, 1992 The final home opener in North Stars history ends in a 5-2 win over St. Louis.

Mar. 11, 1993 At a press conference in Dallas, Norm Green and the Dallas City Council announce that the North Stars will move to Texas beginning with the 1993-94 season. Fifteen games remain in Minnesota North Star history. Seven North Star home games remain in Met Center history.

Apr. 10, 1993 The final victory in Minnesota North Stars history: a 4-3 win over St. Louis at Met Center.

Apr. 13, 1993 The final Minnesota North Star game at Met Center: a 3-2 loss to Chicago. Attendance: 15,445 (sellout).

Apr. 15, 1993 The final game in the history of the Minnesota North Stars: a 5-3 loss at Detroit.

1967-92 DRAFT CHOICES (cont'd)

Year	POS	RD	OV	FROM
1982				
Brian Bellows	RW	1	2	Kitchener
Wally Chapman	C	3	59	Edina HS
Bob Rouse	D	4	80	Billings
Dusan Pasek	C	4	81	Slov Brat Czech
Marty Wiitala	C	5	101	Superior HS
Todd Carlile	D	6	122	North St. Paul
Victor Zhluktov	LW	7	143	CSKA Moscow
Paul Miller	D	8	164	Crookston HS
Pat Micheletti	C	9	185	Hibbing HS
Arnold Kadlec	D	10	206	CHZ Lit, Czech.
Scott Knutson	C	11	227	Warroad HS
1981				
Ron Meighan	D	1	13	Niagara Falls
Dave Donnelly	C	2	27	St. Albert, Alta.
Mike Sands	G	2	31	Sudbury
Tom Hirsch	D	2	33	Patrick Henry HS
Dave Preuss	RW	2	34	St. Thomas Acad.
Jali Wahlsten	LW	2	41	TPS Finland
Terry Tait	LW	4	69	Sault Ste. Marie
Jim Malwitz	C	4	76	Grand Rapids
Kelly Hubbard	D	5	97	Portland
Paul Guay	RW	6	118	Mt. St. Charles
Jim Archibald	RW	7	139	Moose Jaw
Karl Kanervo	D	8	160	TPS Finland
Scott Bjugstad	C	9	181	Univ. of Minn.
Steve Kudebeh	G	10	202	Breck HS
1980				
Brad Palmer	LW	1	16	Victoria
Don Beaupre	G	2	32	Sudbury
Randy Velischek	D	3	53	Providence Coll.
Mark Huglen	D	4	79	Roseau HS
Dave Jensen	D	5	100	Univ. of Minn.
Dan Zavarise	D	6	121	Cornwall
Bill Stewart	RW	7	142	Univ. of Denver
Jeff Walters	RW	8	163	Peterborough
Bob Lakso	LW	9	164	Aurora-Hoyt HS
Dave Richter	D	10	205	Univ. of Michigan
1979				
Craig Hartsburg	D	1	6	Sault Ste. Marie
Tom McCarthy	LW	1	10	Oshawa
Neal Broten	C	2	42	Univ. of Minn.
Kevin Maxwell	C	3	63	U. of N. Dakota
Jim Dobson	RW	5	90	Portland
Brian Gualazzi	RW	6	111	Sault Ste. Marie
1978				
Bobby Smith	C	1	1	Ottawa
Steve Payne	LW	2	19	Ottawa
Steve Christoff	LW	2	24	Univ. of Minn.
Curt Giles	D	4	54	U. of MN-Duluth
Roy Kerling	C	5	70	Cornell Univ.
Bob Bergloff	D	6	87	Univ. of Minn.
Kim Spencer	RW	7	104	Victoria
Mike Cotter	D	8	121	Bowling Green
Brent Gogol	RW	9	138	Billings
Mike Seide	LW/D	10	155	Bloomington, MN
1977				
Brad Maxwell	D	1	7	New Westminster
Dave Semenko	LW	2	25	Brandon
Kevin McCloskey	D	4	61	Calgary
1976				
Glen Sharpley	C	1	3	Hull
Jim Roberts	D	2	33	Ottawa
Don Jackson	D	3	39	Notre Dame Univ.
Ron Zanussi	RW	3	51	London
Mike Fedorko	D	4	75	Hamilton
Phil Verchota	C	5	93	Univ. of Minn.
Dave Delich	C	6	111	Colorado Coll.
Jeff Barr	D	7	129	Michigan State
1975				
Bryan Maxwell	D	1	4	Medicine Hat
Paul Harrison	G	3	40	Oshawa
Alex Pirus	RW	3	41	Notre Dame U.
Steve Jensen	LW	4	58	Michigan Tech
David Norris	LW	5	76	Hamilton
Greg Clause	RW	6	94	Hamilton
Robert Francois	D	7	112	Sherbrooke
Dean Magee	RW	8	130	Colorado Coll.
Terry Angel	RW	9	148	Oshawa
Michel Blais	D	10	164	Kingston
Earl Sargent	RW	11	188	Fargo, ND
Gilles Cloutier	G	12	201	Shawinigan
1974				
Doug Hicks	D	1	6	Flin Flon
Richard Nantais	LW	2	24	Quebec
Pete LoPresti	C	3	42	Univ. Denver
Kim MacDougall	D	4	60	Regina
Ron Ashton	LW	5	78	Saskatoon
John Sheridan	C	6	96	Univ. of Minn.
Dave Heitz	D	7	114	Fargo, ND
Roland Eriksson	C	8	131	Tunadro, Swed.
Dave Staffen	C	9	148	Ottawa
Brian Anderson	D	10	164	New Westminster
George Taylor	D	11	179	Flin Flon
Don Hay	RW	12	193	New Westminster
1973				
Blake Dunlop	C	2	18	Ottawa
Johnny Rogers	RW	2	25	Edmonton
Rick Chinnick	RW	3	41	Peterborough
Tom Colley	C	4	57	Sudbury
Lowell Ostlund	D	5	73	Saskatoon
Dave Lee	LW	6	89	Ottawa
Lou Nistico	C	7	105	London
George Beveridge	D	8	121	Kitchener
Jim Johnston	C	9	136	Peterborough
Sam Clegg	G	10	152	Medicine Hat
Russ Wiechnik	C	11	161	Calgary
1972				
Jerry Byers	LW	1	12	Kitchener
Terry Ryan	C	2	29	Hamilton
Tom Thomson	D	4	60	Toronto
Chris Ahrens	D	5	76	Kitchener
Steve West	C	6	92	Oshawa
Chris Meloff	D	7	108	Kitchener
Scott MacPhail	RW	7	116	Montreal Jr. Can.
Bob Lundeen	D	8	124	Univ. of Wisc.
Glen Mikkelson	RW	9	140	Brandon
Steve Lyon	D	10	145	Peterborough
Juri Kudrasov	C	10	147	Kitchener
Marcel Comeau	C	10	148	Edmonton
1971				
Rod Norrish	LW	2	21	Regina
Ron Wilson	D	3	35	Flin Flon
Mike Legge	LW	4	49	Winnipeg Jets
Brian McBrathney	D	5	63	St. Catherines
Al Globensky	D	6	77	Montreal Jr. Can.
Bruce Abbey	D	7	91	Peterborough
Russ Friesen	LW	8	105	Hamilton
Mike Antonovich	C	9	113	Univ. of Minn.
1970				
Buster Harvey	D	2	17	Hamilton
Fred Barrett	D	2	20	Toronto
Dennis Patterson	D	3	34	Peterborough
Dave Cressman	LW	4	48	Kitchener
Henry Lehvonen	D	5	62	Kitchener
Murray McNeill	LW	6	76	Calgary
Gary Geldart	D	7	69	London
Wayne Donaldson	LW	8	101	Peterborough
1969				
Dick Redmond	D	1	5	St. Catherines
Dennis O'Brien	D	2	14	St. Catherines
Gilles Gilbert	G	3	25	London
Fred O'Donnell	RW	4	37	Oshawa
Pierre Jutras	LW	5	49	Shawinigan
Bob Walton	C	6	61	Niagara Falls
Rick Thompson	D	7	72	Niagara Falls
Cal Russell	RW	8	78	Hamilton
1968				
Jim Benzelock	RW	1	5	Winnipeg
Marc Rioux	C	2	15	Verdun
Glen Lindsay	G	3	22	Saskatoon
1967				
Wayne Cheesman	LW	1	4	Whitby Jr. B
Larry Mick	RW	2	13	Pembrooke

Lou Nanne, 1975

North Stars archives

LOU NANNE

When it comes to the history of the Minnesota North Stars, Lou Nanne has seen it all.

A native of Sault Saint Marie, Ontario, Lou joined the North Stars late in their first season after a standout career with the University of Minnesota and the U.S. National and Olympic teams. In his 23 years with the North Stars franchise, Lou was a player, head coach, general manager and team president.

He scored goals, killed penalties, played pranks, made trades, scouted, drafted and ultimately oversaw the entire organization. Lou's heart bleeds Green & Gold.

Lou on the North Stars' Move

The circumstances surrounding the North Stars' move to Texas have never been told. Gordon and George Gund never wanted to leave Minnesota. They loved it here, they were terrific for the community, they never asked for anything more than they should have, and they always paid more than their fair share.

The Gunds wanted to develop a shopping center, and the property by Met Center came up for sale in 1983-84. It was the Met Stadium site owned by the Metropolitan Sports Facilities Commission.

The Gunds had their brother Graham, an architect, take a look and the three of them decided they wanted the property. They started working on the property deal and used John Karr, who was president of the North Stars at the time, as their point man.

Their plans included remodeling the Met Center, as well. They made a bid for the property, and it looked like they had an agreement — at least the Gunds felt they had one — but at the last minute a businessman from Mankato, Art Petrie, got involved and the rug was pulled out from under the Gunds. Ultimately, the Petrie deal fell through and the Met Stadium site was sold to the Ghermezian brothers, who built the Mall of America.

The Gunds were upset. Next they went to the Commission and said, "If we're not going to have that property, we want to talk about remodeling the arena."

Now we're getting into 1986 or 1987. They had plans drawn up that would expand the concourses, have a ticket office at the front, include a restaurant and add 40-some suites. All of this could be done for $15 million at the time.

The Gunds kept saying that, if they received $15 million to improve the building, they would sign a 20-year lease. The Commission turned them down and so did the city of Bloomington.

Gordon and George Gund

Rick Kolodziej

When the Commission turned us down, I asked the Gunds to build 20 suites, which would cost $3.5 million. Gordon said, "I'll do it, but can we sell them?" I said, "I'm sure we can, so let's put them in."

We put in the 20 suites and we were very successful with them.

Around that same time, if you go back in the archives of the Minneapolis paper, you'll find they were saying sports should exist on their own, that they shouldn't have community help.

The Target Center was starting to get underway downtown, and in essence everybody was trying to force the North Stars downtown.

In 1988 and 1989, we tried one more time to get some money from the Commission, but it didn't happen. By 1990, the Gunds were fed up.

Art Savage, one of George's advisors, was looking in San Jose and said they could strike a deal out there. When the North Stars were not going to get any help, and San Jose was willing to build an arena, the Gunds said, "We might as well move to San Jose."

Head Coach Jack Gordon, with Gilles Gilbert, Dennis O'Brien and Tom Reid

North Stars archives

I flew out to see George in Palm Springs, and I said: "George, if you want to leave I can understand that, but the North Stars have always been in Minnesota. Why don't you do a deal with the league? The league is going to give you some trouble about moving, anyway.

"We'll make a deal where you take 30 of the 50 players off the reserve list and leave the remaining 20 players as an expansion team. We'll get somebody to buy an expansion franchise from Minnesota."

George was OK with that, but at first Gordon balked. He said: "No, we're taking the team and not leaving anything behind. They wouldn't help us, so we're just going to leave."

I said, "Gordon, the league is going to fight you if you try to leave, and you might not win." Gordon says, "I know we can win the case." I said: "Well, you're going to spend a lot of money and it's going to be a lot of hassle. If you just do this deal, if we can get an expansion buyer, then you're home free."

Eventually we went to a meeting in Chicago, and Gordon was all set to fight the deal if he didn't like what the league proposed.

Thanks to Bill Wirtz, the Chicago owner, and league president John Ziegler, both of whom liked the Gunds and also wanted a team in Minnesota, an agreement was reached.

Bill proposed that the franchise in Minnesota would be sold for $32 million, which the Gunds would get. They would then pay the $50 million new franchise fee to go to San Jose.

That was a great deal for the Gunds, getting that market for basically $18 million plus all the North Stars' top players and prospects. Howard Baldwin and Morris Belzberg were the guys who came forward and wanted to buy the franchise.

Howard called and said, "Louie, I want you to stay here with the North Stars." At first, I told him no way, I was quitting to go into the money management business, but eventually he talked me into staying because I was the guy on the Minnesota side who had been here from the beginning.

So Howard and Morris bought the team, and we were making plans to move forward. Howard knew that we needed suites, too.

Right after Howard was awarded the franchise, the Timberwolves contacted us and asked if we'd be interested in moving the North Stars downtown. Howard and Morris thought they would do it if they could get a good arrangement.

They had some preliminary talks that went well. One day, Howard says to me, "Tony Tavares is coming in tomorrow."

Tony was working for Spectacor, an arena management company out of Philadelpia, and he was advising Howard on the deal. Howard says, "I want you and Tony to meet with Marv Wolfenson and Harvey Ratner and make a deal to move the team downtown, if it's workable."

Tavares and I went downtown and met with Wolfenson, Ratner and Bob Stein, Marv's son-in-law who was running the Timberwolves. We worked through a lot of details and then I asked, "How about the dasher boards?"

Wolfenson says, "What do you mean?" I said, "We get significant revenue from advertising on the dasher boards, and we want that money." And Marv says, "OK." I said, "We also need the right to sell the space to whoever we want."

Marv says: "There's no way. You have to sell it to the sponsors we have in the building. I'm not allowing someone else in." I said: "That's OK, provided they buy the dasher boards. But say you have Coke and I have Pepsi, you have Burger King and I have McDonald's. When we sell our packages to TV, their cameras shoot the boards along with the action, so we sell the advertiser on the fact that he's getting exposure from the television package in addition to the rink. If your guys don't take the boards, I have to have the right to sell them to my advertisers."

Bob Stein said: "That's fair. That sounds reasonable." But Marv kept saying no. We never could reach a deal on what advertisers we could use on the dasher boards — and that's why the North Stars never moved to the Target Center.

Top: Cesare Maniago and Dennis O'Brien

Lower left: Lou Nanne and Garry Unger

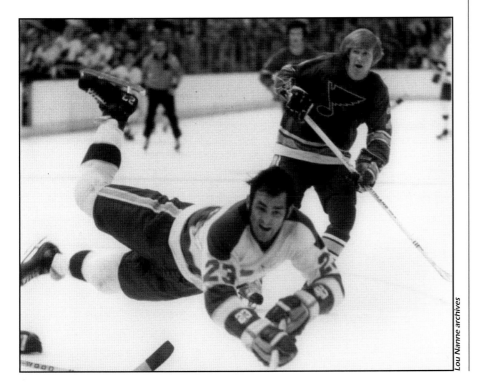

We stayed at the Met. Two weeks later Howard comes into my office and says: "Louie, all of our money problems are over. I just sold controlling interest of the team."

I said, "To whom?" He says, "Norm Green."

The next day, I went down to my lawyer and had the contract written that Howard and I had agreed to earlier, and I came back and said: "Howard, you have to sign this. It's our agreement."

He said, "What do you need that for?" I said, "You and I know about the agreement, but I want to make sure you sign it and Norm Green signs it when he comes here today."

They both signed the agreement. I went home that day and said to my wife, "Mark on your calendar, Howard won't be here in three months." She said, "Why?" I said, "Just trust me."

I knew Norm, and I liked him, but I knew his management style was going to clash with Howard's.

Head Coach
Glen Sonmor

Three weeks later, Howard comes into my office and says, "Why didn't you tell me my management style and Norm's wouldn't mesh?"

I said, "You had already sold the team when you walked into my office." He says, "Well, I'm outta here."

So Howard left, and Morris Belzberg stayed a partner.

Green came to me and said, "I want you and Morris to go to Detroit and find out how they made such a big turnover with season tickets when they were down in the dumps."

Morris and I flew out and met with Jim Lites, who was the son-in-law of owner Mike Ilitch and the president of the Red Wings. We spent the whole day with him going through their strategies and how they did it. When we got back, we had lunch with Norm and I explained what the Red Wings had done. Morris and I gave our thoughts on how we could do similar things.

And Norm says: "Those are lousy ideas. We're not doing any of that." And I'll never forget, Morris Belzberg stood up and said: "That's it — I'm outta here. Buy me out."

So Belzberg left, and it was just Norm and me.

I made a deal with Pillsbury later that year — a whole advertising package to buy some tickets and to purchase and print all the North Star calendars and hand them out.

One morning the team was leaving the building as Norm was coming in, and Norm says, "Where's the team going?" I said: "They're going down to have a team photo taken at Peavey Plaza. Every year we do a different thing with the team — we have them at the Ordway, we have them at First Avenue, we have them do something a little off the wall, and we use it as a calendar."

And he says, "Am I in the picture?" I said, "No." He says, "Is Bobby Clarke in the picture?" I said, "No." He says, "Why not?" I said, "It's just the team — a fun kind of thing."

He says, "How much are we getting for it?" I said, "$25,000, plus season tickets, plus a few other advertising things."

He says, "We can get more than that." I said, "We already made the deal." He says, "I didn't sign it." I said, "I've made the deal."

He says, "Just tell them I haven't signed it and tell them you want more money."

And I said: "Norm, I live in this community. My word is my bond, and I gave my word. We're not changing it."

He says, "Louie, we're not going to be able to continue to work this way." I said: "No, we're not, because I've already got another job, and I'm leaving here in April. So don't worry about that, but we're not changing the Pillsbury deal."

One of the reasons Norm Green had to move the team was because he couldn't get permission from the Bloomington commission to build a shopping area. He wanted to get added revenue by building shops between the Met Center and the Mall of America. The commission wouldn't let him do that.

Then, like the Gunds, he asked for help in putting in suites from the Sports Facilities Commission, and they said no. He knew that he wasn't going to be able to generate enough revenue here, so he decided to move the team to Dallas. Some people thought it was a personal problem he was going through, but it was strictly a financial decision.

It should have occurred to me that Norm was thinking of moving the team when the logo on the uniforms was redesigned. I had put black into the North Stars' uniform years before in the hope it would increase our merchandise sales.

Norm came to me and said: "Louie, we should have a different crest. We have to get somebody to design a different crest." I thought of Bill Mack, who was a terrific artist, so I went to him and asked if he would do a crest for us.

Bill designed the logo in exchange for a couple of season tickets for his father in the Observatory Club. Norm told Bill that he just wanted "Stars" in the logo.

I personally thought the "Stars" should be used as an alternative logo and wanted the North Star logo to be the main one. It had been voted one of the great hockey logos of all-time. Norm said, "We're keeping the North Star logo around, but we're using 'Stars' on the jersey." He maintained that it was strictly a merchandising decision. As it turned out, that logo was easier to transfer to Dallas afterwards.

Marc Bureau in the North Stars' new uniform, 1992

Billy Robin McFarland

Metropolitan Sports Complex, Bloomington, June 16, 1967

William Seaman / Minneapolis Star Tribune

MET CENTER CONSTRUCTION

Walter Bush:

Everybody was nay-saying two or three months before completion, saying we'd never get the building ready. And it was close. But things really ran a lot smoother than people thought it would.

The Met Center was built in about a year, and there were certain things we just couldn't get to before Opening Night. To give you an idea of what was left undone, when the Met was completely finished its total cost was $7 million. On Opening Night, the building had a cost of $4.5 million. So gradually, over time, we just kept adding on, putting another $2.5 million into the building.

Walter Bush lifts the first shovel of dirt at the Met Center ground-breaking, October 3, 1966. Holding the hockey sticks is GM Wren Blair.

Lower left: Building Superintendent Paul Jorgensen oversees early construction of the Met Center, December 8, 1966.

Russell Bull / Minneapolis Star Tribune

North Stars archives

Top:
Looking toward the east end, the lower level of Met Center begins to take shape, June 16, 1967.

Dwight Miller / Minneapolis Star Tribune

Center:
The freezing pipes are laid on the floor of Met Center, August 20, 1967.

John Croft / Minneapolis Star Tribune

Bottom:
The cement floor of Met Center is poured, September 15, 1967.

Russell Bull / Minneapolis Star Tribune

We did a lot of things that hadn't been done before — for example, dugouts where the teams peeled off from the benches and went directly to the locker rooms. That concept was picked up by other teams in the league when they were building new arenas. A few years later we had to put in an extra wall because players were coming together near the locker rooms and there was fighting going on. Some of the best fights took place out of view of the fans.

Considering the cold weather during most of our games, we made a deal with the Pure Oil Company to have tow trucks outside the Met, and we advertised that they could jumpstart anything. That idea also carried over to other buildings in the league.

For the initial game and several thereafter, we had a cleaning crew made up of homeless guys. We'd go downtown and pick up guys from the mission and bring them in. And it just wasn't working. They weren't cleaning the building, they were drinking the spit-backs of beer that were left. Instead of throwing everything away, they were drinking the beer and throwing the cups away. So we put together a hard working group of high schoolers to maintain the building and called them the GLAMOR crowd, for Good Looking Athletic Men of Richfield. In the early years, we had four lights in the ceiling that would illuminate advertising on the ice during intermission. Reverend Johnson from the Episcopal Church had an ad that said "Only God saves more than Gump."

There were a lot of rumors that we were putting the seats in randomly. Well, we really were, but it was because we were trying a new idea. When it happened, many reporters got involved and said we were in such a hurry we just threw the seats in without a design. We just let it go instead of telling them differently. There was no need to get into an argument when we had barely started our first season.

Lou Nanne:

The colored seats were unique, and it's a good thing we had them. On the nights when our crowds weren't so big, the various colors made it appear as though more people were in the building than there actually were. It looked great on TV. The colored seats became a signature of the Met, and people loved them.

Bill Peters, MET CENTER OPERATING ENGINEER:

The original seats of the Met Center were always intended to be random colors. Minneapolis Theater Supply had the initial contract for the Met's seating, and they used a new design called a "splatter technique." The seats consisted of four colors — green, gold, black and white — and four widths from 18 to 21 inches. When we installed the seats, every effort was made to ensure no more than two of the same color went next to each other. The narrow seats went in the corners, and sometimes we had no choice about putting the same colors together because it was all we had for a particular width.

One-inch steel pipes were laid on the Met's floor to make the ice, spaced four inches apart. A chilled salt solution was sent through the pipes to freeze the water and create the ice surface, and certain pipes were used to carry heat away from the surface. The good hockey ice at Met Center was kept frozen at 18 degrees, and it never fluctuated more than three degrees.

The cement floor of the Met was so expertly constructed that it never varied more than one-eighth inch over the 26-year history of the building. Forty anchor points were sunk into the floor to use when we set up things like concert stages and the basketball court. Two anchor points were also placed in the cement at each goal crease for the old net moorings.

Bloomington Historical Society / The Irv Norling Family

North Stars archives

Courtesy of Frank Jirik

Top:
Metropolitan Sports Center in Bloomington, home of the Minnesota North Stars.

Center:
A model of Met Center is examined by (from left) North Stars President Walter Bush, Gerald Moore of the Minneapolis Chamber of Commerce, Metropolitan Stadium Manager Bill Williams, and Bob McNulty, North Stars co-owner and builder of Met Center.

Bottom:
Building Supervisor Frank Jirik chats with Zamboni driver Bill Peters on the new ice of Met Center.

Opening Night at the Metropolitan Sports Center

OPENING NIGHT AT MET CENTER

Al Shaver Remembers

"THERE WAS A NEW GAME IN TOWN—NHL HOCKEY."

It was October 21, 1967, a sunny and gorgeous day in the Twin Cities, but Nancy Giel had a problem. It was an age-old problem faced by fashionable ladies since Eve chose a snarkey, low-cut fig leaf from her wardrobe in the Garden of Eden. Nancy's problem was simply, "What do I wear to a hockey game?" She was familiar with the proper garb for football games on crisp autumn afternoons when she went to old Memorial Stadium

Al Shaver, 1967

to watch her future husband Paul quarterback the Golden Gophers. But on this night, Nancy would be sitting indoors in the brand-spanking-new Metropolitan Sports Center in Bloomington. She knew it would be comfortable in the new building. And, of course, she and Paul would start the evening with dinner somewhere along the 494 strip in Bloomington. She draped herself accordingly. Perhaps they would dine at the classy Camelot Restaurant. They might select Howard Wong's palatial

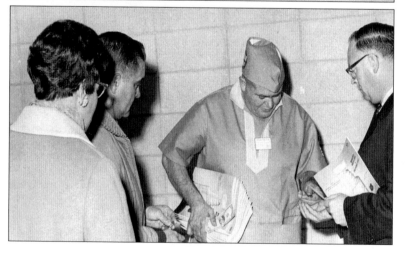

Wong's and Webster's ads from the Opening Night program

palace of Oriental delights. And there was the popular "Champagne Dinner for Two" at Eddie Webster's—just a stone's throw from the new hockey emporium. There was much for Nancy to think about.

When Paul arrived home after his drive-time sportscast on WCCO Radio, he was raring to go—anxious to get the evening's entertainment started. He urged Nancy to "get a move on," which prompted Nancy to reply, "Oh, simmer down Paul, we won't miss the opening puck-off." Later that evening Nancy learned something about the differences in terminology between football and hockey.

Opening Night at Met Center was cause for a few cases of the jitters. The "Noble Nine" certainly had them. These nine men were the original owners of the North Stars. They had pooled their resources to come up with the $2 million franchise fee demanded by the National Hockey League, and had gone into debt for the $5.5 million bucks to finance the construction of Met Center—one of the greatest bargains in sports history. The building was erected by the construction firm of Bob McNulty (one of the Noble Nine), and it was as fine a building for viewing hockey as existed at that time. Along with McNulty in the ownership group were initial club president Walter Bush Jr., John Driscoll, Harry McNeely, "Smokey" Ordway, Bill Rasmussen, Bob Ridder, Gordon Ritz, and Wheelock Whitney. These men were on

The price of this program is 50 cents
(49 cents plus 1 cent Minnesota sales tax)

MINNESOTA NORTH ST☆RS

Official 1967-68 Hockey Program

Walter L. Bush, Jr.	W. John Driscoll	Harry G. McNeely, Jr.
Robert J. McNulty	John G. Ordway, Jr.	William R. Rasmussen
Robert B. Ridder	Gordon H. Ritz	Wheelock Whitney

NORTH STAR OFFICERS

W. John Driscoll . . . Chairman of the Board

Walter L. Bush, Jr. . . . . . President
Robert J. McNulty . . Vice President and Treasurer
Gordon H. Ritz . . . . Governor and Vice President

William R. Rasmussen . . Secretary
Harry G. McNeely, Jr. . . . . Director
John G. Ordway, Jr. . . . . . Director
Robert B. Ridder . . . . . . Director
Wheelock Whitney . . . . . Director

"The Noble Nine"

*Far left:
The north side upper deck and original press box.*

the hook for a lot of money and, although optimism ran high, there was no guarantee that Minnesota would support NHL hockey.

Opening Night jitters were shared by a gentleman named Bill Peters, because that night he would be performing solo three separate times in front of thousands of onlookers. Bill's job was to operate the giant Zamboni machine, with the words "Win Stephens Buicktown" lettered on its sides. It was a job that demanded his full attention, because the slightest distraction could cause him to crash into the end boards, which would be most embarrassing. He also had to make sure his Zamboni was spreading the proper quantity of water while scooping up the snow generated by the players' skates. Everything had to go just right to avoid a mistake that could cause a delay in the game.

A fellow named Art Nickolas also had reason to be uptight. He was the original Met Center Icemaker, which made him responsible for the surface on which the game would be played. With thousands of people seated around the ice, a considerable amount of body heat would be generated. A major increase in the temperature could lead to soft ice, causing increased snow buildup. If the ice got too cold, it could become brittle, causing cracks and chipping.

But those with the most jitters inside Met Center were sitting in a large room down in the arena's lowest level. They were the players who represented the first edition of the Minnesota North Stars, and they were deeply engrossed in thoughts about the inaugural home game of the franchise. Many of them would never have gotten the chance to play in the NHL had expansion not doubled the league's size from six to twelve teams. They wondered how they would be received by the fans.

Their day began with a morning skate followed by some inspirational words from coach Wren Blair and his assistant John Mariucci. Around 11:30 they were herded onto a bus that transported them to downtown Minneapolis and Bob Short's Leamington Hotel. The players were guests-of-honor at the first "Welcome North Stars" luncheon sponsored by Norm McGrew and the Minneapolis Chamber of Commerce. Following lunch, the players were introduced to the curious diners, giving them their first close-up look at the pucksters who would don the green and gold jerseys at Met Center that evening.

A total of 12,951 inquisitive spectators turned up for the home opener. The fans could select from five ticket prices, ranging from a low of $2.80 to the top price of $5.75. As they approached Met Center from 494 and Cedar Avenue, hockey fans noticed brilliant beams probing the skies from a battery of searchlights along the north side of the building. When the throng of "First Nighters" filed into the Met, they had several choices of where to go and what to do. The most popular destination was the Beer Garden located in the northeast corner, where pints of suds were mixed with an assortment of puck-talk. The well-heeled fans headed towards the elevator at the west end, where they were lifted to the top level and the Observatory Club. There, they sipped exotic wines and dined on gourmet delights, all in luxurious splendor.

Shortly before the North Stars and Seals took the ice for warm-ups, organist Norm Grey began to entertain the assembled masses with popular tunes of the '60s. After warm-ups were complete, Bill Peters made the first of his three appearances to recondition the ice. Bill and his Zamboni performed brilliantly—right at the peak of perfection. After the opening ceremonies, it was time for Bob Utecht to issue for the first time his famous challenge of "Let's—Play—Hockey!"

Of course, it was the game itself that was the main attraction and brought nearly 13,000 viewers to rinkside. They went home happy. The honor of scoring the first goal in Met Center history went to Bill Goldsworthy, with assists from Andre Boudrias and Dave Balon. The red light behind the Seals' net was lit later by Ray Cullen from Len Lunde, and by Balon from Boudrias and Captain Bob Woytowich. The game ended in a North Star victory by a score of 3-1. The first game at Met Center was an unqualified success for the home side.

At the 8:23 mark of the 2nd period, Bill Goldsworthy beats Seals goalie Charlie Hodge for the first goal in Met Center history. An assist went to No. 17 Dave Balon.

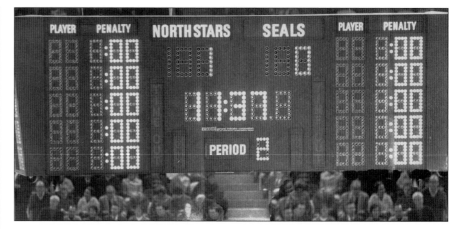

The original scoreboard, immediately after Bill Goldsworthy's first Met Center goal.

Walter Bush Remembers

Because construction time simply ran out, there were parts of the building that weren't finished on Opening Night. We were literally installing seats minutes before the game. As a seat was installed, our ticket manager Dick Arneson would immediately sell it to someone waiting in line at the box office. The locker rooms were done and the hockey office was done, but most of the other offices weren't finished. The press box only had seats up against the back wall, compared to the big gondola that we put in later. At the east end of the press box was the Press Club. There was a lot of activity going on in there—interplay between the media and our staff.

We had a big celebration before the game—a banquet at The Thunderbird Hotel, which was the only place near the Met Center, right in the middle of cornfields. Inside the Met, we had a parade on the ice that included Miss Minnesota and her Court. I rode in the parade with Lieutenant Governor Jim Goetz. We invited many dignitaries up to the Observatory Club in the Met to be part of our celebration. As for the fans, many were very well dressed—coats and ties. And Hamm's was our big sponsor. Lots of Hamm's beer.

People were really impressed with the new modern scoreboard, which if you looked at it now, you would think it came from a small town ice rink. I remember it well. It was a big green thing. There were no pictures on it, but in 1967, that was as good as it got.

The one thing I wasn't worried about on Opening night was the team. They had already been on the road for a number of games, and I'd been with them at training camp. I knew pretty well how we would stack up. I was in my seat at the start of the game. I sat about five rows behind our bench. Later, I'd migrate up to the press box. The game went on, we won, and everybody was happy. After the game, we didn't have any type of mass celebration. We just adjourned to the few offices we had. I didn't go into the dressing room.

There had been so many roadblocks leading up to this night that it seemed like a dream had finally culminated. I thought, "Did this really just happen?" It was quite an accomplishment, like getting to the top of a mountain.

THE BOARD OF DIRECTORS
OF THE MINNESOTA NORTH STARS
OF THE NATIONAL HOCKEY LEAGUE
CORDIALLY INVITE YOU AND A GUEST
TO ATTEND OUR FIRST NHL GAME TO BE PLAYED
IN MINNESOTA, SATURDAY, OCTOBER 21, 1967

MINNESOTA NORTH STARS VS. CALIFORNIA SEALS
METROPOLITAN SPORTS CENTER, BLOOMINGTON, MINN.
SATURDAY, OCTOBER 21, 1967, 8:00 P.M.

THE FAVOR OF A REPLY IS REQUESTED TO:
WALTER L. BUSH, JR., PRESIDENT
320 FIRST NATIONAL CONCOURSE BUILDING
MINNEAPOLIS, MINNESOTA 55402
(612) 339-6371

COCKTAIL SUPPER
THUNDERBIRD MOTEL
5:30 P.M.

Clockwise from upper left: invitation for owners' Opening Night gala; Minnesota beauty queens in the on-ice parade; Minnesota Lieutenant Governor James Goetz (backseat left) and Walter Bush Jr.; fans enjoy the view from the upper deck. The windows of the Observatory Club are in the background.

Head Coach Wren Blair patrols the North Star bench.

Cesare Maniago Remembers

I spent the 1964-65 season with the Minneapolis Bruins, and loved the Twin Cities. When I became the first player chosen by the North Stars in the '67 expansion draft, I couldn't have been happier. It was an honor to come back to Minnesota and to be the first North Star.

Before joining the North Stars, I'd played in the older buildings around the league like the Boston Garden, Maple Leaf Gardens and Chicago Stadium. When I first saw the Met Center, I was in awe. It was a spectacular arena. The color of the seats was mind-boggling, and it really grew on me.

Our first North Star team was comprised of cast-offs from the "Original Six" NHL franchises. We were all fighting for jobs, and developed a

strong camaraderie. I've never been involved with such a tight team as we had in '67. We were 20 guys together, no cliques. We did everything as a team. It was a wonderful experience.

The original owners were a great group of gentlemen, especially Walter Bush and Gordy Ritz. They were the players' best friends. They loved rubbing shoulders with us and would do anything for us.

Naturally, you want to win every game, but we were determined to give the fans a win on Opening Night. We wanted the fans to leave happy and eager to come back. They gave us many standing ovations throughout the night. I had non-stop tingles.

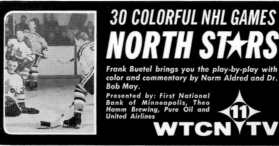

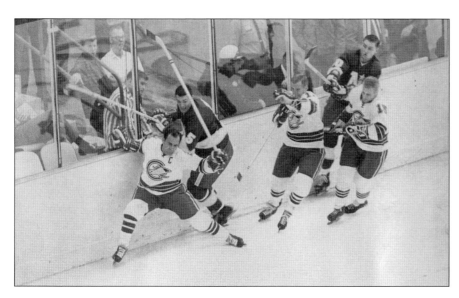

North Stars No. 5 Pete Goegan and No. 10 Ray Cullen battle the Seals along the boards.

WTCN-TV ads from the Opening Night program.

The first event in Met Center history, as seen from the Observatory Club.

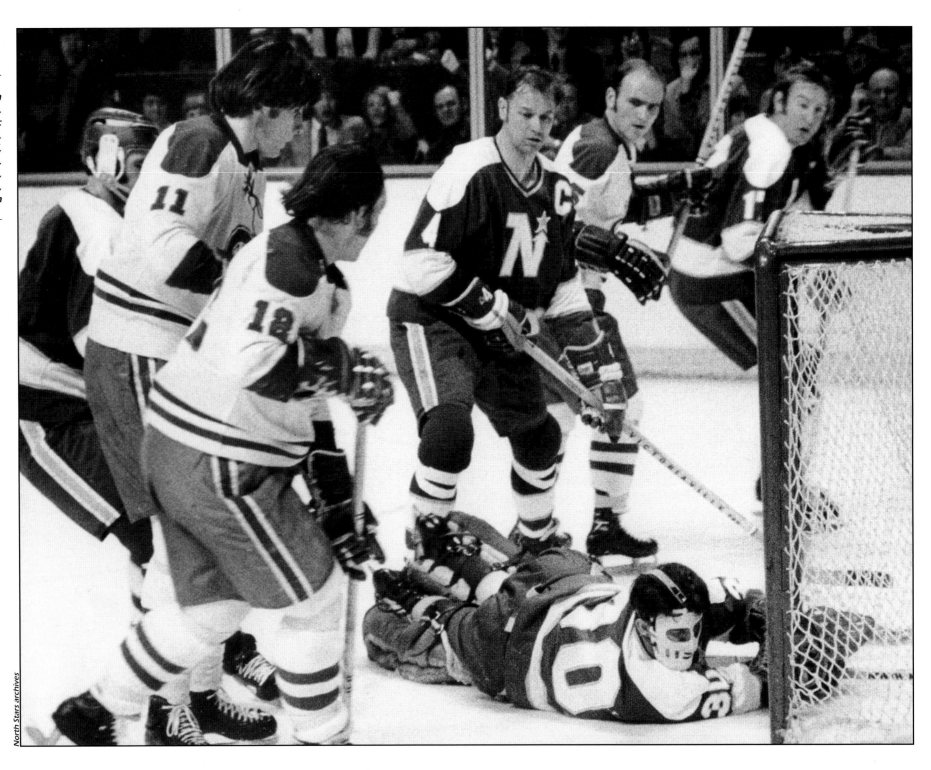

All eyes are on Cesare Maniago. From left: Barry Gibbs, Marc Tardif, Yvan Cournoyer, Ted Harris, Jacques Lemaire, Bob Nevin

North Stars archives

LOU'S NORTH STAR STORIES

HEAD COACHES

Wren Blair

North Stars archives

The North Stars had a number of coaches over the years, resulting in a number of coaching styles. Wren Blair was the first.

Wren was not really a good tactician. He liked speed, he liked pressure, and he liked the team the way he was — very flamboyant. He wanted a lot of flair, flashiness and goal-scoring. He knew he was there to sell hockey, and he did a great job creating a product that was entertaining and exciting.

North Stars archives

He was so tough on everyone that we all hated him and pulled together ourselves. Looking back, he probably did it purposely.

John Muckler

Wren was followed by John Muckler. This was early in his career. Muckler had never coached in the NHL until this time and really wasn't as refined a hockey coach as he became.

When he was with us, Muckler was all about intimidation and yelling and screaming. It was a lot like fire and brimstone. He tried to motivate the team to play hard by getting them fired up. He really didn't develop into a great NHL coach until later, winning Stanley Cups with the Edmonton Oilers. It helped that he had the best team in the world there, but he also learned to handle players better and use more systems.

Charlie Burns

North Stars archives

Charlie Burns coached us for a very short while. Charlie was a hard-working, penalty-killing type of player.

In the '71 playoffs against St. Louis, we needed a checking line, so they moved me up to play on a line with Charlie and Murray Oliver. We not only had a good checking series, we got some goals, so they kept us together and we played as a line for a while. We had a good relationship when we were playing together, but Charlie and I never had a good relationship when he was my coach.

I was a little concerned when Charlie took over, because he used to seem envious of me. And when he took over as coach, he made my life hard. At the end of every practice we'd do a drill skating down and back with our partners. When everybody was done, he'd say, "OK Louie, you go alone now." So I'd have to go with my partners and I'd have to go alone. And he did this constantly.

We had a game against Oakland one night, and we were losing badly with about six minutes left to go in the game. Charlie comes over to me and says, "Louie, get out there and start something." I said, "What do you mean by that?"

As a player, Charlie would never get in a fight — he'd never do anything like that — and all of a sudden here he is ordering one? He says, "You know what I mean." I said, "If you want me to do something, you tell me what you mean. I know what you mean, but I want to hear you say the words." And he says, "Get out there and start a fight." So, I did. When I came back from the penalty box I said: "You would never do something like that."

At the end of the season when he was let go as coach, he came to me and said, "I just want to tell you I picked on you because I knew you could take it. So I used you as a scapegoat."

North Stars archives

I said, "It might have been your way, but I don't appreciate it. I don't think it was very classy."

Jack Gordon

Jack Gordon came in next, and he was the best coach we'd had up to that time. Jack was all about position, checking and balance. He was the first real defensive coach we had. Jack was diligent about defense. He really required that from his players or they didn't play.

Lou Nanne and Jack Gordon, Bloomington Ice Garden

Bloomington Historical Society

Parker MacDonald

Parker MacDonald coached us for a while. Parker was real easy going and laid-back.

We knew Parker would become the coach, because whenever we'd have parties at Wren's house, he made Parker his pool partner. We always said, "Parker, you're going to end up coaching this team, because Wren wants you around as a pool partner."

Ted Harris

Ted Harris followed Jack and Parker. I really enjoyed having Ted as a teammate — he was a great leader on the ice, and I think he was among the best captains we had. Ted was an extremely tough, physical player, and when he became coach, he wanted the team to be that way, too. He worked us hard, and he required us to play hard. But Ted wasn't a great conversationalist and really didn't communicate well. He was a quiet guy, and that's basically the way he coached.

Andre Beaulieu

Andre Beaulieu came after Teddy. He was our assistant coach and didn't have a great deal of experience at a high level. The original owners got rid of Harris during the year, and they didn't want to spend any money hiring a coach, so they put Andre in there. Andre was a nice guy. Unfortunately for him, because of his background the players didn't listen to him the way they should have, didn't work for him as hard as they should have, and didn't respect him the way they should have.

Lou Nanne with Eriksson, Bennett, Pirus and Brasar

Lou Nanne

I myself coached for the last month and a half of the '77-78 season when I took the team over. I knew that I'd coach until the end of the season and then hire a coach. I had coached the University of Minnesota freshman team for four years and some Olympic development leagues for four or five years, and I knew I never wanted to be a coach.

Harry Howell

North Stars archives

Then I hired Harry Howell, who was general manager of the Cleveland Barons when the teams merged.

One of the things that quickly became apparent to me was that the Gunds were going to work in a very businesslike manner with a tight budget. As a matter of fact, I'll never forget when I went to my first meeting, John Karr, the president of the Cleveland team, started asking me about my people and saying: "We've got to make some cuts here. Who's John Mariucci?"

I said: "John Mariucci's a legend. He's the godfather of hockey in Minnesota, and he's an astute hockey man." And Karr says, "We don't hire guys just because they're legends."

I walked out and I said to Mariucci: "You've got a three-year contract." He says, "What are you talking about?" I said: "You and I agreed to a three-year contract. When they come to me and say, 'Who's under contract?' you've already got a contract."

Anyway, Harry Howell had been their GM, and I was going to put him as director of player personnel, but the Gunds asked if we could put him in as coach and I said, "That's fine."

Harry was a terrific Hall of Fame hockey player, a wonderful individual and a very knowledgeable hockey man. I asked him, "Would you like to coach?" and he said: "I'll try it. I've never coached, but I wouldn't mind it."

He coached for a very short time, maybe a month, and he got a heart condition. It wasn't the kind of job that meshed with his personality. I brought in the guy I was originally going to hire as coach: Glen Sonmor.

Glen Sonmor

Glen was the best coach the North Stars ever had, and he was there the longest. He knew how to motivate a team. He knew the type of player he wanted. He knew checking. He knew scoring. He knew offense. He knew defense. He was a terrific coach.

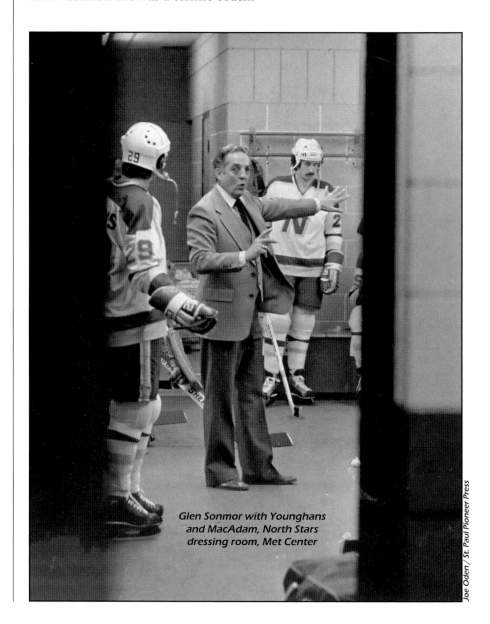

Glen Sonmor with Younghans and MacAdam, North Stars dressing room, Met Center

Joe Oden / St. Paul Pioneer Press

Obviously, the only problems Glen had were his own personal problems with alcohol, and it took us seven or eight years to work through that, off and on. That's why sometimes we had to take him out as coach for a short time and later move him back in.

We were trying to find a way that he could beat his problem, which he eventually did. Afterwards, he was an unbelievable help to many people with alcohol problems.

Murray Oliver

Murray Oliver coached for a very short time. Whenever we'd have a problem with Glen, we'd put Murray in because we knew Glen was coming back. The only time Glen didn't go back was when we played Toronto in the 1983 playoffs.

Murray had to take over for Glen, and Murray came into my office and said: "Louie, we haven't beaten Toronto all year long. I think you've got to come down on the bench and co-coach with me. I don't know if the players are going to listen to me enough."

North Stars archives

I agreed, and we beat Toronto three games to one. Then we played Chicago and the Blackhawks knocked us out.

Bill Mahoney

We followed Glen with Bill Mahoney. He was a real tactician and an excellent hockey man. He was tough and required a lot from the players, but he was successful with the players. He did an excellent job with them and got them all the way to the semifinals.

When I look back at it, I know I made a big mistake when I let him go. The reason I did that was twofold. First, I was having a problem with the players getting upset with Bill. That's when Bobby Smith asked to be traded, and then Al MacAdam asked to be traded, etc.

Staff Photo / St. Paul Pioneer Press

And second, Bill got a little uptight with the media. As a matter of fact, when the media wrote something negative about him, he would tack it to the wall behind his desk, and when reporters came in he would point to it and get confrontational with them.

However, if I had to do it all over again, I would keep Bill. I didn't use enough patience with him and should have tried to work with him better than I did.

Lorne Henning

Lorne Henning came in and did a terrific job for us. He had a wonderful first year. Lorne came from the Islander system and knew how Al Arbour coached, and he did a lot of excellent things.

During the second year, Lorne started getting angry at certain players and just going off on them. He didn't like Kent Nilsson. He didn't like Brian Bellows. We'd lose a game, and Nilsson would be sitting upstairs in the press box. Then Lorne would come to me and say: "You've gotta trade Nilsson. We can't use him here." And I'd say: "Well, Nilsson wasn't even on the ice tonight. We got beat without Nilsson." And he'd say: "I'm never playing Nilsson again. I don't like him, and he's not playing on this hockey club."

Then Lorne did the same thing with Brian Bellows. He tried to get me to trade Bellows. The last straw was when Lorne came in all upset with Craig Hartsburg, who I thought was one of the best defensemen in the league, and said, "You gotta trade Hartsburg to Edmonton. We can get Craig Redmond," who had been the sixth pick overall but never materialized into anywhere near the hockey player Hartsburg was.

I got upset and said: "Lorne, that's it. From now on you coach the team, and I'll manage the team. Don't tell me who to trade and who to get."

Lorne got very close to Keith Acton and Dirk Graham, who were terrific players for us. He wasn't enamored with Ciccarelli, so that caused a little friction between Acton and Graham and Dino.

Things came to a head near the end of '86-87 season. I was away scouting a junior game while the North Stars were playing at the Met. I called Lorne at about midnight for a report on our game. As we discussed various things, he made no mention of a need to call up players from our Springfield farm team.

I arrived back in Minnesota the next day. We had back-to-back home games, and when I got to the Met for the game that night I noticed two of our regular players sitting in the press box. When I asked them what happened, they said they had been benched. Then I looked down at the ice and saw two rookies warming up with the team. They had been called up from Springfield without my knowing it. After the game I talked to the rookies, then went to Lorne and asked, "What's going on?" He said he called up the two players because he thought it might give the team a jolt. He also said he didn't think of making the move until that morning, long after he and I talked the night before. I told Lorne that I had just spoken with the rookies and they said they were informed about the call-up the previous night and arrived in Minnesota the morning of the game.

As GM, I never talked about player contracts with my coaches because I didn't want it to affect their decisions. Therefore, when it came to calling up a player from the minors, it was imperative that the coach discuss with me who he wanted to add to the team and why. There were unique clauses written into the contracts of certain players, and in this instance one of the players called up by Henning would receive a large bonus for playing a few games in the NHL. We could not justify jeopardizing that amount of money simply because he felt the move might give the team a jolt.

A short time later, I got a message from one of the Gunds saying he wanted to talk to me about a letter he received from Lorne. The letter was very critical of the North Stars' scouting department, the assistant coaches and me. Previously, the Gunds had asked if I was considering a coaching change because the team was struggling and I had told them no, believing that Lorne was an extremely capable coach. After telling me about the letter, they asked my thoughts and I said, "I'm going to let him go tomorrow," which I did. Glen Sonmor coached our final two games of the season and we missed the playoffs.

Lorne is a gifted and knowledgeable hockey person, but at times with the North Stars he blurred the lines of his job responsibilities. I felt this was due to his strong desire to be successful after coming from the very successful Islanders organization.

Herb Brooks

Around the time that Henning was let go, John Mariucci died. Herb Brooks and I were at the funeral together, and when we came out of church I looked at him and said, "You know, Herb, John always wanted you to coach here, and I always wanted you to coach here. We've been through this three times. I think now is the time you've got to come and coach."

When I first took over the North Stars and before we had the merger, the first guy I offered the coaching job to was Herb Brooks. He came to my office and I said, "Herb, I want you to come coach the North Stars, and I'll give you a two-year contract." We talked about terms and then he says, "I want a three-year contract."

I said: "Herb, two years. All my people got two years. I'm not going to have a coach out of whack with the rest of the staff." He says again, "Three years." I said, "You're not getting it."

He says: "I really want to coach the Olympics anyway. You're on the Olympic committee, help me get that job." I said, "I'll do what I can, and I know Walter Bush will support you."

He coached the Olympic team to victory over the Soviet Union and won the gold medal in Lake Placid. When he first coached in the NHL, it was with the Rangers.

I got together with him once again when I was looking for a coach, before I hired Mahoney, and he said he would take the position. I worked out a

John Croft / Minneapolis Star Tribune

deal with his agent, Art Kaminsky, and set up a meeting in Princeton, N.J., so he could meet Gordon Gund.

When I got home from playing golf, the day before we were leaving for New Jersey, my phone rang. It was Kaminsky. He says, "Herb's not going with you tomorrow morning."

I said, "Why not?" He says, "He won't take the job unless you pay him $250,000 if you fire him." I said, "Art, no way in the world am I going to pay a guy more to get fired than I am to have him coach."

I called Herb and told him that. He said, "I want a severance check."

I said: "You'll have the rest of your contract if you ever get fired. But I'm not thinking of you getting fired, while I'm hiring you.'"

He says, "No, if I don't get that I'm not coming." So he didn't come.

And that brought us to Maroosh's funeral. I said, "Are you ready to coach the North Stars?" and he said, "Yeah."

Herbie came in — a tremendous coach, but unfortunately for him and for us, we had the most injuries in the history of our organization. We had over 500 man games missed. Everybody was out of our lineup for long periods of time.

It was when we lost Craig Hartsburg and Dan Mandich with career-ending injuries. We lost Tom Hirsch, we lost Brian Bellows, we lost Neal Broten — all our top players were missing games and it was very tough.

It was driving me nuts, and I thought, "I've got to get out of this game." So around January 1988, I decided I'd had enough. I'd gone to the Mayo Clinic and they had given me two years to either change my lifestyle or change my job. The doctors said, "… otherwise you can do severe damage to your body."

I'm obsessive-compulsive, and they gave me some pills for that. But the injuries were driving me nuts and I thought, "I've got to change jobs." So I went to the Gunds and said: "Look, I'm quitting. I want to announce it now. I'll stay as long as you need me, but no longer than the draft." They tried to talk me out of it but I said no. So they sent me on vacation. They said, "Go anywhere you want with your wife for a week, and then come back and talk to us again."

I came back and said, "No, I'm not staying in hockey." That's when they offered me the job to stay as North Stars president, which I took.

Unfortunately, while I was on vacation, Herbie went to the Gunds and said, "I want a five-year contract as GM and coach or I'm quitting at the end of the year."

The Gunds were very upset with Herb for coming to them with an ultimatum at a time like that. Herb said: "I came here to work for Louie. If he's not here, I either get this or I leave."

You don't intimidate the Gunds. When I came back and they told me about it, I went and had a talk with Herb. I'll never forget, he says: "Louie, it's like real estate, where everything is location, location, location. This is timing, timing, timing."

I said, "You don't put a gun to the head of people who have 'screw you' money, Herbie."

He wouldn't back down.

When the season was over, Jack Ferreira was hired as general manager. The Gunds hired him — I didn't interview any of the candidates. They left it to Jack to hire his staff.

When the season was over, the Gunds gave everybody in the hockey department termination letters and told Jack that he had the right to hire back anybody he wanted. And Jack didn't hire Herbie back.

Herbie would have been a wonderful coach for us had he stayed long-term. He didn't really want to be a general manager, he wanted to be a coach. He would have been Ferreira's coach, if he hadn't made the demands.

Pierre Page

Ferreira brought in Pierre Page, who had been an assistant in Calgary and was a fiery coach with a lot of emotion. He was very technical, and did an excellent job moving the team along. In his first season, we qualified for the playoffs after a two year absence. He left for the GM job with Quebec at the same time the Gunds sold the team.

John Croft / Minneapolis Star Tribune

Bob Gainey

Howard Baldwin and Norm Green hired Bobby Clarke as general manager and Bob Gainey as head coach. They were a terrific tandem. Gainey had been a top checking forward in the NHL, and he developed the players into a team that was forthright in checking and position play. His style brought the North Stars to the Stanley Cup Finals in his first year as coach. Gainey was instrumental in developing Mike Modano into a complete player. He taught him the importance of checking and made him a bona fide Frank J. Selke Award candidate for top defensive forward.

Bob Gainey with Assistant Coach Doug Jarvis

Mike Zerby / Minneapolis Star Tribune

1967-68 MINNESOTA NORTH STARS – FIRST OFFICIAL TEAM PHOTO

Front Row (L to R) Cesare Maniago, Dave Balon, Bob Woytowich, Asst. Coach John Mariucci,
President Walter Bush Jr., Head Coach/GM Wren Blair, Mike McMahon, Andre Boudrias, Gary Bauman
Middle Row (L to R) Trainer Stan Waylett, Bill Goldsworthy, Ray Cullen, Wayne Connelly, Bill Masterton, Sandy Fitzpatrick,
Duke Harris, Parker MacDonald, Ted Taylor, Asst. Trainer Al Schueneman
Back Row (L to R) Don Johns, Pete Goegan, Elmer Vasko, Bill Collins, Bob McCord

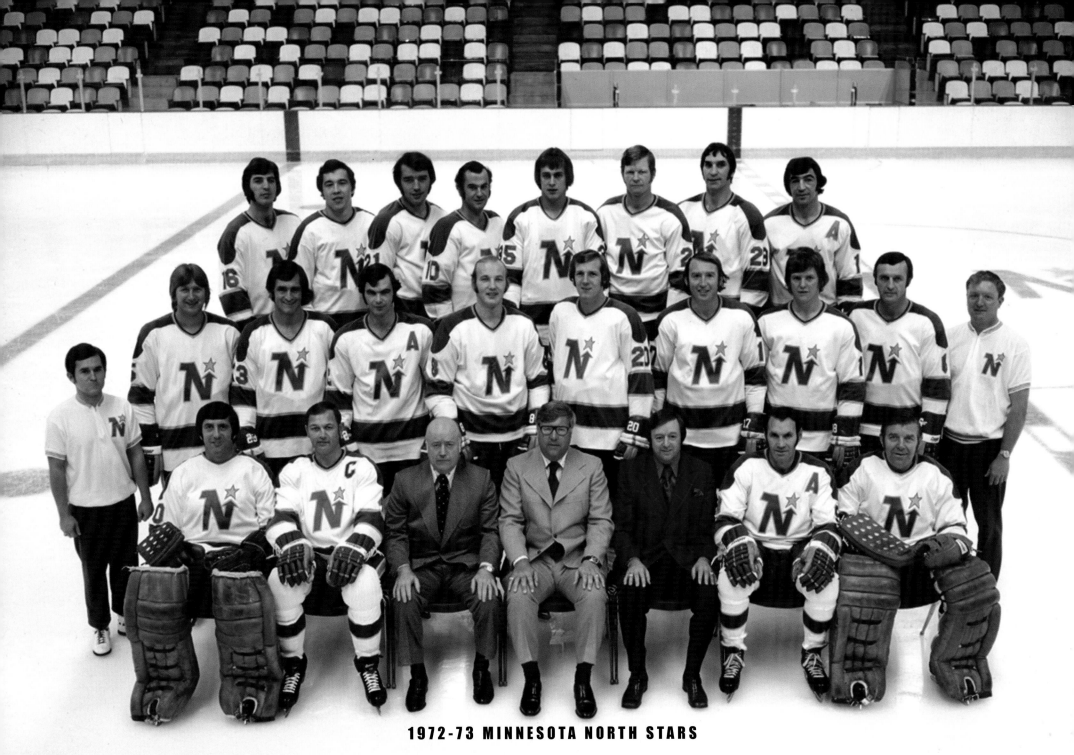

1972-73 MINNESOTA NORTH STARS

Front Row (L to R) Cesare Maniago, Ted Harris, Head Coach Jack Gordon, President Walter Bush Jr., GM Wren Blair, Charlie Burns, Gump Worsley
Middle Row (L to R) Asst. Trainer Dennis Kovach, Dennis O'Brien, Lou Nanne, Barry Gibbs, Bill Goldsworthy, Tom Reid, Bob Nevin, Buster Harvey, Doug Mohns, Trainer Doc Rose
Back Row (L to R) Jude Drouin, Fred Barrett, Danny Grant, Murray Oliver, Gilles Gilbert, Dennis Hextall, Dean Prentice, J.P. Parise

N 1979-80 N
MINNESOTA NORTH ST★RS

GEORGE GUND III
Chairman of the Board

GORDON GUND
Vice Chairman of the Board

Schmidt
BEER

Schmidt
BEER

FRONT ROW: Gary Edwards, Paul Shmyr, Assistant Coach J. P. Parise; Assistant General Manager John Mariucci; Vice-President Walter Bush, Jr.; President John Karr; General Manager Lou Nanne; Coach Glen Sonmor; Assistant Coach Murray Oliver; Gilles Meloche

SECOND ROW: Assistant Trainer Dennis Kovach; Kris Manery, Brad Maxwell, Craig Hartsburg, Tim Young, Kent Erik Andersson, Bobby Smith, Steve Payne, Fred Barrett, Trainer Dick Rose

THIRD ROW: Per Olov Brasar, Gary Sargent, Ron Zanussi, Tom McCarthy, Al MacAdam, Greg Smith, Glen Sharpley, Mike Fidler, Tom Younghans, Mike Polich   NOT PICTURED: Mike Eaves, Jack Carlson.

Best Beer In Any League

1982-83
MINNESOTA NORTH ST☆RS

SITTING (FROM LEFT): Al MacAdam, Tim Young, Jordy Douglas, Neal Broten, Brad Maxwell, Fred Barrett. STANDING: Don Beaupre, Gary Sargent, Gilles Meloche, Craig Hartsburg, Gordie Roberts, Willi Plett, Jim Craig. SEATED ON ZAMBONI: Doc Rose, Brian Bellows, Tom McCarthy, Mike Eaves, Dino Ciccarelli, Randy Velischek, Bobby Smith, Dan Mandich, George Ferguson, Curt Giles, Ron Friest, Steve Payne, Larry Ness.

1989-90 MINNESOTA NORTH STARS

Seated (L to R): *Asst. Coach Doug Jarvis, Head Coach Pierre Page, Stewart Gavin, Perry Berezan, Curt Fraser, Equip. Mgr. Mark Baribeau, Brian Bellows, Curt Giles, Gaetan Duchesne, Dave Gagner, Aaron Broten, Neal Broten, Mike Gartner, Rob Zettler, Larry Murphy*
Standing (L to R): *Asst. Coach Craig Hartsburg, Asst. Coach Dave Chambers, Don Barber, Basil McRae, Shawn Chambers, Frantisek Musil, Dave Mackey, Asst. Equip. Mgr. Lance Vogt, Kari Takko, Jon Casey, Daniel Berthiaume, Mark Tinordi, Mike Modano, Asst. Trainer Dave Smith, Shane Churla, Ville Siren, Neil Wilkinson, Helmut Balderis and Trainer Dave Surprenant*

Jim Gallop / Gallop Studio

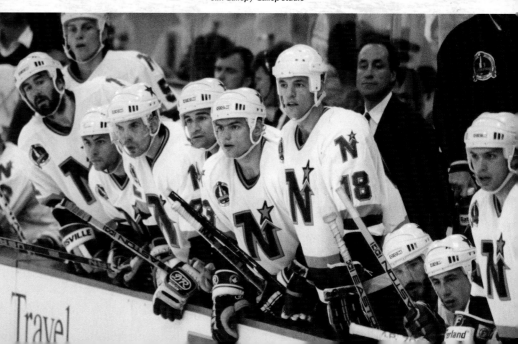

Above, On the bench with Lou Nanne (L to R): *Asst. Trainer Dennis Kovach, Harvey Bennett, Jimmy Roberts, Ron Zanussi, Glen Sharpley.* **North Stars archives**

Right, On the bench with Bob Gainey (L to R): *Neil Wilkinson (back), Stewart Gavin, Neal Broten, Ulf Dahlen, Basil McRae, Brian Bellows, Bobby Smith, Gaetan Duchesne, Shane Churla, Marc Bureau.* **Brian Peterson / Minneapolis Star Tribune**

1980-81 MINNESOTA NORTH STARS – STANLEY CUP FINALIST

Front Row (L to R): Don Beaupre, Paul Shmyr, Asst. Coach J.P. Parise, Chairman Walter Bush Jr., Co-Owner George Gund,
Co-Owner Gordon Gund, President John Karr, GM Lou Nanne, Head Coach Glen Sonmor, Asst. Coach Murray Oliver, Gilles Meloche
Middle Row (L to R): Asst. Trainer Larry Ness, Greg Smith, Craig Hartsburg, Tim Young, Kent-Erik Andersson,
Bobby Smith, Steve Payne, Tom McCarthy, Brad Maxwell, Fred Barrett, Trainer Doc Rose
Back Row (L to R): Curt Giles, Gary Sargent, Ron Zanussi, Brad Palmer, Al MacAdam, Jack Carlson, Don Jackson,
Steve Christoff, Gordie Roberts, Tom Younghans, Mike Eaves, Dino Ciccarelli, Mike Polich

1990-91 MINNESOTA NORTH STARS – STANLEY CUP FINALIST

Front Row (L to R): Jon Casey, Curt Giles, Asst. Coach Doug Jarvis, Head Coach Bob Gainey, Owner Norman N. Green, GM Bobby Clarke, Asst. Coach Andy Murray, Stewart Gavin, Basil McRae, Brian Hayward **Middle Row (L to R):** Asst. Trainer Dave Smith, Asst. Equip. Mgr. Lance Vogt, Asst. GM Doug Armstrong, Perry Berezan, Neil Wilkinson, Mark Tinordi, Bobby Smith, Brian Glynn, Mike Modano, Rob Zettler, Equip. Mgr. Mark Baribeau, Trainer Dave Surprenant **Back Row (L to R):** Doug Smail, Dave Gagner, Gaetan Duchesne, Shane Churla, Chris Dahlquist, Shawn Chambers, Ulf Dahlen, Mike Craig, Jim Johnson, Marc Bureau, Brian Bellows, Brian Propp, Neal Broten

1985-86 Minnesota North Stars at the Ordway Music Theater, St. Paul / Upper right: 1987-88 Minnesota North Stars at First Avenue, Minneapolis
Jim Gallop: The Ordway shoot was a production. The biggest problem was trying to control the amateur musicians and keep them from composing the latest hockey pop hit. And then there were the tennis shoes… The First Ave shoot was also quite a production. Getting the players into make-up and wardrobe alone was a feat. They had to resemble musicians as close as possible, and it took a while for them to get into character. We wanted smoke-fog to create an authentic club atmosphere, and did so by burning 50 packs worth of Camel cigarettes. Jim Gallop / Gallop Studio

COACHING HISTORY

SEASON	HEAD COACH
1967-68	WREN BLAIR
1968-69	WREN BLAIR, JOHN MUCKLER
1969-70	WREN BLAIR, CHARLIE BURNS
1970-71	JACK GORDON
1971-72	JACK GORDON
1972-73	JACK GORDON
1973-74	JACK GORDON, PARKER MACDONALD
1974-75	JACK GORDON, CHARLIE BURNS
1975-76	TED HARRIS
1976-77	TED HARRIS
1977-78	TED HARRIS, ANDRE BEAULIEU, LOU NANNE
1978-79	HARRY HOWELL, GLEN SONMOR
1979-80	GLEN SONMOR
1980-81	GLEN SONMOR
1981-82	GLEN SONMOR, MURRAY OLIVER
1982-83	GLEN SONMOR, MURRAY OLIVER
1983-84	BILL MAHONEY
1984-85	BILL MAHONEY, GLEN SONMOR
1985-86	LORNE HENNING
1986-87	LORNE HENNING, GLEN SONMOR
1987-88	HERB BROOKS
1988-89	PIERRE PAGE
1989-90	PIERRE PAGE
1990-91	BOB GAINEY
1991-92	BOB GAINEY
1992-93	BOB GAINEY

COACHING RECORDS

COACH	YEAR	REGULAR SEASON	PLAYOFFS
Wren Blair	1967-68	27-32-15	7-7
	1968-69	12-20-9	
	1969-70	9-13-10	
John Muckler	1968-69	6-23-6	
Charlie Burns	1969-70	10-22-12	2-4
	1974-75	12-28-2	
Jack Gordon	1970-71	28-34-16	6-6
	1971-72	37-29-12	3-4
	1972-73	37-30-11	2-4
	1973-74	3-8-6	
	1974-75	11-22-5	
Parker MacDonald	1973-74	20-30-11	
Ted Harris	1975-76	20-53-7	
	1976-77	23-39-18	0-2
	1977-78	5-12-2	
Andre Beaulieu	1977-78	6-22-3	
Lou Nanne	1977-78	7-18-4	
Harry Howell	1978-79	3-6-2	
Glen Sonmor	1978-79	25-34-11	
	1979-80	36-28-16	8-7
	1980-81	35-28-17	12-7
	1981-82	34-23-19	1-3
	1982-83	22-12-9	
	1984-85	22-35-10	5-4
	1986-87	0-1-1	
Murray Oliver	1981-82	3-0-1	
	1982-83	18-11-7	4-5
Bill Mahoney	1983-84	39-31-10	7-9
	1984-85	3-8-2	
Lorne Henning	1985-86	38-33-9	2-3
	1986-87	30-39-9	
Herb Brooks	1987-88	19-48-13	
Pierre Page	1988-89	27-37-16	1-4
	1989-90	36-40-4	3-4
Bob Gainey	1990-91	27-39-14	14-9
	1991-92	32-42-6	3-4
	1992-93	36-38-10	

PLAYERS & STAFF

Keith Acton

Keith Acton came to us from Montreal along with Mark Napier in the Bobby Smith trade. He instantly gave us the tenacity we were lacking at center and became one of our key players.

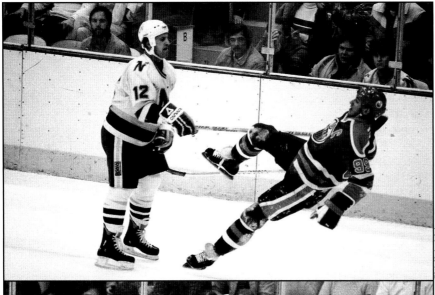

Keith Acton dumps Wayne Gretzky after the whistle, and Gretzky protests to referee Denis Morel when no penalty is called, 2/8/85.

Rick Kolodziej

Rick Kolodziej

Keith played for a number of coaches while with the North Stars, and they all used him to check the opponent's top line. He was a terrific checker with excellent speed.

He was traded to Edmonton for defenseman Moe Mantha during the '87-88 season. It wasn't easy dealing Keith, but we were depleted on defense and he could bring us a solid vet like Mantha.

Kent-Erik Andersson

Kent-Erik Andersson joined us the year after fellow Swede Roland Eriksson became a North Star.

I think Kent was probably the best penalty killer in our team's history. He had great anticipation of what the opponent was going to do. He was an excellent skater, a good puck handler, and most of all he was extremely smart.

Kent-Erik Andersson

North Stars archives

Mike Antonovich

Mike Antonovich was a high school hero at Greenway-Coleraine and had a fabulous career at the University of Minnesota. He was a very creative center who we drafted in 1971, but he chose to play for Glen Sonmor and the Fighting Saints of the WHA.

Mike joined the North Stars for 12 games late in the '75-76 season after the Fighting Saints ceased operations, then returned to the Saints when they started up again in the fall. He rejoined us briefly in '81-82. Even though we were loaded at center, he was one of Glen's favorite players and we wanted to give him a look.

After having a terrific season with our Nashville farm team, Mike signed with New Jersey.

Bob Barlow

A funny thing about head coach Wren Blair was that he could hardly skate. The only time he put on skates was before training camp, when we'd stop to have practice in Toronto on the way to camp in Haliburton.

Wren would put on a brand-new, white North Stars jacket and hold practice in Toronto so the press would come and see him. We'd have no pucks on the ice and skate back and forth for an hour. He'd blow the whistle and say, "Get that oxygen intake up!" And Wren would stand in the center of the ice, blowing the whistle, because he couldn't turn on skates.

Bobby Barlow had played in the American Hockey League, and we got him in training camp in 1968. The first day on the ice in Toronto, Wren Blair is running practice wearing his new white jacket. We're at the George Bell Arena, we have media people there, and Wren's putting

Bob Barlow

North Stars archives

on a show for them. He keeps blowing the whistle, and we keep skating, going around and around endlessly. Barlow finally comes over to Wren and says: "Wren, I can't go anymore. My legs have seized." Wren looks at him and says, "Barlow, once a minor leaguer always a minor leaguer."

Don Beaupre

Don Beaupre

Jim Gallop / Gallop Studio

In the 1980 draft, we had a number of second round picks and our goal was to get some good goaltending for the future. We decided to select Donnie Beaupre and Kelly Hrudey and try to get them back-to-back. So we took Beaupre, but immediately afterwards the Islanders took Hrudey, just in front of our next pick.

I walked over to my good friend, Bill Torrey, after he picked Hrudey and said, "You don't know how much you just hurt me."

Donnie Beaupre was a good goaltender for us throughout his time as a North Star. He came in and had an outstanding rookie year. His sophomore year he went down a bit, but then he bounced back and gave us excellent goaltending for a long time.

Scott Bjugstad

Scott Bjugstad had a tremendous shot and a real knack for scoring. We drafted him out of the University of Minnesota, and he joined the North Stars following his time on the '84 U.S. Olympic team.

He was a big kid who adjusted quickly to the NHL, and in his second season he got 43 goals and 33 assists. The following year, unfortunately, Scott started dealing with injuries and it cost him a lot of ice time. Jack Ferreira eventually sent him to Pittsburgh in a deal for Ville Siren.

Scott Bjugstad

Jim Gallop / Gallop Studio

Wren Blair

Wren Blair was the first general manager and coach of the Minnesota North Stars, and he probably was the biggest character of any executive in the National Hockey League at that time. He was a very high-strung, unpredictable guy.

One of the first games I ever played with the North Stars was against Montreal in Minnesota, and we were under siege right from the beginning — Montreal was putting a lot of pressure on us. Wren turned around facing the crowd, put his hands on the glass behind the bench and said, "Just tell me when they score, just tell me when they score."

During that same game, Montreal continued to dominate us. At one point, the whistle blew stopping play and five of our guys came off the ice. Blair didn't say which line and defensemen he wanted to go out. One of our guys said, "Wren, who's up?" Wren, with his back still turned not watching the game, replied, "Any five, any damn five."

●

The first couple years of existence of the North Stars, Wren felt that the fans didn't know enough to really be critical of the players.

During an exhibition game against Detroit, we had a tough time. On one power play when we couldn't get it out of our zone, he literally stood on the bench with one foot on the dasher board and he turned toward the crowd and started yelling: "Boo the players. Boo. Boo the players."

He was trying to instruct the crowd, and then he lost his balance and he fell right on an extremely sensitive area and lost his breath. All the players on the bench were laughing because we knew what happened to him.

●

We had another night in Pittsburgh where he was very frustrated with us. It was after the second period, and we were getting beat. He came in and as he was walking through the locker room said, "You guys are all

Larry Schreiber / Minneapolis Star Tribune

Wren Blair, with (L to R) MacDonald, Cullen, Collins, Boudrias, 3/7/68

worthless," and he continued walking into the back room. Pittsburgh had a split dressing room, and the back room was a bathroom and lounge area.

We waited and waited and he never came out, and finally the buzzer sounded for us to return to the ice. We knew we could get a delay of game penalty, so we went out to the bench to resume the game. You had to go across the ice from the dressing room to our bench, even if you were a coach. Wren still didn't come out. As it turned out, a policeman locked the door after we left the dressing room and Wren was locked inside. We told Cesare Maniago, who wasn't playing, to start coaching.

Six minutes into the period, there was Wren shaking the glass on the other side of the ice. He had made enough noise to get someone to open the dressing room door. As he came across into the bench, he says to our trainer, "You're fired." Then he says to Cesare, "You're a terrible coach; I'm taking over."

●

Wren Blair fancied himself as a great coach but really didn't know much about playing a position. One day we were practicing in South St. Paul, and Wren was upset with

the way Tom Reid was playing defense. Wren stops the practice, blows the whistle, and is mimicking Tom Reid going backwards and trying to break up a play. Not being able to skate very well, Wren is practically falling over and looking very comical—he thinks he's being funny, but he's funny because of the way he's moving.

He stops and says, "And that's the way Tom Reid plays defense." Later he gets into an argument with Tommy Williams. Then he cuts the practice short, saying, "That's it. Everybody out of here." Wren skates toward the boards, and as he gets there he goes for a big ending by throwing his stick at the bench. The stick hit the top railing of the bench, came right back and hit him right between the eyes.

All four photos: North Stars archives

Moose Vasko

Bob McCord

Lou Nanne

We had a "Welcome Home, North Stars" luncheon the next day, and by then Wren had two black eyes. So he wore sunglasses at the banquet. When he got up in front of the crowd that day, his big line was, "You think it's easy negotiating with these guys?" And he pulled his glasses off to show he had two black eyes.

Dave Balon was the North Stars' lone All-Star selection in the first season, but during the off-season Wren traded him to the Rangers in a deal that brought us Wayne Hillman. The legendary Emile Francis was GM and coach of the Rangers at the time.

We were playing a game at the Met on a Sunday afternoon, and we had a poor first period. At the end of the period, Wren came in to the locker room and started berating the defense, which sat together in a corner. He loved to give the defense a hard time. So he storms in and says "This defense is awful." He looks at Moose Vasko and says "Moose, my captain, you're nothing but a fat piece of shit." He looks next at Bob McCord and says "McCord, my big tough guy – you couldn't fight my mother." He turns to me and says "Lou Nanne, everything I hate in a hockey player. You went to college, you're a defenseman who likes to rush the puck, and you became an American citizen." The last guy he turns to is Wayne Hillman, who he had obtained in the trade for Balon. Wren says, "And you, Hillman,"

Wayne Hillman

then he looks to the ceiling with his hands on his head and says "Oh Emile, how you screwed me, how you screwed me."

At the end of our first season, we had a home-and-home series with St. Louis. We needed to win just one of the games in order to finish ahead of the Blues in the standings. Winning and finishing one slot higher also meant that each player would receive about $500 more in bonus money from the league.

In the first game at St. Louis, we led 2-1 late in the third period when we were called for a penalty. Wren was enraged by the call and threw a towel at the ref. The ref assessed a bench penalty to Wren, so St. Louis had a two-man advantage on the power play. They scored to tie the game during the five-on-three, and then scored to take the lead when we were one man down due to the bench penalty. We lost the game 3-2.

In the locker room after the game, the players were very upset. They felt that Wren had cost them the game, and the bonus money, when he lost control on the bench. Wren felt bad himself, and told the team that the club would pay the difference in bonus money if we wound up behind St. Louis in the final standings.

We lost the next night at the Met, 5-3, and finished the season one point behind the Blues. Wren made good on his promise of the money, but we didn't get home-ice advantage in the playoffs. We were angry and disappointed at losing the final game.

On the Friday night before the big final weekend series with the Blues, Wren hosted a dinner to pull the team together. After we'd eaten, guys were relaxing with a drink. Wren walked past Andre Boudrias, who was drinking a whiskey. Wren says to Andre "I'm going to call your father and tell him you don't drink beer like the rest of the team." Andre looked at Wren and said in his thick French-Canadian accent, "If you trow a party, trow a party, but don't tell people what to drink."

Henry Boucha

Henry Boucha was from Warroad and is one of the best talents the state of Minnesota has produced. He was a big forward and a strong checker. When he came to us from Detroit, he had a bright future. They had him rooming with me, because he was the newest guy on the team and I was the oldest guy.

One night we were playing Boston at the Met. Near the end of the first period, Boucha and Dave Forbes got into it and both took penalties.

Henry Boucha

North Stars archives

I was hurt and sitting in the press box. I was also going to be a guest on Boston television, so I left near the end of the period and was running along the concourse, going from our press box to the TV booth, when I heard a big roar. I thought we had scored, and ran in one of the portals to look, and saw a big scrum on the ice.

I run up to the television booth and ask what happened. They say, "Forbes hit Boucha coming out of the box, and a big melee started." Forbes had butt-ended Boucha as he was skating by him. Henry went down, and then Forbes jumped on Henry, and Murray Oliver jumped on Forbes, and somebody jumped on Murray.

Unfortunately, that did so much damage to Henry's eye that it cost him his career.

Per-Olov Brasar

Per-Olov Brasar came to us from Sweden in 1977. He played a lot with Kent-Erik Andersson, who was a good defensive forward, and Roland Eriksson, who was a very, very clever center. Brasar looked like Stan Laurel, and had the same attitude. He was happy-go-lucky and looked like he had a smile on his face even when he didn't, yet he was extremely talented and a complete player. He could do a lot of things on the ice, and was team MVP in '77-78. Off the ice his passion was horses. He owned horses back in Sweden and was a sulky driver.

Per-Olov Brasar

North Stars archives

Bill Butters

Bill Butters

North Stars archives

Bill Butters came to us from the WHA. He had played at the University of Minnesota, and Sonmor loved him. Billy was a real gamer — tough, mean, and the kind of guy you wanted on the team.

Unfortunately, we got to a point with our defensemen where we just couldn't use him much. When I let him go, I know Billy really felt that I didn't like him much as a player, but it was just that our team was getting better. After he retired, Billy made the biggest transformation of any person I've ever seen. He became a Christian and a real gentleman. He wrote me a letter of apology, saying how he didn't want to harbor any animosity towards me, and how he realized I had just been doing my job.

Billy became a minister and a leader in Hockey Ministries International. When he spoke at Herb Brooks' funeral, his transformation was a revelation to me.

Jon Casey

I signed Jon Casey as a free agent out of the University of North Dakota. I'd watched him play with Grand Rapids High School, and he had been outstanding in the Minnesota state tournament. He also gave North Dakota a lot of good goaltending when he was there.

We almost lost him when his contract ran out. The year that I retired and Ferreira was taking over, Casey's contract was up. Ferreira made a real good move signing him back, and Jon gave the North Stars terrific goaltending and was one of the key reasons they went to the Stanley Cup Finals in 1991.

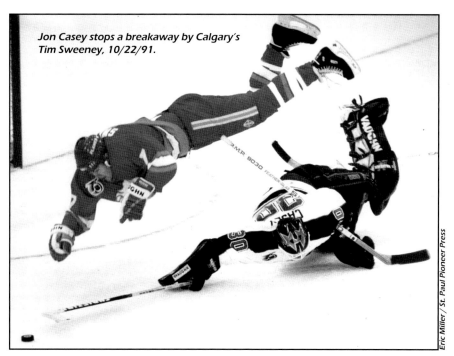

Jon Casey stops a breakaway by Calgary's Tim Sweeney, 10/22/91.

Eric Miller / St. Paul Pioneer Press

Dino Ciccarelli

Shortly after becoming GM, I went out to see Bobby Smith and Brad Marsh, the two top-rated juniors in Canada. Smith was playing with the Ottawa 67's. Brad Marsh was playing with the London Knights, and Dino Ciccarelli was his teammate. Bobby Smith was very impressive, but Ciccarelli also caught my eye. This was in February 1978.

At the end of the year, my scouts were compiling their draft lists. Smith was No. 1, of course. Dino was under-aged and not eligible for the draft. A year later, the draft was changed to only six rounds.

Dino Ciccarelli — first photo after signing with the North Stars, September, 1979.

North Stars archives

After it was over, we were sitting up in the media room in Met Center, and I turned to my scouts and said: "Hey, nobody took that Ciccarelli kid, and we didn't have him high on our list. How come nobody got him?" And Harry Howell, our head scout, said: "Louie, he had a bad injury. He crashed into the goalpost and broke his femur. He's got a steel rod in his leg."

I said, "I'll check him out." I called Dr. Charlie Bull, who had been the Olympic team doctor for Canada in 1968 when I played with Team USA. I had gotten to know him over the years.

I called Dino, introduced myself and asked if he would go to Toronto to see this doctor. Dino agreed, and then I arranged the examination with Charlie Bull. He called me and said: "He's got a rod in his leg, but that shouldn't hamper him. We can get it out in about a year or two, and he should be fine."

I went to see Dino at his house. He said the only other person who had shown interest in him was Scotty Bowman. Dino's father Victor kept saying, "We might like to wait to hear from Scotty Bowman." Finally, I told Victor: "Look, I'm Italian, and I'm from Ontario. You're Italian, and you're from Ontario. You have to go with an Italian."

I gave Dino $25,000 to sign, and he became one of the top goal scorers of all time. He also became the biggest draw we had since Goldsworthy.

Wayne Connelly

Wayne Connelly was one of the most-talented goal scorers we had. One night he and I were sitting out an exhibition game against Detroit at Met Center. Detroit was leading going into the third period. Gordie Howe has the puck, and gets some room, and scores. Connelly turns to me and says: "Louie, you defensemen give Howe way too much room. If I had that much room, I'd score 50 goals."

No sooner had he said that than Howe gets the puck again. Larry Hillman comes to check him and comes a little too close, and Howe passes the puck and then gives Hillman the stick right under the throat. Play stops, a stretcher comes out, and they wheel Hillman off. I turn to Wayne and say, "That's why you don't get that much space — you never touch anybody."

Jim Craig

Jim Craig, as everybody knows, had a magnificent Olympics and was the main reason the U.S. beat the Russians. He signed right away with Atlanta and things didn't go so well for him. He was from Boston, and the Bruins made a deal to get him.

Talk about pressure, the Olympic hero going back to his hometown, a real hockey city. It didn't work out for him there and it looked like he was going to be out of hockey, so I decided to take a chance on him. We signed him and sent him to our farm club in Salt Lake City to get in shape. When he came to the North Stars he played three games, got injured and then retired.

Jude Drouin

North Stars archives

Jude Drouin

Jude was one of the most gifted players the North Stars ever had, and a great acquisition by Wren Blair when he got him from Montreal. Jude was an early version of Neal Broten. He had tremendous balance on his skates, was hard to knock off of the puck and was very effective in traffic. He also had excellent peripheral vision and great instincts for moving the puck.

Off the ice, Jude was happy-go-lucky and enjoyed a good time, so much so that he'd get

Jude Drouin (middle) and Lou Nanne race around the net at the Bloomington Ice Garden, with Dean Prentice close behind, 10/13/71.

Bloomington Historical Society

under Wren's skin a lot. Like Goldy and Gump, Jude enjoyed a cigarette between periods. The three of them smoked together in the back washroom area of our dressing room.

John Flesch

We had a real character on our team named John Flesch, and he had a real hard head. He'd do something wrong, and he'd sit on the bench, and he'd take his stick and hit himself in the head.

The guy was always hitting himself in the head, and everybody thought he was a little goofy because of it. We were in Pittsburgh one night, and the guys talked him into beating his head on the hotel room ceiling, saying, "Bet you can't put it through the ceiling."

John Flesch

North Stars archives

So he gets on the bed and starts jumping, trying to hit his head through the ceiling, bouncing off the ceiling.

One time Chuck Pihl and his wife hosted a Christmas party for the team, and as everyone is leaving the party and saying goodbye, I'm standing beside Mr. and Mrs. Pihl because they're friends of mine. Johnny grabs Mr. Pihl's hand and says goodnight, and then Mrs. Pihl puts out her hand. He grabs her by the shoulders and gives her a coco-bonk right in the head, and she just drops.

He thought he was being affectionate, but that was the last party we had at the Pihl's.

Barry Gibbs

Barry Gibbs came to us from Boston in what was a great acquisition by Wren Blair. Gibbs was not only a very physical defenseman, but he was excellent offensively as well. He provided the North Stars with a long tenure as a two-way player who thrived in any situation on the ice. Without a doubt, Barry is one of the best defensemen in North Stars history.

Barry got in a number of fights and was a good fighter, but one night against Detroit things didn't go so well. Barry was arguing with a Red Wings player, and the next thing you know the kid just dropped his gloves and punched Barry in the jaw. Barry spent the next few weeks all wired up with a broken jaw from that one punch.

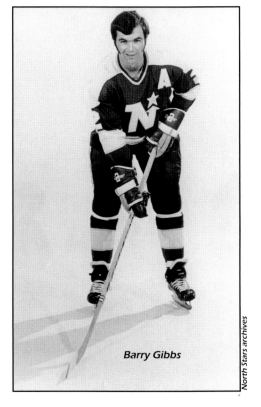

Barry Gibbs

North Stars archives

Bill Goldsworthy

Bill Goldsworthy might have been the most colorful character we ever had on the ice. He was in a class by himself for generating crowd excitement — he had speed, size, strength, and he could come off the wing and score goals like nobody's business.

The hockey camp Wren Blair owned in Haliburton was for boys, ages 8 to 14, so the beds were like Boy Scout beds. When we held training camp there, we were in a barracks with guys like Moose Vasko, who weighed 225 when he was in his best shape.

The camp was out in the wilderness. Wren wouldn't let us have any beer at camp, and both bars in town were off limits. Haliburton was very small and Wren knew everybody. He told the bartenders, "If any of the players come in here, call me." One way a few players outsmarted him was to call a cab driver and have him bring some beer and put it in the woods behind the barracks.

Bill Goldsworthy was a guy who had a knack for getting caught — just couldn't help himself. Goldy goes into town to a bar and, sure enough, the bartender calls Blair.

Goldy gets a cab back and he's walking along the gravel driveway in the woods around midnight. It's really dark. Wren has all the scouts and himself in a half-dozen cars lined up across the road. He sees Goldy's outline and they all turn on their lights. He wanted to show Goldy he could catch him anywhere, any time.

Another example of Goldy getting caught: We were playing Montreal one night. After the game, a bunch of players went to a bar, then headed back to the hotel to beat curfew. Goldy said he was staying to have a few more beers.

He stayed until closing — maybe 2 a.m. When Goldy comes in, he sneaks through the basement of the Sheraton Mount Royal to catch the elevator, rather than going through the lobby. He goes up four floors, the elevator doors open, and who walks in but Wren Blair. Goldy just pulled out his wallet and said, "Take what you need."

●

Blair had a habit of getting on Goldsworthy. One night he was on Goldy every shift: "Goldy, get back on your wing; Goldy, back-check; Goldy, shoot the puck; Goldy, you're not playing worth a damn; Goldy, I'm going to sit you down."

As the clock was winding down in the period, Goldy was coming right by our bench with the puck, and he tried to make a move but got checked.

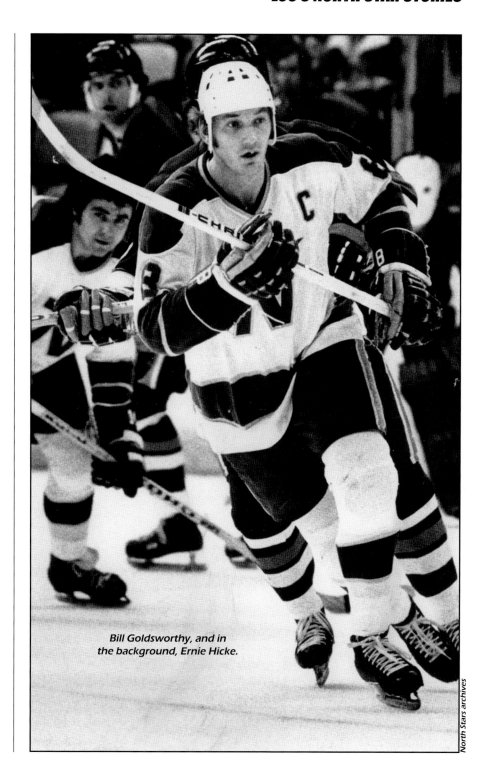

Bill Goldsworthy, and in the background, Ernie Hicke.

North Stars archives

Cesare Maniago and Bill Goldsworthy during a break in practice at the Bloomington Ice Garden, 10/4/71.

Bloomington Historical Society

Wren leaned over and said, "You're going to Waterloo [our farm club] tomorrow."

The buzzer sounded, Goldy's coming toward the bench door and Wren's still yelling at him. Without stopping, Goldy let a right haymaker go and dropped Wren with a shot to the jaw in front of 15,000 people. Then Goldy jumped on top of him. Stan Waylett, the trainer, jumped on top of Goldy to pull him off. Tommy Reid, who was right in front of me, jumped on top of Stan Waylett.

Pretty soon we had about six or seven guys piled on top of each other on the floor of the North Stars bench. Finally it broke up, and as Wren's getting up from being on his back on the bench, he says, "We'll finish this upstairs in the locker room."

Wren goes to his office, which was right in our locker room, and he's trying to open the door, and he's shaking so much he can't get the key in the hole. He finally opens it and says to Goldsworthy, "Sit down." We were all wondering what was happening.

After about 10 minutes Goldy came out and sat down. A couple of minutes later the buzzer goes off and Wren says, "Get back on the ice, everybody. Goldy, you sit on your ass." So we went downstairs and got ready to start play. Reid and I were on defense, Parise and Drouin were up front, and Goldy was the right wing on that line. He didn't come out.

The other team's all ready to go, and the referee says, "Where's the winger?" We look at the bench, and Wren says, "Goldy, get out there." The crowd cheered as Goldy hit the ice. End of crisis.

Goldy was very unpredictable. Some of his antics drove Jack Gordon crazy. One night before a game, he was lying on the training table with an Ace bandage and ice around his ankle. I said, "Kraut, what's the matter?" And he says, "I twisted my ankle at the noon-hour skate." I said, "Goldy, you didn't come downstairs. It was optional, and you didn't skate." He says, "Oh, yes, I did."

Doc Rose caught my eye and pointed to a sign he had made up that said, "One new G.E. refrigerator for sale, with a size 11 shoeprint on the door." Goldy had gotten into an argument with his wife around noon, and he got so frustrated that he kicked the refrigerator, hurting his ankle. He missed the game that night — another mark against him with Gordon.

Danny Grant

The North Stars had a lot of terrific players over the years, really unique guys. Until we got Dino Ciccarelli, Danny Grant was the best pure goal scorer the North Stars ever had.

As a matter of fact, in the early '70s the NHL started a goal-scoring contest. It took place during the summer and was televised across Canada. Each team could send one player to the competition.

I was the vice president of the players' association at that time. I went to a meeting in Toronto the month before the competition and offered a wager to the other reps: "I'll take Danny Grant against the field, I'll take all bets." And Danny did win the competition. He was an unbelievably accurate shooter.

Danny was uniquely skilled in a lot of ways. You could pass the puck and he would take it on his skates, no matter where it was. He made you as a defenseman look real good the way he could accept a pass. He could put the puck in the corner, even when the goalie knew he was going there.

In the shootouts in practice, he used to drive Cesare crazy, because he could always beat him.

Danny Grant

North Stars archives

But Danny wasn't a physical player. One night we were playing the Montreal Canadiens, and John Ferguson was running him. He wasn't going to let Grant have any freedom.

At the end of the first period, we went to the locker room, and Danny O'Shea says: "Grant, you're taking all that abuse from Ferguson. When he runs you, run him back, and you won't see him the rest of the night." And Grant says, "You're right, because I'll be in the hospital with two black eyes that are swollen shut."

Danny was tight with a buck. Going into our last game in Oakland one year, he was tied with the Seals' Norm Ferguson for goal scoring by a rookie.

Before the game Grant says, "Guys, shut out Ferguson tonight, and I'll get a goal and win rookie of the year, and I'll throw a party." Even though we got beat, we shut out Ferguson and Danny did get a goal and win rookie of the year.

It was January of the next season and he still hadn't thrown the party he promised. We were at Howard Wong's one night after a game. I used to get the bill and divide it up. Danny and his wife had to leave early, so he came over and gave me a blank check.

The next day Danny says, "What do I have to deduct from my checkbook?" I said, "Deduct $257.00." He says, "I just had one beer and a hamburger." And I told him: "No, you threw a party. You said you were going to throw a rookie of the year celebration party, you never did, so that was the party last night."

He said, "I was going to have it next week." I said, "OK, you have the party next week." I had already collected money from the other guys, so I gave him the money back and he had the party the following week.

Danny knew how to maximize his earnings, as I mentioned earlier. One night against Boston, Danny had two goals. I was playing right wing with him on a shift with Jude Drouin, and Danny took a shot that I deflected, and it went into the net.

When we went back to the bench and sat down, the announcer said, "Goal by Danny Grant, for a hat trick." Jack Gordon, our coach, walks over and says, "Louie, you got that goal." I said, "Yeah." He says, "Well, go and change it."

Jack walks away and Danny says: "Louie, I've got a bonus in my contract for hat tricks — I get a few hundred bucks. Also, the merchants we have here give us gift certificates for clothes and liquor. Don't change it." I said, "OK, but you've got to pay me $100." He says, "You've got it." I didn't say anything and he gave me $100. So in my career stats, I tell people, I'm credited with one less goal than I actually had.

Danny Grant at the net with Goldsworthy, Maniago and Harris, Bloomington Ice Garden.

Bloomington Historical Society

The Gund Brothers

Gordon and George Gund were the best pro sports owners the Twin Cities ever had. George was an unbelievable hockey enthusiast. I don't know if I've met anybody who likes to play hockey more than George.

He was overweight to the point where we worried about him, and he had to watch his diet. But if he could ever get on the ice, that's all he wanted to do. He bought himself a rink in Sun Valley, Idaho, just so he'd have a place to go and skate at night.

We had a game one night — North Stars alumni playing against various celebrities. The previous morning, I got a call from George. He was in Berlin. He says, "I just wanted to know if I could play in the game tomorrow night." That's the way he was – he owns the team but he still asks me for permission to play. I said, "Sure you're welcome to play." He says, "Great, I'll come back for the game."

The next night we're playing, and the first period has gone by, and here comes George — just in from Berlin — running down the steps.

He played in the alumni game, watched the North Stars game, and then I asked, "Do you want to have a drink?" He says, "No, I've got to go back to Berlin — I've got a meeting there." So he flew all the way from Berlin to play two periods.

With George, you never knew when he was going to pop up. We were playing the seventh game of the Stanley Cup playoffs in Montreal, the night we beat them to advance to the semifinals, and it was the third period.

The game was tied 1-1 and I was nervous as hell. I started walking the corridor. No one was there, obviously, because the game was so good. As I'm walking, I hear someone banging on the entrance door, and I look and there is George Gund, trying to get in.

Gordon Gund

Rick Kolodziej

George Gund

Rick Kolodziej

Security was waving him off. I went up to the guy and said, "Let him in." He says, "No, he hasn't got a ticket." I said, "He owns the team — let him in." So he opened the gate and let George in, and he ended up seeing the last 10 minutes of the game.

George and Gordon were the best owners that anybody could work for. George let Gordon take care of the business end of things.

When I was signing my last contract with them, Gordon said, "Louie, why don't we just have our lawyers represent us so we don't get into any kind of hassle?" So I hired my agent, Arnold Bloom, and Gordon had Ralph Strangis, a Twin Cities attorney.

A month later, we weren't close to an agreement. I finally said to Arnold, "Look, I'm going to handle this myself." I called Strangis, and he called Gordon, who called me and said, "I thought we were going to let our representatives do this."

I said, "It's not going the way I want, and I think we can get this done." So Gordon says, "Why don't you fly out here to Princeton and see me?"

I did that and went to his house. He offered me a drink before dinner. I said fine. He asked if I'd like a cigar. I said fine. We're having drinks and cigars, and are moving into a negotiating mode.

I looked at him and said, "Look, Gordon, we've been going through this for more than a month. All I want is one thing. If you give me that, it's a done deal."

He says, "What do you want?" I smiled and said, "I want to negotiate with George." He says, "No way."

We finally worked our way through it.

One of the funniest things that I have ever seen took place during the 1978 draft in Montreal. After the Gund brothers had purchased the North Stars, at the Board of Governors meetings, I would wait for them to come to the hotel to escort them into our meetings. They were staying at the Château Champlain while everyone else was at the Queen Elizabeth. They did this to maintain privacy while they were negotiating for the North Stars.

When they came to the Queen Elizabeth for the final board meeting, I was waiting at the front door when their taxi arrived. The driver jumped out, opened the trunk, and pulled out a wheelchair. He set it down and took Gordon, who was blind, by the hand, and sat him in the chair. Gordon said, "No, no." He stood up, and George sat down in the chair. Then Gordon started pushing the chair and touching the ground with the cane, as George instructed him on which way to go.

As we all walked into the Board of Governors meeting, people who had not met Gordon could not conceive what was going on. They didn't realize George was suffering from a bad back and Gordon had to push him in a wheelchair into the meeting.

Paul Harrison

Paul Harrison was one of our goaltenders from the 1970's. Eventually, we let him go and he signed with Pittsburgh. That year, we were playing in Pittsburgh one night, and we were playing terribly. I was GM at the time.

At the end of the second period, I couldn't contain myself. I ran down from the Pittsburgh press box and walked into the dressing room to give the team a piece of my mind.

Paul Harrison

North Stars archives

I looked up, and there was Harrison. He said to me: "Oh, hi, Louie. Did you take over our team now?" Here I was standing in the middle of the Pittsburgh Penguins' locker room.

That gaffe cooled me off. I walked out of there and went back to the press box.

Ernie Hicke

North Stars archives

Ernie Hicke

Ernie came to us from the Islanders, and he was a guy who was always upbeat and really enjoyed playing the game. He was gregarious, full of energy and loved by his teammates. Ernie enjoyed life in the NHL, and he partied as hard as he played. We called him "Bubblehead." If they had had bobble-head dolls back then, Ernie would have been perfect.

Doug Hicks

Doug Hicks was our first-round pick and sixth overall in the 1974 draft. As a 20-year-old rookie he made the jump straight from the Western Canada Junior League to the NHL. Doug was a good puck carrying defenseman and one of the better skaters in the league.

When I became GM, budget constraints forced me to trade Doug and his contract to Chicago. Doug was a friend I rode with to games. He became the first player I traded. Following his time in Chicago, Doug had some good years with Edmonton.

Pierre Jarry

Pierre Jarry was a free-spirited guy from Montreal who loved the good life and was extremely loved by North Star fans. He was a good looking guy, like a matinee idol. He never got too concerned about hockey and wasn't real passionate about the game, but when he got on the ice he could really play. He was gifted and talented but didn't last too long with us.

Doug Hicks

North Stars archives

Pierre Jarry, with Tim Young

North Stars archives

Steve Jensen

Steve Jensen was a local product with lots of speed who joined us right after the '76 Olympics. We were going into Philadelphia to play, and one of the writers asked him how he would compare the Russians to the NHL.

Steve was very complimentary to the Russians, and spoke in terms that were almost sacrilegious to some guys in the NHL, especially the Philadelphia Flyers.

Steve Jensen

North Stars archives

Before that game, Doc Rose, our trainer, said to Tom Reid and me: "You better look to help out Steve tonight. I talked to the Philadelphia trainers. The Flyers are going to go after him because of the comments he made in the paper about the Russians."

Sure enough, on Steve's first shift, he goes in a corner and gets run at by Bob Kelly. So immediately we had a little skirmish going on, because they picked on him right away.

Claude Larose

Claude Larose was a great competitor, a guy who worked hard and skated fast, would hit or get hit — it didn't matter — and was a very tough player. He never showed any sign of being hurt, except this one night playing in Detroit.

They had a defenseman named Ron Harris, who was one of the strongest guys in the league. He had no body fat and was built like a Greek god.

During the game, Claude was coming down the boards and looked back to get a pass, and right in front of our bench he got what we call a suicide pass, because Ron Harris was standing there and just creamed him.

Our bench was sitting back a little bit so we couldn't see below us, and the play kept going on. Then we saw one empty glove come over the boards, then a hand, then a stick, then another hand, and then finally Claude climbed over the boards. And he says, "I hit him good that time."

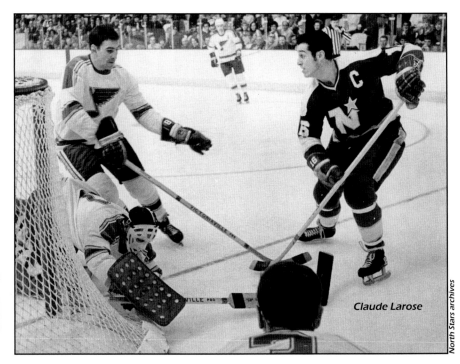

Claude Larose

North Stars archives

Danny Lawson

Danny Lawson came to the North Stars in a trade for Wayne Connelly. Wayne had been a very popular North Star.

Danny was a little different. He had great speed and a great shot, but he was a unique individual.

He roomed with me when he first came to the team. One of the first days, I wake up and head for the bathroom. The whole room is full of steam. Lawson is steaming his clothes to wear that night.

We played in Los Angeles at the end of one season. The game was over, and we were getting on the bus. John Mariucci was on the trip with Wren Blair, and John would get sentimental sometimes, but in a physical way — he'd tap you, or he'd hit you on the head with his knuckles.

So, he's walking down the aisle of the bus, and he's saying, "Good game, good game," and tapping guys. He came to me and hit me in the head with two knuckles, then he sort of pushed Danny in the shoulder and said something like, "You gotta work harder."

And Danny says, "Leave me alone, old man."

John stopped, and I had known him forever, so I knew instantly we had trouble. John turned around and walked off the bus, and I watched him. They were loading the bus with equipment bags, and he started picking up bags and slinging them underneath. I turned to Danny Lawson and

said, "Whatever you do, you shut your mouth and you don't do a thing, or you're going to get killed in the next couple of minutes, I can tell you right now."

He says, "What are you talking about?" I said, "Shut up and don't say another thing."

Danny Lawson

North Stars archives

As I'm saying that, Mariucci climbs back on the bus, and he's only on the first two steps when he says: "OK, Lawson, you think you're a smart guy, huh, calling me an old man? We traded a great guy and a great player for you, a piece of crap. Get off the bus. I'm going to teach you how old I am."

I said, "Danny, don't say a word — nothing."

John says, "Lawson, I'm talking to you." I said, "Danny, not a word."

Now John starts running down the aisle saying, "I'm talking to you." He gets to Lawson and he grabs him by the shirt. I jump in the middle. John lifts Danny out of the seat. I grab John's arms and say: "John, you gotta cool down. You can't do this — you're going to lose your job." He says: "I don't give a damn about my job, I'm going to beat the hell out of this guy. We traded a good guy for him."

A couple other teammates jump in with me, and we pull John off. I turn around, and Lawson does not have one button left on his shirt — he's standing there bare-chested with a suit jacket on, the shirt open, and a tie hanging around his neck. And I always told Danny, "That's as close as you're ever going to come to death until you really die."

Pete LoPresti

Pete LoPresti came from Eveleth on the Iron Range and probably had the easiest going attitude of any goaltender I've ever seen. Usually, goaltenders are either high strung or different or somewhat quirky, but he and Cesare were the most levelheaded, and Pete was by far the easiest going. It didn't matter what happened during the game, it was like water off a duck's back to Pete.

Brian MacLellen levels Robert Nordmark of St. Louis, 2/3/88.

Buzz Magnuson / St. Paul Pioneer Press

Pete LoPresti

North Stars archives

Brian MacLellen

In 1986 we needed to get bigger on the wing, so I obtained Brian MacLellen from the Rangers. Brian was a big, strong forward who played college hockey at Bowling Green. He was the type of player that other teams didn't want to rile because he could be quite physical.

Brian was also one of our most intelligent players, and he's gone on to be a top executive in the NHL.

Cesare Maniago

Cesare Maniago had a penchant for falling asleep early. On our USO trip, we would come back from our visits at about 5 p.m. We'd go to our barracks, and there would be a place where you could buy a drink. It would get to be 5:30, and we'd say, "OK, guys, let's go up and have a shower and then go out for some dinner." And Cesare would say, "No, no, guys, I'm going to have a little rest. Are you going to go to the bar later?" "Yeah." "Well, you wake me up when you get back from dinner."

Every night we'd finish dinner about 8:30 or 9:00, and I'd say, "Let me go get Cesare." He'd say: "No, I'm too tired. I can't get up."

Cesare Maniago in the net, with Bob McCord taking a puck in the shoulder.

North Stars archives

Invariably, I'd come back, I'd go to sleep, and around 3:00 in the morning he'd say, "Louie, Louie, you hear that?" "What?" "All that noise." I'd say, "I don't hear anything." He'd say, "I can't sleep. I gotta get up." I'd say, "Cesare, you've been in bed for 11 hours, no wonder you can't sleep."

We were playing in Buffalo on a Saturday night, so we got there on a Friday night, and Cesare Maniago says, "Louie, come on down to my room and we'll watch the game on TV." Buffalo was playing out of town in Philadelphia, so we wanted to watch the game. I go down to his room and he has his pajamas on, and within 10 minutes, I'm watching the game and he's fallen asleep. I watched the game and listened to him snore for two hours. He didn't even get up once.

John Mariucci

Wren Blair had a penchant for staying up late. He always was up until 3, 4 in the morning. We had a weekend where we lost games both Saturday and Sunday. We usually had an informal practice on Monday, but after losing the weekend pair, Blair stormed into the dressing room and said, "Mandatory practice tomorrow morning at 9."

We knew it was unlikely that he would be there and, sure enough, he wasn't. Mariucci always had to take care of the practices when Wren wasn't there. Wren was never around in the morning, so John essentially ran those practices.

We went down to the ice. John blows the whistle and says: "Everybody sit on the bench. Everyone's tired. Just sit here and we'll tell a few stories." So, John starts telling old stories about when he was with the Blackhawks, and every once in a while as he's talking he blows the whistle. After he'd blown the whistle about 20 times, one of the guys says, "John, why are you blowing that whistle?"

John Mariucci

North Stars archives

And he says, "You never know. Wren might get up and come to the arena, and if he does at least he'll hear the whistle and think we're going through skating drills."

●

We had this kid from Hamilton that I had just signed to a minor league contract. We were in training camp, and we held a scouting meeting to discuss all the players. And John Mariucci says to me: "Louie, we've got a lot of guys here in two different groups. Why don't you let me handle the minor league group — the cuts and assignments — and you guys take care of the majors?"

I said, "Go right ahead."

The next day, Mariucci had a scrimmage, and made some cuts in the team to pare it down. And I'm sitting in my office when my secretary, Sue, says, "A player is here to see you."

The player came in with tears in his eyes and I asked, "What's the matter?" He says: "I don't understand. You signed me to a contract yesterday and you cut me today." I said, "What do you mean I cut you?" He says, "Mr. Mariucci said I was cut."

I called John and said, "What did you do?" He said, "Wasn't that the guy we were going to cut?" I said, "No, that's the wrong guy." We were cutting somebody else. So the kid from Hamilton stayed with us and played in our minor league system.

Bryan Maxwell

One of the first things I did as general manager was try to improve our defense. I took over the team February 10, and four days later Bryan Maxwell was with us.

Jack Gordon had drafted Bryan two years earlier as the fourth overall pick, but he elected to go to the World Hockey Association. He had spent time with the Cleveland Crusaders and Cincinnati Stingers, and was with the New England Whalers when he got into a bit of a squabble with the team and they sent him down to the American League. He was playing in Binghamton when I contacted his agent, Frank Milne, and we consummated a deal that brought him immediately to the North Stars.

Bryan was a big tough defenseman, known almost as an enforcer. When I brought him in, one of the first things I told him was: "We've got a terrific, talented hockey line here in Roland Eriksson, Per-Olov Brasar and Kent-Erik Andersson, three Swedes we've got playing together. A lot of teams like to take liberties with them. Anybody who goes near these three guys, I want you to handle it."

Bryan Maxwell

North Stars archives

We were in Denver playing the old Colorado Rockies. I was coaching and the Swedes were out as a line. One of Colorado's big tough defensemen came over and took Roland Eriksson into the boards in front of our bench.

Bryan was sitting on the bench, stood up and hit the guy with a haymaker — dropped him on the ice.

Obviously, the referee called a penalty. I said to Bryan, "What are you doing?" He says, "You told me to take care of them." I said, "Not while you're on the bench!"

Tom McCarthy

Tom McCarthy could possibly have been the best pure talent that played for the North Stars if he had kept his nose clean and looked after himself. He certainly was the best backhanded passer in the league, a great shooter, and a great stick handler.

As a matter of fact, in the Ontario Junior draft Tom was selected before Gretzky — he went No. 1. McCarthy, Broten and Ciccarelli made a terrific line, with a tremendous ability to move the puck. When they played as a line in the '83 All-Star game at Nassau Coliseum, they were dominating. McCarthy, unfortunately, didn't take care of himself, but he was certainly one of the best talents in the National Hockey League — all-star caliber.

Walt McKechnie

I had played forward on a line with Murray Oliver and Walt McKechnie the week before a game in Vancouver. Now, we were having a pre-game lunch at the Bayshore Restaurant. Jack Gordon came in, and he nodded

at McKechnie and said, "You're out tonight."

That meant McKechnie wasn't dressing. So we finished lunch, and Murray and I were going to go up to our room, but McKechnie said, "Come with me for a walk, and console me. I'm not playing well, and now I get pulled."

Cesare Maniago came along. We started going around the Bayshore boardwalk. And then a seagull flies over, takes a crap, and it lands right on McKechnie.

"That's just the way my luck's going," McKechnie says. "Coaches bench me and birds crap on me."

●

We were playing in St. Louis one night, and we happened to get a delayed penalty call against us. When we did, the puck was down by their goalie, Glenn Hall, so Hall took the puck and came up ice.

At that time it was legal for the goaltender to skate over the red line. McKechnie went to check him and Hall faked, went over the red line, and shot it in the zone.

Walt McKechnie

North Stars archives

It just so happened that the following week we're back in St. Louis, and before the game we're saying things like, "Watch Berenson, he's got a real strong backhand." "Watch Picard, he likes to run you in the corners." And Walt McKechnie pipes up, "Watch Glenn Hall, he's got a great move to his left."

Doug Mohns

Doug Mohns was traded to us from the Chicago Blackhawks. He came to us right after our noon-hour skate. He went around and shook hands with everybody and we all introduced ourselves.

We were playing that night. The buzzer sounded to go out for warm-up, so we all went out. When we came back upstairs to the dressing room, Doug Mohns started yelling, "Who took my package? You guys are a bunch of smart-asses. You think this is a way to welcome somebody to a team?"

We didn't know what he was talking about. He was raving like a maniac: "Come on, give it back to me." Doc Rose, our trainer, says, "Dougie, Dougie, settle down, what's the matter?"

Doug says, "I had a folded piece of paper there on my bench. Where did it go?"

Doc was a clean freak — as soon as you'd leave the dressing room, he'd pick up everything. He saw this paper and threw it in the waste basket. Doc told him he threw it in there. Doug jumped up and plowed through the garbage, found it and pulled it out.

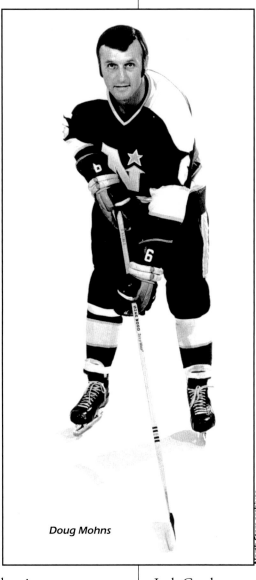

Doug Mohns

North Stars archives

It turns out he had a toupee, and it was inside that folded paper. He thought somebody was playing with his hairpiece, but we didn't even know he had one.

Later, we were playing the Boston Bruins and Doug was my defense partner. Right in front of our bench, he hit Carol Vadnais and had his stick up a little bit. Vadnais dropped his gloves and came at him.

Mohns was a tough guy, so he dropped his gloves and squared off.

The first punch that Vadnais threw knocked Mohns' helmet off. Mohns never wore his hairpiece when he was playing, so now his bald head is showing and his helmet's rolling around. He's holding off Vadnais with his left hand, and dodging punches while he's reaching down on the ice with his right hand to get his helmet. He grabs his helmet and puts it back on his head.

And we're all standing around watching the fight, laughing like crazy because he's not worried about fighting or throwing back a punch, he's just worried about getting his helmet back on his head.

●

Mohns might have been the best skater in the league. He was so fluid, whereas I used to work hard to skate. We were doing drills one day, and defense partners usually pair off. At the end of practice, Jack Gordon says: "Forwards down and back. Defense blues down and back. Yellows down and back." Mohns and I go down and back a couple times. Finally, Mohns looks over and says, "Louie, you don't have to beat up the ice, just skate on it."

Bob Nevin

Bobby Nevin came to us in a trade from New York. I've never seen a player who was so unconcerned about everything. He never got excited about being late. The first time we're rooming together, it's 5:55 and we've got a bus at 6.

I said, "Nevie, we've gotta go, we've got five minutes." He says: "We've got five minutes. That's like a lifetime."

I run to the elevator and get down there in two minutes, with three minutes to spare. And here he comes right at 6. Somebody says, "Hurry up, Nevin," and he says, "The clock says six." And that's the way he handled himself.

●

Nevin loved the grape. He used call wine "the nectar of the gods." We had a party one night at the Minikahda Country Club, hosted by the owners. Nevin was divorced and had a girlfriend in town. She was the complete opposite of him — very high-strung.

Nevin and I are standing at the bar before dinner, talking to some of the people from Minikahda who were hosting us, and one of the ladies comes up to talk to Bobby. She's telling him how happy she is to see him in a North Stars uniform, that she's a big fan and really loves the way Nevin plays.

As she's gushing over him, Nevin's girlfriend is watching from about ten feet away, and her face begins turning the color of her red hair. She

Bob Nevin

North Stars archives

walks over and says, "You leave my boyfriend alone," and throws her glass of wine all over the woman's dress.

Kent Nilsson

Kent Nilsson had all the skills in the world. Some people said he had as much natural skill as Gretzky. He didn't have Gretzky's head, but he was a great skater, a great stick-handler, had great hands, a great shot — anything you could want — but he was a real enigma.

Some nights he would drive you crazy. We were playing against the New York Islanders and lost 1-0. Kent didn't have one shot on goal. As Nilsson was walking out of the dressing room, I grabbed him and said: "Kent, you have a son not even two years old. If somebody came up to you before the game and said your son was kidnapped and you had to play the game and get nine shots on goal, three a period, in order to get him back, do you think you could do it?"

He says, "Of course." I said, "Tonight you got no shots. That's what drives people nuts. Here you've got the ability to get nine shots on goal, you just it said yourself, and you don't shoot the puck enough."

Kent could frustrate a coach enormously, and Lorne Henning was no exception. He would come to me and say, "You gotta get rid of Nilsson." I finally made a deal with Glen Sather for him.

●

When we were playing Toronto in the playoffs, Tiger Williams was running a number of people, but he especially was trying to hit Nilsson. Kent was sitting on the bench, yelling names at Williams, calling him "a gorilla," and Williams yelled that he was going to get Nilsson.

After the game I said, "Kent, you better watch how you talk to Tiger." And Kent says, "He'll never get me — he's not fast enough."

I said: "I'll tell you a story Glen Sonmor told me. When Serge Beaudoin was in Birmingham, he was trying to get a guy, and he couldn't catch him, but Serge yelled at him, 'They still have faceoffs, don't they?' He'll get you at the faceoff."

Murray Oliver

At a home game one night, Murray Oliver was playing forward on the left wing with Jude Drouin. Murray got hit deep in the opposition's zone, and he went down hard. Tommy Reid and I are sitting on the bench, and from our vantage point it looks like Murray is bleeding badly. Jude Drouin comes flying to the bench and says, "I need a towel, I need a towel."

So he gets a towel and goes back there to attend to Murray, and as he gets closer he sees that Murray is just lying on the red faceoff circle and that there's no blood at all. It was just red paint.

●

Bob and Joanie Dayton used to have an annual party for us. The whole team went to their home one night for the annual affair. It was late before we started to leave.

Murray Oliver

North Stars archives

My wife and I were riding with Murray Oliver and his wife, and we said, "Where's Murray?" Nobody could find Murray. We decided, "Let's go get our coats and look for him."

All our coats were piled on a bed in an upstairs bedroom and, as we pulled them off, there was Murray, asleep under the coats.

Danny O'Shea

Danny O'Shea was the North Star version of a Hollywood pin-up. He was big, good-looking and full of life.

Danny came to us as a somewhat unheralded player from the Canadian Olympic team but quickly established himself as a two-way center. He would check the opponent's top line and he was a good playmaker.

He was very popular with his teammates, but he drove Jack Gordon absolutely nuts. Danny was young and single and had a lot of stamina. He would stay out all night but then come to practice in the morning and work as hard as anyone. He dated Loni Anderson in her pre-television days when she was a beauty queen from St. Paul. Danny ultimately drove Gordon to the point where he traded Danny to Chicago for Doug Mohns.

Danny O'Shea

North Stars archives

J.P. Parise

After we merged the two teams, J.P. Parise, who had been in Cleveland, came back to play with the North Stars. J.P. was not only one of the more popular players but one of the most consistent and, to my mind, the best corner man in hockey.

We had an exhibition game up in Duluth against the Winnipeg Jets, who were one of the expansion teams after the merger with the WHA. Winnipeg had a stocky defenseman named Kim Clackson, who was a terrific fighter, and J.P. was working him in the corners, as usual.

Clackson got upset with the way J.P. was banging around in the corner, turned around and dropped his gloves, and they had a little skirmish. Although J.P. was very physical in the corners, he wasn't known as a fighter. After the game, I said to J.P., "You hung in there pretty good with Clackson."

He says, "Louie, tonight I heard the three worst words I've ever heard in my life." I said, "What's that?" He says: "When Clackson grabbed hold of me, the referee said, 'Let them go!' I don't want to fight that guy, except in a phone booth where there's no room for him to throw any punches."

J.P. Parise

North Stars archives

Just before J.P. was traded, we were in Oakland. He was rooming with Fern Rivard, who was one of our goaltenders. For some reason, Fern didn't like taking showers. When he did shower, it didn't last for more than six seconds. Because of that, he didn't have the best hygiene going.

After our practice in Oakland, Fern couldn't have been in the shower more than three seconds. On the way back to hotel, J.P. says, "I know my days are numbered here, because Jack's got me rooming with Fern. I told him I would pay for my own room, or let me have a different roommate, and he wouldn't let me."

Tommy Reid, who was always up to something, said, "J.P., do you know that Fern told me he's using your toothbrush?" And J.P. says, "You gotta be kidding!" He says, "No, you check and see if he's got a toothbrush." Well, J.P. went back to their hotel room, and we went along. Not only did Fern not have a toothbrush, the closet had a little odor from his clothes. J.P. took all Fern's clothes down to Housekeeping and put them in the laundry, then went to the lobby and bought a toothbrush and toothpaste and gave it to Fern.

And J.P. was right — within 10 days, he was traded.

Bill Plager

St. Louis had two Plager brothers, Barclay and Bob, and they were probably as identified with their team as any players in the league at that time. They were the heart and soul of that hockey club.

They had a younger brother named Billy, who came and played with the North Stars when I was there. When you'd say something to Billy, he would take you literally — believe it to the hilt.

One day I came into the locker room before a game, and the guys were kibitzing, and I said to Billy, "You know how much my wife spent on a refrigerator today — $875!"

In 1969 that was a lot of money. I said, "I can't believe a refrigerator could cost that much." He says, "Why does it?" Thinking about all the features, I said, "Well, it does everything — it even answers the phone."

About a week later, my wife Francine says to me, "What are you telling Billy Plager? I was sitting with his wife, and she asked if she could come over and see our refrigerator. I said, 'Why?' and she said she's never seen a refrigerator that answers the phone."

Bill Plager

North Stars archives

Tom Polanic

Tom Polanic was my defensive partner and one of the toughest North Stars ever. He was big, mean and occasionally crude. He could hurt you when he hit you.

One night we're playing Philadelphia, and Tom runs into Reggie Fleming, Philadelphia's tough guy, behind the net. Reggie's nickname around the league was C.H. — Cement Head. Tom wanted to get a piece of Reggie, but the referees jumped in between them.

Polanic, not sounding like a genius himself, says, "Hey C.H. You know what C.H. stands for? It's Cement Head." As if Fleming didn't know.

We were in Oakland and before practice Jack Gordon came to Polanic and said: "After practice, get your gear together. You're going down to Waterloo [our farm team]. We have too many players here."

Polanic was very upset. We're getting dressed in the locker room and he says to me: "They've got too many players now, but we'll see if they do after practice. There might be an opening."

When we started the scrimmage, Tom was running around and killing our guys. It got to the point where Polanic and I went out for a shift, and Danny Grant was sitting on the bench, and Gordon says to him, "Grant, your line is up," and Danny says, "We're not coming out."

Jack said, "Get out there." And Grant says, "No, that guy's crazy — we're not playing against him." Polanic didn't end up taking anybody out, so when the scrimmage was over he went down to the minors.

Dean Prentice

At the start of the 1971-72 season, I was moved to forward and played on a terrific line with Dean Prentice and Murray Oliver. By the end of the year, Murray had 27 goals, I had 21, and Deano had 20.

I had a hat trick in Montreal. One of the North Stars' sponsors was a liquor company, and they gave a case of Canadian Club to any one of us who had a hat trick.

My case of whiskey wasn't delivered until summer. I kept it to share with my linemates. When training camp opened, I gave Dean four bottles, Murray four bottles, and I kept four.

During training camp, there were some initiations that the rookies went through. Dean, Murray, Cesare Maniago and I went out to eat after we had played an afternoon exhibition game in Vancouver.

We all had too much to drink. Dean thought it would be a good night to initiate Jerry Byers, who was a young winger and destined to take Prentice's spot. We went to Byers' room and Dean got carried away. He took a huge basin of ice water and dumped it on Byers.

Dean Prentice

North Stars archives

We actually flooded the room a bit. We lost track of Dean, and eventually found him sleeping in the elevator. We flew home the next day, and afterwards Dean decided he shouldn't be drinking the way he did. He decided to give up alcohol cold turkey.

Dean is a terrific guy and when he makes a decision, he sticks to it. He not only stuck with it then but to this day. He came to the rink and said, "Guys, I don't like the way I've been drinking, and I'm never going to drink again." I said, "That's fine, Dean. Will you give me back my four bottles of Canadian Club?" He said, "No. I'm not drinking again. I don't believe in it."

I said, "I know you don't believe in it, so can I get back my four bottles of CC?" And he said, "I don't believe in it, so I poured them down the sink."

Tom Reid

Tom Reid was a terrific defensive defenseman. He was very consistent — game in and game out you knew you were going to get strong defense from Tommy. His play never varied.

I had three concussions in my career. The third one was the result of a real good check by Dennis Owchar one night in Pittsburgh. At the doctors' suggestion, I had started wearing a helmet after my second concussion to help prevent further ones.

But this night in Pittsburgh I was playing defense with Tom Reid, and I was carrying the puck up ice. I thought I had made a real good move to get by Owchar, but as I slipped the puck through his legs to try to go around him, he hit me with a shoulder right between my shoulder blades and I went down very hard. I hit my head on the ice so hard I eventually had seven stitches, even with the helmet.

I tried to get up, was real dizzy and started going back down again. The next thing I know the trainer, Doc Rose, is on the ice telling me to lie down, that they're going to carry me off.

I said, "There's no way. I've never been carried off the ice, and I'm not going to let anybody carry me off now."

I tried to get up again, and I went right back down. And as I'm going down this time, Tom Reid leans over and says, "Louie, Louie, before you go, can I have your condominium in Florida?"

A few weeks later we were back in Pittsburgh playing the Penguins. They had a real tough kid, Battleship Bob Kelly. One of the few fights I saw Dennis Hextall lose was to Battleship.

On this night, there was a shot coming from the blue line, and Kelly was right between Reid and me. The puck is coming towards the net, and I know the goalie is going to catch it, so I'm thinking, "I've got a chance to give Kelly a shot here with nobody looking."

I raked my stick behind me right across the guy's head. Gilles Gilbert held the puck, the whistle blew, and I sort of bent over and said to Reid,

Tom Reid

North Stars archives

"I got that SOB good that time." And the next thing I heard was, "Like hell you did — he ducked!"

I looked at Tom, and he was bent over and bleeding. I'd knocked out a dozen of his false teeth. And Murray Oliver's going around, "Here's one … here's one … here's one."

So to this day I tell Tommy I got even with him for wanting me dead so he could have my condo.

●

I was paired on defense with Tommy one night when I got checked and lost a contact lens. I could only see out of one eye and yelled to Reid, "Ice the puck, ice the puck!" so I could get to the bench. Tommy ices the puck then asks me, "What's the matter?" I told him I lost a contact and had to put in another one.

I quickly went to the locker room, put another contact in my eye, and went right back onto the ice with a line change. The puck came to Tommy after the faceoff, and right away I holler, "Ice the puck, ice the puck!" I could still only see out of one eye.

As it turns out, in my haste I had put two contacts in the one eye and none in the other.

Dick "Doc" Rose

North Stars archives

When I played for the U.S. at the Olympics in Grenoble, Doc Rose was our trainer. After the Olympics I was joining the North Stars and Doc Rose was obviously going to be out of a training job. When I joined the North Stars, there was talk that one of the two trainers, Al Schueneman, was going to leave, since he was also the trainer for the Chicago Cubs. So I mentioned to Stan Waylett, our head trainer, and to Wren Blair: "If Al retires, one of the guys you should look at is Doc Rose. He's well qualified and terrific with players." They eventually hired him. Doc was so committed to the team, I don't know if anybody hurt more when we lost than he did.

One night we had a particularly tough loss. We got ahead, then we started taking penalties in the third period — penalties I wouldn't even call marginal.

I was upset, Doc was upset, we all were upset with the officials. When a game ends, normally the trainer of the home team takes beer down to the officials' room so they can have a couple after the game.

Doc said to me: "Louie, I took care of those assholes. They're not getting any beer." I said: "Good. Don't give them anything. They don't deserve it." And then he says, "And I did more than that." I said, "What's that?" He says, "I locked them in the dressing room."

I said, "I don't know anything about it."

Early the next morning, I got a call from the executive vice president of the league, Brian O'Neill. He says: "What do you think you're doing? You're causing a problem in the league that you're going to pay for dearly."

I said, "What are you talking about?" He says: "You locked the referees in their room and they didn't get out until one in the morning. They were banging on the door, and finally a security guy heard them."

I said, "Brian, let me do an investigation and I'll get right back to you." So I waited for about six hours and called him back. I said: "Brian, I checked, and I heard there were a lot of fans very upset with the officials, and they were downstairs, too. Apparently, someone must have gotten over by the doorway and locked them in the room."

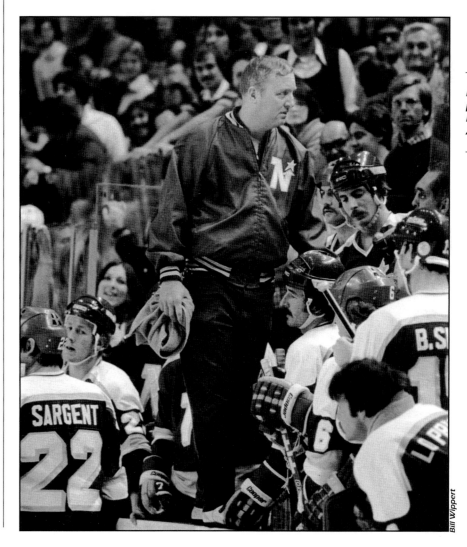

Bill Wippert

Doc Rose patrols the bench at The Aud in Buffalo.

Bobby Rousseau

We were playing a Sunday game in Buffalo, so we were in town a night early. We used to go to Sinatra's bar after dinner. We went in there and Bobby Rousseau was sitting at the bar. He had been in there since the end of practice, drinking Courvoisier cognac. We left at 11 p.m. and Bobby still was there, drinking Courvoisier.

We had no skate the next day and were told, "Be at the rink at 5:15." The rink was right across the street from our hotel, so at 5 o'clock I'm taking the hotel elevator to go to the rink. The elevator stops, the door opens, and Bobby Rousseau is standing there in his overcoat and hat — he always wore a fedora — holding his suitcase.

I said, "Bobby, we're staying here overnight." He says in his French Canadian accent: "No, no, Lou, I got to go myself. There's a big problem — they think I have the heart attack, so they fly me home right now." I said, "What's the matter?" He says, "I don't know, I'm having problem with my heart." He missed the game, they flew him home, his wife, Huguette, was there to pick him up along with an emergency ambulance, and they took him down and gave him all the tests. The problem, of course, was he had too much Courvoisier, but he thought he had a heart attack. He was having palpitations from the cognac.

Bobby Rousseau

North Stars archives

Glen Sather

Glen played one season with the North Stars before they cut him loose in the summer of '76. Upon leaving Minnesota, his parting statement was: "This team – if they want to get it straightened out, they should hire Louie as general manager and me as coach. We'd straighten the team out."

Glen went from the North Stars to the Edmonton Oilers and eventually became the general manager and coach with those great Stanley Cup championship teams.

When he was in Edmonton, he and several friends purchased the Storm Mountain Lodge. It was a historic place and Sather was looking for information to use in advertising.

He called Red Fisher of the Montreal Gazette, the dean of all Canadian hockey writers, and asked if he could provide some information on the lodge. Red was a collector of Native Indian paintings, so he said, "I'll do that, Glen, but you have to pay me with an Indian painting."

Glen agreed and Red provided the material on the lodge. For the next year, when Red saw Sather, he would say: "Where's my painting? You agreed to give me an Indian painting."

Glen made excuses, saying he mailed it but it went to the wrong address. "I got it back and I'll get it to you," Sather said.

A year later, at the NHL draft, Glen sent out invitations to some writers and friends of Red Fisher saying we're going to have a presentation of an Indian painting to honor Red for all that he's done for the sport of hockey.

All the people were gathered in the room. Glen had an easel in the front of the room, and he had the painting all covered up. He stood up and told the story of how Red wanted an Indian painting, and now he was presenting it to him.

Glen then pulled off the cover and there was a photograph of former NHL player Jim Nielson, who is a Cree Indian and was working for the Oilers at the time. In the photo, Nielson was in full Indian head-dress, up on a ladder painting Glen's house. That was the "Indian painting."

Glen Sather

North Stars archives

Al Shaver

When I was general manager, we were playing in Los Angeles one night, and Al Shaver asked me to go on the radio in between periods. In those days we didn't have a color man traveling with Al all the time, so Al would fill in between periods himself.

I came up to the press box, which in L.A. actually sits right at center ice in the middle of the crowd. As I got there, during a commercial break, Al says: "Louie, I'm having a problem. I've got to get to the bathroom real bad. Can you fill in for me?" I said, "Yeah, when we come back on the air just ask me this one question and then you can leave."

Al asked me something, I started talking and he left. I just kept talking, and about twelve minutes later he returned. As he sat down I said, "So that's the way it went." Then he asked another question and didn't miss a beat.

Paul Shmyr

Paul was on our reserve list, and we were able to claim him from Edmonton when the WHA and NHL merged. He was a seasoned veteran and one of the best captains the North Stars ever had. He took over the locker room and really pulled the team together.

He knew when to joke and when to be tough. He called himself Judge Roy Bean. If there was a problem on the team he would wrap himself in a sheet that was his judge's robe and he'd hold court. He handed out decisions on team discipline and fines.

He developed a strong bond with the other players. One night at the Met, Chicago tough guy Dave Hutchinson was getting on one of our players. Shmyr had a broken jaw but still didn't hesitate to take a shot at Hutchinson, and Hutchinson returned fire into Shmyr's jaw.

That's the way Shmyr was, he'd stand up for a teammate no matter what, and he always provided support.

Paul Shmyr

North Stars archives

Bobby Smith

When I took over as GM and coach in February 1978, we were in last place and Washington was second to last. I hoped to have first choice in the draft and take Bobby Smith.

One month later I could see that we'd probably be last or second to last. So, I started bringing up players from the farm system. I signed a couple of college players and played them to see what they could do. We were basically having tryouts.

Max McNab, who was the Washington GM, called and asked, "What are you doing with your lineup?" I said: "I just got this job. I've got to find out who can play and who can't play."

He said, "Do you think you're ever going to catch us?" I said, "I don't think so."

We drafted Bobby Smith, but the WHA also wanted him. He's the only player I ever signed to a one-way contract — meaning he would make the same in the NHL or the minors.

When I was negotiating the contract with Arthur Kaminsky before I drafted Smith, I knew we had to pay him an ungodly amount of money for those days — $250,000.

We didn't have that kind of money, so I called Bill Ramsey, who I had played with at the University of Minnesota and whose family owned Kemps Ice Cream. The Ramseys had been like a second family to me when I was at the U of M. Bill's dad, Dave, was great to me.

I called Bill and said, "I've got a deal for you. I'm signing Bobby Smith. He's going to be a big hit in Minnesota, and I'm giving you an opportunity — we're making a deal now — to have him as your spokesman for Kemps."

I signed him to a three-year contract with Kemps, and they paid part of Smith's contract with the North Stars.

When I got home from negotiating with Kaminsky, I went to see the Ramseys. Dave said to me, "I told Bill that if he keeps dealing with you, he's going to be driving one of our trucks and you're going to be running the ice cream company."

However, it turned out to be a great thing for all parties.

Glen Sonmor

Glen was a guy I adored. I knew he had a drinking problem, and we tried to help him. Whenever Glen drank — and he wasn't supposed to drink at all — he used to put on this cologne I think he bought for a dollar a gallon. We called it his frou-frou juice. Also, when we were traveling and he'd had some drinks the night before, he'd buy every newspaper there was to pretend like he's reading, so he wouldn't have to talk to you and give himself away.

We started the season one year and Glen was going pretty good, and then all of a sudden we get to November and I sit down beside him on the bus, and he's reading his papers, and he's got the cologne on.

Glen Sonmor

North Stars archives

I look at him and say, "Hey, Glen, I'm really happy — I finally thought of what I can get you for Christmas." He says, "What are you talking about?" I said, "Christmas next month. I'm getting your gift — I know what it is. I'm getting you another glass eye."

He says, "Why are you doing that?" I said, "This one's going to be bloodshot, so at least when you come on the bus you can have two bloodshot eyes."

Glen used to get excited during games, and one time in particular he caused a hectic scene on the bench. I was looking down from the press box, wondering what was happening, and all of a sudden I see everybody down on their hands and knees scrambling around. Glen had yelled so hard that his glass eye popped out and rolled under the bench, and he couldn't find it. Everybody was searching for his eye so he could put it back in and they could get the game going.

Dean Talafous

Dean was from Hastings, Minnesota and came to us from the Atlanta Flames. He played college hockey at Wisconsin, where he developed into an NHL talent. His long arms allowed him to be a very effective checking forward and extremely deceptive when handling the puck.

Dean Talafous

North Stars archives

Elmer "Moose" Vasko

Wren used to worry about Moose Vasko's weight a lot, so he had a fine for him: $100 for every pound over 220. Moose knew he couldn't control his weight, but he figured out how to put a piece of metal under the scale so that it would never go over 220. Every time he got weighed, it would stop at 220.

Countless times, Wren would come down and say: "You fat pig, Moose. Get on that scale. I know you're over 220, and it's 100 bucks a pound." Moose would get on, the scale would stop at 220, and Wren would say, "Damn, you look bigger than that."

Moose was usually about 250, of course.

•

Little did I know Moose's beer capacity. At the end of one year, we were playing Pittsburgh on a Saturday night and Philadelphia on a Sunday, and we had to win one of those two games to get in the playoffs. Friday we got into Pittsburgh, and we went to this "Band Box" restaurant, as we called it.

It was four in the afternoon and it was Ray Cullen, Parise, Goldsworthy, Danny O'Shea, Moose and me. We had a few beers and played some pool. At six we decided to sit down and have a steak. When we sit down, Moose is sitting at the bar having a beer, and he says, "What are you guys doing?" I said: "We're going to have a steak. Come on, sit down." And he says: "No, no, I'm going to go back to the room. It's a big game tomorrow, we've got to look after ourselves. I can't eat a steak."

Moose Vasko

North Stars archives

When we were finished, I said, "Guys, I'm going to go back and keep my roomie company." When I open the door, Moose is in bed watching TV.

I look at him and I say: "Moose, I gotta tell you, I'm really impressed. I can't believe your dedication." He says: "Kid, you'll learn. You don't realize when a big game comes, you have to do what you have to do. You look after yourself. Keep your weight down."

I said, "OK, Moose, I'm going to go have a beer." To which he replies: "You want a beer? Have a beer." And I looked over, and he had ordered a case of beer for himself. He didn't have a steak, but he drank the case of beer. I always told Moose, "I know you want to win the Stanley Cup for one reason: so you can buy yourself your own Hamm's beer truck."

•

The year after Moose retired, we were playing in St. Louis. I'm sitting in the locker room before the game, and I pick up one of the programs they always put in locker rooms before games. The St. Louis program always had a feature called "Where Are They Now?" And this particular night, the column featured Moose Vasko, and underneath his photo they had a caption, "Played at 220 … with gusts to 250."

•

Vasko was about six-foot-three and consistently weighed over 225. One time we were playing Philadelphia, and they had a really aggressive team. One guy in particular, Forbes Kennedy, was very tough and a good fighter, but he wasn't that big — probably about five-foot-eight, 170 pounds.

Kennedy went behind the net and right into Vasko, who was freezing the puck on the boards. The whistle blew, and I'll never forget, Moose turned around and looked down at Forbes and said: "Hey Forbes, cut that out. I'm not afraid of you."

Moose was the type of guy who didn't know his own strength. Once at training camp in Haliburton, Lloyd Percival, one of the foremost conditioning coaches in Canada, was putting us through strength testing. You'd grab this grip, and it would register your hand strength. So Moose grabs the grip, and Percival looks at him and says, "Look at you — a big man like you, and you're grabbing that thing like a weakling. You gotta have more strength than that."

Moose says, "No, that's it." Percival says, "Gordie Howe went 290 pounds!" Moose says, "Give me it again," grabbed it, and squeezed so hard he snapped the grip in two.

Stan Waylett

Stan Waylett

Stan Waylett, our original trainer, was a great guy. He was hired by Wren Blair. Previously, he had worked on the assembly line of General Motors in Oshawa, Ontario.

At the first training camp, the players knew Stan had little experience and he was the brunt of many jokes.

Danny O'Shea got a skeletal chart of a man and also a pointer. One night, as the players are getting ready for a game, Danny calls Stan over, and using the pointer says, "Arm, leg, toe, muscle." Danny got a twisted ankle a few weeks later. Stan was cutting tape off the ankle after the game. As he reached in with the scissors, a player said, "Stan, that's an ankle." As he turned to respond, he cut Danny for four stitches in the foot.

Stan Waylett in the North Stars dressing room at Met Center, 2/21/69

Freddie Barrett was a defensive defenseman and a terrific body checker, as good as any in the league. One night Freddie was coming out of the penalty box and he was given a long lead pass for a breakaway. He's rushing the goaltender, loses his balance and crashes into the net. He's lying there sprawled on the ice.

Stan hobbles out there — he had a very bad leg himself — looks at Freddie, and calls for a stretcher. Before it comes, Stan struggles to his feet by leaning on Freddie's leg for support — the one with the broken femur.

Tom Williams squares off with Canuck goalie and future North Star Gary Smith.

North Stars archives

Tom Williams

Tommy came from Duluth, Minnesota and was one of the first U.S.-born players in the NHL. He added great offense to the North Stars with his excellent speed and goal scoring ability. He also brought a very talkative and carefree attitude.

Tommy drove the coaches crazy because he would arrive at the Met five minutes before practice started and be on the ice with a minute to spare. I never saw anyone change from street clothes to hockey gear so fast.

Tommy created a lot of excitement for the fans, with his blond hair flying as he raced down the ice. He was our version of the Golden Jet, but he wasn't a very physical player. One night at the Met he got into a skirmish with Canuck goalie Gary Smith. We told Tommy his gloves must've fallen off by mistake.

Lorne "Gump" Worsley

Gump Worsley was petrified of flying. In fact, we got him out of retirement after he had a terrible flight while with Montreal.

We were flying to Pittsburgh one time, and Gump was sitting in front of me. After take-off, Gump was actually supposed to be sitting with the pilot — if he could see outside he felt a little better, but he still had a terrible, terrible time flying.

We hit an air pocket right in the middle of dinner and food flew all over the place. After everything was calmed down, the North Central Airlines pilot came out, which probably in itself gave Gump a heart attack, thinking about who's flying the plane. The pilot says: "Guys, I'm sorry. We hit a real severe air pocket. We'll have coupons to clean your suits." And Gump says, "How about my shorts?"

Gump Worsley and curious onlookers during practice at
the Bloomington Ice Garden, 10/13/71.

Bloomington Historical Society

Tom Younghans

Tommy Younghans was a great competitor who came from the University of Minnesota. He was fearless, hard-working, an excellent checker and a top penalty killer. He was also one of the most well-liked North Stars.

When I was GM, it came time to negotiate Tom's new contract. His agent was Ron Simon, and we reached a three-week impasse in talks. I had an amount of money to offer Tom that I would not go over, and Simon wanted considerably more.

I called Tommy into my office and told him if he didn't sign I would have to trade him. I offered him an extra $5,000 if he would fire Ron Simon and sign the contract. He said, "OK."

I called Simon and said, "I just signed Younghans, and you're fired." He said, "You can't do that." I said: "I already did, you're history. I'll see you when we negotiate for the next player."

Tom Younghans turns the puck up ice,
as Reid and LoPresti guard the net.

North Stars archives

THE BEST OF THE NORTH STARS

Craig Hartsburg

Rick Kolodziej

The **best defenseman** who ever played for the North Stars was **Craig Hartsburg**. He would have been an All Star for years and years had he not had a career-ending injury. Craig was unbelievably talented. He was very solid defensively and great at handling the puck, setting up plays, and getting the puck out of the zone.

The **best body-checker** was **Leo Boivin**. He hit you the hardest and hurt you the most. He was maybe 5 feet 8 inches tall, but he weighed about 200. He was built like a fireplug, and his checks caused a lot of pain. Another great body-checker we had was **Fred Barrett**. Freddie could stand you straight up.

Leo Boivin

North Stars archives

Fred Barrett

North Stars archives

The **best corner man** would be **J.P. Parise,** without a doubt. He could work the corners better than anybody. **Ulf Dahlen** was also terrific in the corners.

J. P. Parise

North Stars archives

The **best play-makers** would have to be **Neal Broten**, **Bobby Smith** and **Mike Modano**. Smith also was the **best faceoff man** we ever had.

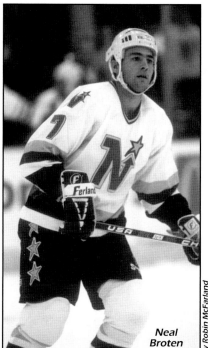

Neal Broten

Billy Robin McFarland

Bobby Smith

North Stars archives

Mike Modano beats Grant Fuhr of Edmonton during Game 3 of the '91 playoffs.

Joey McLeister / Minneapolis Star Tribune

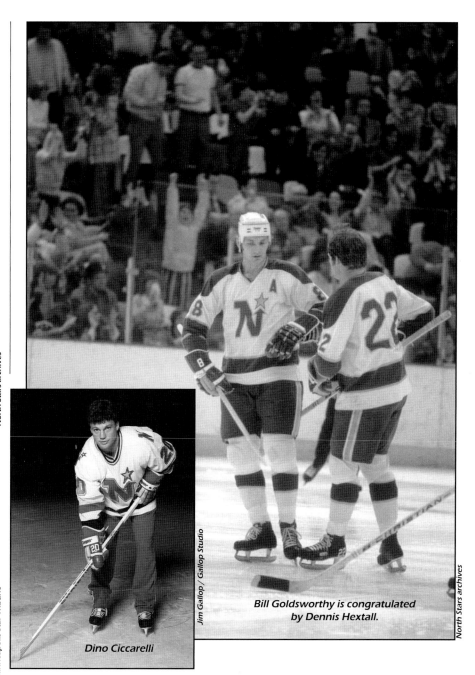

Dino Ciccarelli

Jim Gallop / Gallop Studio

Bill Goldsworthy is congratulated by Dennis Hextall.

North Stars archives

The **best pure goal scorers** would be **Dino Ciccarelli** and **Danny Grant**. **Bill Goldsworthy** would be right behind them. **Wayne Connelly** was another one, but he was here only for a short time.

Steve Payne scores on Billy Smith during Game 4 of the '81 Stanley Cup Finals vs. the Islanders.

Spence Hollstadt / St. Paul Pioneer Press

Tim Young

North Stars archives

The **best slapshot** would probably have to go to **Mike Modano** — he's got as hard a shot as anybody who's ever played with the North Stars. Another guy with a really hard shot was **Brad Palmer**.

The **best backhanded shot**, the **best backhanded passer**, and maybe even the **most talented player** was **Tom McCarthy**.

The **best clutch goal scorer** we ever had was **Steve Payne**. He got more big goals than anyone.

The **best stick handler** was **Tim Young**. He could do things with the stick that were incredible.

The **fastest skater** who played for the North Stars was **Mike Modano.**

Brad Palmer

Tom McCarthy

North Stars archives

Roland Eriksson

North Stars archives

Probably the **purest skater** was **Roland Eriksson** — just a terrific skater.

One of the most **intelligent players** on the ice was **Murray Oliver**. He had an incredible knack for thinking a game through.

If I had to pick one guy to **take a penalty shot** in a game, it would be **Danny Grant**. I just don't ever recall seeing anybody who was as consistently accurate.

Murray Oliver

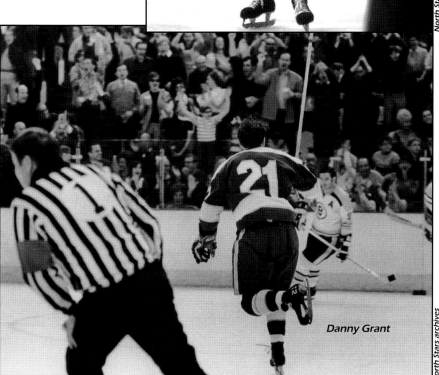

Danny Grant

As far as **facing a penalty shot**, it would be a toss-up. **Cesare Maniago** was always good on breakaways and going one-on-one against a player, but so was **Gump Worsley**. Gump would cut the angles down better than Cesare, but Cesare was a little more athletic. Those two guys were really tough when you came in on them alone.

Gump Worsley during practice at the Bloomington Ice Garden.

Cesare Maniago

Bloomington Historical Society

North Stars archives

North Stars archives

FIGHTERS

Jack Carlson and Dave Richter

Jack Carlson was playing in the WHA when I took over the North Stars. He was a player I wanted. Ted Lindsay was managing the Detroit Red Wings, and they owned Carlson's NHL rights.

I called Ted and made a deal with him. Jack had played in the WHA with the St. Paul Saints and now was playing in Hartford. He was a very popular guy here and from Virginia, Minnesota.

Jack Carlson and Dave Richter were two very similar guys. Off the ice they were quiet and unassuming. On the ice, no one was tougher than these two guys.

If I had to rate the toughest North Star of all time, they'd be tied for No. 1. And I'd rate them in the top five of the all-time toughest in the whole NHL. They could fight like nobody's business.

Jack retired in 1982. Four years later, our team had lost some of its toughness. Glen Sonmor and I were talking and we thought, "One guy we know is tough enough is Jack Carlson."

And we wouldn't have to worry about how much he played, because we'd have him for a specific purpose. So we got him to come back for a time.

Jack Carlson

Rick Kolodziej

We had drafted Dave Richter in the tenth round, all because of John Mariucci. John had seen Richter play for Michigan.

He looked like Clark Kent off the ice, a big guy with glasses. We brought him to training camp in 1980, and he was just starting to learn to play at a higher level, but boy oh boy, if someone did something wrong, he'd drop his gloves and fight.

It got so bad that we used to say, "When Richter drops his gloves, the other teams go for a line change." Nobody wanted to stay out there and fight him.

I not only never saw him lose a fight, I don't know if anybody even got a punch in on him. He had a long reach, and he was left-handed, and he could stand back and throw punches so effectively that the fights didn't last too long. Richter was as good a fighter as I've seen in the National Hockey League.

Rick Kolodziej

Dave Richter

Dennis O'Brien

Dennis O'Brien was a great teammate. He was as game as anybody in the league. He's one guy who would fight for his teammates, he'd fight for himself, he'd fight for fun.

Dennis O'Brien takes control in front of the North Stars net.

North Stars archives

We were playing Vancouver in an exhibition game, and late in the third period we had a 5-on-5 brawl. Unfortunately for Dennis, he grabbed Orland Kurtenbach. You talk about one of the great names in fighting, that was Kurtenbach.

After everything broke up and we were going to the penalty box, I looked and O'Brien's eyes were swelling shut. Soon, he had two black eyes. When he came in the locker room after the game, somebody asked him, "O'Bee, what happened?"

He says, "I don't know. I grabbed Kurtenbach, and before I knew it I got hit with a left and a right in each eye, and I was down."

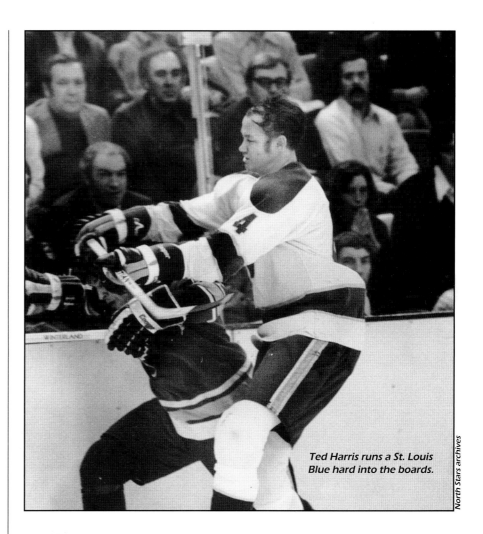

Ted Harris runs a St. Louis Blue hard into the boards.

North Stars archives

Ted Harris

Ted was another of the best fighters in the league. He was tall and he'd stand straight up and throw punches.

We were in St. Louis one night, and we always had tough games with them. Teddy hit someone with a hard check, and Bobby Plager, a tough guy for the Blues, came up to say something to him. Next thing you know, they squared off at center ice. I can still see the fight. Teddy must have hit him fifteen times, and Bobby never landed a punch.

Dennis Hextall

Another one of our top fighters was Dennis Hextall. Hexie was rangy and probably weighed 175 pounds — he was like a greyhound.

I don't know if I ever played with a better-conditioned athlete.

Off the ice, he wears glasses, and he's a quiet guy, like Richter. But once a game started, if you were playing against Hextall, you knew you were in for a tough night. He'd hit you with the stick as quick as look at you, he'd hit you clean, he'd hit you dirty — all he wanted to do was win,

and he would compete like that.

One night in Boston, he started what turned into a five-on-five fight. Dennis was on the ice with Goldsworthy, Harris, Parise and me when Wayne Cashman hit Dennis in the corner. As Cashman was skating away, Dennis took a two-handed shot and slashed Cashman across the ankle.

Cashman dropped his gloves and went at Dennis. And as the Bruins always did when one of their guys got into a fight, they all went toward the fight, and we went, too. It was one of many big brawls we had with the Bruins.

Dennis Hextall throws a big right hand to an Islander.

North Stars archives

Brad Maxwell

Brad Maxwell was a left-handed fighter, and he would throw down with anybody. He could handle the puck, he could shoot the puck as hard as anybody, and he could fight.

For the most part, Brad always won. Being a left-hander, he could surprise an opponent. One night in Detroit he beat Joey Kocur, who was a terrific fighter.

After the game, I went down in the locker room and said to Brad, "You did a nice job in the fight." He says: "It's a good thing I had a helmet. That kid can punch." I said, "What do you mean?" He says, "Look at my helmet."

Kocur had hit him with a right hand and cracked the helmet.

Al MacAdam

I think Al might have been, pound for pound, the best fighter in the league. I remember him taking on Curt Fraser in Vancouver, who was as tough a guy as there was, and winning decisively.

I had the misfortune to fight Al in Oakland earlier in his career. When you're fighting, usually people grab your jersey and throw punches. But he grabbed my arm perfectly, so when I'd throw a punch it seemed to always land an inch from his head. Then he popped me a good one and caught me for four stitches over the eye. I remember saying during the fight, "Just let go and throw punches."

Dave Hanson

Dave was a tough guy who was with us for a year in the late '70s. He played one of the Hanson brothers in *Slap Shot*. Along with being tough, he was extremely competitive and would do anything to stay in the league.

During a summer camp at Augsburg, he asked me what he needed to work on. I told him, "Improve your skating but, remember, the less you handle the puck, the longer you'll stay in the NHL."

Ron Friest

One tough guy we had was Ron Friest, out of Windsor, who we wound up losing because of a back injury.

We had about 60 guys in camp one season. We drafted Ronnie and brought him in. In the first scrimmage, a kid from western Canada went after Friest, and Friest beat the hell out of him.

Before you know it, Friest had five fights in the first two days. Glen Sonmor was up there wringing his hands in joy.

One of the kids that Friest knocked down bit him, and we had to take Friest to the hospital for five stitches in his finger. We joked that we had to check the other player for rabies.

Friest went to the minors and worked hard and developed into a good hockey player. He was one of the reasons we beat the Maple Leafs in the playoffs. Then he got the back injury and never came back. He was another guy in the Richter mold — very quiet and unassuming off the ice, but when he dropped the gloves, he could throw as good as anyone.

Willi Plett

Willi Plett was one of the toughest guys in the league and one of the most feared when it came to fighting. He was very protective of his teammates, and wouldn't hesitate to initiate something on the ice in order

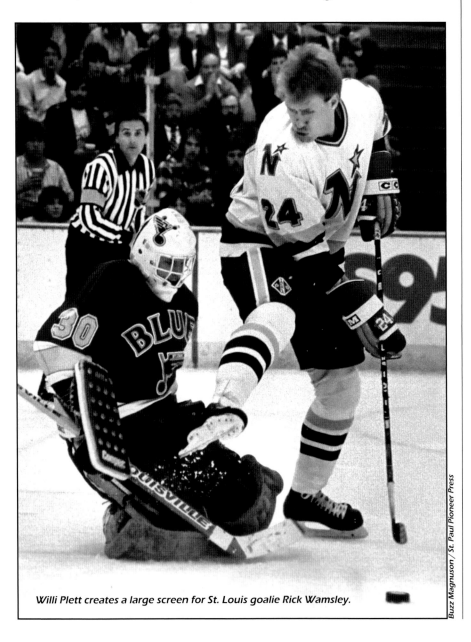

Willi Plett creates a large screen for St. Louis goalie Rick Wamsley.

Buzz Magnuson / St. Paul Pioneer Press

to turn a game around. He played with a great deal of flamboyancy, had good skills and was an accomplished player as well as being tough. He was great on the power play at screening the goalie and creating havoc in front of the net.

When we played Calgary in 1981 in the semifinals, Plett was the leader of Calgary's big, tough lineup. We knew they were tougher than us physically, and that they would try to intimidate us. Sonmor and I felt we had the advantage in speed and puck movement.

In those days, if two players got into a fight and other guys jumped in, the team would always pay the fines for "third man in" and bench-clearing brawls. So guys didn't mind helping their teammates out.

We stayed in Banff at the Banff Springs Hotel to be away from Calgary. We had a team dinner the night before the game. I told the players: "Gentlemen, you might not like this, but Glen and I feel that this team can't beat us if we just play hockey. So, I'm telling you, if anybody gets in a fight, or jumps into a fight, or gets a misconduct, we are not paying the fines. You're going to have to pay your own fines. We think that if we stay on the ice and let them try to chase us and intimidate us, we're going to win the series."

The players grumbled about standing up for one another, but I said again, "We're not paying any fines, and we're going to win the series by playing hockey."

And we did, four games to two.

When the series was over, we had more admiration than ever for Plett as a player and wanted him in our lineup.

Basil McRae

Basil was with the Maple Leafs and then became a free agent. We had lost toughness through retirement, injuries or trades — Jack Carlson, Dave Richter, Dan Mandich — and needed somebody to fill that void.

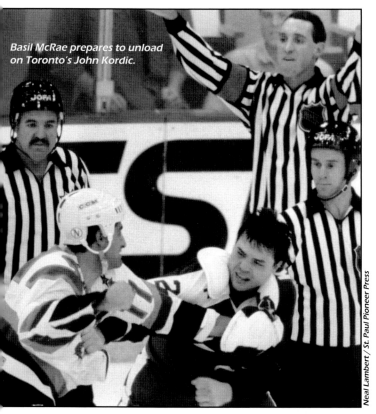

Basil McRae prepares to unload on Toronto's John Kordic.

Neal Lambert / St. Paul Pioneer Press

Several teams wanted Basil, but I had a good relationship with his agent, Bill Waters. I told Bill, "We don't want Basil to come here just to fight. If he comes here, we're going to give him a lot of ice time, because we want him to play, too."

He signed with us and we also brought in Terry Ruskowski from Pittsburgh, another tough kid.

We have a saying in the hockey business about tough guys who try to become goal scorers: They come in as crushers, then try to be rushers, and wind up as ushers.

We weren't worried about Basil McRae getting into that mode. He knew his job, but he also was intent on improving as a player.

Link Gaetz

Link Gaetz was a devastating fighter. He came out of Juniors with hundreds of minutes in penalties. He was 6 feet 3 inches and over 220. When we drafted him in 1988, Sonmor was so excited I thought he was going to have a heart attack. Glen said, "We've found the Missing Link."

We drafted Mike Modano in the first round, and we drafted Gaetz in the second.

When you draft a player and he's there, he comes down to the draft table to meet the staff. Modano was sitting at the table, and Gaetz comes down, and I look at him and he's got two black eyes.

I said, "What happened to you?" He says, "I got into a little skirmish and a couple of guys blindsided me." I said, "I think I need to draft a lawyer in the third round."

He was in the lineup very quickly, and if anybody fooled around with any of our players, Gaetz was right there. He was extremely tough. But he had problems off-ice and had a short career.

Neal Broten

Probably the most publicized fight in North Stars history, next to our battle in Boston, occurred in a game against Edmonton. Neal Broten checked Gretzky, and Gretzky got mad, and they squared off, and Broten dropped Gretzky.

One thing about Neal people didn't realize was that he was a tough little kid, and he had great balance on his skates. It was publicized across Canada like it was the second coming — Gretzky in a fight. It was with Broten, and Broten got him.

TOUGHEST OPPONENTS

Bob Probert

Probert had unusual stamina. The longer a fight went, the tougher he got. He seemed to enjoy taking a punch early in a fight, because it would set him up to finish a guy off as the fight wore on.

John Ferguson

John's teammates loved him because they knew he was always there to back them up. He wouldn't allow anyone to take liberties with them. He enjoyed fighting and would go at the drop of a hat, with anyone. Losing wasn't in his vocabulary.

John once made a vow to be the meanest, rotten-est, most miserable cuss in the NHL. And he lived up to that vow.

In a game against us, he got angry at Danny Lawson. At the time, Lawson's jaw was broken and wired shut. Ferguson knew it, but he didn't hesitate to drop Lawson anyway.

John Ferguson (left), with Colorado Rockies GM Ray Miron and Lou

Lou Nanne archives

REFEREES

Dave Newell

With Glen Sonmor as coach, we had a lot of occasions to have run-ins with referees. Sonmor is like me: During the game we never see a referee we like. After the game, we love them all.

Glen had a real tough time with Dave Newell. We were going into a game one night, and Glen came into my office and said: "Louie, I don't want to coach tonight. Newell's refereeing, and I get so pissed off at him that I always get bench penalties. Maybe I should just sit upstairs tonight and have Murray Oliver coach."

I said: "You can't do that. Just control yourself."

He says, "Okay, but I'm going to have Murray help me out."

He said to Murray: "Listen. Any time I get on the referees, you just grab my shoulder and tell me, 'Cut it out — leave the referees alone.'"

Glen says, "I'm going to write it on my hand — 'Leave the referees alone.'" And he did.

Eight minutes into the game, Newell makes a call and Glen gets upset and starts yelling at Newell, and Murray grabs Glen by the shoulder and says, "Glen, remember, leave the referees alone."

Glen says, "Okay, fine."

Six minutes later, Glen's all over Newell again. Murray grabs him and says, "Leave the referees alone." Glen says, "Okay, fine."

Then right away in the second period we get a penalty, and Glen jumps all over Newell, and Murray grabs him and says, "You're supposed to leave the referees alone." And Glen says, "I'm not leaving them alone, and if you touch me one more time I'm going to send you right to the press box."

Andy Van Hellemond

Once we were playing our archrivals, the Blackhawks, and Andy Van Hellemond made a horrible call on us. We were outplaying them. We were really playing hard, and I thought it was a very cheap penalty. The Blackhawks scored on the power play, and they beat us by a goal.

Van Hellemond went back to the Registry Hotel in Bloomington, and I stayed in my office. About 2:30 in the morning I was still steaming, and I picked up the phone and called the Registry Hotel and asked them for Van Hellemond's room.

They put me through. And I said, "You awake?" He says, "Now I am." I said, "You should be. You've kept me awake all night with your horseshit refereeing." And I hung up.

Andy Van Hellemond disallows a North Star goal, despite the protests of Bill Goldsworthy, Tom Reid, Dennis Hextall and Pierre Jarry, 12/03/75.

Roy Swan / Minneapolis Star Tribune

GMs Vote on Refs

One year we had a general managers meeting in Phoenix, and I was chairman. Every general manager raised the subject of refereeing. There were 21 teams in the league, so we each had 1/21st of a vote, and the general managers' voting was only worth 25 percent toward making decisions on referees.

Also at the meeting were Brian O'Neill, the league's executive vice president, and Scotty Morrison, who was at that time head of the referees.

I said: "Gentlemen, today we're going to do something we haven't done before. We're going to vote as a bloc. I'm going to put all 15 referees on the board, and we're going to rate them, and that way we'll have a stronger voice because our 25 percent is going to be in agreement." Scotty Morrison says, "You can't do that." I said: "Oh yes, I can. We're at a meeting, there are no bylaws against it, and we're doing it today." So that's what we did — we voted as a bloc for a few years, so we could affect which referees, at the end of the year, were rated the poorest and weren't brought back. They took that option away from us later on.

Disallowed Goal

We were playing at home one night against the New York Rangers, and right near the end of the first period we scored a goal but there was no red light. The referee went over and consulted with the goal judge and asked him why he hadn't turned the light on, and the goal judge said, "I'm not sure it went in the net."

The referee waved off the goal. I was up in the press box, and I could see on the video replay that the puck went in the net but the light didn't turn on. Well, I was furious. We didn't have instant replay in those days in the league, so the goal was nullified. So during the last minute of the

period, I ran down and stood right behind the goal judge. As they pull his cage back, he turns around and sees me, and the first thing he says to me is, "It was in, wasn't it?"

I said: "You're damned right it was in. Why didn't you turn the light on?" He says, "I wasn't sure it was in." I said: "If I want a neutral goal judge, I'll go to Boston. Anytime something here gets close, you turn the light on and let the referee be the one to nullify it."

John McCauley and Jim Gregory

Another time, we had what I thought was a real bad job of refereeing from Denis Morel. It was December 23, and John McCauley was the Referee-in-Chief, and I knew he was in Boston at the Copley Hotel because I had talked to him earlier in the day.

I was still fuming in my office at three in the morning, so I called him. It was 4 a.m. there. I said, "I want John McCauley's room," and they said, "He's not taking any phone calls." I said, "This is an emergency, and you'd better go upstairs and tell him to answer the phone."

And they did. He says, "Hello, it's John McCauley." I said, "Yeah, and it's Lou Nanne. I'm still sitting in my office because your referee screwed me tonight." And I hung up.

Similarly, there must have been 10 times that I called Jim Gregory at 2, 3, 4 in the morning, when he was the Referee-in-Chief. His wife always picked up the phone, and she used to say, "Hi, Louie," then hand Jim the phone.

When I retired as GM, one of the first calls I got was from Jim Gregory, and he said, "Rosalie, my wife, just wanted me to thank you for retiring, because now she'll be able to sleep nights."

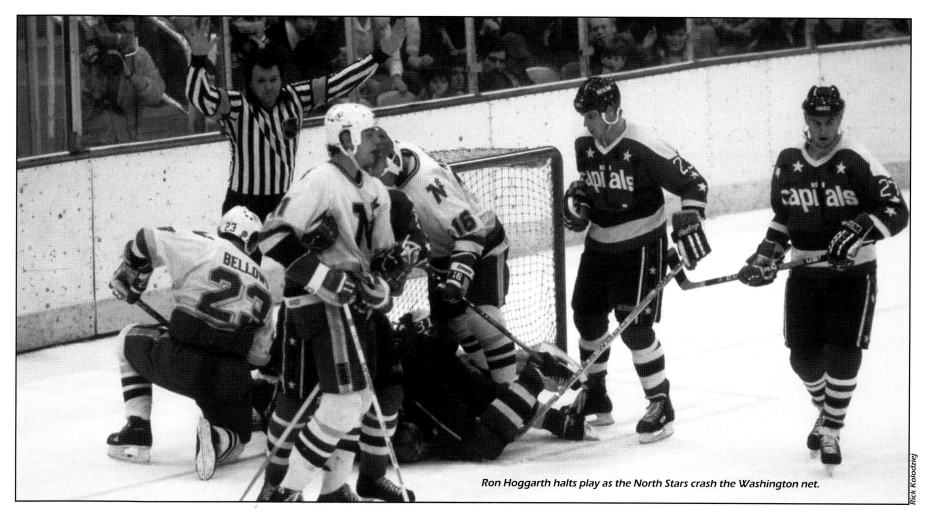

Ron Hoggarth halts play as the North Stars crash the Washington net.

Rick Kolodziej

Ron Hoggarth

Ron Hoggarth and I used to get into numerous confrontations when he was refereeing. One time Hoggarth was refereeing our game with Toronto, and we lost 6-5 in overtime. After the game was over, I went down, and Al Weisman, who was a big 6-foot-5-inch security guy, says: "Louie, Louie, you're not allowed in the referees' room. They told me to keep you out."

The transom is open, and Hoggarth says, "Yeah, don't let him in here —

he just wants to tell me I'm horseshit." I said, "No, I promise you I won't tell you you're horseshit." So he says, "Okay, Al, let him in." So I opened the door and said, "I just wanted to tell you you're damn brutal."

A couple of occasions were really odd. This one time, we won a game 6-3 at home. I went down to the referees' locker room afterwards, and Ron says, "What's on your mind?" I said: "Well, Ron, I can't be a hypocrite. I always complain to you when we lose a game and I figure your refereeing was brutal. We won tonight, and I want to tell you that I still think you were brutal."

THE MEDIA

Spectrum Sports

Gordon and George Gund entered into an agreement with the Twins in the early '80s to form a sports channel called Spectrum Sports. At the time, the North Stars were more successful than the Twins, and the agreement seemed amicable for both parties.

However, when Carl Pohlad bought the Twins in 1984 and they won the World Series three years later, he came to the Gunds to dissolve the agreement. The Gunds, being as wealthy as he was and feeling that the agreement had been done in good faith, declined to do so.

Carl threatened legal action, and the Gunds were very happy to oblige. This happened to be one time that Pohlad did not come out ahead, and a settlement was reached with one of the conditions being that the terms would never be discussed publicly.

Years later the Twins started up another sports channel called Victory Sports and lost a lot of money before dissolving it. Looking back now, had they stayed with Spectrum Sports over the years, this could have proven to be extremely profitable for them and might have made a big difference in whether the Gunds had continued to own the North Stars and operate in Minnesota.

The Boston Bruins, for instance, are part of the New England Sports Network with the Red Sox, and one of the reasons that they thrive is the success of their sports channel.

Wally Shaver tapes a pregame interview with Lorne Henning in a Met Center locker room. Frank Mazzocco compiles his game notes in the background. Empty locker rooms were used as TV studios on game nights.

North Stars archives

Hockey Writers

We had some real characters covering us. One of the funniest was Charley Hallman from the *St. Paul Pioneer Press*. Charley was the type of guy who had to have a story, and if you weren't around he'd come up with one anyway.

One time I came back to town and read where I was trading a player. I was even quoted about it. I called Charley all incensed and said: "How can you say I'm trading this guy? I haven't even talked about him, and I certainly haven't talked to you."

He said, "I tried to get you for four days and couldn't, but I knew that's what you'd say if I could, so I went ahead with it."

When I hired Bill Mahoney as coach, everybody knew I'd been interviewing coaches and we'd scheduled a press conference for the following day to announce our decision. At 4:00 in the morning my doorbell rings, and my wife wakes me up and says, "Somebody's at the door and I don't know who it is."

I walked to the door in my pajamas, and there are Charley Hallman and Charley Walters from the St. Paul newspapers. They said, "We've got to know, who's the new coach?"

They wanted to get a scoop in the afternoon newspaper, the *St. Paul Dispatch*. I said, "I'm not telling you." They said, "We're not leaving until you do."

They waited and we talked for a couple of hours. Finally I said: "I've got to go back to bed. The new coach is Bill Mahoney." So they got their scoop.

In the early years, we had Dwayne Netland covering us for the *Minneapolis Tribune* in the morning and Dan Stoneking covering us for the *Minneapolis Star* in the afternoon. And every now and then we would set them up.

We'd wait until we saw them coming into our locker room, then we'd huddle off to the side and pretend we heard one of our players just got traded. We'd get the reporters to go scurrying after Wren Blair or Jack Gordon to ask about the trade.

Sid Hartman used to come with a big old tape recorder, and he learned very early not to put it down. One day he put it down and Tommy Reid grabbed it and put it in the freezer. Sid was running around the locker room screaming for his tape recorder when he couldn't find it. Finally Doc Rose said: "Sid, Sid, it must be in here. I'm getting some ice and it looks like a tape recorder." And Tom Reid yelled: "It was hot news, hot news. We had to cool it off."

One year, Tom Reid and I decided to pull a prank on a young writer from Duluth named Scott Dahl. He wanted to do a story on the North Stars and research for a book, so Jack Gordon gave him permission to take part in practice. He would come onto the ice and stumble around, but eventually he got familiar with the team and almost felt like a part of it.

Tommy and I set him up pretty good. Tom said to him: "Why don't you go over and ask Louie if you could take his sister out for drinks and dancing this weekend? She lives with him and he's very protective of her, so he might give you some grief."

So Scott came over and asked me about going dancing with my sister and I said, "Are you trying to be a smart guy or something?" He said, "No, I want to take her dancing." I said, "My sister has a severe leg problem and I don't appreciate you making fun of her." He says, "I didn't know." I said, "I don't believe that. When we're on the ice for practice today, I'm going to run this stick through your stomach."

He backed off and we went out to the ice. When he was near me during drills, I started saying: "Hey Jack, let's scrimmage. I've got somebody I gotta get. Let's scrimmage." I said this loud enough for Scott to hear, but not loud enough for coach Jack Gordon to hear.

A few minutes later, Jack blows his whistle and says, "OK, we're going to scrimmage." I turned to Scott and said, "Now I'll get even with you." He skated off the ice and never practiced with us again.

WCCO-TV Prank

We had a highly touted rookie in training camp. He was sitting next to Tommy Reid and me in the locker room, and Tom says, "Hey Louie, our rookie is going to be on TV tonight." The rookie said: "Really? I didn't hear anything about that."

Tom said: "Yeah, they sent me to tell you. They want you at WCCO Television at 6 p.m. for the 6:20 sportscast." The rookie said, "What should I do?" I said: "Take a cab down there, the team will reimburse you. The station is at 11th & Marquette. Get there by six because they will want to put makeup on you. Then, they'll put you on the sports." He said, "Oh, okay, fine."

So the rookie went downtown to WCCO, found his way to the sports studio, sat there for the entire telecast, never got interviewed and came back to the Met. No one from WCCO talked to him because nobody had any idea what he was doing there.

SPANNING THE GLOBE

Vietnam USO Tours

I set up a couple of USO tours in the early 70's, and one was to Vietnam. I had Tommy Reid, J.P. Parise and Murray Oliver with me. It was scorching hot, and it was in the middle of the war, and the first thing we were told was, "If you hear any incoming shells or rockets, put your helmet on and jump under the bed."

We spent a couple of weeks flying around in helicopters, which was very unnerving to J.P. When we were in Saigon, at the end of each day we'd return by helicopter to the Saigon Hotel. It was a hotel and a barracks that was fortified by cement-filled barrels.

They had a little room off the bedrooms where we could sit at the end of the day. J.P. didn't drink much before, but after the helicopter flying, he would buy a pint of vodka and drink it.

One night I went behind the bar to mix drinks, and I thought I saw a cockroach, but on second glance it was actually a black knife with a black laced loop attached to it.

J.P. is terrified of creatures — snakes, cockroaches, even monkeys. I thought, if I could get this knife in J.P.'s bed, he might think it's a big cockroach and it would be worth a laugh. I made an excuse for leaving, went in J.P. and Murray's room and put the knife under J.P.'s covers at the foot of the bed.

Around 2 a.m., J.P. said he was going to take a shower and go to bed. When J.P. walked into the shower, Tommy and I hid in the armoire in the room and Murray pretended to be reading. It's very quiet and J.P.'s singing to make noise and feel more comfortable. He's toweling himself as he comes out, and now he starts walking towards the armoire.

I had roomed with J.P. and knew he always slept nude, but I started wondering, "What if he's going to wear pajamas? If I open the door right now, he'll have a heart attack. He'll think it's the Viet Cong coming out of here." I'm starting to laugh but also I'm thinking, "Please, don't let this happen."

He comes right towards us. He opens the armoire and Tommy jumps out, and I fall out. J.P. starts backpedaling 100 mph, throwing punches and kicking, and then sees it's us. He says: "Bad joke, guys. Bad joke. Get out of my room."

As we're leaving, I'm thinking, "He's still got the knife in the bed." And sure enough, we hear another scream. He thinks his foot has hit a cockroach.

While in Vietnam, Lou Nanne, Murray Oliver, Tom Reid and J. P. Parise meet with General Fred C. Weyand, U.S. Army.

Lou Nanne archives

Barry Gibbs and Lou Nanne (top) and Cesare Maniago visit wounded soldiers.

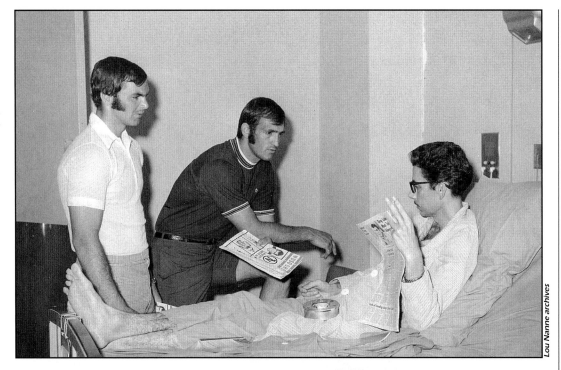

Lou Nanne archives

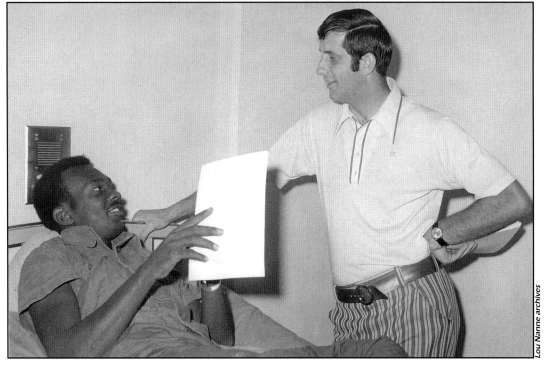

Lou Nanne archives

The other USO tour was to Japan, the Philippines, Okinawa and Guam. I went with Murray Oliver, Cesare Maniago, Barry Gibbs and Ted Hampson. We visited people who were shot up in firefights — some only a few hours earlier. They were transported to these locations from Vietnam.

We would go to hospitals, make small talk and also talk hockey. Many servicemen were hockey fans, and we brought some hockey films and souvenirs with us.

It was a unique experience — very humbling. I'll never forget, one guy had been badly burned and he was bandaged from head to toe. And he says: "Hockey players! Oh, I love that sport — it's so tough." And I said: "Please, don't talk to me about being tough. We don't know anything compared to guys like you."

I saw so many guys who had lost legs or arms but would say, "When I go back, I'm going to ski, I'm going to golf, I'm going to do this on one leg, I can do it."

My son, 10 years later, lost his leg, and when he was coming out of the coma and he had no leg, the thing I said to him was: "Michael, remember I told you about those guys in Vietnam, how they said they were going back, and they were going to ski, and they were going to enjoy all the sports that they wanted to play, and enjoy life the same way? You could do it like they're doing it."

Those USO trips were something that I treasured and never forgot.

Excerpts from Tom Reid's Vietnam Journal:

Vietnam USO: 24 May 1972 — 6 June 1972
Overnight stays in Saigon, Da Nang, Ca Mau

…Upon arrival in Saigon we were briefed on details, especially a lot of bombing — hit the floor fast.

…At the 3rd Field Hospital, the soldiers were very glad to see someone from "the world" other than soldiers.

…Flew from Saigon to Da Nang in a C-130 cargo plane used for paratroopers. No windows and very hot. Everyone calls Da Nang "Rocket City," so we are a little nervous.

…Visited the 95th EVAC hospital. Only 50 men there, which was good. Some had malaria and others had shrapnel wounds.

…Visited the Tactical Communications installation on Monkey Mountain. Men were planted all around the towers so the North Vietnamese could not destroy them. We returned to the hotel under an armed guard escort because it was after curfew.

…Flew to Long Thanh by Huey helicopter. Chopper had no sides where passengers sit. I was really scared. So was J.P. An awful feeling when we banked, I could see nothing but the ground 1,500 feet below. Nothing holding me in but a seat belt.

…Helicopter flight to the Eunis fire base was at high altitude because the Viet Cong below had heat-seeking missiles. Return flight was terrifying. Flew at 4,200 feet with no sides.

…In Ca Mau, we could hear gunfire from howitzers two miles away. The Viet Cong destroyed a South Vietnamese outpost.

Other spots visited:

11th Combat Aviation Group	79th Artillery Unit
196th Infantry	Tan Son Nhut
336th Tactical Fighter Wing	Bac Lieu

The First European North Star

The first European player to be drafted and signed by the North Stars was Roland Eriksson from Sweden. GM Jack Gordon drafted Eriksson in 1974. I had played against him in the '74 World Championships in Helsinki and was glad Gordon was able to select him.

Roland Eriksson (middle) is welcomed to the North Stars by Tom Reid, Head Coach Ted Harris, Lou Nanne and Assistant Coach Andre Beaulieu.

North Stars archives

Eriksson was still playing for Sweden in 1976 when the World Championships were in Katowice, Poland. I was on the U.S. team and we were staying in the same hotel as the Swedes. I talked to Eriksson at length about joining the North Stars, and he indicated that he was ready. He began playing for us at the start of the '76-77 season, becoming the first North Star from Europe.

Roland did a great job for us for two years before deciding to return home.

The Russians

One night late in my playing career, we played the Russians in an exhibition game at the Met. I had been playing against the Russians since 1960, first when I was at the University of Minnesota and then with the U.S. National team and Olympic team, so I was very familiar with them.

When the game was over, I invited four of the Russians — Makarov, Petrov, Ragulin and Lutchenko — to my home. I was always trying to get players from behind the Iron Curtain to defect. As they walked into my house, they looked around and said "Louie, you live like the ministers of Russia." I said, "If you come over here and play in the NHL, you'll live like ministers of Russia, too."

Makarov, a terrific player, said, "We don't leave the Mother Country." I said: "You're playing for the Red Army. It's about time you went out and made a little money for yourself." He replied, "No, that is our life and that's why we play." He was a top player on their club at the time, and he was a guy who just would not leave. The others felt the same way.

In 1982 when I was general manager, I drafted Viktor Zhlutkov from the Soviet National team and tried to get him to come to Minnesota. He was from Latvia, as was our team doctor George Nagobads, and I had George working on Zhlutkov.

Helmut Balderis was another Soviet we wanted. Every time I went to a World tournament, I would talk to those two guys, Balderis and Zhlutkov, trying to get them to defect and join the North Stars.

Jack Ferreira eventually drafted Balderis, but not until years later when I was team president. Helmut was a terrific player on the World scene. Unfortunately, by the time he came to Minnesota he was near the end of his career.

The North Stars and Soviet Union Olympic team prior to their exhibition game at Met Center, 1/4/83.

Frantisek Musil's Defection

In 1983 I drafted Czech defenseman Frantisek Musil in the second round. I had watched him play in the World Championships, and he looked like a terrific young player. The Quebec Nordiques at that time had the Stastny brothers, who had defected from Czechoslovakia, and they were tearing up the NHL.

I drafted Frantisek, went to the World Championships in Munich, and talked to him about defecting. I said, "After the last game of the tournament, I'll have a police escort get us to the airport and take you back." He says, "Let me think about it, and I'll talk to you later in the week." They always had security watching the Czech team. He didn't come with us in '83. Then in 1984, the third Canada Cup came along, and Musil was playing on the Czech team and I was managing the U.S. team. I'd call him every day and try to encourage him to defect at the end of the tournament. Again, it didn't happen.

Finally, I went to Toronto and hired the same Czech contact who had helped get the Stastnys out of Czechoslovakia. He said if he personally got Musil out, it would cost $250,000, with $25,000 up front for expenses.

That had been his price to get the Stastnys out, too. I said, "OK." Back then, you didn't have to pay the defectors a signing bonus, so it was almost like a wash. I gave him the $25,000, and for the next two years, he'd fly over to Europe and watch them play in different championships, and he'd say, "He's coming, he's coming."

In 1986, I got a call from Rich Winter in Edmonton, and Rich says, "Louie, I'm the agent for Frantisek Musil." Winter had convinced him to defect.

He says, "Musil's going to be vacationing in Umag, Yugoslavia, starting tomorrow." I said, "I'll fly over and meet him in Zagreb at the American Consulate, and I'll get him out from there." He says: "OK, I'm com-

ing, too, but you'll have to give me a little time. We'll meet there in two days." I made airline reservations to fly to Trieste, Italy, which is right on the Yugoslavian border. Bob Bruce, from KSTP, was around the office while all this was going on, and he says, "Louie, do you mind if I come with a cameraman?"

I said, "What are you going to do?" He says: "I'd just like to film it. I won't say anything, won't do anything — I'll stay out of the way." I said, "You better, because I'm not looking after you." He says, "Just tell me what flight you're on."

So we ended up in Trieste, and I rented a car. I said to Bruce and his cameraman, "I'm going to make a dry run to Umag tonight to see what I have to do to drive through the border, to see if I'm going to have to put him in the trunk to sneak him out tomorrow."

We drove to Umag, couldn't find him, and drove back. As we're coming back across the border, I see the Yugoslav guards all have guns, and that they stop you and check the car. I see the Italian gate — just a wooden gate — 100 yards farther down, and I figure I can drive slowly and then just gun it and go right through the wooden arm and be on the other side, if that's what I gotta do.

So the next day we drive down to Zagreb. We get to the American Consulate, and I go up to the door, and there's a Marine sitting behind a bulletproof window. I said to him: "My name's Lou Nanne. I'm supposed to meet Frantisek Musil here." He says, "We don't know any Frantisek Musil." I said, "He's a Czech guy who wants to defect, and he should be here with Rich Winter."

He says, "We don't have anybody here." I said, "Would you let me talk to the consulate?" So he rings upstairs, gives me the phone, and I ask the guy if a Frantisek Musil has come here with Rich Winter. "Yeah," he says, "but I sent them to Belgrade."

I said: "Belgrade? What did you do that for?" He says, "Well, that's where they process people who want to defect."

I said: "You've gotta help me. This guy who wants to defect is a hockey player." He says, "Sorry, I can't help you."

Fortunately for me, I had Bruce and his cameraman there. I said: "Would you come down here for a minute? I've got a person from ABC here with a cameraman, and if you don't come down we're going to do a story on how you won't give any help to an American citizen who needs it here in Zagreb."

He comes down and I said, "Do you want to go on camera and say you won't help me?"

He says: "No, I'll help. What do you want me to do?" I said: "Make a call, stop them from being processed there, and tell them to drive back here. Otherwise it will take two years to get him out of that holding area."

So he did that.

I said: "I'll tell you what. I want to take you and your whole staff out to dinner. Pick the best restaurant in Zagreb."

They said great. So there's six of us, and we're eating and drinking wine, and we're having a real good time. All of a sudden I get tapped on the shoulder, and there's a guy dressed like a maitre d' in a black suit and tie. I tried to order cheesecake from him.

Finally, the consulate says: "Louie, that's the Secret Police. They want to see your passport." Then the consulate pulls out his green passport and says: "Diplomatic group here. They're with me."

I ask: "How do I get this guy out? I'm willing to put him in the trunk and drive through the border." He says: "No, you don't have to do that.

Just get him a visa. If you can get a visa for him immediately, we can just put you on a plane. Tomorrow morning you call back to the States to get an OK for an immediate H-1 visa, then you take him to get a passport picture."

I said, "Let's get on the phone right now, and I'll call Senator Dave Durenberger." I called and said, "Senator, this guy is going to tell you what I need," and then he told the senator what I had to do. I called my secretary, Sue Thomas, and said: "Go down to Immigration right now, get this kind of visa. Write up a contract for Musil with these figures on it, so they know he's got a job and he's got money. Fax everything back to this guy's office so we have it in the morning."

Which they did. Musil got in at midnight. The consulate said, "There's a 1:30 flight out of here tomorrow to London," and we decided to try for it, and then get a ticket in London to Minnesota.

The first thing in the morning, Musil and I went to get his passport picture. I walked in and said to the guy, "I need a passport picture." He says, "Come back at four." I said, "No, no, I need it right now." He says, "I can't do it." So I pull out my wallet, give him $20, and he says, "I'll have them in five minutes."

The next sticking point was the Ford Taurus, my rental car from Italy. I didn't know what to do with it, so I drove over with Musil to Hertz. I said to the guy, "Can you drop off cars?" and he says, "Yes." I said, "Here's my car," and I gave him the keys. He walks outside with me and says, "I can't take that — it's from Italy, we're in Yugoslavia." I said, "I don't care if I end up owning it." A Taurus was only worth $4,200 or $5,200 in the States at that time, and I've got a player I'm saving $250,000 on. I gave him $20 and the keys.

When I got the drop-off charges, the bill was only $427.

We went straight to the airport, got on the plane, and sat there waiting nervously with Rich Winter, Bob Bruce and the cameraman. In a communist country, there are police all over the airport, all around the airstrip, and I'm wondering if anybody will notice that he's leaving for London. Finally, the plane takes off, and we open a bottle of wine to celebrate.

We get to London, we're going through British immigration, and we discover Musil hasn't got the visa he needs — he's got one for the States but not for England.

I said, "This kid's defecting, and he's going to be a professional hockey player back in Minnesota, we're taking him there." The guy was sympathetic, and he says: "Listen, we'll hold him right here. You go get two tickets on the next flight out of England to the United States, and we'll let him go."

I went upstairs and the next flight was on the Concorde to Canada, so I got two tickets on the Concorde. Our other three traveling companions got tickets on the same flight, and we all left. In the air, the pilot announced we had a guy defecting from Czechoslovakia, a hockey player, and they made a big thing out of it — they were toasting Musil and taking us for a tour of the cockpit.

When we landed, we were met by immigration officials, and they just whisked us through Customs and out to a waiting car. They drove us to La Guardia in New York City and got us to Minnesota.

Oddly enough, about half a year later, my son Marty made the U.S.A. World Juniors team, and the World Championships were in Pistany and Trencin in Czechoslovakia. My wife and I wanted to go see our son play, and I wanted to scout the tournament, so we went.

When we got there I knew we might have a little trouble, because some people were very upset, so as soon as we landed we went right to the rink where the U.S. was ready to play. I went right up into the director's office, because I know the Czech officials from World hockey. And I'll never forget, I walk in, and Miro Schubert, the top Czech hockey official, looks at me and

Courtesy of Joe Janasz

Upon arrival in Minnesota, Frantisek Musil and his representatives are led through a back corridor of the Minneapolis–St. Paul International Airport by North Stars executive Joe Janasz (far right).

says, "Oh Louie, how could you come back here after what you did to us?" I said, "I didn't do anything to you." He says, "You stole our player." I said: "No, your player just wanted to defect and play hockey. In America, we have freedom of choice. He made the choice. He just happens to play for me." So they were kind to me and everything was OK.

Then a few months later, in June, I drafted two guys for the following year, Dusan Pasek and Igor Liba. By the following July, an agreement was in place between the NHL and Czechoslovakia, and you could buy a player's rights to get him out of the country.

Swedish Hockey Federation

I had a Swede under contract to the North Stars named Lars Lindgren, and he was playing defense for us. One day he came to me and said: "Lou, I'd like to go back to Sweden and play. My kids are getting old enough, and I want them to grow up there."

I said, "I'll let you go back on one condition: If we need you at the end of the season for the Stanley Cup playoffs, if we've got some injuries, you have to come back and play." He agreed.

We made the playoffs and did have a couple of defensemen injured. I called Lindgren and said, "Lars, I need you to come over next week when the playoffs start." He said, "OK, I'll tell my team and get permission to come."

Kent Nilsson

Jim Gallop / Gallop Studio

A day later I get a call from Curt Berglund, who was heading up the Swedish federation, and he said: "We are not allowing Lindgren to come back. We want to use him for the Swedish national team in the World Championships."

I was upset, but there was nothing I could do.

A year later, we were out of the playoffs. When you're eliminated, the hockey federations from various countries start calling to see if they can use your players. Kent Nilsson, our outstanding forward, called me personally to say he needed to get his equipment because he was going to Sweden to play for the national team.

I said: "No, you're not. You're under contract to me and I have to give permission to you. You're not going."

Curt Berglund called and said, "Lou, you guys are out of the playoffs. We need Nilsson."

I said: "Curt, do you remember last year when I needed Lindgren? You screwed me last year with Lindgren, so I'm doing the same to you with Nilsson. Now we're even."

John Mariucci in Finland

There was a free agent, Ilkka Sinisalo, playing in Finland, and there was a lot of talk that he was going to come over, sign with the NHL and join one of the teams. I sent John Mariucci to Finland to scout him. Ilkka played way up in northern Finland, and I told John, "When you get there, give me a call and let me know what he looks like."

And John says, "There's no use paying those high phone rates from the hotel — I'll call you collect, you don't answer, then you just direct dial me."

I said, "OK, fine." So John took off for Finland, and a day later somebody from the airline came to the Met and brought me two suitcases. I opened them up, and they were John's. He had his overcoat in one, he had a teapot, he had a lot of winter clothes packed. He had gotten to the airport late and his luggage didn't make the plane.

A collect call came from John Mariucci for Lou Nanne and I said, "He's not here." And before I could ask for a number to return the call, the operator disconnected me.

I didn't get a call back from John until the next day, and the same thing happens again, so I still don't know where he is. So the third day I get a collect call from John Mariucci for Lou Nanne, and I hear him say, "Take the damn call — I'm freezing to death, I got no clothes, and I can't give you a report."

I took the call and said, "What's the matter?" He said, "It's 500 miles north from Helsinki, I got no clothes, and I don't have a credit card for a car."

I said, "Buy a coat and catch the train." John did that, saw Sinisalo, but Philadelphia signed him about a week later.

BEHIND THE SCENES

Lou's Contract Negotiations

In 1966, they announced the expansion was coming in 1967. After the Original Six protected 30 players, everyone else on the reserve list became a free agent.

This meant I was finally able to get off the Blackhawks' reserve list. I was planning to play with the 1968 Olympic team. In July 1967, Wren Blair came back from the draft, called and asked me to come to his office, which was in the Midland Bank building.

He said he'd like me to sign. We talked about it for three or four days, and finally he gave me a sales pitch about how anybody growing up Canadian should play in the National Hockey League if he gets the chance.

He said I should sign, and that he'd give me a two-year contract for $20,000 a year, which was above the average in the National Hockey League. But I was making a little more than that selling envelopes for Harvey Mackay, so he says, "We'll give you a job selling advertising in the summer, too, so you'll make more money, but at least you'll be playing hockey."

I said, "I'll agree to those terms." So he says: "Wait right here. I'll go upstairs and get the contract typed."

While he was doing that, I called George Lyon, who was somewhat of a mentor, and said, "George, I agreed to a contract." He says, "How much?" I said, "Forty thousand bucks for two years." He says: "You're stupid — I'm never going to talk to you again. That's not nearly enough — you've got to get more money than that."

Herb Brooks and Lou Nanne, United States National Team, 1967

Lou Nanne archives

I said: "The players were only making an average of $12,000 in the league last year. This year they'll probably make $13,000 or $14,000." He says, "Still, that's not enough." I said: "You're right. I want to play with the Olympic team anyway."

I hung up the phone and called upstairs and said: "Wren, don't bother. I'm not signing. I'm going to play with the Olympic team."

He starts screaming at me: "You'll never play for the North Stars. You do that to me once, I never forget. You're done. I'm never talking to you about playing again."

I said, "That's your prerogative, but I'm playing with the Olympic team." So I left the office, didn't talk to Blair anymore, and started training with the Olympic team.

Murray Williamson was our manager-coach for the Olympics, and in September we were practicing at Wakota Arena in South St. Paul.

I'm standing in the corner waiting my turn to take a shot, and I turn around and Wren Blair is right behind the screen. The North Stars had broken camp, come back home, and had a couple of defensemen hurt.

And Wren says to me, "Louie, I'll pay you $500 a game to play five games for us." I said, "I'll do it if it's OK with Murray."

And Murray starts yelling at me, "You wouldn't be eligible for the Olympics," and then he starts screaming at Wren, and pretty soon they are challenging each other to a fight.

Finally, I said: "Forget it, Wren. If I'm not eligible to play in the Olympics, I'm not playing."

When I returned to Minnesota following the Olympics, Walter Bush called me in to his office and got involved in my contract talks with the North Stars. I suggested the team offer me a personal service contract. In addition to playing for the North Stars, I would do public speaking on behalf of the team, run the North Stars Hockey Camp, and sell North Stars advertising through Colwell Press. Walter and I each had a dollar amount in mind for the three-year personal service contract, and we jotted them down on a piece of paper. I asked for $120,000 and Walter offered $110,000. We settled on the amount of $116,000, taking into account the playoff shares from the previous season. I was now a full time North Star.

●

In 1972, the WHA was beginning and I was in a position to sign a contract with a team in their league. St. Paul was getting a team and the Saints were interested in a few North Stars.

That's the way Ron Simon's career started as an agent. He was my personnel lawyer. I had the players come to my house and we had a meeting.

Cesare Maniago was one of his first clients; Goldy and Dennis Hextall, too. Phil Esposito called me and said: "Why don't you use my agent, Arnold Bloom? He's a tax lawyer, and he's got a gimmick that the North Stars don't know about, that no one knows about."

I decided not to hire Arnold Bloom and said: "No, Wren's already pissed at me. I'm going to do this myself."

I was prepared to sign my contract at that time for $36,000 for the next season. Wren says, "OK, next week we'll go play golf at Olympic Hills and talk contract."

We get there, Wren says, "What's your handicap?" and I said, "16." He said his was 20, so I had to give him four shots. We're playing $2 a side, $2 for the match, and $2 for a press.

We start playing, he pars the first five holes, and I say, "Why am I giving you strokes?" and start hinting that he has a phony handicap.

He says, "No, no, it's accurate," and then he double-bogeys the sixth and the seventh. He says: "Are you happy now? You were just trying to get to me. Screw you and your contract." And then he walks off the course.

I went home, called up Arnold Bloom, and he represented me. He got me a five-year contract that averaged about $55,000, with a trust that deferred half my money. The North Stars couldn't get a deduction on that deferred money. With the trust growing through investments, it worked out very well for me. Phil Esposito, Fred Stanfield and I were the only three guys in the league with contracts like that.

Lou Becomes General Manager

When I took over the North Stars in February of 1978, that season was going to be my last as a player. Management came to me and said: "We want you available as a player. You can broadcast if you're not in the lineup." Early on I was doing TV only, then I had to play again. Teddy Harris was our coach, and they fired him and then took on Andre Beaulieu as the next coach. We were in a terrible losing streak — especially after Beaulieu took over.

Andre would go around the locker room asking questions, and I was the oldest guy on the team — 37, with 10 years in the league — but he never asked me a thing. Both Andre and Teddy seemed to be under the impression that I wanted their coaching jobs, which I never wanted.

A week before we went to New York for a game, there was a party for the team at one of the clubs in town. Bob McNulty and Gordie Ritz said, "We have some questions to ask you about the way the team's playing and what they should do."

I gave a few opinions and McNulty said, "Could you write that on paper for me, before you go on the road trip?"

On Monday, I flew out to Philadelphia to broadcast the game of the week for NBC. We were never on the game of the week, so NBC had hired me to do the color on Mondays, and then I would fly to the game on Tuesday, wherever we played.

After this game, I took the train from Philadelphia to New York, because were going to play the Islanders on Tuesday and the Rangers on Wednesday. On Tuesday, there was a huge snowstorm in New York and the game was cancelled because our team couldn't get in until late Tuesday night.

On Wednesday, we played the Rangers, and we got beat 3-0. I was back in my hotel room and got a call from McNulty and Ritz. They said, "When you get in tomorrow, come down to McNulty's office."

I asked, "What about?" And he said, "We want to talk to you about taking over as general manager for the rest of the year — we're going to let Jack Gordon go." I said: "I don't have any interest in taking over the team for two months. What do you expect me to do in two months?"

At that time, I'd also had some discussions with Alan Eagleson about working for the players' association. I wasn't prepared to settle for a two-month job.

McNulty and Ritz said, "What do you want?" I said: "I want two years. I won't take any more money than I'm making as a player right now, but I need a two-year contract."

I went to McNulty's office on Thursday morning and they asked me to a meeting of the full board the next morning at the Minnesota Club in St. Paul. They said, "We want you there, because we're going to tell the board that we want to hire you, and they will want to question you."

The first question I got was, "Who would you hire as coach for this team?" And I said, "Glen Sonmor." They said, "Well, you can't hire Sonmor, because he was part of the WHA, and the WHA almost wrecked our franchise."

I said, "If you ask me to do a job, you can't put these restraints on me, because I can't be successful without hiring my own people."

They sent me outside, discussed it for a while, brought me back in, and asked more questions. Then I was told: "OK, we're going to hire you. We'll have a press conference at 1 p.m. to announce you as the new general manager and coach."

I went back to the Met Center for a 9:30 practice. Before I went on the ice, I called over Doc Rose, our trainer. I said, "Doc, in a half hour I want you to come down and just say that there's a meeting I have to go to that Bob McNulty wants me to attend, and get me off the ice."

We're going through practice, and two minutes before Rose comes down, Andre blows the whistle, gets us in a circle, and says: "Guys, we haven't scored in 30-some power plays. We've really got a problem." And, sure enough, he turns to me and says, "Louie, give me some ideas — what should we do with the power play?" It's the first time he ever asked me a question. And I knew I was taking over the team and was going to fire him in about 30 minutes, so I said, "Just do what you gotta do."

And that's when I took over: February 10, 1978. I addressed the team, and I'll never forget what I said, because I'd been so close to them for so long.

I said: "Gentlemen, things change. Yesterday I was your teammate, today I'm your boss. But before we go any further, I want you to understand one thing. I know all you guys in this room, I like you, I consider you my friends. However, being your friend is not going to deter me from doing my job the way I think I have to do it. And after I do my job, if you don't consider me your friend, that's your prerogative, but I still will look at you as friends."

When I went through the payroll, one of our three highest-paid players was Doug Rombough, who we had traded J.P. Parise for, and who had spent part of the year in the minors on our farm team and part of the year with us. He roomed with me for a while, as a matter of fact.

A second guy was Bill Hogaboam, who was my neighbor and used to ride to the rink with me and Doug Hicks for games. And Dougie Hicks was the third guy.

One of the first deals I made, I traded Hicks, who I just loved as an individual. Then I traded Bill Hogaboam to the Red Wings — he was making about $150,000 when our average salary on the team was maybe $60,000.

Then I went to Rombough, and I said, "Dougie, I've got to buy you out." And he says: "You can't do that, Louie. We roomed together, we played together." I said: "Dougie, I can't help it. We can't afford you, and I can't trade you, so I'm going to buy you out. I want you to take your money, and if you can get another job, fine, but I've already tried, and nobody is going to take you right now."

He said, "I won't take a buyout." I said: "If you don't take it, I'm going to have to do what I have to do. And what I'm going to do is put you with a different minor league team every week for the next year. I really think you should be wise enough to take this, because I've got to get this payroll down. We're losing tons of money here." Ultimately, Rombough agreed to the buyout.

The Cleveland Merger

When I went to the NHL draft in June of 1978, I didn't know anything about Cleveland and the North Stars talking about a sale and a merger.

We had meetings the day before the draft, and were talking a lot of trades.

Dennis Maruk, Cleveland Barons

North Stars archives

Al MacAdam, Cleveland Barons

North Stars archives

I found myself sitting in a general managers meeting next to Harry Howell, who was the GM for Cleveland. I said to Harry: "I would like to make a deal for one of your players, Al MacAdam. Let me know what it would take."

And then there was a knock at the door, and Bob McNulty and Gordie Ritz motioned for me to come out into the hallway. They said: "Don't make any deals. You're going to have more players than you can handle. We might buy another team."

When the GM meeting was over, Bob and Gordie were outside again and said: "You have to go up to a suite and meet George and Gordon Gund, the owners of the Cleveland Barons. We're putting a deal together for them to buy us."

I had no idea what was going on. I was thinking, "Are we going to Cleveland?"

I knocked on their door and the room was all filled with cigar smoke. There was a man in there who said, "I'm Gordon Gund." I walked over to the table and put my hand out, and he put his hand out and missed mine by a foot. We tried again and missed. I thought to myself, "Why is this guy playing with me?" Then, he says, "I can't see."

Obviously, I didn't know until that instant he was blind. We shook hands and he said, "This is my brother George."

I heard, "Hi, Lou," but I couldn't see anybody. George was under the table smoking a cigar. He had a bad back, so he was lying on a board under the table.

Then they said, "This is our lawyer, Mr. Watson." I heard, "How are you doing?" but again I didn't see anybody. As it turned out, he was in the bathroom because he couldn't stand smoke. So he would open the door and close the door and open the door and close the door. I thought,

"What am I getting myself into here?"

Gordon said, "We're in the midst of making a deal to purchase the North Stars, and we're trying to put together a deal that the league will accept." I said: "Well, they're in a board meeting right now. Let me go see what's going on."

I went downstairs, and it was being agreed upon by the teams that Cleveland could purchase the North Stars. I found Ritz and he said: "There's no structure yet. McNulty was able to get a special committee to look at the deal."

When the meeting reconvened, someone said, "We can't allow two teams to be put together." And Montreal GM Sammy Pollock said: "Gentlemen, if you get one bag of shit and put it together with another bag of shit, all you get is a bigger bag of shit. Let 'em do it. It will solve a couple of problems for us."

When the meeting was over, I went through a wastebasket and found lists of players that Pollock, Sinden and Ed Snider liked. They had listed the players they thought would be valuable to get. They would allow Cleveland to buy the North Stars, but the North Stars could only protect ten players from Cleveland and two goaltenders. However, they wanted us to protect less.

I went back upstairs and said to Gordon Gund: "They will do ten skaters and two goalies. They're saying they won't, but they will. And they already have announced among one another that the deal will get done. Don't give in to anything but protecting ten and two."

During the night, we're working on protecting players, and we get a call from Max McNab with Washington. He had the first pick of our unprotected players. He said: "Louie, I talked with the league and was told — rather than taking one of your players — I can have the first pick in the second round. I

Gilles Meloche, Cleveland Barons

North Stars archives

think that's more fair for us, to give us a chance to get a good young player."

I said, "I won't do that." We wrangled for a while, and I said the only way I would do that is if he agreed not to take either of two players we were looking at in the draft in the second round.

The first thing in the morning, the draft starts. I go right to the draft at 8 a.m. and don't even get a chance to talk to the new owners until I see them at the table. I tell them that in the second round Washington is going to be picking before us, and Gordon says, "I want to talk to you about that."

I said, "I've already made a deal, I'll talk to you later about it." I had put down Steve Payne and Steve Christoff as the players Washington couldn't draft. They made a pick, and I was able to draft the two players I wanted.

It worked pretty well for us. We added Bobby Smith, Steve Payne, Steve Christoff, Curt Giles and Al MacAdam to our roster in those two days.

We went back to Minnesota and had a meeting, and the Gunds said to me: "You've got 65 players here under contracts and $4.7 million in contracts. You've got to get it down to $2.2 million."

I started buying out and trading players. A month later at our meeting, I said, "We've gotten rid of almost 20 players, and we're down to $2.5 million in salaries."

I was feeling real good about cutting off $2 million in salaries and not losing any of the players we wanted. And I'll never forget, Gordon said, "So you've got another $300,000 to go."

Right then, I knew it was going to be like Harvard Business School working for these guys. It was a tremendous experience to work for people like that, because it was an education in economics. It was all bottom line.

Arbitration

In the summer of 1978, after putting the Cleveland Barons and North Stars together, we had a lot of players. The Gunds felt our payroll was too high, and they told me to reduce it.

One way I felt I could get rid of a few players was to sign some free agents, then give up a number of players as compensation.

I went to Gary Sargent, who was a free agent and an All-Star defenseman for Los Angeles. Gary was from Bemidji and said he would like to come back to Minnesota.

I called L.A. to try to make a deal with them. In exchange for Sargent, they wanted Gilles Meloche and Greg Smith, who I felt were two of the best players coming over from Cleveland.

I decided to sign Sargent and go to arbitration. This was the first arbitration case for compensation in NHL history. After signing Sargent, I submitted an official offer of Steve Jensen, Dave Gardner and Rick Hampton — players on our team that I thought were expendable. L.A. asked for Meloche and Smith, as I thought it would.

We didn't agree, so a couple of weeks later, we headed to Toronto for the arbitration hearing. I submitted a brief that I did myself and argued my case in front of Judge Ed Houston.

Jack Kent Cooke owned the Kings. Rather than send his GM, George McGuire, Jack Kent sent his brother and lawyer, Don Cooke.

We sat in Houston's office in Toronto and each gave our side of things — why we thought what we were requesting should be the proper reward in the case for Sargent.

The judge said he would let us know in three or four days. Don Cooke got up and walked out, and then Judge Houston asked me a couple of questions unrelated to the case — about some players in the league. He was a big hockey fan and just wanted to discuss players haphazardly.

We're sitting there, the phone rings and the judge points to the phone and mouths, "Jack Kent Cooke." It was a little humorous, sitting there and listening to Cooke try to talk the Judge into voting for him.

Three days later I got word that I won the case. And we ended up with Gary Sargent, who was a tremendous defenseman capable of having a long career in the NHL.

The North Stars had a real good run for five years. Unfortunately, that ended when we went through our rash of injuries. We lost Sargent along with Tom Hirsch and Dan Mandich and Craig Hartsburg and David Quinn, who we had drafted No. 1 as a defenseman out of Boston University — five tremendous defensemen lost to injuries. It really hurt us.

The arbitration left me feeling confident, so I went back out and signed Mike Polich, who was playing for the Canadiens' farm team in Halifax. Mike had been up with the Canadiens during the year, and they had won the Stanley Cup.

I had tried to make a deal with Montreal, but Sammy Pollock wanted too much. So, I decided to go to arbitration again. Then, as I walked to the Telex machine to request arbitration, it started receiving a message. I looked down and it said Pollock had announced his retirement.

This was a break for us. It meant that Pollock wasn't going to be in front of Judge Houston arguing the benefits of Polich and why he should have a second-round pick instead of a fourth-round.

The Canadiens also announced Irv Grundman would succeed Pollock.

Irv was a great guy and a wonderful businessman, but he wasn't a hockey man. So we ended up going to arbitration and I won that case, too, and we ended up giving a fourth rounder to Montreal for Polich.

Gary Sargent

The NHL/WHA Merger

The NHL was talking merger with the WHA, and these talks had been going on for some time. There were four teams that were going to come in from the WHA — Edmonton, Quebec, Hartford, and Winnipeg — and the other teams going out of the WHA league would be getting a payment.

We had a Board of Governors meeting in 1979 at Ocean Reef in Florida, and we weren't getting anywhere on the merger. It was 11:30 at night, my wife and I had just gotten back from the Board of Governors dinner, and the phone rang.

It was Bill Wirtz and he said, "Louie, I need you to come down to my boat right now." Bill had a 125-foot yacht, the "Blackhawk," docked there. When I got there, 11 of the 21 NHL governors were on the boat. Wirtz just needed a majority to get the merger through.

Bill says to me, "Louie, you've got to come up with a plan that satisfies the people in this room, so we get their 11 votes at tomorrow's meeting and can get the merger done."

I asked each of the owners, "What do you need in order for you to vote for the merger?" They gave many different answers.

A couple things happened that were amazing. One was that Wayne Gretzky stayed in Edmonton because of Frank Griffith, the Vancouver owner.

Frank had Bill Hughes there as his representative, and Bill said, "Frank is adamant about the fact that the 18-year-old, Wayne Gretzky, should stay in Edmonton, because he's the face of their franchise."

This was really a magnanimous thing for the Vancouver owner to say. I should have kept all the notes, because I can't remember the entire structure of the deal now. But whatever we got them all to agree to that night, I wrote on a piece of paper. When the night was over, I had figured out that the only thing we could do was to let each WHA team protect two players and two goaltenders. Then teams could reclaim players.

There was strong opposition to Quebec coming into the league, because Molson owned the Montreal Canadiens and Labatt's owned Quebec, and Molson didn't want its rival brewery in the league.

Wirtz gave my piece of paper to John Zeigler. When I got to the league meeting in the morning, Zeigler says, "Look, we have to have an owner read this and explain it, so I'm going to give your notes to Peter O'Malley from the Washington Capitals, and he'll read your notes, and we'll vote on it, and we'll get this done."

Peter was reading my notes, and my writing is not the best, and he read one of the things wrong, and it changed Vancouver's vote. So we lost the vote 11-10 and everybody stormed out of the meeting. This was a Thursday or Friday, so everybody went back home.

About two days later, Gil Stein, who was assistant to John Zeigler, called me and said: "Louie, I'm going over your notes. That's not what Peter said on this one point." I said, "Peter didn't read my writing correctly."

"Explain it to me, and I'll fly out to Vancouver and explain it to them so they change their vote back."

I explained the concession we made to Vancouver, and Stein flew to Vancouver and the Canucks changed their vote.

With those 11 votes, Ziegler called a meeting in Chicago. The funny thing is that Montreal now knows that it's going to lose the vote, so the Canadiens make a public announcement that they're changing their vote. They didn't want people mad at the brewery up in Montreal, and they knew the merger would now happen.

A year later, we had a general managers meeting in Miami Beach. And after the meeting, Edmonton's GM, Larry Gordon, told me he was very upset with me. He said I had cost him Bengt Gustafson in the merger, which I had — I couldn't let teams protect everybody. So he got mad at me and I got mad at him. We ended up in a fight — the only time I know of two general managers getting into fisticuffs.

Fogged-out Game

On December 22, 1979 we were going to play Quebec at home on a Saturday night. That day, there was a terrible fog over the Twin Cities. Quebec didn't play the night before and was supposed to have flown in then, but unbeknownst to us, they hadn't. Due to the fog, they were delayed getting in on game day.

The North Stars scrimmage on the night of the fogged-out game vs. Quebec, 12/22/79.

Pete Hohn / Minneapolis Star Tribune

Finally, it was getting too late, and we told the media around 5 p.m. that Quebec wasn't going to be able to make it in due to the fog. Our team was already at the building when we called the game. We were somewhat concerned, because we had 6,000 or 7,000 fans who obviously didn't know it and had made an effort to get to the game.

I had a talk with Glen Sonmor, and I told him that we had to do something for the fans who came to the game. We divided the team into two different units, putting them in home and away jerseys, and had a regular game for the fans who had made it to the building.

One thing that came out of that was a new league rule. Up until that time, teams could come in the day of the game, even if they hadn't played the night before. The league put a rule in that if you are not playing the night before a game, you must be in that city or be fined.

The Brawl in Boston

Boston Garden was a place where the North Stars had a terrible time winning. We played some tremendous games in there and never won. One game we ended up tied 4-4, and Gump Worsley faced 67 shots on goal — he just played unbelievably well. I remember Tom Reid joking to Gump in the locker room after the game, "If you had stopped one more shot, we'd have won."

We had come close but had never won a game there in our history. It continued that way from when I was a player to when I was GM.

We were going into Boston one night right near the end of the '81 season, and it looked like we were going to be playing Boston in the playoffs. Glen Sonmor had the team in Boston, and I was in Victoria, British Columbia, scouting a Juniors game. I remember talking to Glen

in the morning and him saying, "We gotta make a statement, and I think we should do it tonight." I said, "That's fine."

He says, "Okay, we're going to let Boston know we're coming to play in the playoffs."

So that night in Victoria, at the end of the first period, I came downstairs and ran into Bart Bradley. He was the head scout for Boston. And Bradley says to me, "You got a score on the game in Boston." And I said, "Oh Bart, I don't think the game's over yet." He says: "What do you mean it's not over yet? They start at 7 and it's 10:30 in the East." I said, "I just got a hunch it's going to be a long one tonight."

The game ended up being the highest penalized in the history of the NHL. A fight started six seconds into the game and by the end the benches were half empty because of all the players thrown out of the game. It got so wild that at the end of the game as Gerry Cheevers, Boston's head coach, was leaving the ice, Glen Sonmor yelled out at him: "We're not through yet! You come on down to my locker room and they're going to take your head home in a basket." The North Stars lost the game 5-1.

The next morning, I got a call from John Ziegler, saying that he wanted a hearing between Sonmor, Cheevers and myself. I said: "John, we were telling you earlier this year that we thought that there were too many teams trying to take advantage of our players, and that if you wanted a war, we were going to give you a war. Now you've got it. Maybe when we get to the playoffs, the war won't be over." He gave us a considerable fine.

What eventually occurred was we played Boston in the first round of the playoffs. We went into Boston for the first two games, beat them both games there, came back to Minnesota, and beat them the first game here. It was a best-of-five and we swept them.

Glen Sonmor on The Brawl

Every time we played in Boston, we were ridiculed and called "soft" by the Boston newspaper because of the way the Bruins dominated us. It was pretty clear that we would face Boston in the first round of the playoffs, so I felt it was time for us to make a stand. I called Louie, and he agreed.

We had our usual team meeting before our pre-game meal at about 1 p.m. I talked to the players about the newspaper articles and how the Bruins always tried to intimidate us and said: "Tonight we're going to make a stand. At the first sign of intimidation by the Bruins, we're going to war, and we're not going stop." Their reaction was positive. I went on to say, "I can't guarantee we'll win the game by making a stand, but I can guarantee we won't ever win a game here until we make a stand."

On a bulletin board I had a list of the Bruins' players and next to it a list of ours. Then I went down the two lists and showed our guys that man-for-man we were just as tough as the Bruins were.

Before we went out on the ice to start the game, my final words were, "We make our stand at the first sign of intimidation — not the third time they try to intimidate us, not the second time — the first."

At the opening faceoff, Boston's Steve Kasper took the draw against Bobby Smith and then raised his stick and clipped Bobby's chin. That was it. Bobby dropped his gloves, and six seconds into the game the battle was on. There were some real donnybrooks, and I distinctly remember Al MacAdam just pounding a guy.

We lost the game, but it was one of the very few times I was happy after a loss. And, of course, we won the first two playoff games in Boston a few weeks later and got the sweep.

Dino Ciccarelli

Dino Ciccarelli

Back in 1988, Ciccarelli high-sticked one of the Toronto Maple Leafs, Luke Richardson, and they charged him with assault and had him spend the night in jail. I had to go back to Toronto for the trial.

They had a prosecuting attorney who was a little arrogant, and he had a mustache. When I was on the stand, he said to me, "Mr. Nanne, I played hockey in Juniors and I think I know the game quite well." I said, "You obviously weren't very good because you didn't go any farther than that."

One of his questions to me was, "Why don't you believe that Dino Ciccarelli intentionally high-sticked Luke Richardson?" I said, "Because if he wanted to hurt him, he's so good at handling the stick, he could take that mustache off your face without you knowing it."

The judge got excited and told me not to make references like that. Dino got off with just a fine.

Dino was such a feisty guy on the ice, and he could incite a crowd no matter where he was. He always had his family at the Toronto games, and the Maple Leafs ran at him constantly.

Two or three times in Toronto, after somebody took a cheap shot at him and missed, he would get the puck and shoot it right at the player's back as the player headed to the bench.

The Target Center and the Met Center

A crucial meeting took place when Minnesota was awarded an NBA franchise, the Timberwolves. The Gunds had come very close to buying Kansas City's NBA team, which eventually moved to Sacramento. John Karr, the North Stars president, thought he had a deal with them for about $8.5 million.

The Gunds didn't get it, and Marv Wolfenson and Harvey Ratner were able to get an expansion franchise for Minnesota. They came over to talk about a deal to play in Met Center. They didn't get what they wanted from the Gunds and Karr, so they decided to build their own arena — what became the Target Center.

Marv Wolfenson and Bob Stein, the team president, called and asked me to come down to Marv's office. I was the general manager. They said: "Maybe you can help us. Here's our plans."

They showed me the plans for the new building. I came back and told Gordon Gund, "These guys are definitely going to build this arena, and I think we should make a deal to play in it."

He said, "See if you can talk them out of it."

I invited Marv, Harv and Bob Stein to a hockey game for dinner. I'll never forget our statements. Marv said, "Louie, you're here to tell us you're going to join us in the new venture," and I said, "No, I'm here to ask you to fill that hole that you're making."

Marv said: "Louie, I made $200 million in the fitness business. If I have to lose $200 million, I'll lose it. But I'm going to build that arena."

And that's when we knew it was going to happen. They offered us a deal to split revenues, but Gordon figured they'd never get it done, so we didn't become partners with them. Gordon also thought that, even if they did get it done, they'd lose money on it, which they did.

●

Norm Green spent about $7 million refurbishing the Met and did a magnificent job making it a better building and an attractive venue. He was trying to compete with the new Target Center, and hoping he'd get money from the Metropolitan Sports Commission, but they turned him down. He tried to get approval to build a shopping center connecting the Met to the Mall of America, but the city of Bloomington turned him down. These things upset him because he couldn't generate more revenue, and it's one of the reasons he moved the team, if not the main reason.

When the North Stars left, the Met Center was in such good shape that it only cost about $1 million a year to operate. I tried to get a franchise for a proposed new WHA in the Met, but failed. The Sports Commission wouldn't use the Met for anything and they began talk of tearing it down.

I hoped that the Commission would donate the building for high school events rather than tear it down. There could be graduations, hockey, basketball, volleyball, tennis, wrestling, regional playoffs and all the state tournaments. I really believed they would have no problem generating enough income to take care of the building.

In my bones, I just know that the Sports Commission was so paranoid about having a venue that might attract events away from downtown Minneapolis and the Target Center, that they wanted the Met Center gone. There was no reason for that building to be taken away other than protection for the Target Center. It was just unfortunate.

The ironic thing was, a year after the North Stars left, a poll of NHL players was taken by one of the major sports publications and Met Center was named the No. 1 hockey venue in the league. Our ice was so good that every hockey player just loved coming to Minnesota to skate — it was the best.

Greg Smith

As general manager I had an open door policy with the players. On one specific occasion, Greg Smith came to my office with a concern. He wanted to know why Glen Sonmor wasn't using him on power plays. I said: "Glen's the coach, you need to ask him. I don't get involved in his decisions." Smith responded, "Well, I thought that you might have an idea as to why." I said, "Let me tell you something, if I were coaching this team you wouldn't be playing as much as you are on regular shifts, let alone the power plays."

I said that to Greg, not because I believed it, but because I knew it would get back to the rest of the team. I didn't want the other players thinking they could divide the coach and general manager.

Michael Nanne's Accident

We beat out Calgary in the 1981 playoffs. During the series, Norm Green, then one of the Calgary owners, invited Calgary GM Cliff Fletcher, me and our wives to the Mediterranean. We took our kids to stay with family in Sault Ste. Marie, and went to spend a week on Green's boat in the Mediterranean. And, we and the Fletchers were going to spend another week in Paris.

The day we arrived in Nice we had dinner with the Fletchers and the four us went walking the boardwalk.

We went back to our rooms around midnight. All night, I was tossing and turning. I told Francine: "I just don't feel right. I'd like to go home. I don't want to go to Paris."

I had no sooner finished saying that when the phone rang. It was my sister, calling from Sault Ste. Marie, where we left our kids. She said,

Greg Smith

North Stars archives

"Louie, Michael's been in a motorcycle accident, you've got to come home. Michael's OK, but you've got to come home."

That's all she would tell me. We got a flight out of Nice early in the morning to Paris, Paris to Montreal, and Montreal to Sault Ste. Marie. I got off the plane in Montreal, called the Soo, and they said, "Michael is still alive."

When we got to the hospital a few hours later, the doctors said, "If he lives 72 hours, he should make it." He was in a coma. He had a broken femur, a broken shoulder bone, and had lost his spleen. After 72 hours, we thought he made it, but gangrene had set in his leg.

The doctor said we had a decision to make: take the leg or take a chance on the gangrene turning into a life-threatening situation.

We said: "There's no decision at all. We'll just have to take his leg." And I called Dr. Harvey O'Phelan, the renowned orthopedic surgeon in the Twin Cities, and he concurred.

The doctors in the Soo took Michael's leg and flew him to Victoria Hospital in London, Ontario on a medical plane. Our owner, Gordon Gund — as wonderful as the Gunds always were — sent his plane up so Francine and I could fly there.

Michael stayed in a coma for a week before he was out of danger. We took an apartment in London for a month. Bob Short, a Minneapolis businessman and a wonderful person, sent his plane for our family to come back to Minnesota.

Michael went right into the University Hospitals and stayed there for another month. He wound up graduating from the university and is now a dentist. He married a girl from the Soo that he met up there the next year and went on to have a wonderful family.

Bill Goldsworthy's Illness

Bill Goldsworthy, after his career was over, ended up staying in Memphis, and he did some minor-league coaching. I got a call from an individual in Memphis, who said he was a minister and that he had gotten very close to Goldy. He wanted me to know that Goldy was in serious trouble and didn't want anybody to know about it.

I asked him what Goldy's problem was and he says he's got AIDS, that he's coming back to Minnesota, and he needs help but he won't see anyone. A few days later, Bill was back in the Twin Cities. I was able to reach him and he agreed to go out to lunch.

I go to pick him up and here's Goldsworthy, taking oxygen and smoking a cigarette. At lunch, I asked what was the problem and he said: "Louie, I've got an illness. I'm not sure what it is."

I said: "You haven't called anybody? Why don't you talk to your friends?" He said, "I just don't want to."

I said: "Goldy, I know you've got AIDS. We really have to get this story out so you can see your friends, and they can help you." He was very leery about it, and skeptical, and I said: "Goldy, true friends are still your friends, and the ones that don't want anything to do with you really weren't your friends. The best thing to do is make people aware of your situation, then you can get on with your life."

He said he would do it, and asked that Gary Olson from the *St. Paul Pioneer Press* write the story. We called Gary and told him. I also called Tommy Reid and J.P. Parise, who wanted to help. We all knew Goldy's financial situation was not good.

We decided to put on a fundraising night for Bill Goldsworthy. It turned out to be a rousing success. We made quite a bit of money for him. We took over as the guardians of his money and gave Goldy an allowance every month. He also had a chance that night to be reminded of how much people thought of him. He passed away in 1996 at age 51.

PRANKS & SUPERSTITIONS

Tom Reid

Tommy was always a practical joker. At one of my parties, Tommy was acting as bartender, and I had just bought a number of bottles of vodka, and people are drinking, and I'm not paying attention, don't realize what's going on.

A couple of weeks later, I invite Bob and Joannie Dayton over for dinner. I ask them if they'd like something to drink before dinner, and Joannie Dayton says, "Sure — vodka." So I make her a vodka and water. A few minutes later she said: "That wasn't too bad — not too strong. I'll have another one." So I make her another one. Pretty soon I give her another one.

Then she says, "I'm feeling a little tipsy," so I didn't give her any more.

After they leave, I'm cleaning up and I make myself a vodka. I take a drink, and it's only water. Reid had taken the vodka bottle after

Tom Reid gets tangled with Cesare Maniago.

North Stars archives

it was finished, filled it with water and put the cork back on, so here I'm serving my guests water. And Joannie said she was tipsy. I think she didn't want to embarrass me.

J.P. and Goldy used to room together a lot, and they were always pulling pranks on one another, but the rest of us used to like to get them as well. One night in Long Island, before J.P. and Goldy came back to their room, Tommy Reid went in and unlocked the adjoining door to our rooms.

Later, when J.P. and Goldy had turned the lights out and gone to bed, Tommy opened the door very quietly, crawled in on his hands and knees, got between their two beds, reached up and grabbed J.P. by the ankle.

J.P. says to Goldsworthy, "Kraut, cut that out!" And from about 15 feet away, Goldy says, "What are you talking about?" When he realized it couldn't be Goldsworthy, J.P. came flying out of that bed.

We were on a road trip in St. Louis, staying at the Chase Park Plaza Hotel. Andre Beaulieu had been named coach a few weeks beforehand, and Tommy Reid thought it was time for Andre to be "initiated."

While we were all out to eat, Tommy excused himself, got a live

lobster from the restaurant, and took it back to the hotel. He pretended to be staying in Andre's room and asked the front desk for a key, which they gave him. Then he went up to Andre's room and put the lobster in Andre's bed.

When Andre jumped into bed later that night, the lobster climbed on top of him and he went nuts. The next day, the team skated for 45 minutes without touching a puck.

Bill Goldsworthy and J.P. Parise battle the Penguins.

North Stars archives

J.P. Parise and Dennis Hextall

J.P. Parise was just terrified of cockroaches and mice and snakes and that type of thing. One night before a game, Dennis Hextall put a dead mouse in J.P.'s skate. As J.P. was getting ready for the game, he put his foot into the skate and stepped on the mouse. He threw the skate across the room, jumped up on the bench and started swearing in French.

Murray Oliver

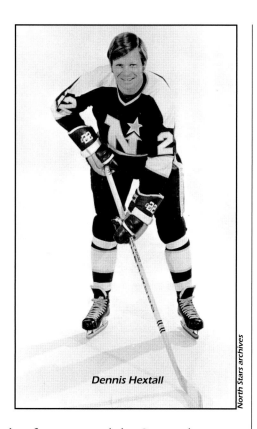

Dennis Hextall

North Stars archives

Murray Oliver and I roomed together for quite a while. One night we played a game in Minnesota against Chicago, and right after the game took a charter to Chicago to play them again. We arrived in Chicago at two in the morning and went directly to the hotel.

Tom Reid and I knew that Murray always carried a briefcase, and as we're walking into the lobby of the Marriott, Tom runs ahead to Murray and undoes one of the buckles on the briefcase. I undid the other one, and the briefcase popped open. A bottle of Scotch that Murray liked to travel with bounced out on the marble floor, and rolled and bounced until it stopped right at the foot of our coach, Jack Gordon.

Murray was chasing the bottle and swearing and looked up as he reached for it and there was Jack Gordon, standing there fuming. It looked like Jack had passed gas — he always turned red when he got mad.

One superstition I had involved Murray Oliver. In the locker room before a game, I wouldn't tie my skate laces until Murray tied his. Murray had been told about this by a few teammates, but I didn't know that he knew. One night before we took the ice, Murray leaned forward to tie his skates, and I leaned forward to tie mine. Then, Murray leaned back without tying his skates. I had to do the same thing. He went on to do this four or five times, and he was aware he was driving me crazy. Finally, I couldn't take it anymore and said to him, "If you don't tie those skates I'm gonna come over there and strangle you."

Willi Plett

Willi Plett lived in Burnsville during his years as a North Star, and his next-door neighbor was a fellow named Mark Pevan. Mark was in charge of all of the concessions at Met Center. Willi and Mark constantly pulled pranks on each other, but it got to a point where Willi was getting upset.

One night after a game, Willi took a jack and lifted Mark's car two inches above the pavement. When Mark got to the car at one in the morning after his post-game work, he stepped on the gas pedal but didn't go anywhere. He finally figured out why.

After the next home game, Mark collected all of the unsold and discarded popcorn in huge plastic bags. Late that night, he spread the popcorn all over Willi's front lawn. There was no snow on the ground, but it was covered in a blanket of popcorn.

The following week, Willi called the *Star Tribune* newspaper and ran a classified ad for Mark's new car. He listed the car at $10,000 below its normal asking price and included Mark's phone number. Mark was swamped with calls about the car for a week.

Gary Smith and Cesare Maniago

Gary Smith was a great guy and a good goaltender, but he had a funny superstition. When Gary played his first game with our team, he comes in the locker room after the first period, and we're all sitting down resting, and all of a sudden here he is undressed.

Gary Smith

North Stars archives

I thought he was going home — I thought something had happened. But he runs into the shower. Every period of every game, he used to undress, take a shower, and dress back up again.

The only other goaltender I ever saw undress during a game was Cesare Maniago. We were in Toronto and Ted Harris was our coach. It was customary not to give a goaltender any crap, even if he let in a bad goal.

At the end of the first period, Toronto had scored a couple of soft goals and Harris gave Cesare hell about it. Cesare said, "You can go screw yourself." He took his equipment off, said, "I'll meet you guys at the bar after the game," and left.

We finished the game with one goalie in net and none on the bench.

Jim McKenny

Jim McKenny was a player I got from Toronto in a trade, and he was one of the funniest guys in the league. He's a broadcaster now in Toronto.

The year before I got McKenny, he was playing in Tulsa, and he had played with Gary Smith, our goaltender, who was another character.

Right after I took over, I said to Gary, "I want you to go to the minors." He says: "Louie, I'm the best goaltender on the team. Why am I going to the minors?" I said, "We can't make the playoffs, so I've got to look at some other goaltenders here and hopefully build this team up."

So Gary went down to the minors, and I called our coach for a report after the last game of the year. I said, "How did the game go?" He says: "Well, everything went well, except for one thing. Gary let in a shot from McKenny from behind center ice. McKenny needed one more point to set the record for defensemen, so when the shot came Gary just stepped aside and let it go in the net."

Jim McKenny

North Stars archives

John Mariucci

One of my funnier moments happened in New York in 1969. We were playing the Rangers on a Sunday night, and we got beat. It was a well-played game, but the Rangers came back and beat us. Wren Blair was not very happy about that, so he said, "Curfew for everybody at 11." Well, it was 10 when the game was over, so it hardly gave us enough time to get showered, changed, and have a quick beer and burger.

Ten of us decided to go to Parker MacDonald's room and order up some beer and food from the hotel. At 11:30, the phone rings and it's Mariucci checking rooms for Blair.

I picked up the phone and said hello. Mariucci says: "Louie? Don't you know there's curfew? You're supposed to be in your room." I said, "I am in my room."

He says, "I'm calling 204." I said, "You got 206." This went on for about five calls — Maroosh calling Parker's room, me answering, telling him he had the wrong room.

Finally, I said, "John, please don't call again, because Danny O'Shea's sleeping." John's upset and calls the operator and starts screaming at her for giving him the wrong room and tells her if it happens one more time, he'll get her fired.

I never told John that story until just before he died. He never realized that all night long he was calling the right room.

Lou's Superstitions

I had a lot of weird superstitions. The first one I had and the one that was the most consistent was I wanted to follow Bill Goldsworthy out onto the ice. Why, I don't know.

One night, Goldy turns around and says: "Damn it, Lou, you've got to quit following me. I haven't scored a goal in the last five games." I said: "Goldy, I've been following you for a year and a half. You got 48 last year."

He says: "No, I'm bugged. You've got to follow somebody else."

We're back in the locker room before the game, the buzzer sounds and there's no Goldsworthy. I figure he's pulling a prank and is trying to get away from me, so I hide in the skate room. After the whole team is gone, the next thing I hear is Goldy coming, running full speed from the bathroom and down the stairs. And here I come behind him. He says, "Damn it, don't follow me!"

I said: "We're the only two left. I gotta follow you now." He scored a goal that night and we didn't have to worry about our dueling superstitions anymore.

●

We were in the playoffs in Toronto, and it got to the point I was so nervous about the game that I couldn't go to it. I went to the rink, but when the players went to the locker room, I walked out and found a movie theater. The title of the movie was "When Time Ran Out," which I thought might be a bad omen.

The movie finished, I'm still sitting there, and another movie starts. The usher came down, grabbed me by the shoulder and said, "Mr. Nanne?" I said, "Don't tell me the score, don't tell me the score."

He said: "I'm not telling you the score. I'm telling you that you didn't pay for the second movie." I thought: "Oh, the heck with it. I'll go to a bar we used to go to when we had good luck against the Maple Leafs."

I was sitting in the bar, the game was on, obviously, but I didn't want to hear the score, so I walked out. I'm walking down the street, and a man and his son are on the other side of the street, and he yells over, "What's the matter, Nanne, can't you take it?"

I yelled back, "Take what?" He said, "You guys are behind 2-1 and you leave?" It was the end of the second period.

I thought, "There's nothing I can hurt now — we're already behind — so I might as well go to the game."

I walked into the back end of the arena. Doc Rose saw me and said, "Did you see that call at the end of the period? Wasn't that terrible?"

He didn't know I wasn't at the game. I said, "You're right," and I ran down to the officials' room, knocked on the door and said to the referee, "That was a lousy call!"

I gave him all this static about a bad call when I wasn't there. Then, I went upstairs; we ended up tying the game and winning 3-2 in overtime.

●

My superstitions got ridiculous by the time I became general manager. I had heard somewhere that an empty toilet paper roll was good luck. I had one with me before a big game and we won, so I kept it.

Well, we got to the playoffs, I had the toilet paper roll in my pocket, and I'm having dinner with the Gunds in their hotel suite before a game. When they asked how I felt about the game, I said, "I'm feeling good because I got my lucky toilet paper roll." I told them it was a lucky charm. They told me I was crazy and getting crazier.

It turns out we won the game that night. The next time I saw them, both Gund brothers had toilet paper rolls in their pockets. Here they are, multimillionaires walking around with toilet paper rolls in their pockets.

Word started getting around about my superstitions, and it led to an appearance on the Oprah Winfrey Show in 1987. I was on with the women's basketball coach from the University of Maryland, talking about being obsessive-compulsive and superstitious.

Lou as a Dangerous Teammate

Many times when I went to body-check someone, I would get one of my own teammates instead. It got to be a running joke amongst the team. One night I went to hit Serge Savard behind the net in Montreal. Freddie Stanfield was trailing him, and Serge sidestepped me, and I knocked Freddie flying.

Another game, Murray Oliver was playing center ice and I was playing right wing. Murray was coming to check one of the Detroit Red Wings right at the blue line at the very same time I was coming to hit him, and the guy stopped and I ran into Murray. He looked up at me and said, "Louie, their team is in red."

Another night we had a faceoff to the right of the goaltender in Chicago's zone, and I was playing on the line with Goldsworthy and Dennis Hextall. Hextall was battling for the puck after the drop, and I came running in there and hit the opposition guy. Then I turned and looked at Hextall, and he's bleeding. I said, "Hexie, get off the ice, you're bleeding!" And he says, "Yeah, you just cut me with your stick."

It all came to a culmination one night when we were playing in Vancouver. Jack Gordon, our coach, came in and said: "Louie, I want you to play the forward line tonight on the wing with Goldsworthy and Hextall. You take the left side."

Jack announced the change to everyone. I always followed Goldsworthy out onto the ice, and as we're filing out, Goldy turned around and I saw he had a piece of tape across his helmet that read, "Louie, I'm on your side."

In the second period, we had a penalty, and Gordon says, "Goldsworthy and Nanne, kill the penalty up front." So we jumped on the ice and were forechecking, killing the penalty. Then we were crisscrossing, going after the puck as it was being brought up ice, and the puck carrier

dished it off. I kept coming and I hit Goldsworthy — he went flying, his stick went flying, and his helmet went flying.

And I heard Goldy say, "Well, I'm happy it's over and I don't have to worry about it anymore."

OFF THE ICE

Behind Bars

We had a game one night in Philadelphia, and had a few beers later. After we were done there, some of us wanted to get a hamburger. Tom Reid, Andre Boudrias and I went to a place across the street from the Warwick Hotel called Dewey's.

As we were heading back to the hotel, in walked Bill Goldsworthy, Billy Orban, J.P. Parise and Cesare Maniago. Orban wound up in a fight with another customer. He dispatched him rapidly, but the owner called the cops. Orban hears him calling and takes off across the street to the hotel, comes to the room that Tommy Reid and I are in and says: "You gotta hide me. I might be in some trouble."

Back at Dewey's, the cops came in as Goldsworthy was helping the guy Orban had punched off the floor. He was bleeding, so there was blood all over Goldy's coat. The cops, thinking Goldy was fighting, grabbed him and threw him in the paddy wagon. They took J.P., too.

Cesare went to the hotel, told Wren, and he came running across the street and said to the cops: "What are you doing? Those are my guys." One of the policemen said, "These guys are going to jail." Blair said, "You don't take them without me." They said, "That's not a problem," and they grabbed him and threw him in the paddy wagon. So on their way down to the jail, J.P. told me, Wren says: "You know, guys, this is kind of exciting. I've never been in paddy wagon before."

They got fined a little bit, and we had to keep Orban out of Philadelphia — they had a warrant out for him.

•

When I first took over the North Stars as general manager and coach, our first road trip was going to be in St. Louis. I had let the majority of the staff go, so I was staying home to scout the University of Minnesota Gophers game. They were playing Colorado, and we had a couple prospects in the game.

I sent the team to St. Louis under the direction of our trainer, Doc Rose. I was in bed about 3 a.m., the phone rings, and it's Doc, saying: "We got some problems down here. Gary Smith, Harvey Bennett, and Brad Maxwell got in an altercation in the bar tonight. They were taken to jail; I got them out."

When I got to St. Louis, I assembled the whole team in my room, and I proceeded to rip them all, and especially those three guys. As I'm berating them for their behavior, Gary Smith leaned over to Harvey and Brad and said, "You guys said Louie was going to love us for sticking together."

What happened was someone swung a beer bottle at Bennett, who was the wrong guy

Dennis O'Brien and goalie Pete LoPresti

North Stars archives

to swing at, and Harvey dropped him in the bar. The guy got back up and then Maxie took care of him. The police were called, and they took the three of them to jail. While they're sitting in jail, Maxie told Gary Smith that they weren't going to be in any trouble because Louie really liked his team sticking together.

Dennis O'Brien always played aggressively and would take on anybody, whether he could win or not. Sometimes his fun-loving attitude got him in a little trouble.

One night in Atlanta, a bunch of us went downtown to a bar called The Mousetrap. After a while, all of us had left except for O'Brien, Ted Harris, and Danny Grant. Dennis got rowdy, so the bouncer asked him to leave. He went outside and needed to urinate, and did so on the side of the building.

The bouncer saw him and came out, and they got in a skirmish. The police were called. As the cops were taking Dennis away, Ted Harris stepped in and said, "I'm the captain of the team — Dennis is with us." So they said, "You two are going, too," and they threw Ted and Danny Grant in the paddy wagon.

Murray Oliver and I got word of it in our room about 11:45, and I went around to different players' rooms and collected money for bail. When I got enough, I found a bail bondsman, and went to the jail to get them out after 1 a.m.

When I got there, they were taking mug shots of the guys and Harris was livid. He was embarrassed and wanted to kill O'Brien. We got them out and thought everything was okay.

When we got on the bus the next day, we found out that the newspaper had somehow gotten hold of the story. It ended up that Dennis got fined, and the North Stars took some heat when it became public.

We had some classic drinkers on our team, and they were led by Moose Vasko. Moose was unbelievable! I always knew when Moose had been out especially long the night before or had even more than he normally drank, because before the game he'd always look at me and say: "I know this team really well. I know how they play. So I'll stand up and meet the play. You go back and get the puck."

After practices we'd go either to a Holiday Inn or Howard Wong's and we'd sit down for lunch, and Moose would start drinking beer at 11 in the morning.

Andre Boudrias

North Stars archives

One time, Moose, Wayne Hillman, Andre Boudrias, Danny O'Shea and I went to Howard Wong's right after practice. I had to go from Minneapolis to Albert Lea to give a speech that night, so about one o'clock when my lunch was finished, I left for Albert Lea. I went down in a snowstorm, went to the banquet, gave the speech and drove back.

As I'm coming back up 35W and getting close to 494, it's 12:50 in the morning. I thought to myself, "Ah, I'll just take a look." Al Baker was always good to the guys — he'd never kick them out, even at closing.

So I drive over there, and I get in at 12:55, and sure enough, there they are, sitting right there. I walked in and I said: "I can't believe you could sit here that long and drink that much. Didn't you have dinner?" And Wayne Hillman pipes up and says: "Nah, I called Teresa," who was his wife, "and asked her what's for dinner, and she said, 'Crap.' I told her just make enough for herself, I wouldn't be home."

One of our earliest road trips of the 1968-69 year was to L.A. I'd never played in L.A. before, so I asked Moose Vasko, "Where are you going?" He says, "Down to Melanie's." I said, "Okay, I'll meet you there — I'll get a cab."

I walked into Melanie's and sitting at the bar was Moose Vasko, Bob McCord, Andre Boudrais and Parker MacDonald. I sat down and Moose said, "Get him a beer." I got the beer, sat there, drank the beer, had another beer, and the whole time — about 25 minutes — no one talked. All they did was drink beer. Then I knew we had some serious drinkers. I finally said: "I gotta go. The company is too stifling in here.

Bob McCord

North Stars archives

Wren Blair

Wren Blair was always unpredictable. We were playing the last game of a season in Oakland and the game didn't mean anything in the standings. So the day before, at 4:00 in the afternoon, J.P. Parise, Bill Goldsworthy, Ray Cullen, Danny O'Shea, Cesare Maniago, Al Shaver and I went down to a bar-restaurant in Jack London Square.

Three, four hours later, Shaver gets paged. Al took the call and it was Blair, wanting to know if he could come and drink with us. There's an unwritten rule that players and coaches don't drink in the same bar, but we said, "It's not a problem." Wren came in, and we stayed late.

Wren knew our team wasn't in the greatest shape for the game, so he said to John Mariucci: "You coach. I'm going to watch the game from upstairs and see how these guys play."

At the end of the first period, we were down 5-0, and Wren came into the locker room and proceeded to rip everybody apart. He started calling Moose Vasko "fat ass" and saying, "He's up all night and drinking." He berated the whole bunch of us and said: "I treat you guys like men and you take advantage of me. That's it. Things are going to change."

He turns to me and says: "That hockey school you're running this summer? You're not working it. And Goldsworthy and Parise, you're not working for him."

I was under contract to run the hockey school for the North Stars, and it didn't matter whether I worked or not, I would still get paid.

He yelled at every one of the guys who was in the bar with him, saying how terrible it was to treat him like that and play so poorly after he let us stay out.

North Stars archives

Ray Cullen

On the plane home the next day, Danny O'Shea came up to a few of us including Ray Cullen and said: "Cully, I've been thinking about it all night, and it's really bothering me. I'm going to tell Blair he's not going to drink with us anymore." Cully, our captain, said, "Sure, go ahead." Danny pulled the curtain into first class, and Wren was in the first seat right in front of us. Danny says, "Blair, just want to let you know that the guys on the team were talking, and you're never allowed to come and drink with us again."

Wren came to Cullen and said: "Did you hear that? What do you think?" And Cully says: "You heard him. You did us wrong, so you're not allowed to drink with us anymore."

This was in April. I worked as the sales rep for advertising with the North Stars during the summer. In July, Blair calls and asks me to come to the office. I'm assuming that means he's trading me.

I sit down in his office and I'm waiting for him to tell me where I'm going. Instead, he makes small talk for a while, then says, "I've been thinking about this all summer. Do you think the guys would let me drink with them again?" I said, "If you promise not to treat us like you did the last time, I'll talk to the guys and see if I can get an okay." He says, "I'd really appreciate it if you would do that for me." All summer — he thought about it the whole summer!

Harrowing Flight

In the early '80s, the team was flying to Boston to play a game. We were on a commercial flight, sitting in the back of the plane. Shortly after takeoff, we noticed flames shooting out of the right engine. The captain came on the intercom to tell us we were returning to the Minneapolis airport, where they were preparing for an emergency landing.

On the plane, people were yelling, screaming and praying. Our team tried to stay composed. Meanwhile, all I could think about was this: If this plane crashes, the league will need to hold a dispersal draft to restock the franchise … they'll need to bring kids up from our minor league team … they'll quickly need to hire a new coach and GM … they shouldn't miss more than three games in the schedule. Instead of life and death, I was worried about the franchise. Ultimately, the plane made a safe return to the airport.

Las Vegas

We had a stretch of games where we were playing really well, and we were getting ready for a game in Los Angeles. I said to our coach, Glen Sonmor: "If we win tonight, maybe we should take the guys to Las Vegas for a day as a reward. They've been playing terrific." Glen said, "Good idea, let's do it."

I went upstairs at the L.A. Forum and asked King's owner Jerry Buss, who had connections in Vegas, if he could get us fifteen rooms in Vegas. He said, "Sure." Well, we won the game, then hopped on a plane to Vegas and stayed an extra day.

When we got back to Minnesota, Glen and I got off the airplane first and walked right into Nichole Meloche and Cathy Maxwell. Nichole says to me, "Aren't our husbands gone enough, do you have to keep them away longer?" I said, "They played well and we wanted to reward them with an extra day in Vegas." She said, "Then you should've had the wives flown out, too." I replied, "We were giving them a day of freedom, and we didn't want you around hassling Gilles."

Nichole and I feuded all the time, and that's why I gave her the retort that I did. She and Cathy Maxwell gave me static about a lot of things.

We had a banquet at the Decathlon Club one night, and everybody was enjoying themselves during the cocktail hour. Nichole and Cathy walked up to me and said, "We understand you want to send us to Russia." I said, "What are you talking about?" Cathy said, "When Brad signed his contract this summer, you told his agent that if you had your way you'd send Nichole and me to Russia." I said, "There's absolutely no truth to that, because I've got nothing against the Russians."

Charlie Burns

Charlie Burns and Tom Reid

Charlie Burns and Tommy Reid were rooming together when Charlie was asked by Wren Blair to take over as coach. He was a player one day and our coach the next.

Not long after, Charlie and Tommy overslept and were going to be late for practice. Tommy wakes Charlie at 8:45 and practice is at nine. They rush to the Met and get there right at nine, and we're already on the ice. Tommy gets dressed and comes out on the ice, and then Charlie comes out and fines Tommy $25 for being late.

The Swedes

Right before I took over the team, we had a party before Christmas at Ernie Hicke's house, and we were sitting in Hicke's basement. Hicke and Dennis O'Brien fancied themselves as good drinkers, and Ernie says to O'Brien, "Let's show these Swedes how to drink."

So he called over Roland Eriksson and Per-Olov Brasar and says, "Okay you're going to have to match us drink for drink." So they sat there drinking vodka, drink after drink after drink. After about an hour, I looked and both Ernie and Dennis were lying on the floor, and the two Swedes were saying, "I thought those guys knew how to drink."

Ernie Hicke

North Stars archives

Per-Olov Brasar

North Stars archives

Michelle Nanne

I drafted Tommy McCarthy the same year I signed Dino Ciccarelli. Two years later, they were 20-year-olds and my daughter Michelle, who was 17, was working as an usher at Met Center. I had a rule for her: Never date a player.

Ciccarelli and McCarthy walked into my office one day and asked if they could talk to me. "We understand you won't let Michelle go out with any of the hockey players." I said, "That's right."

They said, "We'd like to take her out," and I said, "No." They asked, "What if one of us takes her out?"

And I said: "If she sneaks out with you and I find out about it, which I will, because I know a lot of people in town and they will tell me immediately, then whoever takes her out, you're going to be playing in Oklahoma City the next day.

"You have two-way contracts, and I have the freedom to move you for three years up and down like a toilet seat. So if you take my daughter out on a Thursday, Friday you'll be playing in Oklahoma City, you can bet on that. And you'll be playing for $20,000 instead of $75,000."

They never got to take her out. Eventually, she married Tino Lettieri, goalie for the old Kicks soccer team.

Cattle Raising

In early May one year, I was having dinner with Cesare Maniago, Murray Oliver and our mutual friend Pete Karos. While we were looking at the menu, we started talking about all of the meat we ate during the season. Back then, we ate steak before every game. I owned a 10-acre hobby farm on a lake near Litchfield, and since part of the property was fenced I suggested we buy a couple of cows. We figured we could raise the cattle, have it slaughtered, split up the beef, and then freeze it so we'd have plenty for the next season at a lot less cost.

I called someone at a stockyard in South St. Paul and had two cows delivered to my farm. I put them in a field right beside the farmhouse, gave them a salt block, and watched them all summer long. When September came around and training camp was about to start, I was all excited about the beef. I called the gentleman who had delivered the cows and asked

Bear wrestling with Craig Cameron (far left) and Lou (far right).

him to come get them, slaughter them and quarter them. He said, "No problem."

The next day he calls me and says: "Louie, what the hell did you do to these cows? They've each lost 45 pounds." I said, "What do you mean?" He said, "Didn't you feed them?" I said, "I gave them a salt block and they had the grass." He said: "The grass is knee high. Did you think they'd stand on their hind legs and eat from the top down? You starved them. You've got to feed them, too."

So, we traded the two skinny cows for two fat cows, paid the difference, and got our meat.

Bear Wrestling

At the end of one season, our breakup party took place at a restaurant in Bloomington called La Cantina, owned by Nick Minotti. We went over there at 3 p.m. and we started having a few beers and telling stories.

About 5 p.m., they brought a big brown bear in and wanted to know if anybody wanted to wrestle the bear. Nick, the owner, was going to wrestle the bear as were some others in the bar. Craig Cameron and I said we wanted to wrestle the bear.

Nick went up there first, and the bear took him and threw him right off the stage. He landed on the stairway and hurt his back, which actually bothered him for quite a while.

The other guys went in one by one, and the bear put them down pretty quickly. I was watching, and as the bear came at them, he raised up on his hind legs. So when my turn came, as the bear stood up and came at me, I'd hit him in the chest and then I'd grab him and try to throw him. I can tell you right now, you can never throw a bear — it's unbelievable the kind of balance they've got.

So I'd hit him in the chest, grab him, try to throw him, couldn't throw him. Then we'd break up, he'd come at me again, and I'd hit him in the chest and try to throw him. This went on for about five minutes, and the bear didn't get me down. The trainer finally said: "Okay, we've had enough for now. We'll do it again tonight."

We drank a little while longer, and we were getting ready to leave when Nick comes up to me and says, "Look Louie, if you stay around and wrestle the bear again tonight at eight, I'll buy the beer for all of you until then."

I said, "Sure." When they were ready for the evening show, they announced, "Lou Nanne is going to wrestle the bear." This kid jumps up and comes over to me and says: "Louie, I'm on the wrestling team at Mankato State. Can I wrestle the bear, too?"

I looked at him, and he had this lightweight Members Only jacket on, and I said: "I'll tell you what. If you let me wear your jacket to wrestle the bear, I'll let you go first."

I wanted to wear the jacket because the bear, even though he was declawed, would scrape you a little bit on the arms. He says, "Sure."

He goes out and the bear grabs him right away and throws him down and he's done. I said, "Give me that jacket," and I put it on. As the bear would come at me and I'd hit him in the chest, he'd come down my arms with his paws, and that jacket had pulls all the way down both sleeves. I continued to hit him in the chest and then try to throw him. I never threw him, but he never got me down.

Finally the trainer comes and says: "You're making the bear mad. You can't be hitting him like that." That was the end of our wrestling match.

THE BLACKHAWK RIVALRY

I've never seen a better rivalry in sports than we had with the Chicago Blackhawks. Every game in Chicago Stadium was wild. You had to be very cautious if you were a North Stars fan sitting in the crowd. If there wasn't enough action on the ice, people in the crowd would start fighting.

Bobby Hull swoops past Cesare Maniago, trailed by Doug Mohns.

North Stars archives

For one of our playoff games at Chicago Stadium in 1982, tickets had sold out far in advance, and when the game started, the fans without tickets broke down the doors. Fans were coming up the fire escapes, sitting in the aisles all over the building, and hanging from the rafters that night.

The stadium was supposed to seat 16,666. I talked to Bob Pulford at the end of the game and their best estimate was at least 21,000 people were in the stadium. Amidst the frenzy, we won 7-1.

Usually, Chicago's security was tough and took no guff. Our fans were much more civilized than Chicago's, but we still put on extra security. Many Blackhawk fans would travel to Met Center, and anything could happen.

A skirmish in the corner sends a pane of plexiglass into the crowd, 11/4/72.

Bloomington Historical Society

From 1981 to 1985, we actually faced the Blackhawks four times in the playoffs. Twice we ended up with more points than they did during the year, and twice they ended up with more than us. The real upset was in the 1981-82 season when we had 94 points and they had 72, but they got very strong goaltending from Murray Bannerman and put us out. Our rivalry got to the point that if there was a Blackhawks game coming, the demand for tickets was enormous.

The North Stars line up to congratulate Cesare Maniago after a 5-3 win over Chicago, 11/4/72.

Bloomington Historical Society

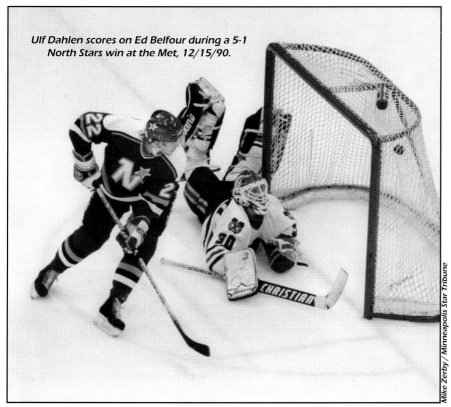

Ulf Dahlen scores on Ed Belfour during a 5-1 North Stars win at the Met, 12/15/90.

Mike Zerby / Minneapolis Star Tribune

One night we were delayed getting into Chicago. We had played elsewhere the night before, and coming into Chicago that day the weather was horrendous.

We got to Chicago Stadium at the time the game was supposed to start, and we still had to get dressed, we had to have warm-up — the whole works. When the game finally started, Bob Pulford, who was their general manager, came up to me and said: "Louie, you're not going to believe this. We've sold out of alcohol in the building." Because of the delay, they had completely sold out of beer and whiskey by the time the game started.

Our advertising agency took our rivalry with the Blackhawks a step further when they ran an ad in the newspaper the week before a game showing an Indian head in the sights of a gun and saying, "We have the Hawks in our sights."

My switchboard operator came to me and said, "Mr. Nanne, there's an Indian chief on the phone who's called here about ten times and says he has to talk to you."

I get on the line and the chief introduces himself and says, "Mr. Nanne, I'd like to tell you how offended I am by your ad in the paper about the Blackhawks."

I said, "First of all, Chief, the ad agency did this. We should have approved it, but we didn't. You have to remember this is sports — we weren't meaning to denigrate the Indians in any way."

He says, "We think it's way off base and we want an apology." I got a little upset. I said, "Chief, do you ever watch television?" He says, "Yeah." I said, "Do you watch on Thursday nights?" He says, "Yeah." I said, "Do you know what's on Thursday nights?" He says, "What?"

Lou Nanne clashes with Bobby Hull, as Bob Barlow looks on.

Lou Nanne archives

I said: "The Untouchables. I'm Italian, and all they do is kick the crap out of us every Thursday night. I watch it and don't get all worked up about it. I think it's the same with this hockey game. You shouldn't get that concerned. And by the way, my wife's part Indian, so I think I understand."

I thought I remembered my wife telling me she was part Indian, but when I got home I said: "Remember, Francine, if anybody calls, you are part Indian. I know you're French, and I think the French and the Indians got together sometime." She says, "Yeah, I think I'm a sixteenth Indian." I said, "OK, then I didn't lie to him."

Denis Savard

Denis Savard was one of the true treasures in the league — a terrific player. Every time we played the Blackhawks, he was the guy we knew we had to stop. When the Blackhawks played us, they were concerned about stopping Dino Ciccarelli.

Glen Sonmor used to get very upset when the Blackhawks singled out Ciccarelli or Broten. If somebody took a run at either of them, especially when the teams' benches were side by side, he'd just lean around the glass and yell, "Savard, the next time one of your teammates hits Broten or Ciccarelli, we're getting Plett after you!"

Then, Savard would tell his coach, "Lay off those guys."

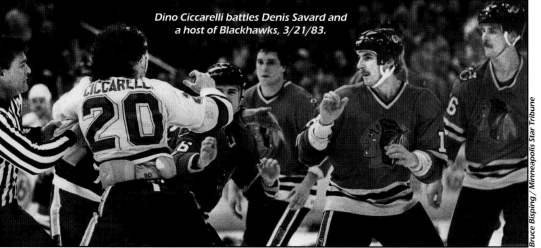

Dino Ciccarelli battles Denis Savard and a host of Blackhawks, 3/21/83.

Bruce Bisping / Minneapolis Star Tribune

Al Secord

Chicago's Al Secord developed into a very good hockey player and was one of the toughest guys in the league. One reason I signed Dino Ciccarelli was his attitude toward Secord.

When I scouted Ciccarelli, his goal-scoring ability and the feisty way he played were very impressive. I asked a London, Ontario, newspaperman, "Does Ciccarelli always play that aggressively, being such a small guy?"

He said: "Louie, we got a guy in the league named Al Secord, and he's as tough as they come. Every time Hamilton comes in here to play London, Secord's job is to get Ciccarelli — hit him, get him off the ice,

bother him. Last month, Ciccarelli scored a goal, and we ran a picture in the London Free Press. Right behind him in the photo was Secord, coming to get him.

"Ciccarelli saw the photo, came down to the paper, got the glossy, signed it, 'Hey Al, isn't this your man?' and shipped it off to him."

I heard that and fell in love with Dino right there.

Secord would always mount battles with the North Stars, and he was one of the reasons why I went out and got guys like Jack Carlson and Dave Richter and Basil McRae. We were playing Chicago in our division and we had to measure up to them.

Chicago Stadium

One of the most electric atmospheres I've experienced in hockey was at the '91 All-Star Game at Chicago Stadium. The game was played three days after the start of the Gulf War.

Before the opening faceoff, the building went dark, the big pipe organ started playing, and Wayne Messmer began singing the National Anthem. The whole crowd immediately joined in, and people were waving flags and sparklers and lighters. As I said, the atmosphere turned absolutely electric. It was incredible to look at the fans, all singing.

About five minutes into the game, Dave Gagner scored the first goal and the crowd roared. I'm sure it was the loudest ovation a North Star ever got in Chicago.

Rick Kolodziej

Don Beaupre and Harold Snepsts stand guard, with Al Secord lurking around the net, 4/23/85.

PLAYOFF HISTORY

1971

We played St. Louis in the playoffs in 1968 and 1970 and lost to them both times. It was an albatross hanging around our necks. We desperately wanted to get past them and have the opportunity to meet one of the established Original Six teams. Sure enough, in the 1971 playoff quarterfinals we caught St. Louis again.

That year, Jack Gordon put together a different line for the playoffs. He moved me up from defense to right wing to play on a checking line with Murray Oliver and Charlie Burns. St. Louis was ahead in the series two games to one, and Game 4 was in Minnesota. In that game, Charlie Burns got the winning goal in a 2-1 victory. In Game 5 back in St. Louis, I scored the winning goal in a 4-3 win. Then we returned to Minnesota and closed them out 5-2 with Bobby Rousseau scoring the game winner. When we finally beat St. Louis in the playoffs, it was one of the most exhilarating moments that I'd experienced in sports, and it was the first major hurdle cleared by the North Stars franchise.

We went on to play Montreal in the semifinals. At the time, no Original Six team had ever lost a playoff game to an expansion team. The hockey public was looking past us and essentially handing the series to Montreal. However, we were very upbeat after the St. Louis series and committed to playing our best.

We opened up in Montreal, and the Canadiens waxed us 7-2. Things turned around in the next game and we beat them 6-3. I scored the winning goal and we became the first expansion team to win a playoff game against an Original Six team.

We came back to Minnesota with a lot of confidence, but Montreal went right back ahead with a 6-3 win. In Game 4, J.P. Parise scored a

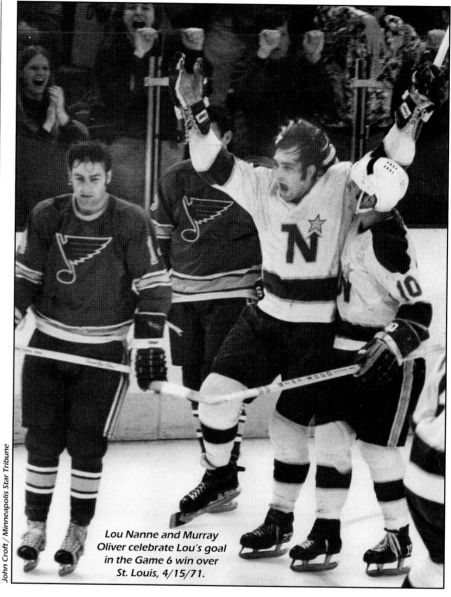

John Croft / Minneapolis Star Tribune

Lou Nanne and Murray Oliver celebrate Lou's goal in the Game 6 win over St. Louis, 4/15/71.

big goal for us and we went on to win 5-2. Game 5 was in Montreal and we got trounced 6-1.

Then came one of the big moments in North Stars history. We returned to Minnesota for Game 6 and it was a terrific hockey game, back and forth all night long. We were losing 3-2 in the final seconds of the third period

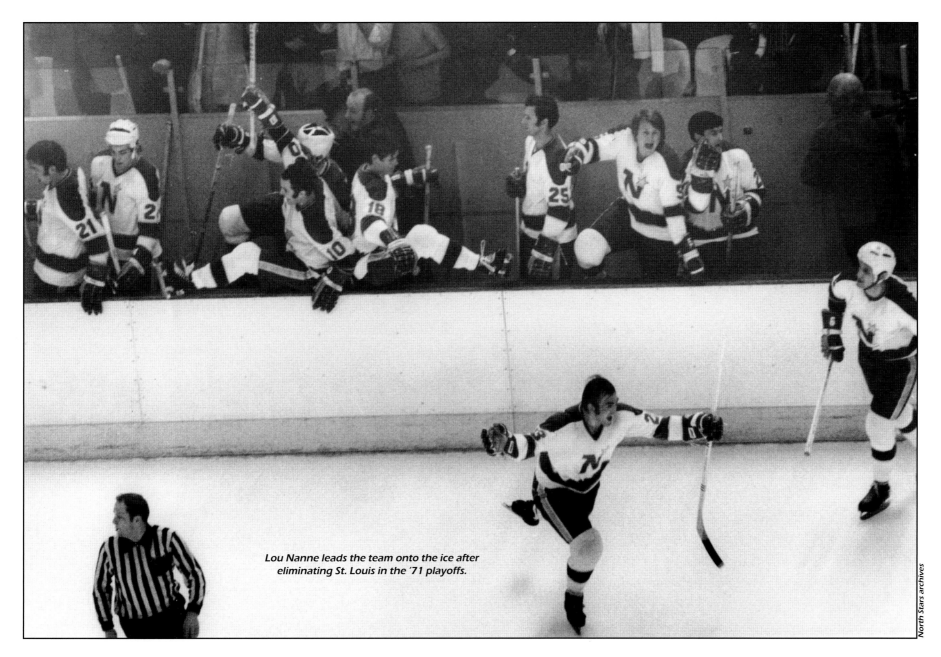

Lou Nanne leads the team onto the ice after eliminating St. Louis in the '71 playoffs.

North Stars archives

when Teddy Hampson scored an apparent goal right at the buzzer. The crowd went crazy, but the red goal light never came on and we lost 3-2.

Replays later proved that the goal was scored 7/100th of a second after the green end-of-game light went on. We were that close to tying the game. Many people were thinking the puck had crossed the line in time, but the goal light would block out the end-of-game light, and the red light never quite made it on.

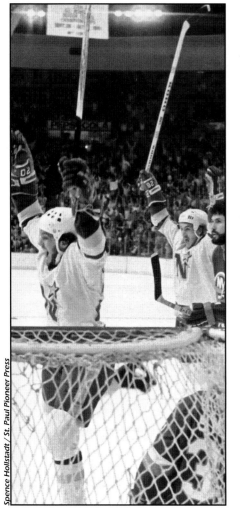

Dino Ciccarelli and Steve Payne celebrate a goal in Game 4 of the '81 Stanley Cup Finals. The North Stars win the game 4-2 to keep the series alive. Defending for the Islanders are Gord Lane and goalie Billy Smith, 5/19/81.

1981

Another big series occurred in 1981. We had never won a game in Boston during our 14 years of play, and we had just had the big fight night in the last regular season game we played in Boston a month earlier.

We were getting ready to go to Boston when Glen Sonmor received a letter from a woman who claimed to be a mystic. She sent him an eye patch, which he wore on the bench.

We swept the Bruins in three straight. Steve Payne, an outstanding playoff performer, scored the winning goal in two of the games, including an overtime goal in Game 1, our first ever win at Boston Garden.

From there we went on the defeat Buffalo four games to one, with Payne getting another game-winner in overtime. Then we faced Calgary and beat them four games to two. We were a Cinderella team in the Stanley Cup Finals against the great New York Islanders, who were the defending Cup champions. They knocked us out in five games.

Glen Sonmor had put together a line of rookies — Neal Broten, Dino Ciccarelli and Brad Palmer — and they played terrific throughout the playoffs. Dino was on fire. He set two NHL rookie playoff scoring records with 14 goals and 21 points. Nobody received more abuse in front of the net than Dino, and it all started in the '81 playoffs, specifically the Islanders series.

The atmosphere inside the Met during the '81 Cup finals was something I've never experienced before or since. In our first game home versus the Islanders, the crowd was roaring 30 minutes before the opening faceoff and never stopped. Glen and the players could not believe the noise they heard in the dressing room. It sent chills down everyone's spine.

I had friends from Canada who were watching on TV and marveling at the atmosphere. Many of them called asking for tickets because they wanted to come from Sault Saint Marie and be a part of the bedlam. As I scouted games in Canada during the following years, I was often approached by strangers who said they became North Stars fans because they were enthralled by the Met Center crowd during the '81 Cup finals.

Gordie Roberts, Neal Broten and Dino Ciccarelli celebrate a goal on Chicago's Murray Bannerman during a 6-5 North Stars win in the '84 playoffs. Defending for Chicago is Rick Paterson, 4/5/84.

We took the momentum from our great playoff run into the next season. We had an outstanding year, only to be upset by Chicago in the first round of the playoffs. We finished the regular season with 94 points, which was the highest point total in team history at that time.

We went to training camp the following fall of '82 and played an exhibition game against Edmonton. I'll never forget the feeling that came over me as I watched the Oilers from the stands. They were so fast, so talented and so young that I said to Glen Sonmor, "We're in deep trouble. That team's going to be around for a long time giving us a lot of problems." Sure enough, we faced them in the '84 conference finals and they swept us in four games. We had come through Chicago and St. Louis, but when we ran into Edmonton it was like running into a buzz saw. That was the start of the Oilers' run of Stanley Cups.

1991

The North Stars' great playoff run of '91 was interesting because the key players had come from three different administrations. Previous GM Jack Ferreira had acquired Mark Tinordi, Stewart Gavin and Ulf Dahlen. Holdovers from my time as GM were Brian Bellows, Neal Broten, Dave Gagner and Mike Modano. New GM Bobby Clarke did a wonderful job of solidifying the lineup by adding Brian Propp and bringing back Bobby Smith. Coach Bob Gainey had the team playing great defense and hitting their stride at playoff time. Bellows, Gagner, Modano and Smith sparked the offense, and Jon Casey was outstanding in net.

The team took North Stars fans on a whirlwind ride with series wins over Chicago — the top team in the league during the regular season — St. Louis and Edmonton.

We faced Pittsburgh in the finals, and at one point it looked like the Cup would be ours. We led the series two games to one with Game 4 at the

Jeff Wheeler / Minneapolis Star Tribune

Bruce Bisping / Minneapolis Star Tribune

Top: Dave Gagner beats Oilers' goalie Grant Fuhr in Game 4 of the '91 Campbell Conference Finals. The North Stars win the game 5-1. Trailing the play is Edmonton's Craig Muni, 5/8/91.

Bottom: The Penguins turn the tide on Jon Casey and the North Stars with a 5-3 win in Game 4 of the '91 Stanley Cup Finals, 5/21/91.

Met. In the end, the brilliance of Mario Lemieux was overpowering. He put the Penguins on his shoulders and carried them to victory. Pittsburgh won the series 4-2, but it was another magical playoff run. There was incredible electricity inside the Met as well as outside among thousands of tailgating fans.

TRADES & DRAFTS

1979 Draft

One of the best players the Minnesota North Stars ever had was Neal Broten. We were going into the draft in 1979, which they had cut down to six rounds, and Neal was playing at the University of Minnesota.

We had a second-round pick, and we were planning on taking Broten. Right before the draft started, I made a trade with the Montreal Canadiens to acquire Bill Nyrop. I had talked to Nyrop a great deal that year. He was sitting out from the Canadiens and said he was going to retire. He said if I got his rights, he'd return to play.

I was willing to give up a second-round pick, because Bill Nyrop was a premier defenseman when he was playing for the Canadiens. So I gave them our second rounder, and then had to do something to get back a second-rounder so we could get Broten.

Just about fifteen minutes before the draft, I made a deal with Edmonton. Dave Semenko was our property through the merger with the WHA, but he didn't want to come to Minnesota. I called Glen Sather and gave him the rights to Dave Semenko in exchange for a second-round pick. We took Broten.

I had gotten a call from Washington's Max McNab, who said, "We're taking Broten with our second-round pick unless you give us something to leave him alone."

Craig Hartsburg

Jim Gallop / Gallop Studio

I said: "Well Max, if it happens, it happens. I'll talk to you when your pick comes." They were picking right after Edmonton, and I didn't want them to jump ahead. When Edmonton's pick came, it was traded to the North Stars, and we got Broten.

One thing I wasn't so thrilled about afterwards. We had a pick in the next round, and I had gone down to scout guys playing in the WHA, particularly Craig Hartsburg, Rob Ramage and Michel Goulet. I saw this 18-year-old kid, Mark Messier.

He had not scored much in the WHA that year, but he was a tremendous talent to watch at eighteen. Edmonton beat us to him.

The 1979 draft was the greatest draft of all time in the National Hockey League. It was tremendous. I remember going up to see Bobby Smith the year before, and in that game were Bobby Smith and Steve Payne playing for Ottawa, and Wayne Gretzky and Craig Hartsburg playing for Sault Ste. Marie.

Gretzky wasn't eligible, but my cousin told me: "You watch this kid on our team. You won't see him all night long, and at the end of the night he'll have three points."

Hartsburg was a year younger, and I remember seeing him and thinking, "I wonder who's going to get that player next year; he's going to be great."

Our plan going in was to try to get two guys we really wanted in the first round, Craig Hartsburg and Ray Bourque. I remember going to

Montreal to scout a junior. I bumped into Jacques Lemaire and Guy LaPointe, who were there watching the game for the Canadiens.

They looked at me and Jacques said: "You come to see Bourque? He plays like that every night." Ramage, Hartsburg, Goulet and others were playing in the WHA, while Bourque was in Juniors. We had the sixth pick and the tenth pick, and we thought we'd pick Hartsburg and Bourque. We ended up with Hartsburg as the sixth pick and wound up taking Tommy McCarthy with the tenth because Boston took Bourque with the eighth pick.

1987 Draft

We drafted Dave Archibald first in 1987. He was playing in the Western League, and we were looking for a big centerman. We were hoping to get a defenseman first, but Boston took Glen Wesley before us, so we took Archibald. I made a mistake there — a couple of my scouts, Murray Oliver and Dick Bouchard, were very passionate about Joe Sakic.

We weren't the only ones who missed on Sakic. Phil Esposito told me a similar story. He had seen Sakic play when he was general manager of the Rangers and said, "Why don't we take Sakic?" But his scouting staff really liked Jayson More, instead, and Sakic slipped down to fifteenth before Quebec got him.

Ironically, Dave Archibald was traded to the Rangers by Jack Ferreira in exchange for Jayson More.

Brent Ashton, Fred Barrett and Steve Christoff

In the fall of '83, we were trying to get left winger Brent Ashton from New Jersey, but I couldn't seem to satisfy their GM, Max McNab, who was looking for a defenseman.

I had been talking to Los Angeles at the same time, so I ended up making a three-way deal. New Jersey had an interest in Kings defenseman Dave Lewis, so I traded Steve Christoff, who we had re-acquired a few months earlier, and Fred Barrett to Los Angeles for Lewis. I immediately traded Lewis to New Jersey for Ashton.

Brent Ashton

Rick Kolodziej

Steve Christoff

North Stars archives

Brent was a hard worker and skated well, but he just couldn't seem to find the back of the net for us. He eventually went to Quebec along with Brad Maxwell in exchange for Tony McKegney and Bo Berglund. He scored much more in Quebec.

Brian Bellows

As we were getting ready for the season in 1981, we had a lot of defensemen. I looked around the league trying to decide who might end up near the bottom, to try to make a deal with them.

Brian Bellows

Jim Gallop / Gallop Studio

I called Detroit and offered Greg Smith and Donnie Murdoch and our No. 1 pick for Detroit's No. 1 pick. The Red Wings accepted.

Detroit ended up second to last in the league, so now Boston had the first pick and we had the second pick. I wasn't sure if Boston was going to pick Brian Bellows or Gord Kluzak, two great prospects.

We liked both players, but we felt we needed a forward more than a defenseman. Also, I had called Barrie MacKenzie, Kluzak's coach at Notre Dame and a former North Star, and he said: "Kluzak's a tremendous hockey player. If I have any question about him, it's that he does get injured sometimes. He might be prone to injuries."

That was enough for me to think we should go for Bellows. I always felt that to get a great player, you do what you gotta do. I called Harry Sinden in Boston and offered him Brad Palmer and Dave Donnelly in exchange for not picking Bellows.

We were willing to give up two players just to ensure that we got Bellows. He had a long career and scored almost 500 goals. Unfortunately for Boston, Kluzak had a career-ending injury early on.

Dino Ciccarelli and Mike Gartner

When I was president of the North Stars in 1988-89, just before the trading deadline I went into the general manager's office, where they had been talking about trades all day long. As I was sitting there, it seemed pretty evident that the coach, Pierre Page, wanted to trade Dino Ciccarelli and Bob Rouse to Washington for Mike Gartner and Larry Murphy.

Five minutes before the deadline, Pierre said to Jack Ferreira, "Are we going to do the deal?" Jack says, "I don't know if it fits into the budget."

This was the first major deal for Ferreira and Page, and I didn't want to let the budget stand in the way. I said to Jack, "If you want to make the deal, make the deal and I'll take care of the budget."

They made the trade — a major one, since Ciccarelli, Rouse, Gartner and Murphy were four very good players. It was a unique situation seeing Dino get traded away from the North Stars, because I had never discussed trading him when I was GM.

Mike Gartner

Rick Kolodziej

Gartner and Murphy played very well for the North Stars. Murphy was a gifted offensive defenseman who wound up playing in the league forever. It was a trade that I think worked out very well for both teams.

Jude Drouin and J.P. Parise

Jude and J.P. were traded to the Islanders in separate deals within days of each other in January of '75. J.P. was actually traded first. The Islanders were in need of a good corner man, and J.P. was the best. They came to the North Stars offering Ernie Hicke and Doug Rombough, and Jack Gordon made the deal.

Craig Cameron

North Stars archives

Two days later, Drouin was sent to the Islanders for Craig Cameron. Jude rankled the coaches with his carefree attitude and it also got to Gordon. At the time, Jack was looking to add size to our forwards, so he brought in Cameron.

Drouin and Parise led the Islanders in a sensational run in the playoffs that year. They weren't there for the Islanders' Stanley Cups, but I've always felt Jude and J.P. laid the foundation. They were two terrific players we lost at once, and it led to some lean years.

Mike Eaves

Mike Eaves played very, very well for us in the early '80s, but it seemed that he was getting prone to concussions. We decided to trade Mike because we were not sure how long his career would last. We sent him and Keith Hanson to Calgary and we got Steve Christoff back along with a second-round draft pick, which we used to select Frantisek Musil.

Mike Eaves

North Stars archives

Dave Gagner

We were looking to acquire Dave Gagner from the Rangers. The scouts liked him a lot and when we played the Rangers we liked him, too. We got him in October of 1987 along with tough guy Jay Caufield in exchange for Jari Gronstrand and Paul Boutilier.

Dave had an outstanding career in Minnesota. He was one of the top guys we had come to us.

The trade talks started in an unusual way. We were looking for a center and Gagner wasn't playing that much for the Rangers.

I called New York and asked for General Manager Craig Patrick. His assistant said he was in Sweden, but she didn't know exactly where.

I hung up and took out my book of scheduled games around the world, and I thought, "What game would I see if I were in Sweden?" I found one in a small town in northern Sweden, way north of Stockholm. I called Information in that town and asked for the name and number of their nicest hotel, then I called there and said, "Can I speak to Craig Patrick?'"

The guy says, "He just left for dinner — I saw him walk out of the lobby." I said, "Where did he go?" He says, "I don't know." I said, "Can you give me the name and number of the nicest restaurant in town?" So he did.

I called the restaurant ten minutes later and said, "There's a tall, thin, balding man there named Craig Patrick. Would you tell him to come to the phone?"

Craig comes to the phone and I say, "Craig, it's Louie." He says, "How did you find me? Even I didn't know I was coming here until ten minutes ago."

We started talking a trade and it led to us getting Gagner.

The same thing happened with Gene Ubriaco. I had him coaching for me in Baltimore, and after our games were over, I always liked to call our farm teams and see how they did that night. So I was sitting in my office, and it was about 1:30 a.m. Eastern time in Baltimore, so I called Ubriaco at home. He wasn't there. I called Information in Baltimore and asked, "What's a great Italian restaurant in Baltimore?"

The operater said, "Sabatino's." I got the number, called, and said, "Is there a Gene Ubriaco there?" "Yes, he is."

Curt Giles and Bob Brooke

Curt Giles came to me and asked to be traded, so in '86 we sent him to the Rangers with Tony McKegney for Bob Brooke and a draft pick. Curt was in New York for one season, and I saw him the following summer. He told me he'd like to come back to the North Stars. Fortunately for us, in November of '87, New York was willing to deal him. We got him back for minor leaguer Byron Lomow.

Bob Brooke

Gilles Gilbert and Fred Stanfield

Fred Stanfield

North Stars archives

Gilles Gilbert, our goaltender, had become a free agent in 1972, the year the WHA was starting. He was in Los Angeles negotiating and it looked like Gilles would sign with the new league.

Harry Sinden, the Boston manager, needed a goaltender very badly.

Sinden contacted Gilbert's agent and basically agreed on contract terms if he could get Gilles' NHL rights. At the draft, Sinden met with Wren Blair. It was late in the evening and Sinden offered Fred Stanfield, a very good forward, for Gilbert. Wren wanted to hold him up. He insisted on Stanfield and a No. 1 draft choice. They argued for a while and then Sinden agreed.

They spent a long time trading stories and talking of old times. Then Wren said: "I'm going upstairs to talk to my guys. Don't forget, Stanfield for Gilbert."

He didn't mention the first-round pick. Wren went upstairs, told the scouts what he was doing, then came back to Sinden's room and said, "Okay, it's a deal: Stanfield for Gilbert," again not mentioning the draft pick.

My friend Harry Sinden later told me: "I just sat there and didn't say anything. So we kept our first-round pick."

Danny Grant

Danny was with us for a long time, and he was tremendous, but Danny was the kind of player who was mostly offense. Somehow, management decided it wanted a different type of player, and we traded him to Detroit for Henry Boucha. Danny went on to play very well for the Red Wings.

We missed him as a teammate. He kept everyone loose and was one of the best storytellers ever. He was one of the most accurate shooters to ever play the game.

Marc Habscheid and Don Barber

In January of '85, we traded Mark Napier to Edmonton for Gordie Sherven and Terry Martin. Gordie was with us until December of '85,

Don Barber

Rick Kolodziej

and then we traded him back to Edmonton with Don Biggs in exchange for Marc Habscheid, Donnie Barber and Emanuel Viveiros.

Habscheid had a great season for us in 1988-89 when Pierre Page put him on a line with Neal Broten and Brian MacLellen. Pierre gave Habscheid an opportunity to really develop, and he did, but unfortunately he signed with Detroit as a free agent after that season.

Bill Hogaboam

Bill Hogaboam came to us from the Red Wings for Dennis Hextall in February of '76. Bill was a really nice kid who bought Cesare's house right around the corner from me, and we'd ride to the Met together with Brad Maxwell, Blake Dunlop or Doug Hicks.

When I became GM of the North Stars, one of the first things I had to do was get the contracts in line, and Hogaboam had the biggest contract. I didn't want to just buy Bill out and leave him out of hockey, so I arranged to get him back to the Red Wings. I called up Ted Lindsay and worked a deal where I could buy Hogie out for a third of the money and Detroit would pick up the rest of his contract. We freed up money we could use in other ways.

Paul Holmgren

I tried many times to get Paul Holmgren from Philadelphia. He was a big strong right-winger from St. Paul. I used to sit at the draft and try to work him into deals with Philadelphia.

One year I was trying so hard to get Holmgren that after Keith Allen, their general manager, went to sleep at the Elizabeth Hotel, I got a big sheet of paper and I'd write down one of our players and say "for Holmgren and" some other consideration, then I'd knock on Allen's door and shove the offer under the door.

I was keeping Keith Allen up all night. We finally got Holmgren in 1984 in exchange for the rights to Paul Guay and our third-round pick. So, Holmgren was able to play for the North Stars before his career ended.

Brian Lawton

We had drafted Ron Meighan in 1981 as our first-round pick — he played in the Ontario league. During his first training camp with us, we were playing an exhibition in Fargo and I decided his style of play was not going to fit in with our team.

I thought, who can I trade him to that might end up near the bottom of the league? I decided Pittsburgh might have a tough time making the playoffs and thought maybe I could make a deal.

Baz Bastien was Pittsburgh's general manager. I talked trade with him for a month. Finally, we sent Meighan and Anders Hakansson and our No. 1 pick for George Ferguson and their No. 1 pick.

Brian Lawton

There's good and bad news about that. Fortunately for us, Pittsburgh ended up last so we got the first pick. Unfortunately for us, we didn't pick Pat LaFontaine or Steve Yzerman, who turned out to be superstars.

LaFontaine and Brian Lawton were rated "1" and "1A" by NHL Central Scouting as well as by our scouts.

I remember going to Kitchener to see the players the scouts were talking about. I saw Yzerman and told a friend of mine, "I just saw a right-handed Broten."

That was a big tribute, because Neal Broten was playing extremely well for us at the time. As it turned out, Yzerman was even more than that.

We needed a big center and Brian Lawton showed a lot of skill. His dad was a big man and we thought Brian might grow into a big center that could play against someone like Brian Trottier. We took him. He had a nice career, but it was average, at best, when compared to Yzerman's or LaFontaine's.

Al MacAdam

Through the merger with Cleveland, one of the real assets we acquired was Al MacAdam. He seemed like everybody's favorite, every coach's favorite. However, sometimes players don't read it that way.

When Bill Mahoney took over as coach, MacAdam was playing on a line with Bobby Smith and Steve Payne. Even after Bobby got traded, Al continued to play extremely well.

At the end of the season, he walked into my office with his wife, Anne, which was very unusual. Players had started to get agents by that time, but Al wasn't using anybody. They sat down before me, and I remember Anne said, "Louie, we're in here because we'd like to get traded." I was in shock. I said, "Why would you want to be traded?"

Anne says, "We don't think Mahoney appreciates Al." I said: "I want to tell you he not only appreciates him, I think Al's his favorite player. I really believe that you're misreading this."

Al says: "No, I want to go. I don't think he respects my ability and I think it might be better off for me to leave." And that's when I ended up having to trade Al. I traded him to Vancouver for Harold Snepsts, and Mahoney was real disappointed because he loved Al.

Al MacAdam

North Stars archives

Dennis Maruk

We opened the 1978-79 season with a game at Montreal. We had four centers at the time — Timmy Young, Glen Sharpley, Dennis Maruk and our top draft pick, Bobby Smith. I was now the general manager, and after two periods I noticed that Bobby Smith had hardly played.

Well, I decided right then and there I needed to deal one of my centers because Bobby Smith was the future of the franchise and with four centers he might not develop as quickly as he should. Maruk was the logical choice to go because Washington had been expressing interest in him. Furthermore, Young and Sharpley were much more diligent defensively.

Dennis Maruk

Jim Gallop / Gallop Studio

I traded Maruk to the Capitals for a first-round draft pick, which we used to select Tommy McCarthy. I reacquired Dennis from Washington in 1983 for a second-round pick.

Brad Maxwell and Tony McKegney

Tony McKegney

Jim Gallop / Gallop Studio

Brad Maxwell was another player who asked to be traded, and it happened at the same time we were looking for more scoring. I had been talking to Quebec, trying to get Tony McKegney, and they were interested in Maxwell. They also wanted Brent Ashton. I ended up sending Ashton and Maxwell to the Nordiques for McKegney and Bo Berglund. That was a funny deal because about two months after he was there, Brad's wife Cathy came to me and said, "We wanted to be traded, but not to Quebec." I said: "Well, you don't get to say where you're going. You wanted to go, you went." Eventually, I got him back.

Kevin Maxwell

We set our budgets in July and didn't deviate. One October, I had a contractor give an estimate on how much it would cost to expand my office to the empty office next door, so we could meet there with the scouts.

The estimate was $15,000. Next time I saw Gordon, I said, "I'd like permission to spend $15,000 to fix up the office." He said: "It's not in the budget, is it? If it's not in the budget, we don't do it." I said to him, "Gordon, it's only $15,000." He said, "No, we go by the budget."

At the time, Max McNab was badly in need of a centerman in Washington. He wanted Kevin Maxwell. I had been asking for a third-round draft choice, and Max wanted to give me a fourth.

He was desperate. He called one day, we didn't make a deal, and he called the next. I said, "Max, I have to tell you now that there's no use talking unless you give me a third-rounder and $15,000."

He says, "What are you talking about?" I said: "I would've given you him for a third-rounder before, but I changed my mind. If I deal him, I have to replace him. I need some cash."

He hung up on me. And then the next day, he called up, we made the deal, and I had the $15,000 to remodel the office. I told Gordon how I came up the money and he said, "I can't argue with that." From that point on we always called the scouts' room the Kevin Maxwell office.

Gilles Meloche

Gilles Meloche was one of the North Stars' top goaltenders. He was a great person, too. He came to us in the merger with Cleveland and played very well.

As salaries went higher, Meloche came into my office with his lawyer, Mike

Adams, and we started negotiating a contract. They wanted in the neighborhood of $150,000, which was exorbitant for us.

I said, "Fine, we'll talk again."

Then, I picked up the phone and called Glen Sather and said: "I'll make a deal with you. I've got to trade a goaltender I can't afford — Gilles — but you guys are doing well there and selling out, so maybe you can afford him."

So we ended up making a three-way trade and Gilles went to Edmonton for Paul Houck. Then Edmonton immediately traded Gilles to Pittsburgh for Marty McSorley.

Paul Holmgren, Dave Richter and Gordie Roberts congratulate Gilles Meloche after his 2-0 shutout of St. Louis. The win gave the North Stars a three-game sweep of the Blues in the '85 playoffs.

Rick Kolodziej

Mike Modano

During 1987-88, Mike Modano and Trevor Linden were the two top-rated players in Junior hockey. We had a tremendous number of injuries and it looked like we were going to miss the playoffs.

I went to scout Linden and Modano, and also talked about them at length with our scouts. When it came right down to it, two of our scouts at most thought we should pick Linden. I felt strongly that we needed a franchise-type player who could bring fans out of their seats and create excitement.

I'll never forget, when we were in Kalamazoo having our meetings, Gordon Gund came in with his wife, Lulie, to meet some of the guys we were having in for interviews. And one thing the Gunds never did was interfere — they never interfered at all. But Lulie Gund had the opportunity to talk to the guys, and she was really taken by Linden, so she was hoping we were going to pick Linden. In fact, during the car ride to the airport, Lulie continued to talk with Linden, while Modano sat with headphones on, listening to music. Our thoughts were that we needed somebody to really establish a franchise tag, so we picked Modano.

Right after the draft, Jack Ferreira took over as GM and Page as coach. Modano went back to Juniors to play while we were trying to sign him, and Linden came in and had a very good rookie season with Vancouver. We took a lot of static in the paper for the decision we made, but we felt very confident that in the long run there would prove to be a big difference between the two players.

Linden has had a solid career, but Modano has been the face of the Stars franchise and a premier player in the NHL. Soon Mike will be the highest scoring U.S.-born player and a Hall of Famer.

Kent Nilsson

I traded Kent Nilsson because Lorne Henning wouldn't use him. I called Glen Sather in Edmonton and said: "Glen, have I got a player for you. Nilsson is about as talented as anyone in the league, and if he comes there with Gretzky and Messier, he'll be phenomenal."

Glen says, "What do you want for him?" I said, "I want a second-rounder for him." He says: "I'm not giving you a second-rounder. I'll give you a fourth rounder for him, because I hear he's going home next year."

I said: "I know this guy, and I know he can play, and I know that he won't go home if he gets in that situation. So here's the deal I'll make. You give me a fourth-round pick. If you win the Stanley Cup this year, which I know you'll do if you get Nilsson, it becomes a third-round pick. And then if he doesn't go home, it becomes a second-round pick."

Sather agreed, Nilsson went to the Oilers, they won the Stanley Cup, he didn't go home, and we got a second-round pick.

Willi Plett

Jim Gallop / Gallop Studio

Willi Plett

In 1982, getting Willi Plett became a big deal to us. We had always coveted him, because he was a dominant physical force on the ice. I was very concerned about Bill Nyrop, who I had convinced to come back to play. He seemed to be out of the lineup too often.

Steve Christoff had done very well for us — a good scoring wing — but we had depth there. I packaged Christoff and Nyrop together with a second-round pick, and we got Willi Plett from Calgary.

Willi played for us for five years and did extremely well. We got a lot out of him.

Dave Richter

In November of '85, we were looking at Todd Bergen, a very talented player for Philadelphia. But he had a stomach problem, and we weren't sure how bad it was. The Flyers really coveted Dave Richter, who wasn't playing much for us at the time. They had Eddie Hospodar, who was a very physical player, a tough guy — not as good a fighter as Richter but a guy who would stand up for his team.

We decided to trade Richter with Bo Berglund, and we got Hospodar and Bergen. Hospodar played for us a while and did an admirable job. Bergen never came around with the injury, and I guess he had more desire to play golf, so he retired from hockey after half a year with our Springfield farm team.

Gordie Roberts and Mike Fidler

Mike Fidler was a terrific talent who came to the North Stars in the Cleveland merger. Mike was also a bit of an enigma. Every now and then he'd get a little rambunctious, and it got to the point where Glen Sonmor was getting a little upset with him. At that time in the late '70s we needed to improve our defense. I called Hartford because it was

close to where Fidler had grown up and I thought he might be someone they'd be interested in. In exchange, I asked for defenseman Gordie Roberts. Whalers' GM Jack Kelly needed a forward and felt he could part with Roberts, so we made the deal.

Gordie came to us and had an outstanding career. The funny part of the trade is the comment Jack Kelly made afterward. He said, "No matter how this deal works out, you've gotten the best of it." I asked why, and he said, "Because Gordie Roberts has the best-looking wife in hockey."

Mike Fidler

North Stars archives

Glen Sharpley

Sharpley was a powerful skater, a good shot, a goal scorer, and a competitor. He was a guy who liked to be controversial. If you told him the sky was blue, he'd say it was pink. He could really agitate.

One night in Toronto, Steve Jensen was on the ice right before a faceoff deep in Toronto's zone. Jensen skated over to Sharpley and asked, "Where do you want me?" and Sharpley looked at him and said, "In the press box." So, he used to drive Sonmor a bit crazy.

Glen Sharpley

North Stars archives

We liked this big left winger, Ken Solheim, that Chicago had. So, in December 1980, we traded Sharpley to Chicago for Solheim and a second-round pick, which eventually turned out to be Tom Hirsch.

Sharpley wasn't in Chicago long before he damaged his eye, and it cost him his career.

Bobby Smith

The guy I wanted to trade the least of all was Bobby Smith. He was my first draft pick ever and a sensational guy. He was someone I was hoping would spend his whole career with the franchise. However, as can happen with great talents, when coaches play a different style, or don't use them the way they think they should be used, the player gets frustrated.

That's what happened to Bobby. At the All-Star Game in Long Island, we were having dinner — including Gordon Gund and his wife — and Art Kaminsky walks over and asks if he can talk with me for a minute.

He said, "I'm here to tell you that Bobby Smith wants to be traded, and we want to let you know right now."

I said, "You're nuts, we're not trading him." And then I said, "We're having dinner, Art, and I don't think it's right to bring this up."

As we played the rest of the year out, Bobby came to me once or twice and said: "Louie, I'm not happy here. I'd like to be traded." I said, "Bobby, let's just wait and see how things go. I'm sure we're going to get settled and be happier again."

The following season starts and Mahoney isn't playing Bobby as much as he wants. Smith isn't sharp and during one game, Sid Hartman, one of my close personal friends from the *Star Tribune*, comes over and says: "What's the matter with Bobby? You're going to have to trade him if he plays like that."

Finally, Bobby comes in my office and says: "Louie, you know I've got a lot of money, because you paid me a lot of money. You know I like school — my brother's a lawyer, he went to school with your brother — and I've always had an interest in going back to school. So, I'm telling you right now, you either trade me or I'm going to quit and go to college."

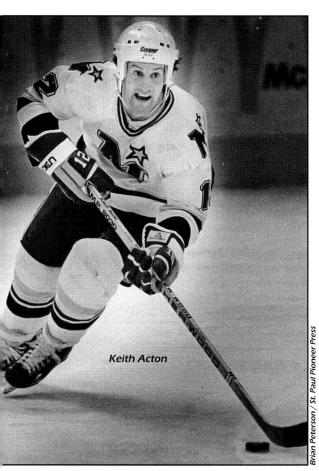

Keith Acton

Brian Peterson / St. Paul Pioneer Press

I asked him to wait a couple of months, and he said: "No, if I wait a couple of months the only thing that'll be different is I'll be in your office with golashes on because there's snow outside. I'm not waiting."

There was no talking him out of it, so I said: "Do me a favor then. Don't tell anybody, because I don't want it to hurt your value. If I can get something that I can go to my owners with, we'll do it if we have to."

I checked around and made the best deal I could for the North Stars. Bobby went to Montreal and played great for them there, too. In return, the Canadiens sent us Mark Napier, Keith Acton and a draft pick that turned out to be Kenny Hodge Jr. They were a big factor for us in playing well — especially Acton. The best offer other than that was Smith for Boston's Keith Crowder.

The announcement of the trading of Bobby Smith obviously caused a huge media thing here. One of the newspaper writers I thought was very clever, Doug Grow, wrote an article saying something like, "Lou Nanne just traded away a treasure. Hold onto the lakes. Hold onto the birds. He'll trade a mosquito." It was a very comical article and very appropriate — I had traded away a real valuable thing.

The only funny part about the whole deal was when Sid Hartman came up to me before the game that night and said, "Are you crazy trading Bobby Smith?" I turned around to Sid, pretended I was incredulous, and said, "Sid, I only did that because you told me to do it. Otherwise, I would have never traded him — I love Bobby Smith." Sid says, "I didn't tell you that." I said: "Yes you did, and I can't get him back. What am I going to do?" And he says: "Are you nuts? I didn't tell you that." I had Sid all worked up over the deal.

Mark Napier

Rick Kolodziej

Mark Tinordi

Another good trade Jack Ferreira made was Brian Lawton and Igor Liba to the Rangers for Mark Tinordi and Paul Jerrard. Lawton was an average center for us, but New York was very interested in him. Tinordi hadn't really established himself in New York yet, and Jack saw a lot of potential in him. Mark came in and did extremely well for the North Stars. He was a key player in the Stars' 1991 run for the Stanley Cup.

Tim Young

Tim Young was one of the most gifted players who ever wore a North Stars uniform. He would have been even better with more intensity.

Young had unusual talent handling the puck. In January 1979, he scored five goals during a game in New York. It was amazing the way he played that night.

When Dennis Maruk rejoined the North Stars in 1983, we had too many centers. I was talking a deal with Winnipeg GM John Ferguson while I was traveling. I told him I was looking to move Tim Young and I needed a defenseman. He had a defenseman, Craig Levie, and we liked the way he could handle the puck. He also had a prospect named Tom Ward, who was from Richfield and who they had drafted from the University of Minnesota. So, we gave them Tim Young for Levie and Ward.

As we discussed the deal, Ferguson asked, "What's Timmy make?" I said, "I don't have my contract book with me, but I know he's got a two-way contract." John says, "Just tell me this: Did you negotiate his contract?" I said, "Yeah." He said: "If you negotiated it, I don't have a problem. I know it's a good contract." So we made the deal over the phone while I was traveling, and Timmy went to Winnipeg.

Ron Zanussi

Ron Zanussi was a tough-checking wing who developed into a good goal scorer. The thing with Ron is he took criticism too seriously. He was the type of player that Glen Sonmor loved, but Ron would get frustrated when Glen got on him. Ron finally came to me and asked to be traded, so I dealt him to the Maple Leafs.

Ron Zanussi

North Stars archives

Trades Never Made

Wren Blair always worried because he thought the owners liked me. We were in Detroit in 1970 or so. We were playing pretty well. Wren always loved Nick Libett from the Red Wings. So he went to Ned Harkness, the Red Wings GM who had been at Cornell and RPI previously. When he was at RPI, Harkness tried to recruit me to play college hockey. He now wanted to get me for the Red Wings. He couldn't tamper, so he would call Bob May, the former North Dakota coach and a mutual friend, and say, "Ask Louie if he'll report if I trade for him."

I told May: "Yes, I want to play hockey. Plus, growing up in the Soo, the Red Wings were always my favorite team."

We beat Detroit that night and I had a good game. I was on the way out of the building when Harkness came over and said, "I'm going to make a deal for you. You're going to be here Wednesday."

Blair and Harkness agreed on the deal: Cesare Maniago and me for Nick Libett and Gary Bergman. Then, the North Stars ownership wouldn't let Wren make the deal, which really irritated him, of course.

●

I was almost traded during the 1975-76 season, but I didn't know it at the time. Emile Francis was the GM for St. Louis and is now a very good friend, and he made a trade for me. Ted Harris was our coach, and he was uneasy about me playing for him because he thought I wanted to coach the North Stars. I kept reassuring him that I had no interest in coaching and that coaching didn't pay enough. Jack Gordon told Ted that Emile was trying to make a trade for me, and Ted convinced him to do it, so they made a deal to send me to St. Louis for Rick Wilson.

When they took the trade to the owners for approval, the owners once again said no and turned it down. I never knew about it until a few

years later when I became GM and Emile said to me, "You're the North Stars General manager today, but I almost had you in a trade for Rick Wilson," and he filled me in on the details.

●

There is one trade that stands out in my mind as the one that got away: I was trying to deal Glen Sharpley to Edmonton for Glenn Anderson. Glen Sather and I talked about that trade off and on for a long time, and I thought it was going to get done time and time again, but we never did get it done. I was hoping they would give up on Anderson early in his career, but Sather is a very intelligent hockey man and they kept him.

●

Once when I was GM, I was looking to add a left-winger. I called George McGuire of the Los Angeles Kings and asked if he had anyone he was looking to deal. He said he wanted to trade Glen Goldup, who was a left-winger, so I said, "Don't do anything until I come out to watch your next home game."

I flew to Los Angeles to watch Goldup and was in the Kings' press lounge before the game. In walked two gorgeous women. One of them, a Playboy Playmate of the Year, was married to Kings center Charlie Simmer, who played his Junior hockey in my hometown. His wife and her friend sit down at my table, and after she introduces me to her friend she adds, "She's Miss April, and Glen Goldup's girlfriend." We had a nice chat, and then I went to watch the game.

I wasn't impressed enough with Goldup to make a deal, so I took an early flight back to Minneapolis. I no sooner walk into my office than the phone rings. It's George McGuire wondering why I left without making a deal. I told him, "I looked at Goldup and wasn't interested, but I'll give you a first-round pick for his girlfriend."

Gordie Roberts, Tom Hirsch, Brian Bellows and Keith Acton (obscured) celebrate Steve Payne's goal vs. Edmonton, 2/8/85.

Rick Kolodziej

THEY WORE THE NORTH STAR

*I*n the following pages you will see images

of most and statistics for all of the players in

North Star history. The entries have been

divided between skaters and goalies.

From the bench, Dino Ciccarelli extends his congratulations to Steve Payne, 2/8/85.

Acton, Keith

Ahrens, Chris

Andersson, Kent-Erik

Antonovich, Mike

Archibald, Dave

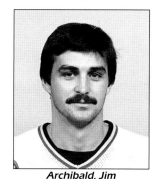
Archibald, Jim

Arnason, Chuck

Ashton, Brent

Babe, Warren

Baby, John

Balon, Dave

Barber, Don

Barlow, Bob

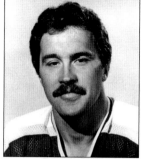

Barrett, Fred

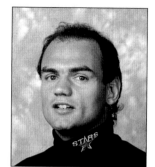

Beaudin, Norm

Bellows, Brian

Bennett, Harvey

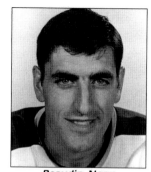

Berezan, Perry

Berger, Mike

Bergloff, Bob

Bergman, Gary

Beverley, Nick

Bialowas, Dwight

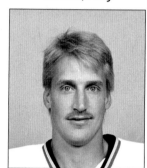

Bjugstad, Scott

Black, James

Blackburn, Don

Boh, Rick

Boivin, Leo

Boo, Jim

Boucha, Henry

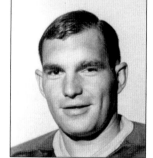

Boudrias, Andre

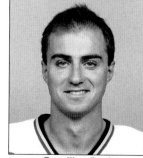

Boutilier, Paul

Brasar, Per-Olov

Brooke, Bob

Broten, Aaron

Broten, Neal

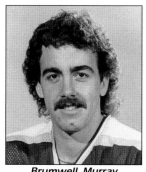
Brumwell, Murray

Bureau, Marc

Burns, Charlie

Butters, Bill

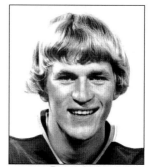
Byers, Jerry

Caffery, Terry

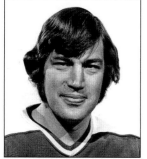
Cameron, Craig

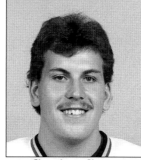
Carlson, Jack

Chambers, Shawn

Charlebois, Bob

Chernoff, Mike

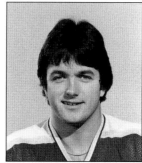
Chicoine, Dan

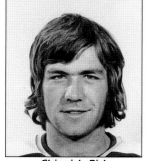
Chinnick, Rick

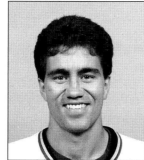
Chisholm, Colin

Christoff, Steve

Churla, Shane

Ciccarelli, Dino

Colley, Tom

Collins, Bill

Connelly, Wayne

Coulis, Tim

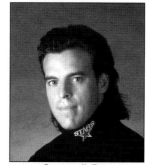
Courtnall, Russ

Craig, Mike

Cressman, Dave

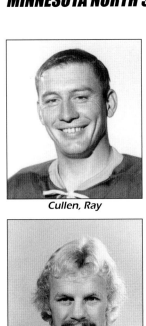
Cullen, Ray

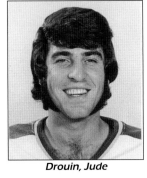
Dahlen, Ulf

Dahlquist, Chris

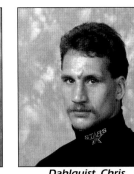
DePalma, Larry

Dineen, Gary

Dineen, Gord

Dobson, Jim

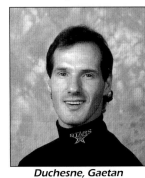
Drouin, Jude

Duchesne, Gaetan

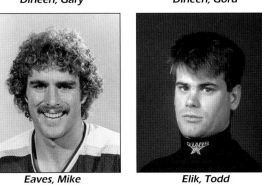
Dunlop, Blake

Eaves, Mike

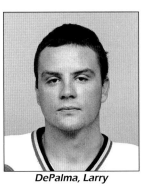
Elik, Todd

Engele, Jerry

Erickson, Grant

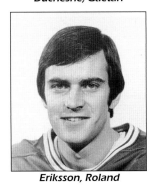
Eriksson, Roland

Fairbairn, Bill

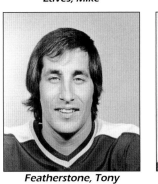
Featherstone, Tony

Fidler, Mike

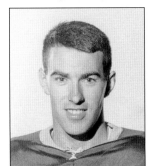
Fitzpatrick, Sandy

Flesch, John

Flockhart, Rob

Fraser, Curt

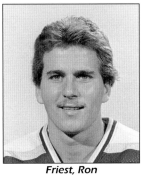
Friest, Ron

Gagner, Dave

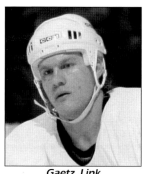
Gaetz, Link

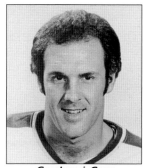
Gallimore, Jamie

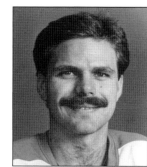
Gambucci, Gary

Gartner, Mike

Gavin, Stewart

Geldart, Gary

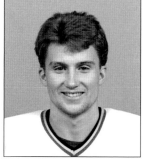
Gibbs, Barry

Gilchrist, Brent

Giles, Curt

Glynn, Brian

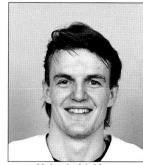
Goegan, Pete

Goldsworthy, Bill

Gotaas, Steve

Graham, Dirk

Grant, Danny

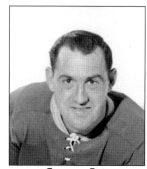
Gratton, Norm

Gronstrand, Jari

Habscheid, Marc

Hakansson, Anders

Hall, Murray

Hallin, Mats

Hampson, Ted

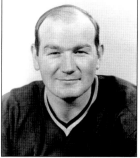
Hanson, Dave

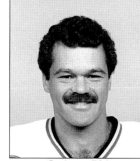
Harris, Duke

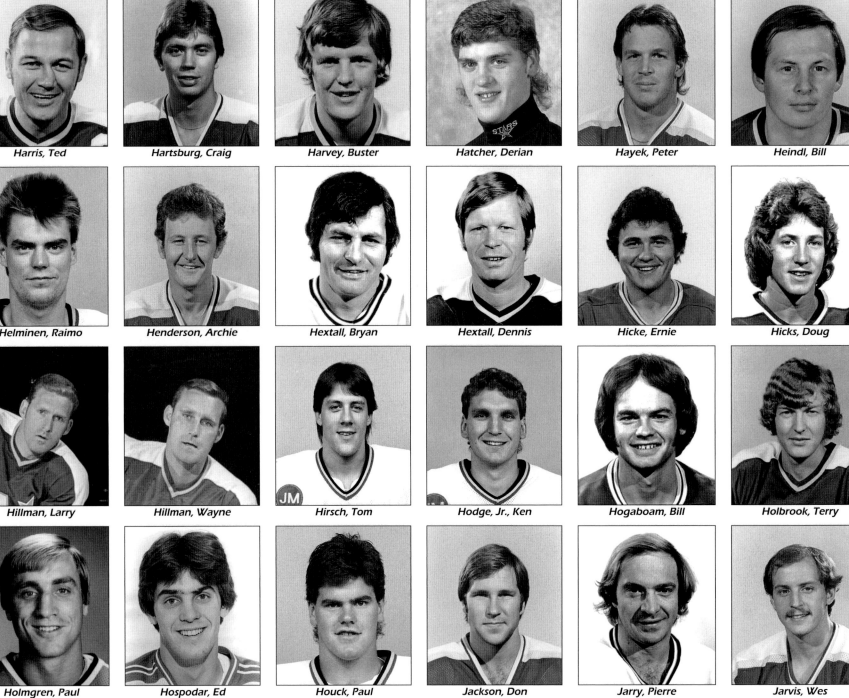

Harris, Ted	Hartsburg, Craig	Harvey, Buster	Hatcher, Derian	Hayek, Peter	Heindl, Bill
Helminen, Raimo	Henderson, Archie	Hextall, Bryan	Hextall, Dennis	Hicke, Ernie	Hicks, Doug
Hillman, Larry	Hillman, Wayne	Hirsch, Tom	Hodge, Jr., Ken	Hogaboam, Bill	Holbrook, Terry
Holmgren, Paul	Hospodar, Ed	Houck, Paul	Jackson, Don	Jarry, Pierre	Jarvis, Wes

Jensen, Dave

Jensen, Steve

Jerrard, Paul

Johnson, Jim

Johnson, Mark

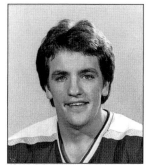

Johnston, Joey

Johnston, Marshall

Kaminski, Kevin

Klatt, Trent

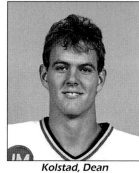

Kolstad, Dean

Labossiere, Gordie

Laird, Robbie

Langlais, Alain

Larose, Claude

Larson, Reed

Lawson, Danny

Lawton, Brian

Levie, Craig

Ludwig, Craig

Lunde, Len

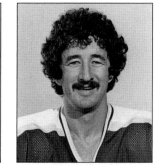

MacAdam, Al

MacDonald, Parker

MacKenzie, Barrie

MacLellen, Brian

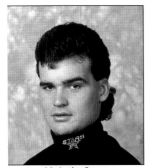

Maltais, Steve

Mandich, Dan

Manery, Kris

Mantha, Moe

Marcetta, Milan

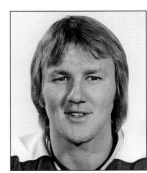

Martineau, Don

Martinson, Steve

Maruk, Dennis

Masterton, Bill

Matvichuk, Richard

Maxwell, Brad

Maxwell, Bryan

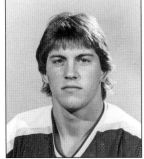

Maxwell, Kevin

McCarthy, Tom

McCaskill, Ted

McCord, Bob

McDougall, Kim

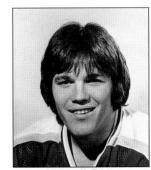

McElmury, Jim

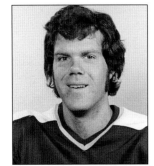

McIntosh, Bruce

McKechnie, Walt

McKegney, Tony

McKenny, Jim

McMahon, Mike

McPhee, Mike

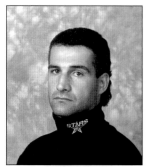
McRae, Basil

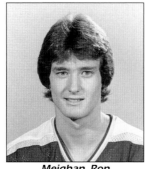
Meighan, Ron

Meissner, Barrie

Melin, Roger

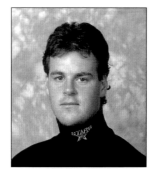
Messier, Mitch

Micheletti, Pat

Miszuk, John

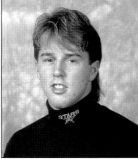
Modano, Mike

Mohns, Doug

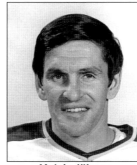
Muloin, Wayne

Murphy, Larry

Musil, Frantisek

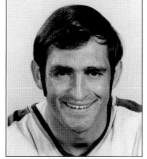
Nanne, Lou

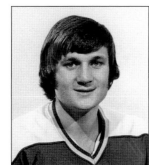
Nantais, Richard

Napier, Mark

Nevin, Bob

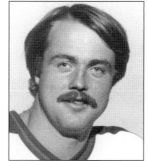
Nilsson, Kent

Norrish, Rod

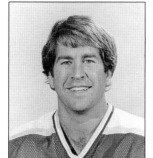
Nyrop, Bill

O'Brien, Dennis

Oliver, Murray

Orban, Bill

O'Shea, Danny

Palmer, Brad

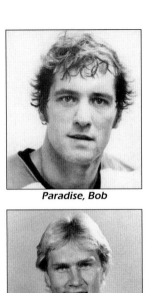
Paradise, Bob

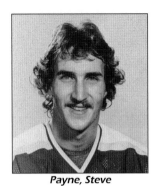
Parise, J.P.

Payne, Steve

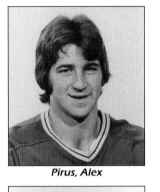
Pedersen, Allen

Pirus, Alex

Plager, Bill

Plett, Willi

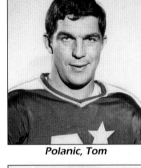
Polanic, Tom

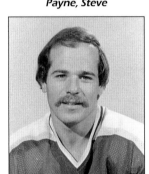
Polich, Mike

Potvin, Jean

Poulin, Dan

Prentice, Dean

Price, Pat

Pronovost, Andre

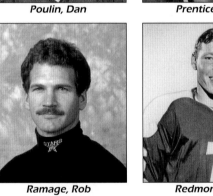
Propp, Brian

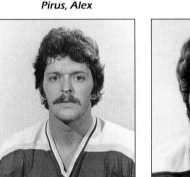
Pryor, Chris

Ramage, Rob

Redmond, Dick

Reid, Tom

Richter, Dave

Roberts, Gordie

Roberts, Jim

Rogers, Johnny

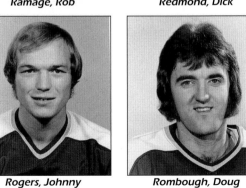
Rombough, Doug

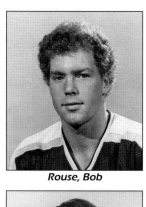
Rouse, Bob

Rousseau, Bobby

Roy, Stephane

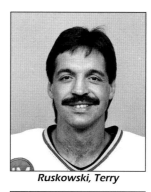
Rupp, Duane

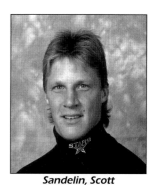
Ruskowski, Terry

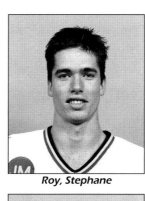
Sandelin, Scott

Sargent, Gary

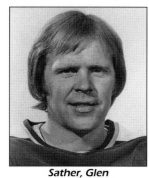
Sather, Glen

Schreiber, Wally

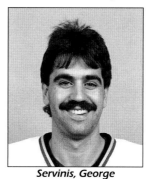
Seguin, Danny

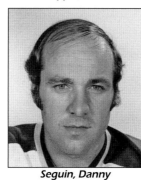
Servinis, George

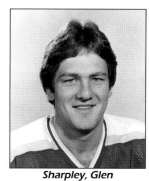
Sharpley, Glen

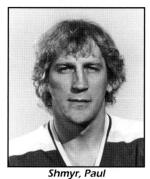
Shmyr, Paul

Sjodin, Tommy

Sly, Darryl

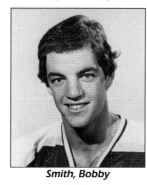
Smith, Bobby

Smith, Derrick

Smith, Greg

Snepsts, Harold

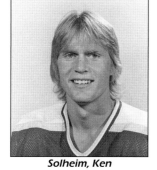
Solheim, Ken

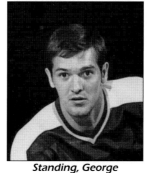
Standing, George

Stanfield, Fred

Talafous, Dean

Talbot, Jean-Guy

Taylor, Ted

Thyer, Mario

Tinordi, Mark

Tomlinson, Kirk

Toomey, Sean

Vasko, Elmer

Velischek, Randy

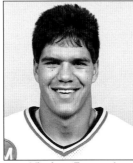
Viveiros, Emanuel

Whitlock, Bob

Wilkinson, Neil

Williams, Tommy

Wilson, Ron

Woytowich, Bob

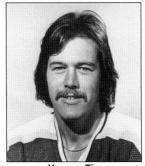
Young, Tim

Young, Warren

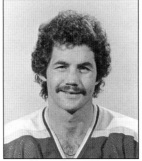
Younghans, Tom

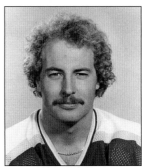
Zanussi, Ron

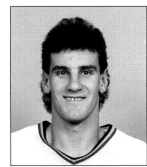
Zemlak, Richard

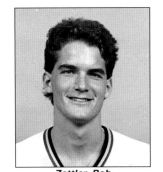
Zettler, Rob

PHOTO UNAVAILABLE

Balderis, Helmut
Barrault, Doug
Barrett, John
Berglund, Bo
Berry, Brad
Berthiaume, Daniel
Biggs, Don
Caufield, Jay
Ciccone, Enrico
Contini, Joe

Cook, Bob
Donatelli, Clark
Douglas, Jordy
Duggan, Ken
Evans, Kevin
Ferguson, George
Fontas, Jon
Hardy, Mark
Hayward, Brian
Horvath, Bronco
Janssens, Mark
Johns, Don
Keczmer, Dan

Keissling, Udo
Langevin, Dave
Lappin, Peter
Leiter, Ken
Lindgren, Lars
Mackey, Dave
MacLoed, Pat
Magee, Dean
Markell, John
Martin, Terry
Martin, Tom
McHugh, Mike
Miller, Kip

Mitchell, Roy
More, Jay
Myllys, Jarmo
Osiecki, Mark
Pasek, Dusan
Pavelich, Mark
Quinn, Dan
Robinson, Scott
Shaw, David
Sherven, Gord
Simpson, Reid
Sinisalo, Illka
Siren, Ville

Smail, Doug
Smith, Brian
Smith, Randy
Stewart, Bill
Taglianetti, Peter
Terry, Bill
Thiffault, Leo
Tuer, Al
Trimper, Tim
White, Tony

T H E   G O A L I E S

Bauman, Gary	Beaupre, Don	Broderick, Ken
Casey, Jon	Craig, Jim	Edwards, Gary
Gilbert, Gilles	Harrison, Paul	Janaszak, Steve
Levasseur, Lou	LoPresti, Pete	Maniago, Cesare
Mattson, Markus	Melanson, Roland	Meloche, Gilles
Middlebrook, Lindsay	Rivard, Fern	Sands, Mike
Smith, Gary	Takko, Kari	Wakaluk, Darcy
Wetzel, Carl	Worsley, Gump	

PLAYER STATISTICS

PLAYER / SEASONS	GP	G	A	TP	PM
KEY: GP = Games Played G = Goals A = Assists TP = Total Points PM = Penalty Minutes					
Acton, Keith '83-88	343	87	148	235	380
Ahrens, Chris '72-77	52	0	3	3	84
Andersson, Kent-Erik '77-82	322	59	68	127	56
Antonovich, Mike '75-76, '81-82	14	0	2	2	8
Archibald, Dave '87-90	162	28	44	72	46
Archibald, Jim '84-87	16	1	2	3	45
Arnason, Chuck '78-79	1	0	0	0	0
Ashton, Brent '83-85	97	11	17	28	69
Babe, Warren '87-89, '90-91	21	2	5	7	23
Baby, John '78-79	1	0	1	1	2
Balderis, Helmut '89-90	26	3	6	9	2
Balon, Dave '67-68	73	15	32	47	84
Barber, Don '88-91	74	23	24	47	44
Barlow, Bob '69-71	77	16	17	33	10
Barrault, Doug '92-93	2	0	0	0	2
Barrett, Fred '70-83	730	23	123	146	663
Barrett, John '87-88	1	0	1	1	2
Beaudin, Norm '70-71	12	0	1	1	0
Bellows, Brian '82-92	753	342	380	722	537
Bennett, Harvey '77-78	64	11	10	21	91
Berezan, Perry '88-91	132	15	22	37	65
Berger, Mike '87-89	30	3	1	4	67
Bergloff, Bob '82-83	2	0	0	0	5
Berglund, Bo '84-86	36	8	9	17	10
Bergman, Gary '73-74	57	3	23	26	66
Berry, Brad '91-93	70	0	3	3	115
Beverley, Nick '76-78	109	9	31	40	24
Bialowas, Dwight '74-77	116	8	37	45	24
Biggs, Don '84-85	1	0	0	0	0
Bjugstad, Scott '83-88	222	68	58	126	116

PLAYER / SEASONS	GP	G	A	TP	PM
Black, James '92-93	10	2	1	3	4
Blackburn, Don '72-73	4	0	0	0	4
Boh, Rick '87-88	8	2	1	3	4
Boivin, Leo '68-70	97	4	18	22	46
Boo, Jim '77-78	6	0	0	0	22
Boucha, Henry '74-75	51	15	14	29	23
Boudrias, Andre '67-69	127	22	44	66	48
Boutilier, Paul '86-87	10	2	4	6	8
Brasar, Per-Olov '77-80	167	27	79	106	12
Brooke, Bob '86-90	137	26	51	77	276
Broten, Aaron '89-90	35	9	9	18	22
Broten, Neal '80-93	876	249	547	796	459
Brumwell, Murray '80-82	22	0	3	3	18
Bureau, Marc '90-93	118	16	31	47	165
Burns, Charlie '69-73	268	27	53	80	60
Butters, Bill '77-79	72	1	4	5	77
Byers, Jerry '72-74	24	0	2	2	6
Caffery, Terry '70-71	8	0	0	0	0
Cameron, Craig '71-72, '74-76	182	20	18	38	57
Carlson, Jack '78-79, '80-82, '86-87	124	18	6	24	264
Caufield, Jay '87-88	1	0	0	0	0
Chambers, Shawn '87-91	198	15	47	62	206
Charlebois, Bob '67-68	7	1	0	1	0
Chernoff, Mike '68-69	1	0	0	0	0
Chicoine, Danny '78-80	25	1	2	3	12
Chinnick, Rick '73-75	4	0	2	2	0
Chisholm, Colin '86-87	1	0	0	0	0
Christoff, Steve '79-82	145	60	50	110	91
Churla, Shane '88-93	236	14	22	36	1,194
Ciccarelli, Dino '80-89	602	332	319	651	642
Ciccone, Enrico '91-93	42	0	1	1	163
Colley, Tom '74-75	1	0	0	0	2
Collins, Bill '67-70	220	47	30	77	113

PLAYER / SEASONS	GP	G	A	TP	PM
Connelly, Wayne '67-69	129	49	37	86	51
Contini, Joe '80-81	1	0	0	0	0
Cook, Bob '74-75	2	0	1	1	0
Coulis, Tim '83-86	28	3	3	6	111
Courtnall, Russ '92-93	84	36	41	77	49
Craig, Mike '90-93	176	48	43	91	293
Cressman, Dave '74-76	85	6	8	14	37
Cullen, Ray '67-70	208	71	91	162	70
Dahlen, Ulf '89-93	241	94	91	185	22
Dahlquist, Chris '90-92	116	3	19	22	101
DePalma, Larry '85-89, '90-91	121	18	14	32	362
Dineen, Gary '68-69	4	0	1	1	0
Dineen, Gord '87-89	15	1	2	3	23
Dobson, Jim '79-82	8	0	0	0	4
Donatelli, Clark '89-90	25	3	3	6	17
Douglas, Jordy '82-84	82	16	18	34	40
Drouin, Jude '70-75	319	79	183	262	187
Duchesne, Gaetan '89-93	297	45	45	90	185
Duggan, Ken '87-88	1	0	0	0	0
Dunlop, Blake '73-77	100	18	30	48	18
Eaves, Mike '78-83	207	55	78	133	50
Elik, Todd '91-93	108	27	50	77	173
Engele, Jerry '75-78	100	2	13	15	162
Erickson, Grant '69-70	4	0	0	0	0
Eriksson, Roland '76-78	158	46	83	129	22
Evans, Kevin '90-91	4	0	0	0	19
Fairbairn, Bill '76-78	57	9	21	30	2
Featherstone, Tony '73-74	54	9	12	21	4
Ferguson, George '82-84	128	14	22	36	33
Fidler, Mike '78-81	103	33	42	75	61
Fitzpatrick, Sandy '67-68	18	3	6	9	6
Flesch, John '74-76	90	11	17	28	94
Flockhart, Rob '79-81	12	1	3	4	2

PLAYER / SEASONS	GP	G	A	TP	PM
Fontas, Jon '79-81	2	0	0	0	0
Fraser, Curt '87-90	53	7	6	13	118
Friest, Ron '80-83	64	7	7	14	191
Gaetz, Link '88-90	17	0	2	2	86
Gagner, Dave '87-93	440	187	217	404	575
Gallimore, Jamie '77-78	2	0	0	0	0
Gambucci, Gary '71-72, '73-74	51	2	7	9	9
Gartner, Mike '88-90	80	41	43	84	34
Gavin, Stewart '88-93	289	39	47	86	232
Geldart, Gary '70-71	4	0	0	0	5
Gibbs, Barry '69-75	375	35	121	156	600
Gilchrist, Brent '92-93	8	0	1	1	2
Giles, Curt '79-86, '87-91	760	40	177	217	625
Glynn, Brian '90-92	103	10	23	33	107
Goegan, Pete '67-68	46	1	2	3	30
Goldsworthy, Bill '67-77	670	267	239	506	711
Gotaas, Steve '88-89, '90-91	13	1	3	4	8
Graham, Dirk '83-88	226	67	79	146	291
Grant, Danny '68-74	463	176	177	353	161
Gratton, Norm '74-76	66	21	15	36	22
Gronstrand, Jari '86-87	47	1	6	7	27
Habscheid, Marc '85-89	113	31	45	76	48
Hakansson, Anders '81-83	77	12	4	16	38
Hall, Murray '67-68	17	2	1	3	10
Hallin, Mats '85-87	44	3	2	5	90
Hampson, Ted '70-72	96	9	20	29	10
Hanson, Dave '79-80	22	1	1	2	39
Hardy, Mark '88-89	15	2	4	6	26
Harris, Duke '67-68	22	1	4	5	4
Harris, Ted '70-74	246	11	52	63	294
Hartsburg, Craig '79-89	570	98	315	413	818
Harvey, Buster '70-74	199	49	59	108	66
Hatcher, Derian '91-93	110	12	19	31	266

PLAYER / SEASONS	GP	G	A	TP	PM
Hayek, Peter '81-82	1	0	0	0	0
Heindl, Bill '70-72	14	1	1	2	0
Helminen, Raimo '86-87	6	0	1	1	0
Henderson, Archie '81-82	1	0	0	0	0
Hextall, Bryan '75-76	58	8	20	28	84
Hextall, Dennis '71-76	328	84	216	300	567
Hicke, Ernie '74-77	199	68	52	120	169
Hicks, Doug '74-78	300	18	48	66	224
Hillman, Larry '68-69	12	1	5	6	0
Hillman, Wayne '68-69	50	0	8	8	32
Hirsch, Tom '83-85, '87-88	31	1	7	8	30
Hodge, Jr., Ken '88-89	5	1	1	2	0
Hogaboam, Bill '75-79	109	19	25	44	26
Holbrook, Terry '72-74	43	3	6	9	4
Holmgren, Paul '83-85	27	6	8	14	84
Horvath, Bronco '67-68	14	1	6	7	4
Hospodar, Ed '85-86	43	0	2	2	91
Houck, Paul '85-88	16	1	2	3	2
Jackson, Don '77-81	27	0	7	7	41
Janssens, Mark '91-92	3	0	0	0	6
Jarry, Pierre '75-78	115	38	48	86	36
Jarvis, Wes '82-83	3	0	0	0	2
Jensen, Dave '83-86	18	0	2	2	11
Jensen, Steve '75-78	171	42	46	88	141
Jerrard, Paul '88-89	5	0	0	0	4
Johns, Don '67-68	4	0	0	0	6
Johnson, Jim '90-93	194	8	39	47	307
Johnson, Mark '81-82	10	2	2	4	10
Johnston, Joey '68-69	12	1	0	1	6
Johnston, Marshall '67-71	49	0	5	5	16
Kaminski, Kevin '88-89	1	0	0	0	0
Keczmer, Dan '90-91	9	0	1	1	6
Kiessling, Udo '81-82	1	0	0	0	2

PLAYER / SEASONS	GP	G	A	TP	PM
Klatt, Trent '91-93	48	4	19	23	38
Kolstad, Dean '88-89, '90-91	30	1	5	6	57
Labossiere, Gord '70-72	38	10	7	17	4
Laird, Robbie '79-80	1	0	0	0	0
Langevin, Dave '85-86	80	0	8	8	58
Langlais, Alain '73-75	25	4	4	8	10
Lappin, Peter '89-90	6	0	0	0	2
Larose, Claude '68-70	142	49	60	109	215
Larson, Reed '88-89	11	0	9	9	18
Lawson, Danny '68-71	96	13	16	29	25
Lawton, Brian '83-88	303	71	91	162	250
Leiter, Ken '89-90	4	0	0	0	0
Levie, Craig '83-84, '85-86	51	8	15	23	52
Lindgren, Lars '83-84	59	2	14	16	33
Ludwig, Craig '91-93	151	3	18	21	207
Lunde, Len '67-68	7	0	1	1	0
MacAdam, Al '78-84	459	138	202	340	268
MacDonald, Parker '67-69	104	21	32	53	22
MacKenzie, Barrie '68-69	6	0	1	1	6
Mackey, Dave '89-90	16	2	0	2	28
MacLellen, Brian '86-89	211	64	86	150	247
MacLeod, Pat '90-91	1	0	1	1	0
Magee, Dean '77-78	7	0	0	0	4
Maltais, Steve '91-92	12	1	2	3	2
Mandich, Dan '82-86	111	5	11	16	303
Manery, Kris '78-80	88	20	23	43	32
Mantha, Moe '87-89	46	10	19	29	14
Marcetta, Milan '67-69	54	7	15	22	10
Markell, John '84-85	1	0	0	0	0
Martin, Terry '84-85	7	1	1	2	0
Martin, Tom '88-89	4	1	1	2	4
Martineau, Don '74-75	76	6	9	15	61
Martinson, Steve '91-92	1	0	0	0	9

PLAYER / SEASONS	GP	G	A	TP	PM
Maruk, Dennis '78-79, '83-89	309	80	156	236	234
Masterton, Bill '67-68	38	4	8	12	4
Matvichuk, Richard '92-93	53	2	3	5	26
Maxwell, Brad '77-85, '86-87	471	82	217	299	1,031
Maxwell, Bryan '77-79	43	3	11	14	87
Maxwell, Kevin '80-82	18	1	7	8	15
McCarthy, Tom '79-86	385	146	187	333	293
McCaskill, Ted '67-68	4	0	2	2	0
McCord, Bob '67-69	139	7	26	33	109
McDougall, Kim '74-75	1	0	0	0	0
McElmury, Jim '72-73	7	0	1	1	2
McHugh, Mike '88-91	12	0	0	0	2
McIntosh, Bruce '72-73	2	0	0	0	0
McKechnie, Walt '67-71	112	9	13	22	77
McKegney, Tony '84-87	108	28	41	69	68
McKenny, Jim '78-79	10	1	1	2	2
McMahon, Mike '67-69	117	14	44	58	92
McPhee, Mike '92-93	84	18	22	40	44
McRae, Basil '87-92	323	32	58	90	1,567
Meighan, Ron '81-82	7	1	1	2	2
Meissner, Barrie '67-69	6	0	1	1	4
Melin, Roger '80-82	3	0	0	0	0
Messier, Mitch '87-91	20	0	2	2	11
Micheletti, Pat '87-88	12	2	0	2	8
Miller, Kip '91-92	3	1	2	3	2
Miszuk, John '69-70	50	0	6	6	51
Mitchell, Roy '92-93	3	0	0	0	0
Modano, Mike '88-93	317	123	186	309	257
Mohns, Doug '70-73	162	12	48	60	148
More, Jayson '89-90	5	0	0	0	16
Muloin, Wayne '70-71	7	0	0	0	0
Murphy, Larry '88-91	121	18	75	93	94
Musil, Frantisek '86-91	271	14	46	60	547

PLAYER / SEASONS	GP	G	A	TP	PM
Nanne, Lou '67-78	635	68	157	225	356
Nantais, Richard '74-77	63	5	4	9	79
Napier, Mark '83-85	97	23	46	69	19
Nevin, Bob '71-73	138	20	32	52	6
Nilsson, Kent '85-87	105	29	77	106	22
Norrish, Rod '73-75	21	3	3	6	2
Nyrop, Bill '81-82	42	4	8	12	35
O'Brien, Dennis '70-78	470	27	75	102	836
Oliver, Murray '70-75	371	83	118	201	62
Orban, Bill '68-70	30	1	7	8	17
O'Shea, Danny '68-71	208	39	70	109	186
Osiecki, Mark '92-93	5	0	0	0	5
Palmer, Brad '80-82	95	26	27	53	40
Paradise, Bob '71-72	6	0	0	0	6
Parise, J. P. '67-75, '78-79	588	154	242	396	509
Pasek, Dusan '88-89	48	4	10	14	30
Pavelich, Mark '86-87	12	4	6	10	10
Payne, Steve '78-88	613	228	238	466	435
Pedersen, Allen '91-92	29	0	1	1	10
Pirus, Alex '76-79	155	30	26	56	94
Plager, Bill '67-68, '73-76	60	0	5	5	61
Plett, Willi '82-87	317	70	63	133	1,137
Polanic, Tom '69-71	19	0	2	2	53
Polich, Mike '78-81	225	24	29	53	57
Potvin, Jean '78-79	64	5	16	21	65
Poulin, Dan '81-82	3	1	1	2	2
Prentice, Dean '71-74	168	48	46	94	40
Price, Pat '87-88	14	0	2	2	20
Pronovost, Andre '67-68	8	0	0	0	0
Propp, Brian '90-93	147	41	73	114	107
Pryor, Chris '84-88	62	1	4	5	67
Quinn, Dan '92-93	11	0	4	4	6
Ramage, Rob '91-92	34	4	5	9	69

PLAYER / SEASONS	GP	G	A	TP	PM
Redmond, Dick '69-71	16	0	3	3	20
Reid, Tom '68-78	615	17	106	123	617
Richter, Dave '81-86	120	4	14	18	397
Roberts, Gordie '80-88	555	33	224	257	832
Roberts, Jim '76-79	106	17	23	40	33
Robinson, Scott '89-90	1	0	0	0	2
Rogers, Johnny '73-75	14	2	4	6	0
Rombough, Doug '74-76	59	8	11	19	39
Rousseau, Bobby '70-71	63	4	20	24	12
Rouse, Bob '83-89	351	9	58	67	735
Roy, Stephane '87-88	12	1	0	1	0
Rupp, Duane '68-69	29	2	1	3	8
Ruskowski, Terry '87-89	50	6	13	19	78
Sandelin, Scott '91-92	1	0	0	0	0
Sargent, Gary '78-83	187	32	71	103	120
Sather, Glen '75-76	72	9	10	19	94
Schreiber, Wally '87-89	41	8	10	18	12
Seguin, Danny '70-71	11	1	1	2	4
Servinis, George '87-88	5	0	0	0	0
Sharpley, Glen '76-81	318	98	138	236	176
Shaw, David '91-92	37	0	7	7	49
Sherven, Gord '84-86	45	2	14	16	19
Shmyr, Paul '79-81	124	4	24	28	163
Simpson, Reid '92-93	1	0	0	0	5
Sinisalo, Ilkka '90-91	46	5	12	17	24
Siren, Ville '88-90	91	3	23	26	118
Sjodin, Tommy '92-93	77	7	29	36	30
Sly, Darryl '69-70	29	1	0	1	6
Smail, Doug '90-91	57	7	13	20	38
Smith, Bobby '78-84, '90-93	572	185	369	554	489
Smith, Brian '68-69	9	0	1	1	0
Smith, Derrick '91-92	33	2	4	6	33
Smith, Greg '78-81	209	15	61	76	376

PLAYER / SEASONS	GP	G	A	TP	PM
Smith, Randy '85-87	3	0	0	0	0
Snepsts, Harold '84-85	71	0	7	7	232
Solheim, Ken '80-83, '84-85	114	16	20	36	27
Standing, George '67-68	2	0	0	0	0
Stanfield, Fred '73-75	111	24	46	70	22
Stewart, Bill '85-86	8	0	2	2	13
Taglianetti, Pete '90-91	16	0	1	1	14
Talafous, Dean '74-78	277	61	90	151	59
Talbot, Jean-Guy '67-68	4	0	0	0	4
Taylor, Ted '67-68	31	3	5	8	34
Terry, Bill '87-88	5	0	0	0	0
Thiffault, Leo '67-68 (playoffs only)	0	0	0	0	0
Thyer, Mario '89-90	5	0	0	0	0
Tinordi, Mark '88-93	314	29	88	117	872
Tomlinson, Kirk '87-88	1	0	0	0	0
Toomey, Sean '86-87	1	0	0	0	0
Tuer, Al '87-88	6	1	0	1	29
Trimper, Tim '84-85	20	1	4	5	15
Vasko, Elmer '67-70	145	2	13	15	113
Velischek, Randy '82-85	88	6	11	17	38
Viveiros, Emanuel '85-88	29	1	11	12	6
White, Tony '79-80	6	0	0	0	4
Whitlock, Bob '69-70	1	0	0	0	0
Wilkinson, Neil '89-91	86	2	14	16	217
Williams, Tom '69-71	116	25	65	90	34
Wilson, Ron '84-88	113	19	52	71	60
Woytowich, Bob '67-68	66	4	17	21	63
Young, Tim '75-83	564	178	316	494	401
Young, Warren '81-83	5	1	1	2	0
Younghans, Tom '76-82	382	41	36	77	356
Zanussi, Ron '77-81	244	49	75	124	353
Zemlak, Richard '87-89	77	1	6	7	320
Zettler, Rob '88-91	80	1	12	13	154

GOALIE STATISTICS

GOALIE / SEASONS	GP	GA	SO	GAA	W-L-T
Bauman, Gary '67-69	27	97	0	3.64	5–13–6
Beaupre, Don '80-89	316	1,111	3	3.74	126-125-45
Berthiaume, Daniel '89-90	5	14	0	3.50	1-3-0
Broderick, Ken '69-70	7	26	0	4.33	2-4-0
Casey, Jon '83-84, '85-86, '87-93	325	988	12	3.28	128-126-42
Craig, Jim '83-84	3	9	0	4.91	1-1-0
Edwards, Gary '78-80	51	165	0	3.44	15-18-15
Gilbert, Gilles '69-73	44	143	2	3.39	16-22-5
Harrison, Paul '75-78	35	138	1	4.18	6-22-3
Hayward, Brian '90-91	26	77	2	3.14	6-15-3
Janaszak, Steve '79-80	1	2	0	2.00	0-0-1
Levasseur, Lou '79-80	1	7	0	7.00	0-1-0
LoPresti, Pete '74-79	173	660	5	4.06	43-101-20
Maniago, Cesare '67-76	420	1,283	26	3.17	143-192-71
Mattson, Markus '82-83	2	6	1	3.60	1-1-0
Melanson, Roland '84-86	26	102	0	4.17	7-11-5
Meloche, Gilles '78-85	328	1,104	9	3.51	141-117-52
Middlebrook, Lindsay '81-82	3	7	0	3.00	0-0-2
Myllys, Jarmo '88-91	12	46	0	5.85	1-9-0
Rivard, Fern '68-70, '73-75	55	190	2	3.98	9-27-10
Sands, Mike '84-87	6	26	0	5.17	0-5-0
Smith, Gary '76-78	39	148	1	3.92	10-19-9
Takko, Kari '85-91	131	438	1	3.87	33-67-14
Wakaluk, Darcy '91-93	65	201	2	3.44	23-31-6
Wetzel, Carl '67-68	5	18	0	4.02	1-3-1
Worsley, Gump '69-74	107	261	3	2.62	39-37-24

KEY: GP = Games Played GA = Goals Against SO = Shutouts
GAA = Goals-Against Average W-L-T = Wins, Losses, Ties

GOALIE SCORING AND PENALTIES

GOALIE	G	A	TP	PM	GOALIE	G	A	TP	PM
Bauman, Gary	0	0	0	2	Melanson, Roland	0	0	0	9
Beaupre, Don	0	3	3	128	Meloche, Gilles	0	4	4	37
Casey, Jon	0	11	11	112	Myllys, Jarmo	0	0	0	2
Edwards, Gary	0	1	1	26	Rivard, Fern	0	0	0	10
Gilbert, Gilles	0	0	0	6	Sands, Mike	0	0	0	2
Harrison, Paul	0	0	0	12	Smith, Gary	0	0	0	18
Hayward, Brian	0	0	0	2	Takko, Kari	0	1	1	2
LoPresti, Pete	0	3	3	6	Wakaluk, Darcy	0	3	3	40
Maniago, Cesare	0	1	1	47	Worsley, Gump	0	2	2	34

KEY: G = Goals A = Assists TP = Total Points PM = Penalty Minutes
NOTE: Goalies not listed did not record a point or a penalty.

Don Beaupre plays the puck, 12/29/84.

Rick Kolodziej

NORTH STARS TOP 10 LISTS — REGULAR SEASON

GAMES PLAYED

1.	Neal Broten	876
2.	Curt Giles	760
3.	Brian Bellows	753
4.	Fred Barrett	730
5.	Bill Goldsworthy	670
6.	Lou Nanne	635
7.	Tom Reid	615
8.	Steve Payne	613
9.	Dino Ciccarelli	602
10.	J.P. Parise	588

GOALS

1.	Brian Bellows	342
2.	Dino Ciccarelli	332
3.	Bill Goldsworthy	267
4.	Neal Broten	249
5.	Steve Payne	228
6.	Dave Gagner	187
7.	Bobby Smith	185
8.	Tim Young	178
9.	Danny Grant	176
10.	J.P. Parise	154

Barrett

North Stars archives

Broten

Rick Kolodziej

Parise, Drouin, Gibbs & Reid

Pete Hohn / Minneapolis Star Tribune

Pirus, Parise & Smith

D.R. Brewster / Minneapolis Star Tribune

Giles

Billy Robin McFarland

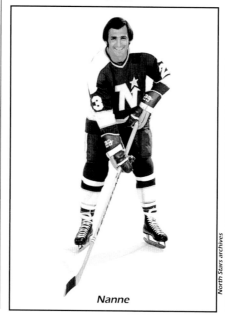

Nanne

North Stars archives

Bellows

Rick Kolodziej

Smith

North Stars archives

ASSISTS

1.	Neal Broten	547
2.	Brian Bellows	380
3.	Bobby Smith	369
4.	Dino Ciccarelli	319
5.	Tim Young	316
6.	Craig Hartsburg	315
7.	J.P. Parise	242
8.	Bill Goldsworthy	239
9.	Steve Payne	238
10.	Gordie Roberts	224

Young

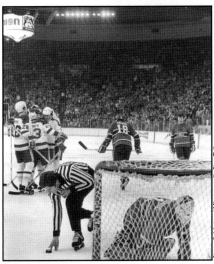

Ciccarelli

Roberts

Goldsworthy

POINTS

1.	Neal Broten	796
2.	Brian Bellows	722
3.	Dino Ciccarelli	651
4.	Bobby Smith	554
5.	Bill Goldsworthy	506
6.	Tim Young	494
7.	Steve Payne	466
8.	Craig Hartsburg	413
9.	Dave Gagner	405
10.	J.P. Parise	396

Churla

O'Brien

PENALTY MINUTES

1.	Basil McRae	1,567
2.	Shane Churla	1,194
3.	Willi Plett	1,137
4.	Brad Maxwell	1,031
5.	Mark Tinordi	872
6.	Dennis O'Brien	836
7.	Gordie Roberts	832
8.	Craig Hartsburg	818
9.	Bob Rouse	735
10.	Bill Goldsworthy	711

Maxwell

GAMES BY A GOALIE

1.	Cesare Maniago	420
2.	Gilles Meloche	328
3.	Jon Casey	325
4.	Don Beaupre	316
5.	Pete LoPresti	173
6.	Kari Takko	131
7.	Gump Worsley	107
8.	Darcy Wakaluk	65
9.	Fern Rivard	55
10.	Gary Edwards	51

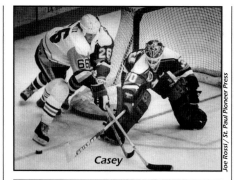
Casey

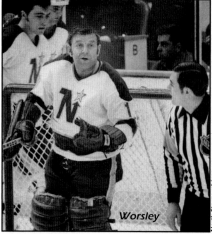
Worsley

GOALS-AGAINST AVERAGE

1.	Gump Worsley	2.62
2.	Cesare Maniago	3.17
3.	Jon Casey	3.28
4.	Gilles Gilbert	3.39
5.	Gary Edwards	3.44
tie	Darcy Wakaluk	3.44
7.	Gilles Meloche	3.51
8.	Don Beaupre	3.74
9.	Kari Takko	3.87
10.	Gary Smith	3.92

Meloche

Hextall & LoPresti

WINS BY A GOALIE

1.	Cesare Maniago	143
2.	Gilles Meloche	141
3.	Jon Casey	128
4.	Don Beaupre	126
5.	Pete LoPresti	43
6.	Gump Worsley	39
7.	Kari Takko	33
8.	Darcy Wakaluk	23
9.	Gilles Gilbert	16
10.	Gary Edwards	15

Velischek & Beaupre

Rivard

Takko

Maniago

Edwards

Gilbert

NORTH STARS ALL-TIME TEAM
Selected by Lou Nanne and Glen Sonmor

FORWARDS
Left Wing
J.P. Parise   Steve Payne   Brian Bellows
Center
Mike Modano   Bobby Smith   Neal Broten
Right Wing
Bill Goldsworthy   Al MacAdam   Dino Ciccarelli

DEFENSE PAIRINGS
Craig Hartsburg and Gary Sargent
Doug Mohns and Brad Maxwell
Ted Harris and Curt Giles

GOALIES
Gump Worsley   Cesare Maniago

ALL-TIME OPPOSITION TEAM
Selected by Lou Nanne and Glen Sonmor

FORWARDS
Wayne Gretzky   Gordie Howe   Mario Lemieux

DEFENSEMEN
Bobby Orr   Denis Potvin

GOALIES
Patrick Roy   Terry Sawchuk

UNHERALDED SUPERSTAR
Peter Stastny

AL SHAVER'S NICKNAMES

Rick Kolodziej

Axe	Gary Smith
Bat	Bill Masterton
Bazz	Basil McRae
BeeBee	Brian Bellows
Big Bird	Jack Carlson
The Bird	Wren Blair
Blah	Bobby Barlow
Bood	Andre Boudrias
Bomber	Tommy Williams
Brots	Neal Broten
Butts	Billy Butters
Cat	Andre Beaulieu
Cully	Ray Cullen
Cyclops	Glen Sonmor
Doc	trainer Dick Rose
Eaver	Mike Eaves
Frankie	Frantisek Musil
Gags	Dave Gagner
Gator	Gaetan Duchesne
Gibby	Barry Gibbs
Gilly	Gilles Gilbert and Gilles Meloche
Hartsy	Craig Hartsburg
Hexy	Dennis Hextall
Jeep	J. P. Parise
Jughead	Tommy McCarthy
Kraut	Bill Goldsworthy
Lots	Brian Lawton
Mandy	Dan Mandich
Maxie	Brad Maxwell and Bryan Maxwell
Millie	Milan Marcetta
Modo	Mike Modano
Muzz	Murray Oliver
O'Bee	Dennis O'Brien
Oly	Per-Olov Brasar
Pee Wee	Dennis Maruk
Pengy	Curt Giles
Potsy	Dino Ciccarelli
Rosie	Claude Larose
Rosko	Terry Ruskowski
Sarge	Gary Sargent
Scoop	Gary Edwards
Sharps	Glen Sharpley
Slats	Glen Sather
Slick	Nick Beverley
Smitty	Bobby Smith, Gary Smith and Greg Smith
Spud	Al MacAdam
Stork	Dean Talafous
Swoop	Freddie Barrett
Tin Man	Mark Tinordi
Tuna	Danny Grant
Woody	Keith Acton
Woyto	Bob Woytowich
Zoo	Ron Zanussi

A bench-clearing brawl breaks out at Met Center in a game against the Vancouver Canucks. The North Stars win 9-4, 3/28/78.

NORTH STARS YEAR-BY-YEAR

North Stars archives

March 14, 1971: *Donna Peterson of Albert Lea became the two-millionth fan to attend a North Stars game at Met Center. She was escorted to cer ice by team president Walter Bush for a ceremonial face-off between Phil Goyette of the Buffalo Sabres and North Star Jude Drouin. As a prize for being the historic fan, Donna and a guest were invited to join the North Stars on a road trip the following season. She and her sister attended games Montreal and Boston. While on the trip, Donna met North Star standout J.P. Parise. Four years later, J.P. and Donna became husband and wife.*

SEASON RECORDS & TEAM LEADERS

(Asterisks indicate North Star records)

1967-68

27-32-15 • 69 points • 4th Place, West Division

Goals: Wayne Connelly 35
Assists: Andre Boudrias 35
Points: Wayne Connelly 56
Penalty Minutes: Dave Balon 90
Goalie Wins: Cesare Maniago 22

Playoffs: Beat Los Angeles, 4-3 • Lost to St. Louis, 4-3

1967-68 SEASON RESULTS

GM#	DATE	OPP'T	RSLT	SCORE	RECORD	GM#	DATE	OPP'T	RSLT	SCORE	RECORD
1	10/11	@ STL	T	2-2	0-0-1	41	1/18	PHI	L	4-2	14-18-9
2	10/14	@ OAK	L	6-0	0-1-1	42	1/20	@ TOR	L	5-1	14-19-9
3	10/15	@ L.A.	L	5-3	0-2-1	43	1/21	PIT	W	4-3	15-19-9
4	10/18	@ PIT	T	3-3	0-2-2	44	1/24	@ STL	L	5-2	15-20-9
5	10/21	OAK	W	3-1	1-2-2	45	1/25	@ PHI	W	3-0	16-20-9
6	10/25	STL	W	3-2	2-2-2	46	1/27	OAK	W	3-1	17-20-9
7	10/28	CHI	L	4-2	2-3-2	47	1/28	DET	W	2-1	18-20-9
8	11/1	PIT	L	4-1	2-4-2	48	1/31	L.A	W	6-1	19-20-9
9	11/2	@ PHI	W	3-1	3-4-2	49	2/3	@ DET	L	8-1	19-21-9
10	11/4	L.A.	T	2-2	3-4-3	50	2/4	OAK	W	4-3	20-21-9
11	11/8	STL	W	5-1	4-4-3	51	2/7	@ L.A.	W	4-2	21-21-9
12	11/11	TOR	W	2-1	5-4-3	52	2/10	@ OAK	W	5-2	22-21-9
13	11/15	MTL	L	5-1	5-5-3	53	2/11	PHI	L	3-2	22-22-9
14	11/18	PHI	T	2-2	5-5-4	54	2/14	@ PIT	L	6-3	22-23-9
15	11/19	@ NYR	L	5-2	5-6-4	55	2/15	NYR	L	6-2	22-24-9
16	11/22	@ TOR	L	3-0	5-7-4	56	2/17	STL	T	2-2	22-24-10
17	11/25	CHI	L	4-1	5-8-4	57	2/21	BOS	W	5-3	23-24-10
18	11/26	@ CHI	L	2-1	5-9-4	58	2/22	@ PHI	L	7-3	23-25-10
19	11/29	@ BOS	L	5-1	5-10-4	59	2/24	@ DET	L	3-1	23-26-10
20	11/30	@ MTL	T	1-1	5-10-5	60	2/25	OAK	T	3-3	23-26-11
21	12/2	@ STL	W	5-1	6-10-5	61	2/28	@ OAK	L	6-3	23-27-11
22	12/3	@ CHI	W	4-3	7-10-5	62	3/2	MTL	L	3-2	24-27-11
23	12/6	TOR	T	1-1	7-10-6	63	3/7	PIT	T	2-2	24-27-12
24	12/9	PIT	L	3-2	7-11-6	64	3/9	NYR	T	1-1	24-27-13
25	12/10	@ PIT	W	7-4	8-11-6	65	3/10	@ PHI	L	2-0	24-28-13
26	12/13	L.A.	W	4-0	9-11-6	66	3/13	PHI	L	4-2	24-29-13
27	12/15	@ L.A.	W	3-0	10-11-6	67	3/16	L.A.	L	2-1	24-30-13
28	12/16	@ OAK	W	1-0	11-11-6	68	3/17	DET	W	5-1	25-30-13
29	12/21	@ PHI	L	6-0	11-12-6	69	3/20	@ L.A.	T	3-3	25-30-14
30	12/23	@ PIT	L	4-0	11-13-6	70	3/23	PIT	W	3-0	26-30-14
31	12/25	STL	L	1-0	11-14-6	71	3/24	@ PIT	T	4-4	26-30-15
32	12/27	@ NYR	T	3-3	11-14-7	72	3/27	@ LA	W	5-3	27-30-15
33	12/28	@ MTL	L	6-2	11-15-7	73	3/30	@ STL	L	3-2	27-31-15
34	12/30	BOS	W	5-4	12-15-7	74	3/31	STL	L	5-3	27-32-15
35	1/3	L.A.	W	6-0	13-15-7						
36	1/6	@ OAK	T	5-5	13-15-8						
37	1/10	PHI	W	6-4	14-15-8						
38	1/13	OAK	T	2-2	14-15-9						
39	1/14	@ BOS	L	9-2	14-16-9						
40	1/17	@ STL	L	5-0	14-17-9						

1968-69 SEASON RESULTS

GM#	DATE	OPP'T	RSLT	SCORE	RECORD	GM#	DATE	OPP'T	RSLT	SCORE	RECORD
1	10/11	@ OAK	W	5-1	1-0-0	41	1/11	PHI	L	4-2	9-25-7
2	10/16	@ CHI	L	10-4	1-1-0	42	1/12	STL	L	2-0	9-26-7
3	10/17	MTL	L	3-1	1-2-0	43	1/15	PIT	L	3-1	9-27-7
4	10/19	L.A.	W	4-1	2-2-0	44	1/16	@ BOS	L	5-1	9-28-7
5	10/22	OAK	L	3-2	2-3-0	45	1/19	STL	L	3-1	9-29-7
6	10/24	@ PHI	T	3-3	2-3-1	46	1/23	@ PIT	W	3-1	10-29-7
7	10/26	NYR	L	3-0	2-4-1	47	1/25	L.A.	W	3-2	11-29-7
8	10/30	BOS	L	4-2	2-5-1	48	1/26	@ BOS	L	4-3	11-30-7
9	11/2	@ STL	W	2-0	3-5-1	49	1/29	@ MTL	L	4-0	11-31-7
10	11/3	@ NYR	L	2-1	3-6-1	50	2/1	CHI	T	5-5	11-31-8
11	11/6	TOR	L	1-0	3-7-1	51	2/2	@ PHI	W	3-2	12-31-8
12	11/7	@ DET	L	5-2	3-8-1	52	2/5	@ TOR	T	5-5	12-31-9
13	11/9	DET	W	6-4	4-8-1	53	2/8	MTL	L	6-3	12-32-9
14	11/13	PHI	W	4-3	5-8-1	54	2/9	PIT	W	3-1	13-32-9
15	11/16	L.A	W	3-2	6-8-1	55	2/12	@ TOR	L	7-1	13-33-9
16	11/17	@ STL	T	3-3	6-8-2	56	2/15	DET	W	6-2	14-33-9
17	11/20	CHI	L	2-0	6-9-2	57	2/16	@ STL	L	6-0	14-34-9
18	11/23	@ MTL	L	4-3	6-10-2	58	2/19	L.A	W	7-4	15-34-9
19	11/24	@ CHI	L	6-0	6-11-2	59	2/23	TOR	W	7-2	16-34-9
20	11/27	OAK	T	3-3	6-11-3	60	2/24	@ L.A.	T	1-1	16-34-10
21	11/30	@ TOR	T	3-3	6-11-4	61	2/26	@ OAK	L	6-5	16-35-10
22	12/1	@ BOS	L	4-0	6-12-4	62	3/1	DET	L	4-2	16-36-10
23	12/4	TOR	L	4-2	6-13-4	63	3/3	@ CHI	L	6-1	16-37-10
24	12/7	@ L.A.	L	3-2	6-14-4	64	3/5	OAK	W	5-2	17-37-10
25	12/8	@ OAK	W	4-1	7-14-4	65	3/9	STL	T	2-2	17-37-11
26	12/11	PIT	L	4-2	7-15-4	66	3/11	BOS	T	3-3	17-37-12
27	12/14	NYR	W	4-1	8-15-4	67	3/13	@ MTL	T	4-4	17-37-13
28	12/15	@ DET	L	5-2	8-16-4	68	3/15	PHI	T	2-2	17-37-14
29	12/17	OAK	L	3-2	8-17-4	69	3/16	@ STL	W	3-2	18-37-14
30	12/19	@ PHI	T	5-5	8-17-5	70	3/19	NYR	L	4-2	18-38-14
31	12/21	@ PIT	W	3-1	9-17-5	71	3/20	@ PHI	L	5-2	18-39-14
32	12/22	@ NYR	L	4-2	9-18-5	72	3/22	PHI	L	5-1	18-40-14
33	12/25	STL	L	2-0	9-19-5	73	3/23	@ PIT	L	5-0	18-41-14
34	12/26	L.A.	T	4-4	9-19-6	74	3/25	PIT	L	3-1	18-42-14
35	12/28	CHI	L	5-2	9-20-6	75	3/29	@ OAK	L	7-2	18-43-14
36	12/31	@ DET	L	6-3	9-21-6	76	3/30	@ L.A	T	3-3	18-43-15
37	1/4	BOS	T	2-2	9-21-7						
38	1/5	@ NYR	L	5-1	9-22-7						
39	1/7	MTL	L	6-3	9-23-7						
40	1/9	@ PIT	L	7-2	9-24-7						

1968-69

18-43-15 • 51 points • 6th Place, West Division

Goals: Danny Grant 34
Assists: Ray Cullen 38
Points: Danny Grant 65
Penalty Minutes: Bill Goldsworthy 151
Goalie Wins: Cesare Maniago 18

No Playoffs

1969-70

19-35-22* • 60 points • 3rd Place, West Division

Goals: Bill Goldsworthy 36
Assists: Tom Williams 52
Points: J.P. Parise 72
Penalty Minutes: Barry Gibbs 182
Goalie Wins: Cesare Maniago 9

Playoffs: Lost to St. Louis, 4-2

1969-70 SEASON RESULTS

GM#	DATE	OPP'T	RSLT	SCORE	RECORD	GM#	DATE	OPP'T	RSLT	SCORE	RECORD
1	10/11	PHI	W	4-0	1-0-0	41	1/18	PHI	L	4-2	10-17-14
2	10/15	@NYR	L	4-3	1-1-0	42	1/24	PHI	L	6-0	10-18-14
3	10/16	@DET	W	3-2	2-1-0	43	1/25	OAK	L	4-1	10-19-14
4	10/18	@STL	L	4-2	2-2-0	44	1/28	@MTL	L	5-4	10-20-14
5	10/19	@CHI	W	4-1	3-2-0	45	1/29	@BOS	L	6-5	10-21-14
6	10/22	BOS	L	3-2	3-3-0	46	1/31	TOR	L	4-2	10-22-14
7	10/25	PIT	L	4-1	3-4-0	47	2/1	@CHI	L	7-4	10-23-14
8	10/29	MTL	W	4-1	4-4-0	48	2/4	PIT	L	7-5	10-24-14
9	11/1	@PIT	L	6-3	4-5-0	49	2/7	MTL	T	1-1	10-24-15
10	11/2	@PHI	L	6-2	4-6-0	50	2/8	@PIT	L	6-3	10-25-15
11	11/5	@MTL	T	2-2	4-6-1	51	2/11	@OAK	L	2-1	10-26-15
12	11/8	STL	W	5-2	5-6-1	52	2/14	CHI	L	5-2	10-27-15
13	11/12	PHI	W	4-2	6-6-1	53	2/15	STL	T	3-3	10-27-16
14	11/15	DET	T	2-2	6-6-2	54	2/18	STL	T	1-1	10-27-17
15	11/19	OAK	L	4-2	6-7-2	55	2/19	@CHI	L	3-2	10-28-17
16	11/20	@STL	L	3-1	6-8-2	56	2/21	BOS	L	4-2	10-29-17
17	11/22	L.A.	W	4-1	7-8-2	57	2/25	L.A.	T	3-3	10-29-18
18	11/26	PIT	T	4-4	7-8-3	58	2/28	@PHI	L	6-2	10-30-18
19	11/29	@TOR	L	5-2	7-9-3	59	3/1	TOR	W	8-0	11-30-18
20	11/30	@NYR	T	2-2	7-9-4	60	3/4	PHI	T	2-2	11-30-19
21	12/3	TOR	T	5-5	7-9-5	61	3/7	@TOR	W	8-3	12-30-19
22	12/6	@MTL	W	4-3	8-9-5	62	3/8	@DET	T	2-2	12-30-20
23	12/7	@BOS	T	2-2	8-9-6	63	3/11	STL	L	9-1	12-31-20
24	12/10	CHI	W	8-5	9-9-6	64	3/14	PIT	W	6-3	13-31-20
25	12/11	@DET	T	2-2	9-9-7	65	3/15	@NYR	W	4-2	14-31-20
26	12/13	NYR	L	5-2	9-10-7	66	3/17	@STL	T	5-5	14-31-21
27	12/15	@L.A.	T	4-4	9-10-8	67	3/18	DET	L	6-2	14-32-21
28	12/17	@OAK	L	3-1	9-11-8	68	3/21	BOS	W	5-4	15-32-21
29	12/20	@L.A.	T	3-3	9-11-9	69	3/22	@BOS	L	5-0	15-33-21
30	12/23	@STL	L	5-3	9-12-9	70	3/24	OAK	T	2-2	15-33-22
31	12/25	CHI	T	4-4	9-12-10	71	3/25	@PIT	L	2-0	15-34-22
32	12/27	OAK	L	5-3	9-13-10	72	3/28	@L.A.	L	4-2	15-35-22
33	12/30	@L.A.	T	0-0	9-13-11	73	3/29	@OAK	W	8-3	16-35-22
34	1/3	NYR	T	3-3	9-13-12	74	3/31	L.A.	W	5-2	17-35-22
35	1/4	@PHI	L	3-1	9-14-12	75	4/4	@PHI	W	1-0	18-35-22
36	1/7	@TOR	T	3-3	9-14-13	76	4/5	@PIT	W	5-1	19-35-22
37	1/10	L.A.	L	6-4	9-15-13						
38	1/14	STL	W	5-2	10-15-13						
39	1/15	@OAK	T	1-1	10-15-14						
40	1/17	NYR	L	3-1	10-16-14						

1970-71 SEASON RESULTS

GM#	DATE	OPP'T	RSLT	SCORE	RECORD	GM#	DATE	OPP'T	RSLT	SCORE	RECORD
1	10/10	@PHI	L	2-1	0-1-0	41	1/10	@CHI	W	3-2	14-19-8
2	10/15	PIT	W	4-2	1-1-0	42	1/14	MTL	T	3-3	14-19-9
3	10/17	DET	L	3-2	1-2-0	43	1/16	BUF	L	4-3	14-20-9
4	10/18	@DET	W	2-1	2-2-0	44	1/17	@DET	W	2-0	15-20-9
5	10/21	@MTL	W	3-1	3-2-0	45	1/21	STL	W	5-3	16-20-9
6	10/24	NYR	L	4-1	3-3-0	46	1/23	PHI	T	2-2	16-20-10
7	10/28	CHI	L	4-3-0	47	1/24	@NYR	L	6-2	16-21-10
8	10/31	@TOR	W	3-1	5-3-0	48	1/27	@CAL	L	6-2	16-22-10
9	11/1	@BOS	L	5-0	5-4-0	49	1/29	@VAN	W	2-1	17-22-10
10	11/4	MTL	L	4-3	5-5-0	50	1/31	CAL	W	7-1	18-22-10
11	11/7	STL	T	1-1	5-5-1	51	2/3	DET	T	4-4	18-22-11
12	11/8	@CHI	T	3-3	5-5-2	52	2/6	CHI	L	6-2	18-23-11
13	11/11	L.A.	W	3-1	6-5-2	53	2/7	@BOS	T	4-4	18-23-12
14	11/14	VAN	T	3-3	6-5-3	54	2/10	@NYR	L	4-3	18-24-12
15	11/17	@STL	W	5-3	7-5-3	55	2/11	@MTL	L	6-2	18-25-12
16	11/18	BOS	L	8-4	7-6-3	56	2/13	PHI	T	2-2	18-25-13
17	11/21	BUF	W	3-0	8-6-3	57	2/14	PIT	W	5-4	19-25-13
18	11/22	@NYR	L	2-0	8-7-3	58	2/17	CAL	W	3-2	20-25-13
19	11/24	@VAN	L	3-2	8-8-3	59	2/18	@DET	L	5-3	20-26-13
20	11/27	@CAL	W	3-2	9-8-3	60	2/21	TOR	L	4-1	20-27-13
21	11/28	@L.A.	W	3-2	10-8-3	61	2/24	L.A.	W	5-1	21-27-13
22	12/2	CAL	W	3-2	11-8-3	62	2/25	@TOR	T	1-1	21-27-14
23	12/5	CHI	L	4-1	11-9-3	63	2/27	DET	L	4-2	22-27-14
24	12/6	@BUF	L	1-0	11-10-3	64	2/28	@BUF	L	5-2	22-28-14
25	12/9	PIT	T	2-2	11-10-4	65	3/2	BOS	L	6-0	22-29-14
26	12/10	@MTL	L	6-1	11-11-4	66	3/6	VAN	W	3-1	23-29-14
27	12/12	@PIT	W	1-0	12-11-4	67	3/7	PHI	W	3-1	24-29-14
28	12/13	@CHI	L	5-2	12-12-4	68	3/10	STL	W	4-0	25-29-14
29	12/15	@STL	L	2-1	12-13-4	69	3/13	@PIT	T	0-0	25-29-15
30	12/16	MTL	T	1-1	12-13-5	70	3/14	BUF	L	5-0	25-30-15
31	12/19	NYR	L	5-3	12-14-5	71	3/16	@L.A.	W	7-2	26-30-15
32	12/20	@BOS	L	7-2	12-15-5	72	3/21	@VAN	W	6-3	27-30-15
33	12/25	TOR	W	6-3	13-15-5	73	3/23	L.A.	W	3-1	28-30-15
34	12/26	@STL	T	1-1	13-15-6	74	3/25	@PHI	T	2-2	28-30-16
35	12/30	BOS	L	6-2	13-16-6	75	3/28	@BUF	L	4-2	28-31-16
36	12/31	@PIT	L	4-1	13-17-6	76	3/30	VAN	L	2-1	28-32-16
37	1/2	@L.A.	T	3-3	13-17-7	77	3/31	@CAL	L	4-1	28-33-16
38	1/5	TOR	L	2-0	13-18-7	78	4/3	@PHI	L	3-2	28-34-16
39	1/6	@TOR	T	4-4	13-18-8						
40	1/9	NYR	L	1-0	13-19-8						

1970-71

28-34-16 • 72 points • 4th Place, West Division

Goals: Bill Goldsworthy and Danny Grant 34
Assists: Jude Drouin 52
Points: Jude Drouin 68
Penalty Minutes: Barry Gibbs 132
Goalie Wins: Cesare Maniago 19

Playoffs: Beat St. Louis, 4-2 • Lost to Montreal, 4-2

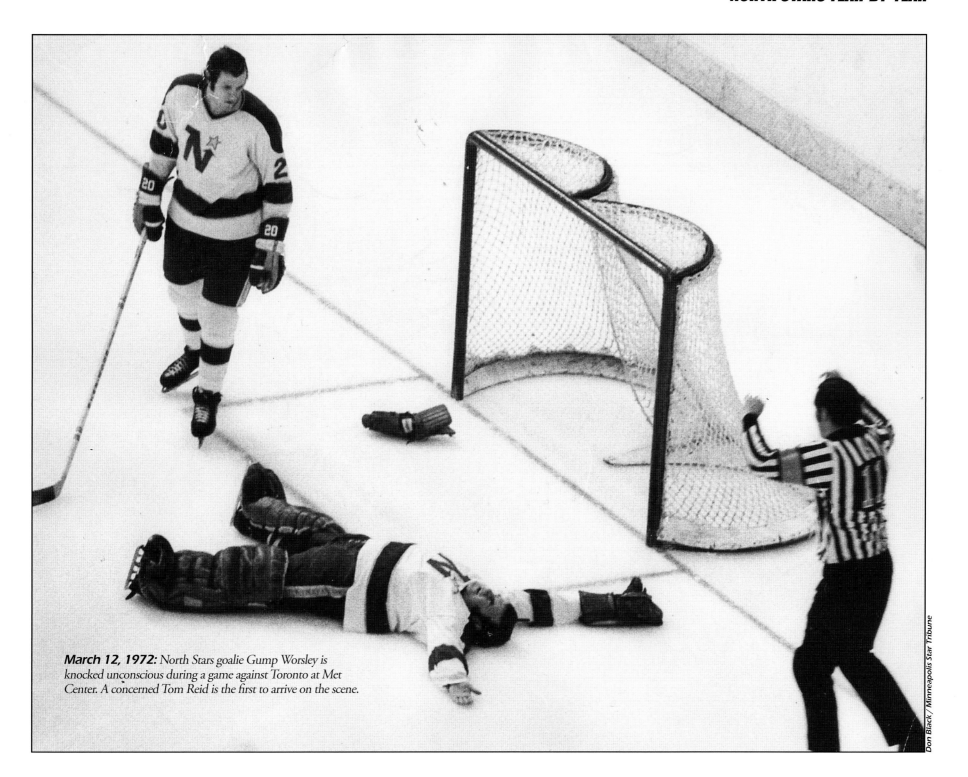

March 12, 1972: North Stars goalie Gump Worsley is knocked unconscious during a game against Toronto at Met Center. A concerned Tom Reid is the first to arrive on the scene.

Don Black / Minneapolis Star Tribune

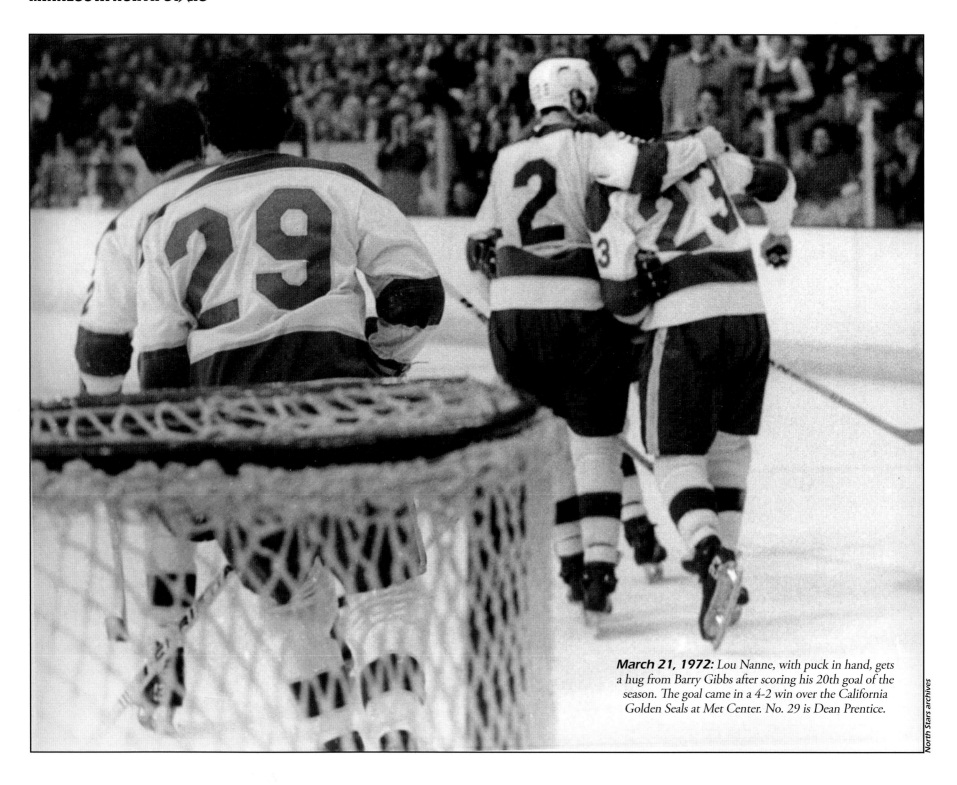

March 21, 1972: Lou Nanne, with puck in hand, gets a hug from Barry Gibbs after scoring his 20th goal of the season. The goal came in a 4-2 win over the California Golden Seals at Met Center. No. 29 is Dean Prentice.

1971-72 GAME RESULTS

GM#	DATE	OPP'T	RSLT	SCORE	RECORD
1	10/9	@DET	W	4-2	1-0-0
2	10/14	MTL	T	1-1	1-0-1
3	10/16	CHI	L	3-2	1-1-1
4	10/17	@BUF	W	3-2	2-1-1
5	10/20	VAN	W	7-0	3-1-1
6	10/23	BUF	W	5-1	4-1-1
7	10/24	@L.A.	W	6-3	5-1-1
8	10/27	@STL	W	2-1	6-1-1
9	10/28	PIT	W	2-0	7-1-1
10	10/30	@TOR	T	1-1	7-1-2
11	10/31	@BOS	L	5-2	7-2-2
12	11/3	TOR	W	2-1	8-2-2
13	11/6	STL	W	5-1	9-2-2
14	11/7	@PHI	W	3-0	10-2-2
15	11/10	DET	L	2-1	10-3-2
16	11/13	MTL	L	5-1	10-4-2
17	11/16	@PIT	W	5-1	11-4-2
18	11/18	PIT	W	4-3	12-4-2
19	11/20	NYR	W	4-1	13-4-2
20	11/21	@PHI	T	1-1	13-4-3
21	11/23	@VAN	W	2-1	14-4-3
22	11/26	@CAL	W	2-1	15-4-3
23	11/27	@L.A.	W	3-1	16-4-3
24	12/1	CAL	W	4-1	17-4-3
25	12/4	PHI	W	3-1	18-4-3
26	12/5	@BUF	L	3-1	18-5-3
27	12/8	@TOR	L	3-1	18-6-3
28	12/11	@MTL	L	4-3	18-7-3
29	12/12	@CHI	L	5-3	18-8-3
30	12/15	STL	W	4-1	19-8-3
31	12/18	CHI	L	4-1	19-9-3
32	12/19	@NYR	T	1-1	19-9-4
33	12/21	L.A.	W	3-2	20-9-4
34	12/25	NYR	L	2-1	20-10-4
35	12/26	@DET	L	5-1	20-11-4
36	12/30	BOS	T	2-2	20-11-5
37	1/1	@L.A.	W	3-2	21-11-5
38	1/5	DET	W	4-2	22-11-5
39	1/8	VAN	L	5-1	22-12-5
40	1/11	@VAN	T	2-2	22-12-6
41	1/12	@CAL	L	2-0	22-13-6
42	1/15	@STL	L	7-2	22-14-6
43	1/16	@CHI	L	3-2	22-15-6
44	1/18	CAL	T	1-1	22-15-7
45	1/19	@DET	W	4-1	23-15-7
46	1/22	TOR	W	4-1	24-15-7
47	1/23	L.A.	W	5-3	25-15-7
48	1/27	@MTL	W	6-5	26-15-7
49	1/29	NYR	W	4-2	27-15-7
50	1/30	@NYR	T	1-1	27-15-8
51	2/2	@TOR	L	3-2	27-16-8
52	2/3	@BOS	L	6-1	27-17-8
53	2/5	BUF	T	3-3	27-17-9
54	2/6	CHI	L	5-0	27-18-9
55	2/9	L.A.	W	4-1	28-18-9
56	2/10	@STL	W	3-1	29-18-9
57	2/12	PHI	W	5-1	30-18-9
58	2/16	DET	W	4-2	31-18-9
59	2/19	BOS	L	6-4	31-19-9
60	2/20	PIT	W	2-0	32-19-9
61	2/24	MTL	L	4-2	32-20-9
62	2/26	STL	L	3-2	32-21-9
63	3/2	@PHI	L	3-0	32-22-9
64	3/4	@PIT	L	4-2	32-23-9
65	3/5	CHI	W	2-1	33-23-9
66	3/8	BOS	L	5-4	33-24-9
67	3/12	TOR	T	2-2	33-24-10
68	3/14	BUF	L	4-3	33-25-10
69	3/16	VAN	W	6-2	34-25-10
70	3/18	@MTL	L	4-3	34-26-10
71	3/19	@BOS	L	7-3	34-27-10
72	3/21	CAL	W	4-2	35-27-10
73	3/23	@BUF	T	4-4	35-27-11
74	3/25	@PIT	L	3-2	35-28-11
75	3/26	@NYR	W	5-0	36-28-11
76	3/28	PHI	T	2-2	36-28-12
77	3/31	@CAL	W	2-1	37-28-12
78	4/2	@VAN	L	4-1	37-29-12

1971-72

37-29-12 • 86 points • 2nd Place, West Division

Goals: Bill Goldsworthy 31
Assists: Jude Drouin 43
Points: Bill Goldsworthy 62
Penalty Minutes: Barry Gibbs 128
Goalie Wins: Cesare Maniago 20

Playoffs: Lost to St. Louis, 4-3

September 13, 1972:
The North Stars begin training camp with a jog through the concourse of Met Center.

Richard Olsenius / Minneapolis Star Tribune

1972-73

37-30-11 • 85 points • 3rd Place, West Division

Goals: Danny Grant 32
Assists: Dennis Hextall 52
Points: Dennis Hextall 82
Penalty Minutes: Dennis Hextall 140
Goalie Wins: Cesare Maniago 21

Playoffs: Lost to Philadelphia, 4-2

1972-73 SEASON RESULTS

GM#	DATE	OPP'T	RSLT	SCORE	RECORD
1	10/7	@MTL	L	3-0	0-1-0
2	10/11	CAL	W	5-2	1-1-0
3	10/14	VAN	T	3-3	1-1-1
4	10/15	@NYR	L	6-2	1-2-1
5	10/18	@ATL	W	6-0	2-2-1
6	10/21	ATL	L	3-2	2-3-1
7	10/24	@STL	W	2-1	3-3-1
8	10/25	TOR	L	4-3	3-4-1
9	10/28	PHI	W	2-1	4-4-1
10	10/29	@BUF	L	2-1	4-5-1
11	11/1	STL	T	3-3	4-5-2
12	11/4	CHI	W	5-3	5-5-2
13	11/8	CAL	W	5-2	6-5-2
14	11/10	@ATL	L	5-1	6-6-2
15	11/11	NYI	W	3-0	7-6-2
16	11/14	L.A.	W	4-1	8-6-2
17	11/15	@PIT	L	7-1	8-7-2
18	11/18	@TOR	T	4-4	8-7-3
19	11/19	@CHI	W	5-1	9-7-3
20	11/22	TOR	W	3-1	10-7-3
21	11/25	@L.A.	W	3-0	11-7-3
22	11/26	@VAN	W	3-1	12-7-3
23	11/29	ATL	W	5-0	13-7-3
24	12/2	BUF	W	8-6	14-7-3
25	12/3	@BUF	L	7-4	14-8-3
26	12/6	@MTL	L	6-3	14-9-3
27	12/7	@PHI	L	6-2	14-10-3
28	12/9	DET	W	7-0	15-10-3
29	12/10	@CHI	L	5-1	15-11-3
30	12/13	PHI	W	7-2	16-11-3
31	12/16	NYR	W	5-1	17-11-3
32	12/17	@DET	L	6-4	17-12-3
33	12/20	@CAL	W	5-2	18-12-3
34	12/23	@NYI	L	4-2	18-13-3
35	12/27	MTL	W	3-2	19-13-3
36	12/29	BOS	L	2-0	19-14-3
37	12/31	@DET	T	4-4	19-14-4
38	1/6	CHI	L	2-0	19-15-4
39	1/8	@MTL	T	3-3	19-15-5
40	1/10	MTL	L	6-0	19-16-5
41	1/11	@BOS	T	1-1	19-16-6
42	1/13	NYI	W	8-1	20-16-6
43	1/16	@NYI	W	1-0	21-16-6
44	1/18	@PHI	L	6-1	21-17-6
45	1/20	CHI	T	3-3	21-17-7
46	1/21	@DET	W	5-3	22-17-7
47	1/23	L.A.	T	5-5	22-17-8
48	1/25	@BUF	L	5-2	22-18-8
49	1/28	@CHI	L	5-1	22-19-8
50	2/1	@ATL	L	3-1	22-20-8
51	2/3	@PIT	L	2-1	22-21-8
52	2/4	PIT	W	4-3	23-21-8
53	2/7	BOS	L	3-2	23-22-8
54	2/8	@STL	L	3-2	23-23-8
55	2/10	DET	W	3-1	24-23-8
56	2/11	VAN	W	6-3	25-23-8
57	2/14	STL	W	5-2	26-23-8
58	2/17	BOS	W	5-2	27-23-8
59	2/18	@PHI	L	5-1	27-24-8
60	2/21	STL	L	5-2	27-25-8
61	2/24	BUF	W	4-2	28-25-8
62	2/25	@NYR	L	6-5	28-26-8
63	2/28	CAL	W	7-3	29-26-8
64	3/3	ATL	W	3-0	30-26-8
65	3/4	@PIT	W	5-2	31-26-8
66	3/7	PIT	W	10-4	32-26-8
67	3/10	@TOR	L	4-3	32-27-8
68	3/11	NYI	W	2-1	33-27-8
69	3/13	L.A.	T	2-2	33-27-9
70	3/15	TOR	W	5-2	34-27-9
71	3/17	@L.A.	W	4-3	35-27-9
72	3/18	@CAL	L	2-0	35-28-9
73	3/20	NYR	L	6-1	35-29-9
74	3/22	@BOS	L	5-3	35-30-9
75	3/25	@NYR	W	2-1	36-30-9
76	3/27	VAN	W	4-3	37-30-9
77	3/28	@STL	T	3-3	37-30-10
78	3/30	@VAN	T	3-3	37-30-11

1973-74 SEASON RESULTS

GM#	DATE	OPP'T	RSLT	SCORE	RECORD
1	10/10	MTL	L	5-2	0-1-0
2	10/13	BUF	L	4-3	0-2-0
3	10/14	@CHI	T	1-1	0-2-1
4	10/17	PIT	L	4-2	0-3-1
5	10/18	@DET	T	4-4	0-3-2
6	10/20	STL	T	4-4	0-3-3
7	10/23	@TOR	T	2-2	0-3-4
8	10/25	@NYI	T	1-1	0-3-5
9	10/27	@MTL	L	4-2	0-4-5
10	10/28	@BOS	T	3-3	0-4-6
11	10/31	BOS	L	5-0	0-5-6
12	11/3	CHI	W	5-4	1-5-6
13	11/7	LA	W	5-2	2-5-6
14	11/10	DET	L	4-2	2-6-6
15	11/13	@PIT	L	5-2	2-7-6
16	11/14	VAN	W	6-3	3-7-6
17	11/17	NYR	L	6-3	3-8-6
18	11/21	MTL	L	4-3	3-9-6
19	11/22	@STL	L	2-1	3-10-6
20	11/24	CAL	W	6-3	4-10-6
21	11/28	@CAL	L	5-1	4-11-6
22	11/30	@VAN	W	5-4	5-11-6
23	12/1	@L.A.	T	1-1	5-11-7
24	12/6	TOR	L	4-1	5-12-7
25	12/8	DET	W	3-0	6-12-7
26	12/9	@CHI	L	5-3	6-13-7
27	12/11	L.A.	W	6-3	7-13-7
28	12/13	@BOS	L	4-2	7-14-7
29	12/15	BUF	W	4-3	8-14-7
30	12/19	ATL	W	4-2	9-14-7
31	12/22	@L.A.	L	5-2	9-15-7
32	12/23	@CAL	T	2-2	9-15-8
33	12/26	NYI	W	1-0	10-15-8
34	12/28	@VAN	W	5-3	11-15-8
35	12/30	@NYR	W	4-3	11-16-8
36	1/2	PIT	W	8-4	12-16-8
37	1/5	PHI	T	3-3	12-16-9
38	1/6	@DET	W	9-6	12-17-9
39	1/9	DET	T	2-2	12-17-10
40	1/10	@PHI	L	7-4	12-18-10
41	1/12	NYI	L	4-3	12-19-10
42	1/15	@STL	W	5-3	13-19-10
43	1/17	@MTL	L	6-1	13-20-10
44	1/19	TOR	W	5-3	14-20-10
45	1/23	@L.A.	L	3-1	14-21-10
46	1/25	@VAN	W	5-4	15-21-10
47	1/27	@CAL	T	2-2	15-21-11
48	1/31	@TOR	L	3-1	15-22-11
49	2/2	NYR	L	3-1	15-23-11
50	2/3	@NYR	T	5-5	15-23-12
51	2/5	@NYI	L	6-2	15-24-12
52	2/6	MTL	W	4-3	16-24-12
53	2/9	@TOR	W	4-1	16-25-12
54	2/10	@BOS	L	4-0	16-26-12
55	2/13	VAN	T	3-3	16-26-13
56	2/16	@STL	W	4-2	17-26-13
57	2/17	CAL	W	7-1	18-26-13
58	2/20	BOS	T	5-5	18-26-14
59	2/23	ATL	L	5-3	18-27-14
60	2/27	CHI	L	3-1	18-28-14
61	2/28	@PHI	T	2-2	18-28-15
62	3/2	NYR	L	3-1	18-29-15
63	3/6	BUF	T	4-4	18-29-16
64	3/8	@ATL	L	3-1	18-30-16
65	3/10	STL	W	8-1	19-30-16
66	3/13	ATL	W	5-1	20-30-16
67	3/16	PHI	L	4-2	20-31-16
68	3/17	@BUF	L	5-2	20-32-16
69	3/19	CAL	W	6-3	21-32-16
70	3/23	PIT	W	5-1	22-32-16
71	3/24	@CHI	L	6-0	22-33-16
72	3/26	L.A.	W	5-1	23-33-16
73	3/27	@PIT	T	3-3	23-33-17
74	3/30	@ATL	L	4-1	23-34-17
75	3/31	@BUF	L	6-1	23-35-17
76	4/2	PHI	L	6-3	23-36-17
77	4/6	@NYI	L	4-2	23-37-17
78	4/7	@PHI	L	6-2	23-38-17

1973-74

23-38-17 • 63 points • 7th Place, West Division

Goals: Bill Goldsworthy 48
Assists: Dennis Hextall 62
Points: Dennis Hextall 82
Penalty Minutes: Dennis O'Brien 166
Goalie Wins: Cesare Maniago 12

No Playoffs

1974-75 SEASON RESULTS

GM#	DATE	OPP'T	RSLT	SCORE	RECORD	GM#	DATE	OPP'T	RSLT	SCORE	RECORD
1	10/9	PIT	L	4-2	0-1-0	41	1/15	NYR	L	5-3	11-25-5
2	10/12	WSH	W	6-0	1-1-0	42	1/18	@STL	L	5-4	11-26-5
3	10/16	VAN	T	1-1	1-1-1	43	1/19	@DET	T	4-4	11-26-6
4	10/19	BUF	L	2-1	1-2-1	44	1/23	MTL	L	7-0	11-27-6
5	10/20	@CHI	L	6-0	1-3-1	45	1/25	K.C.	W	4-1	12-27-6
6	10/22	@VAN	W	3-2	2-3-1	46	1/28	@NYI	L	6-2	12-28-6
7	10/25	@ATL	T	2-2	2-3-2	47	1/29	NYI	L	4-3	12-29-6
8	10/26	@NYI	L	4-0	2-4-2	48	2/1	@K.C.	W	3-2	13-29-6
9	10/30	BOS	T	3-3	2-4-3	49	2/2	ATL	L	5-3	13-30-6
10	11/3	@BOS	L	10-1	2-5-3	50	2/5	CHI	L	2-1	13-31-6
11	11/4	@MTL	L	6-1	2-6-3	51	2/6	@BOS	L	3-2	13-32-6
12	11/6	@TOR	L	7-4	2-7-3	52	2/8	PHI	W	5-0	14-32-6
13	11/7	@PHI	L	2-0	2-8-3	53	2/9	@ATL	W	3-2	15-32-6
14	11/9	TOR	W	7-5	3-8-3	54	2/12	NYI	L	4-2	15-33-6
15	11/13	DET	W	7-4	4-8-3	55	2/15	NYR	L	9-2	15-34-6
16	11/14	@BUF	L	5-3	4-9-3	56	2/16	CAL	W	8-4	16-34-6
17	11/16	K.C.	W	3-1	5-9-3	57	2/19	ATL	L	4-2	16-35-6
18	11/18	@MTL	L	9-4	5-10-3	58	2/22	VAN	W	4-1	17-35-6
19	11/21	STL	W	3-2	6-10-3	59	2/23	@K.C.	L	4-2	17-36-6
20	11/23	CAL	W	3-1	7-10-3	60	2/25	TOR	L	9-2	17-37-6
21	11/24	@WSH	T	4-4	7-10-4	61	2/26	@CAL	W	3-1	18-37-6
22	11/27	WSH	W	6-4	8-10-4	62	3/1	@L.A.	L	7-4	18-38-6
23	11/30	CHI	W	5-3	9-10-4	63	3/4	VAN	W	6-4	19-38-6
24	12/1	@CHI	L	3-0	9-11-4	64	3/5	PHI	L	9-2	19-39-6
25	12/3	@VAN	L	6-5	9-12-4	65	3/8	@TOR	L	5-3	19-40-6
26	12/4	@L.A.	L	4-1	9-13-4	66	3/9	STL	L	5-4	19-41-6
27	12/6	@CAL	L	5-3	9-14-4	67	3/12	@ATL	L	9-4	19-42-6
28	12/8	@BUF	L	5-0	9-15-4	68	3/15	CHI	L	5-2	19-43-6
29	12/10	MTL	L	5-3	9-16-4	69	3/16	DET	W	4-3	20-43-6
30	12/12	@PHI	L	6-0	9-17-4	70	3/18	L.A.	L	5-3	20-44-6
31	12/14	BUF	W	4-2	10-17-4	71	3/20	@WSH	W	5-1	21-44-6
32	12/18	@NYR	L	7-0	10-18-4	72	3/22	@PHI	L	4-0	21-45-6
33	12/21	PIT	W	8-7	11-18-4	73	3/23	NYI	T	3-3	21-45-7
34	12/26	@DET	T	4-4	11-18-5	74	3/25	K.C.	W	2-1	22-45-7
35	12/28	@STL	L	4-2	11-19-5	75	3/26	@NYR	W	4-2	23-45-7
36	12/30	NYR	L	8-1	11-20-5	76	3/29	@STL	L	2-1	23-46-7
37	1/2	@PIT	L	6-3	11-21-5	77	3/30	@PIT	L	4-1	23-47-7
38	1/4	BOS	L	8-0	11-22-5	78	4/1	STL	L	7-3	23-48-7
39	1/6	@K.C.	L	5-2	11-23-5	79	4/4	@VAN	L	4-1	23-49-7
40	1/8	L.A.	L	4-2	11-24-5	80	4/6	@CHI	L	3-0	23-50-7

1974-75

23-50-7 • 53 points • 4th Place, Smythe Division

Goals: Bill Goldsworthy 37
Assists: Dennis Hextall 57
Points: Dennis Hextall 74
Penalty Minutes: Dennis Hextall 147
Goalie Wins: Cesare Maniago 11

No Playoffs

October 1975: *Pete LoPresti, Tom Reid, Lou Nanne and Ernie Hicke pose with a few of their fans at the "Welcome North Stars" luncheon.*

1975-76

20-53*-7 • 47 points
4th Place, Smythe Division

Goals: Bill Goldsworthy 24
Assists: Dennis Hextall 35
Points: Tim Young 51
Penalty Minutes: Dennis O'Brien 187
Goalie Wins: Cesare Maniago 13

No Playoffs

January 28, 1976: Dennis Hextall and Bill Goldsworthy (background) create a stir in front of the Kansas City Scouts' net. Keeping an eye on Hextall are goalie Denis Herron and defenseman Jean-Guy Legace. The North Stars win 9-3. (This is the final Met Center appearance of the Kansas City Scouts before they move to Denver and become the Colorado Rockies. At the start of the 1982-83 season, the Rockies become the New Jersey Devils.).

1975-76 SEASON RESULTS

GM#	DATE	OPP'T	RSLT	SCORE	RECORD	GM#	DATE	OPP'T	RSLT	SCORE	RECORD
1	10/8	VAN	L	3-2	0-1-0	41	1/14	TOR	L	6-5	13-26-2
2	10/11	PHI	L	9-5	0-2-0	42	1/17	WSH	W	7-3	14-26-2
3	10/15	CAL	W	4-1	1-2-0	43	1/18	@ BUF	L	4-1	14-27-2
4	10/18	CHI	L	3-1	1-3-0	44	1/21	VAN	W	5-1	15-27-2
5	10/19	@ CHI	L	3-2	1-4-0	45	1/23	@ VAN	L	8-3	15-28-2
6	10/22	@ CAL	L	4-2	1-5-0	46	1/25	@ PIT	T	1-1	15-28-3
7	10/24	@ VAN	L	4-2	1-6-0	47	1/27	@ NYI	L	4-3	15-29-3
8	10/26	@ L.A.	L	4-2	1-7-0	48	1/28	K.C.	W	9-3	16-29-3
9	10/29	K.C.	W	2-0	2-7-0	49	1/31	PHI	T	3-3	16-29-4
10	11/1	PIT	W	7-3	3-7-0	50	2/1	@ NYR	L	3-2	16-30-4
11	11/5	STL	L	4-1	3-8-0	51	2/4	@ DET	L	5-0	16-31-4
12	11/7	@ ATL	L	3-2	3-9-0	52	2/7	BUF	L	4-3	16-32-4
13	11/9	@ CHI	L	3-0	3-10-0	53	2/8	@ TOR	L	4-1	16-33-4
14	11/11	@ MTL	L	6-0	3-11-0	54	2/11	BOS	L	5-2	16-34-4
15	11/13	@ BOS	L	6-0	3-12-0	55	2/14	DET	L	3-2	16-35-4
16	11/15	NYR	L	5-2	3-13-0	56	2/15	CAL	L	7-3	16-36-4
17	11/18	@ STL	W	5-1	4-13-0	57	2/17	@ L.A.	L	2-1	16-37-4
18	11/19	MTL	L	6-0	4-14-0	58	2/18	@ CAL	L	6-3	16-38-4
19	11/22	ATL	L	6-3	4-15-0	59	2/20	@ VAN	L	7-0	16-39-4
20	11/26	NYI	L	9-1	4-16-0	60	2/22	@ K.C.	W	6-3	17-39-4
21	11/29	WSH	W	5-3	5-16-0	61	2/24	NYI	L	7-2	17-40-4
22	12/3	TOR	W	3-1	6-16-0	62	2/26	@ PHI	L	3-2	17-41-4
23	12/6	K.C.	W	4-0	7-16-0	63	2/28	NYR	W	5-3	18-41-4
24	12/7	@ PHI	L	6-1	7-17-0	64	3/1	@ TOR	L	4-2	18-42-4
25	12/9	@ NYI	L	6-0	7-18-0	65	3/2	PIT	L	6-2	18-43-4
26	12/11	@ K.C.	W	5-3	8-18-0	66	3/6	@ PIT	L	5-0	18-44-4
27	12/13	CHI	W	2-1	9-18-0	67	3/7	VAN	L	4-3	18-45-4
28	12/14	@ WSH	T	4-4	9-18-1	68	3/10	ATL	L	4-1	18-46-4
29	12/17	ATL	W	3-2	10-18-1	69	3/13	CHI	L	4-1	18-47-4
30	12/18	@ BUF	L	5-2	10-19-1	70	3/14	BUF	L	8-2	18-48-4
31	12/20	DET	W	5-3	11-19-1	71	3/16	@ NYI	W	3-1	19-48-4
32	12/21	@ NYR	L	2-0	11-20-1	72	3/17	@ NYR	L	3-1	19-49-4
33	12/26	@ WSH	T	1-1	11-20-2	73	3/21	L.A.	T	4-4	19-49-5
34	12/27	@ MTL	L	2-1	11-21-2	74	3/23	PHI	T	3-3	19-49-6
35	12/29	L.A.	W	2-1	12-21-2	75	3/24	@ K.C.	W	4-1	20-49-6
36	12/31	BOS	L	6-1	12-22-2	76	3/27	@ STL	L	6-3	20-50-6
37	1/3	@ STL	L	3-2	12-23-2	77	3/28	@ CHI	L	5-3	20-51-6
38	1/7	MTL	L	2-1	12-24-2	78	3/30	STL	L	5-3	20-52-6
39	1/8	@ DET	L	5-0	12-25-2	79	4/2	@ ATL	L	4-2	20-53-6
40	1/10	STL	W	2-0	13-25-2	80	4/4	@ BOS	T	2-2	20-53-7

1976-77 SEASON RESULTS

GM#	DATE	OPP'T	RSLT	SCORE	RECORD	GM#	DATE	OPP'T	RSLT	SCORE	RECORD
1	10/6	@NYR	L	6-5	0-1-0	41	1/12	@VAN	L	5-3	10-22-9
2	10/7	@BOS	L	6-2	0-2-0	42	1/15	@BOS	T	3-3	10-22-10
3	10/9	COL	W	4-1	1-2-0	43	1/16	@PHI	L	4-2	10-23-10
4	10/12	NYR	L	10-4	1-3-0	44	1/18	@NYI	L	7-2	10-24-10
5	10/16	BUF	L	2-1	1-4-0	45	1/20	ATL	T	4-4	10-24-11
6	10/17	@CHI	L	3-0	1-5-0	46	1/22	BUF	W	4-3	11-24-11
7	10/20	ATL	W	4-3	2-5-0	47	1/23	TOR	L	5-2	11-25-11
8	10/22	@COL	T	3-3	2-5-1	48	1/26	@L.A.	W	3-2	12-25-11
9	10/23	CHI	W	4-3	3-5-1	49	1/29	@VAN	L	4-3	12-26-11
10	10/27	@TOR	W	5-3	4-5-1	50	1/30	@COL	L	4-2	12-27-11
11	10/30	TOR	L	5-1	4-6-1	51	2/2	@PIT	L	5-2	12-28-11
12	10/31	@PHI	L	9-1	4-7-1	52	2/5	VAN	T	5-5	12-28-12
13	11/3	MTL	L	5-2	4-8-1	53	2/6	@CHI	W	3-0	13-28-12
14	11/6	@NYI	L	5-2	4-9-1	54	2/9	COL	L	8-6	13-29-12
15	11/7	@WSH	L	4-1	4-10-1	55	2/12	DET	T	2-2	13-29-13
16	11/10	PIT	W	3-2	5-10-1	56	2/13	@BUF	L	6-2	13-30-13
17	11/13	NYI	L	3-2	5-11-1	57	2/15	@WSH	T	3-3	13-30-14
18	11/14	@BUF	T	4-4	5-11-2	58	2/17	WSH	T	4-4	13-30-15
19	11/17	CLV	T	3-3	5-11-3	59	2/19	CHI	W	6-2	14-30-15
20	11/19	@MTL	L	6-3	5-12-3	60	2/20	@COL	L	3-2	14-31-15
21	11/20	@TOR	L	8-3	5-13-3	61	2/23	BOS	W	2-1	15-31-15
22	11/24	STL	L	4-2	5-14-3	62	2/25	@ATL	L	6-2	15-32-15
23	11/27	WSH	W	6-1	6-14-3	63	2/26	VAN	W	3-0	16-32-15
24	11/28	@NYR	L	4-1	6-15-3	64	3/1	PHI	L	5-2	16-33-15
25	12/1	PHI	T	2-2	6-15-4	65	3/5	COL	W	6-3	17-33-15
26	12/4	NYR	L	11-4	6-16-4	66	3/6	STL	W	3-2	18-33-15
27	12/7	@PIT	L	6-2	6-17-4	67	3/8	@NYI	W	3-1	19-33-15
28	12/8	ATL	L	5-0	6-18-4	68	3/9	@NYR	L	6-4	19-34-15
29	12/10	@ATL	T	3-3	6-18-5	69	3/12	@STL	T	3-3	19-34-16
30	12/11	@STL	T	1-1	6-18-6	70	3/13	NYI	T	5-5	19-34-17
31	12/14	PHI	T	3-3	6-18-7	71	3/16	MTL	L	5-2	19-35-17
32	12/18	VAN	L	3-1	6-19-7	72	3/18	@CLV	T	2-2	19-35-18
33	12/21	CHI	T	3-3	6-19-8	73	3/20	DET	W	2-1	20-35-18
34	12/22	@CLV	L	4-3	6-20-8	74	3/22	PIT	L	4-2	20-36-18
35	12/28	L.A.	W	8-3	7-20-8	75	3/26	@CHI	L	7-2	20-37-18
36	12/30	@MTL	T	5-5	7-20-9	76	3/28	STL	W	5-4	21-37-18
37	1/1	@STL	L	3-1	7-21-9	77	3/29	CLV	W	4-2	22-37-18
38	1/5	L.A.	W	5-2	8-21-9	78	3/31	@DET	W	3-1	23-37-18
39	1/6	@DET	W	7-2	9-21-9	79	4/2	@L.A.	L	7-2	23-38-18
40	1/8	BOS	W	3-1	10-21-9	80	4/3	@VAN	L	6-3	23-39-18

1976-77

23-39-18 • 64 points • 2nd Place, Smythe Division

Goals: Ernie Hicke 30
Assists: Tim Young 66
Points: Tim Young 95
Penalty Minutes: Dennis O'Brien 116
Goalie Wins: Pete LoPresti 13

Playoffs: Lost to Buffalo, 2-0

North Stars archives

1977-78

18-53*-9 • 45 points
5th Place, Smythe Division

Goals: Tim Young 23
Assists: Roland Eriksson 39
Points: Roland Eriksson 60
Penalty Minutes: Jerry Engele 105
Goalie Wins: Pete LoPresti 12

No Playoffs

September 23, 1977:
The North Stars defense takes a break during training camp. Left to right: Nick Beverley, Lou Nanne, Doug Hicks, Dennis O'Brien, Fred Barrett, Tom Reid.

1977-78 SEASON RESULTS

GM#	DATE	OPP'T	RSLT	SCORE	RECORD	GM#	DATE	OPP'T	RSLT	SCORE	RECORD
1	10/12	@MTL	L	7-3	0-1-0	41	1/14	@STL	L	5-2	9-27-5
2	10/15	VAN	L	5-3	0-2-0	42	1/18	NYI	L	5-2	9-28-5
3	10/19	@ATL	L	5-1	0-3-0	43	1/21	CHI	L	4-1	9-29-5
4	10/20	CLV	L	7-4	0-4-0	44	1/22	ATL	L	4-3	9-30-5
5	10/22	DET	L	4-2	0-5-0	45	1/26	@BUF	W	2-1	10-30-5
6	10/23	@BUF	L	4-1	0-6-0	46	1/28	CLV	L	2-1	10-31-5
7	10/26	BOS	W	3-0	1-6-0	47	1/29	@WSH	W	4-0	11-31-5
8	10/27	@DET	L	3-1	1-7-0	48	1/31	@ATL	L	7-4	11-32-5
9	10/29	WSH	W	7-4	2-7-0	49	2/1	@PIT	L	6-1	11-33-5
10	11/2	NYI	W	3-2	3-7-0	50	2/4	BUF	L	4-2	11-34-5
11	11/5	CHI	L	5-2	3-8-0	51	2/8	@NYR	L	3-0	11-35-5
12	11/7	@MTL	W	5-3	4-8-0	52	2/11	VAN	W	3-2	12-35-5
13	11/9	@CHI	T	2-2	4-8-1	53	2/12	COL	T	3-3	12-35-6
14	11/11	@VAN	L	4-2	4-9-1	54	2/16	@PHI	W	4-2	13-35-6
15	11/12	@L.A.	T	2-2	4-9-2	55	2/18	@TOR	L	5-4	13-36-6
16	11/16	PIT	W	7-4	5-9-2	56	2/19	@WSH	L	2-1	13-37-6
17	11/19	PHI	L	7-2	5-10-2	57	2/22	L.A.	W	4-1	14-37-6
18	11/22	@ATL	L	4-2	5-11-2	58	2/24	COL	L	3-2	14-38-6
19	11/23	NYI	L	9-2	5-12-2	59	2/25	@VAN	L	5-1	14-39-6
20	11/26	COL	T	4-4	5-12-3	60	2/28	@STL	L	7-1	14-40-6
21	11/29	ATL	W	4-3	6-12-3	61	3/1	STL	L	3-2	14-41-6
22	12/1	@BOS	L	4-2	6-13-3	62	3/4	DET	L	3-1	14-42-6
23	12/3	NYR	L	4-0	6-14-3	63	3/5	@DET	L	4-3	14-43-6
24	12/4	@NYR	T	4-4	6-14-4	64	3/8	CHI	L	4-3	14-44-6
25	12/6	@NYI	L	4-2	6-15-4	65	3/11	@STL	T	1-1	14-44-7
26	12/7	@TOR	L	6-3	6-16-4	66	3/13	MTL	L	5-2	14-45-7
27	12/10	BUF	L	4-2	6-17-4	67	3/16	@BOS	L	7-2	14-46-7
28	12/11	@CHI	L	8-3	6-18-4	68	3/17	@CLV	T	4-4	14-46-8
29	12/14	MTL	W	3-2	7-18-4	69	3/19	NYR	T	7-7	14-46-9
30	12/16	TOR	L	8-5	7-19-4	70	3/21	PIT.	W	7-1	15-46-9
31	12/17	@COL	L	5-1	7-20-4	71	3/23	L.A.	L	3-1	15-47-9
32	12/21	@L.A.	L	8-1	7-21-4	72	3/25	PHI	L	4-3	15-48-9
33	12/23	@VAN	W	7-5	8-21-4	73	3/26	@NYI	L	6-3	15-49-9
34	12/27	STL	W	1-0	9-21-4	74	3/28	VAN	W	9-4	16-49-9
35	12/29	@PHI	L	5-2	9-22-4	75	3/29	@CLV	L	7-3	16-50-9
36	1/4	NYR	L	5-3	9-23-4	76	4/1	@COL	L	4-2	16-51-9
37	1/7	BOS	L	3-1	9-24-4	77	4/4	COL	W	5-3	17-51-9
38	1/8	STL	L	3-1	9-25-4	78	4/5	@PIT	L	7-2	17-52-9
39	1/11	TOR	L	4-3	9-26-4	79	4/8	@CHI	L	4-2	17-53-9
40	1/13	WSH	T	2-2	9-26-5	80	4/9	@PHI	W	3-1	18-53-9

1978-79

28-40-12 • 68 points • 4th Place, Adams Division

Goals: Bobby Smith 30
Assists: Bobby Smith 44
Points: Bobby Smith 74
Penalty Minutes: Greg Smith 147
Goalie Wins: Gilles Meloche 20

No Playoffs

1978-79 SEASON RESULTS

GM#	DATE	OPP'T	RSLT	SCORE	RECORD	GM#	DATE	OPP'T	RSLT	SCORE	RECORD
1	10/11	@ MTL	L	5-2	0-1-0	41	1/13	CHI	W	4-3	15-21-5
2	10/14	BUF	L	5-2	0-2-0	42	1/15	@ NYR	W	8-1	16-21-5
3	10/18	VAN	W	7-2	1-2-0	43	1/16	@ PIT	L	5-0	16-22-5
4	10/19	@ CHI	L	6-2	1-3-0	44	1/19	@ COL	L	5-3	16-23-5
5	10/21	@ DET	T	4-4	1-3-1	45	1/20	COL	T	3-3	16-23-6
6	10/25	BOS	T	2-2	1-3-2	46	1/24	TOR	T	2-2	16-23-7
7	10/28	COL	L	1-0	1-4-2	47	1/27	PHI	W	3-1	17-23-7
8	11/1	STL	W	9-1	2-4-2	48	1/28	@ BUF	W	3-1	18-23-7
9	11/4	BUF	W	2-1	3-4-2	49	1/30	@ NYI	W	5-4	19-23-7
10	11/5	@ BUF	L	2-1	3-5-2	50	2/1	DET	W	6-1	20-23-7
11	11/7	@ NYI	L	5-2	3-6-2	51	2/3	BUF	L	2-1	20-24-7
12	11/8	@ NYR	W	5-3	4-6-2	52	2/4	TOR	W	6-4	21-24-7
13	11/10	@ VAN	W	3-2	5-6-2	53	2/14	VAN	W	8-1	22-24-7
14	11/11	@ L.A.	L	8-1	5-7-2	54	2/15	@ PIT	L	6-5	22-25-7
15	11/15	WSH	L	3-2	5-8-2	55	2/17	BOS	T	3-3	22-25-8
16	11/18	NYR	L	7-2	5-9-2	56	2/18	@ PHI	L	3-2	22-26-8
17	11/19	@ BUF	L	9-2	5-10-2	57	2/21	TOR	W	5-1	23-26-8
18	11/22	NYI	L	4-1	5-11-2	58	2/23	@ ATL	T	2-2	23-26-9
19	11/24	@ PHI	L	4-3	5-12-2	59	2/24	ATL	L	6-3	23-27-9
20	11/25	L.A.	L	4-1	5-13-2	60	2/28	NYR	T	4-4	23-27-10
21	11/29	TOR	L	5-3	5-14-2	61	3/1	@ BUF	T	5-5	23-27-11
22	12/1	@ ATL	W	4-3	6-14-2	62	3/3	@ BOS	L	5-0	23-28-11
23	12/2	ATL	W	5-3	7-14-2	63	3/4	@ WSH	L	5-4	23-29-11
24	12/6	L.A.	W	4-0	8-14-2	64	3/7	DET	W	5-1	24-29-11
25	12/9	COL	W	3-0	9-14-2	65	3/10	BOS	L	4-3	24-30-11
26	12/10	@ BOS	T	4-4	9-14-3	66	3/11	@ STL	L	8-2	24-31-11
27	12/13	MTL	L	3-2	9-15-3	67	3/14	MTL	W	4-3	25-31-11
28	12/15	@ WSH	W	6-1	10-15-3	68	3/17	@ TOR	L	6-4	25-32-11
29	12/16	BUF	L	5-2	10-16-3	69	3/18	NYI	L	5-3	25-33-11
30	12/19	VAN	W	5-3	11-16-3	70	3/21	PHI	W	7-3	26-33-11
31	12/20	@ TOR	L	4-2	11-17-3	71	3/24	@ COL	W	3-1	27-33-11
32	12/23	PIT	W	5-3	12-17-3	72	3/25	@ VAN	L	2-1	27-34-11
33	12/26	@ STL	W	6-4	13-17-3	73	3/27	PIT	L	5-1	27-35-11
34	12/27	WSH	W	6-1	14-17-3	74	3/29	@ BOS	L	7-4	27-36-11
35	12/30	@ COL	L	7-2	14-18-3	75	3/31	@ TOR	L	6-2	27-37-11
36	1/3	STL	T	3-3	14-18-4	76	4/1	@ DET	L	3-1	27-38-11
37	1/6	BOS	L	5-2	14-19-4	77	4/3	CHI	W	4-3	28-38-11
38	1/8	@ MTL	L	3-1	14-20-4	78	4/4	@ CHI	L	7-1	28-39-11
39	1/10	@ TOR	T	2-2	14-20-5	79	4/6	@ VAN	T	2-2	28-39-12
40	1/11	@ BOS	L	6-4	14-21-5	80	4/7	@ L.A.	L	7-1	28-40-12

1979-80 SEASON RESULTS

GM#	DATE	OPP'T	RSLT	SCORE	RECORD	GM#	DATE	OPP'T	RSLT	SCORE	RECORD
1	10/11	HFD	W	4-1	1-0-0	41	1/16	STL	W	7-3	22-11-8
2	10/13	CHI	W	5-1	2-0-0	42	1/19	DET	L	5-4	22-12-8
3	10/14	@ BUF	W	5-4	3-0-0	43	1/21	@ BOS	L	3-0	22-13-8
4	10/17	@ TOR	L	6-2	3-1-0	44	1/23	@ QUE	L	6-4	22-14-8
5	10/19	@ WPG	L	3-2	3-2-0	45	1/26	L.A.	T	4-4	22-14-9
6	10/21	@ EDM	T	5-5	3-2-1	46	1/27	@ CHI	L	3-0	22-15-9
7	10/24	STL	W	5-2	4-2-1	47	1/29	@ NYI	T	2-2	22-15-10
8	10/27	NYR	W	7-2	5-2-1	48	1/31	@ PHI	L	4-2	22-16-10
9	10/31	@ DET	W	5-3	6-2-1	49	2/2	VAN	L	5-4	22-17-10
10	11/1	@ MTL	L	5-1	6-3-1	50	2/3	COL	W	6-2	23-17-10
11	11/3	WSH	W	7-1	7-3-1	51	2/9	@ PIT	W	5-2	24-17-10
12	11/6	@ VAN	T	7-7	7-3-2	52	2/10	@ HFD	W	6-2	25-17-10
13	11/9	@ COL	W	6-5	8-3-2	53	2/13	EDM	L	5-3	25-18-10
14	11/10	@ L.A.	T	6-6	8-3-3	54	2/16	ATL	T	2-2	25-18-11
15	11/14	QUE	W	7-2	9-3-3	55	2/18	QUE	W	6-2	26-18-11
16	11/17	BUF	L	4-2	9-4-3	56	2/19	@ ATL	T	4-4	26-18-12
17	11/18	@ CHI	T	3-3	9-4-4	57	2/21	@ NYI	W	5-2	27-18-12
18	11/21	NYI	W	3-1	10-4-4	58	2/23	NYR	W	6-3	28-18-12
19	11/24	DET	T	3-3	10-4-5	59	2/24	@ DET	L	7-5	28-19-12
20	11/25	@ BUF	L	6-2	10-5-5	60	2/26	VAN	W	5-4	29-19-12
21	11/28	@ NYR	T	4-4	10-5-6	61	2/28	@ MTL	L	6-3	29-20-12
22	11/29	@ PHI	L	6-4	10-6-6	62	3/1	CHI	L	4-1	29-21-12
23	12/1	WPG	T	4-4	10-6-7	63	3/2	BUF	T	2-2	29-21-13
24	12/5	EDM	W	6-1	11-6-7	64	3/5	@ QUE	T	3-3	29-21-14
25	12/8	ATL	W	4-1	12-6-7	65	3/8	PHI	L	6-2	29-22-14
26	12/12	@ WSH	W	5-4	13-6-7	66	3/9	@ NYR	L	4-2	29-23-14
27	12/14	@ ATL	L	3-2	13-7-7	67	3/12	MTL	L	4-3	29-24-14
28	12/15	@ STL	W	3-1	14-7-7	68	3/15	@ PIT	L	5-2	29-25-14
29	12/17	TOR	W	5-1	15-7-7	69	3/16	@ HFD	W	6-1	30-25-14
30	12/19	MTL	W	5-2	16-7-7	70	3/18	PIT	W	4-3	31-25-14
31	12/26	WPG	W	6-0	17-7-7	71	3/19	BOS	W	7-4	32-25-14
32	12/27	@ COL	L	4-3	17-8-7	72	3/21	@ WSH	W	4-3	33-25-14
33	12/29	@ L.A.	L	4-3	17-9-7	73	3/23	COL	W	7-1	34-25-14
34	12/31	PIT	W	4-2	18-9-7	74	3/25	TOR	W	7-2	35-25-14
35	1/2	BOS	W	2-1	19-9-7	75	3/28	@ WPG	W	2-1	36-25-14
36	1/5	WSH	T	2-2	19-9-8	76	3/30	@ VAN	L	5-3	36-26-14
37	1/7	PHI	W	7-1	20-9-8	77	4/1	NYI	T	1-1	36-26-15
38	1/9	HFD	W	6-2	21-9-8	78	4/2	@ EDM	T	1-1	36-26-16
39	1/12	L.A.	L	6-5	21-10-8	79	4/5	@ TOR	L	2-1	36-27-16
40	1/15	@ STL	L	2-1	21-11-8	80	4/6	@ BOS	L	4-2	36-28-16

1979-80

36-28-16 • 88 points • 3rd Place, Adams Division

Goals: Al MacAdam and Steve Payne 42
Assists: Bobby Smith 56
Points: Al MacAdam 93
Penalty Minutes: Brad Maxwell 126
Goalie Wins: Gilles Meloche 27

Playoffs: Beat Toronto, 3-0 • Beat Montreal, 4-3 • Lost to Philadelphia, 4-1

1980-81

35-28-17 • 87 points • 3rd Place, Adams Division

Goals: Steve Payne 30
Assists: Bobby Smith 64
Points: Bobby Smith 93
Penalty Minutes: Greg Smith 128
Goalie Wins: Don Beaupre 18

Playoffs: Beat Boston, 3-0 • Beat Buffalo, 4-1 • Beat Calgary, 4-2
Lost to New York Islanders, 4-1 (Stanley Cup Finals)

1980-81 SEASON RESULTS

GM#	DATE	OPP'T	RSLT	SCORE	RECORD	GM#	DATE	OPP'T	RSLT	SCORE	RECORD
1	10/11	HFD	W	9-3	1-0-0	41	1/12	@BOS	L	4-3	20-11-10
2	10/15	BOS	W	3-2	2-0-0	42	1/14	@BUF	T	1-1	20-11-11
3	10/17	@COL	T	5-5	2-0-1	43	1/17	QUE	W	7-1	21-11-11
4	10/18	@CGY	L	6-2	2-1-1	44	1/19	MTL	W	6-3	22-11-11
5	10/22	QUE	W	4-2	3-1-1	45	1/21	@WSH	W	2-1	23-11-11
6	10/24	@EDM	W	4-2	4-1-1	46	1/22	@PHI	L	5-4	23-12-11
7	10/25	WPG	W	4-1	5-1-1	47	1/24	EDM	W	6-1	24-12-11
8	10/29	STL	T	2-2	5-1-2	48	1/26	CGY	W	3-2	25-12-11
9	11/1	PIT	W	6-3	6-1-2	49	1/28	@PIT	L	3-1	25-13-11
10	11/2	CGY	W	8-3	7-1-2	50	1/29	@DET	T	3-3	25-13-12
11	11/7	@VAN	L	3-2	7-2-2	51	1/31	NYR	L	7-3	25-14-12
12	11/9	@CHI	W	7-1	8-2-2	52	2/4	@QUE	L	6-2	25-15-12
13	11/11	@NYI	T	6-6	8-2-3	53	2/5	@MTL	L	7-0	25-16-12
14	11/12	@HFD	W	5-1	9-2-3	54	2/7	@NYI	T	5-5	25-16-13
15	11/15	CHI	W	5-2	10-2-3	55	2/8	@NYR	T	3-3	25-16-14
16	11/17	NYI	L	2-1	10-3-3	56	2/12	TOR	L	4-3	25-17-14
17	11/19	@PIT	W	3-2	11-3-3	57	2/14	HFD	W	7-4	26-17-14
18	11/20	@PHI	T	1-1	11-3-4	58	2/15	VAN	W	7-2	27-17-14
19	11/22	CHI	L	6-2	11-4-4	59	2/18	COL	W	6-2	28-17-14
20	11/26	@QUE	L	5-2	11-5-4	60	2/20	@WPG	W	5-3	29-17-14
21	11/29	@MTL	W	4-2	12-5-4	61	2/21	@TOR	L	5-3	29-18-14
22	12/1	@NYR	W	5-3	13-5-4	62	2/23	NYI	L	4-1	29-19-14
23	12/3	@WSH	T	3-3	13-5-5	63	2/25	@HFD	L	3-2	29-20-14
24	12/6	BUF	T	3-3	13-5-6	64	2/26	@BOS	L	5-1	29-21-14
25	12/7	DET	T	1-1	13-5-7	65	2/28	PHI	L	4-2	29-22-14
26	12/9	@STL	L	4-1	13-6-7	66	3/4	BOS	T	3-3	29-22-15
27	12/10	L.A.	L	7-2	13-7-7	67	3/7	PIT	W	8-5	30-22-15
28	12/13	WPG	W	4-3	14-7-7	68	3/9	MTL	T	1-1	30-22-16
29	12/15	TOR	L	6-3	14-8-7	69	3/11	BUF	W	3-1	31-22-16
30	12/17	@TOR	L	4-2	14-9-7	70	3/12	@CGY	L	6-3	31-23-16
31	12/20	NYR	T	3-3	14-9-8	71	3/14	@L.A.	L	10-4	31-24-16
32	12/23	@DET	W	6-2	15-9-8	72	3/18	EDM	L	5-3	31-25-16
33	12/26	@WPG	W	5-3	16-9-8	73	3/20	@EDM	T	1-1	31-25-17
34	12/27	COL	W	6-4	17-9-8	74	3/22	DET	W	9-3	32-25-17
35	12/30	PHI	W	6-5	18-9-8	75	3/24	L.A.	L	4-3	32-26-17
36	1/3	WSH	W	3-0	19-9-8	76	3/28	@L.A.	L	3-2	32-27-17
37	1/4	@BUF	T	2-2	19-9-9	77	3/29	@VAN	W	4-2	33-27-17
38	1/7	VAN	T	1-1	19-9-10	78	3/31	STL	W	6-3	34-27-17
39	1/9	@COL	L	4-2	19-10-10	79	4/4	@STL	W	5-0	35-27-17
40	1/10	WSH	W	3-2	20-10-10	80	4/5	@CHI	L	8-4	35-28-17

1981-82 GAME RESULTS

GM#	DATE	OPP'T	RSLT	SCORE	RECORD	GM#	DATE	OPP'T	RSLT	SCORE	RECORD
1	10/8	TOR	T	3-3	0-0-1	41	1/9	MTL	T	3-3	15-12-14
2	10/10	NYR	W	7-0	1-0-1	42	1/11	@NYR	L	5-3	15-13-14
3	10/12	@QUE	W	4-2	2-0-1	43	1/13	NYR	L	2-0	15-14-14
4	10/14	@TOR	W	2-1	3-0-1	44	1/16	QUE	W	4-1	16-14-14
5	10/17	@PIT	L	5-2	3-1-1	45	1/17	CHI	W	7-5	17-14-14
6	10/18	@PHI	L	3-2	3-2-1	46	1/20	@COL	W	3-1	18-14-14
7	10/22	STL	T	5-5	3-2-2	47	1/21	@L.A.	T	3-3	18-14-15
8	10/24	L.A.	W	6-3	4-2-2	48	1/23	CHI	W	8-4	19-14-15
9	10/25	@BUF	W	6-3	5-2-2	49	1/25	@TOR	W	9-2	20-14-15
10	10/28	CGY	W	6-1	6-2-2	50	1/27	DET	W	8-6	21-14-15
11	10/31	DET	W	5-4	7-2-2	51	1/28	@STL	L	8-3	21-15-15
12	11/4	@WSH	W	6-1	8-2-2	52	1/30	@NYI	L	4-2	21-16-15
13	11/7	@HFD	L	4-2	8-3-2	53	2/3	@PIT	W	9-6	22-16-15
14	11/8	@BOS	W	4-1	9-3-2	54	2/4	@PHI	T	3-3	22-16-16
15	11/11	WPG	W	15-2	10-3-2	55	2/7	@CHI	L	5-2	22-17-16
16	11/14	QUE	T	5-5	10-3-3	56	2/11	BOS	L	4-2	22-18-16
17	11/18	@WPG	W	6-4	11-3-3	57	2/13	DET	W	6-1	23-18-16
18	11/19	EDM	T	2-2	11-3-4	58	2/15	@TOR	T	3-3	23-18-17
19	11/21	CHI	L	6-4	11-4-4	59	2/17	@EDM	L	7-4	23-19-17
20	11/22	@CHI	T	1-1	11-4-5	60	2/18	@CGY	T	2-2	23-19-18
21	11/25	WSH	T	4-4	11-4-6	61	2/20	WSH	W	7-3	24-19-18
22	11/27	@WPG	T	5-5	11-4-7	62	2/22	HFD	W	8-7	25-19-18
23	11/28	PHI	W	5-3	12-4-7	63	2/24	TOR	W	7-5	26-19-18
24	11/30	COL	T	2-2	12-4-8	64	2/27	BUF	T	5-5	26-19-19
25	12/2	@VAN	L	5-0	12-5-8	65	2/28	@DET	W	5-4	27-19-19
26	12/5	NYI	L	8-5	12-6-8	66	3/3	DET	W	6-4	28-19-19
27	12/9	MTL	T	6-6	12-6-9	67	3/6	VAN	W	3-1	29-19-19
28	12/10	@DET	L	4-1	12-7-9	68	3/8	STL	W	8-1	30-19-19
29	12/12	CHI	W	6-3	13-7-9	69	3/10	NYI	T	4-4	30-19-20
30	12/15	@STL	L	4-2	13-8-9	70	3/13	@STL	W	3-2	31-19-20
31	12/17	WPG	L	4-2	13-9-9	71	3/15	PIT	W	4-3	32-19-20
32	12/19	@EDM	L	9-6	13-10-9	72	3/17	WPG	L	3-2	32-20-20
33	12/22	@VAN	T	4-4	13-10-10	73	3/20	@MTL	L	5-1	32-21-20
34	12/23	@CGY	T	4-4	13-10-11	74	3/22	L.A.	L	4-2	33-21-20
35	12/26	STL	W	6-3	14-10-11	75	3/25	@DET	W	4-3	34-21-20
36	12/28	COL	T	4-4	14-10-12	76	3/27	@BOS	W	6-5	35-21-20
37	12/31	@BUF	L	4-2	14-11-12	77	3/28	@HFD	W	5-2	36-21-20
38	1/2	@TOR	W	6-2	15-11-12	78	3/30	WPG	L	7-5	36-22-20
39	1/5	@STL	L	4-1	15-12-12	79	4/2	@WPG	W	5-2	37-22-20
40	1/6	TOR	T	3-3	15-12-13	80	4/4	@CHI	L	4-3	37-23-20

1981-82

37-23-20 • 94 points • 1st Place, Norris Division

Goals: Dino Ciccarelli 55*
Assists: Bobby Smith 71
Points: Bobby Smith 114*
Penalty Minutes: Dino Ciccarelli 138
Goalie Wins: Gilles Meloche 26

Playoffs: Lost to Chicago, 3-1

1982-83

40*-24-16 • 96 points* • 2nd Place, Norris Division

Goals: Dino Ciccarelli 37
Assists: Bobby Smith 53
Points: Neal Broten and Bobby Smith 77
Penalty Minutes: Willi Plett 170
Goalie Wins: Gilles Meloche 20

Playoffs: Beat Toronto, 3-1 • Lost to Chicago, 4-1

1982-83 SEASON RESULTS

GM#	DATE	OPP'T	RSLT	SCORE	RECORD	GM#	DATE	OPP'T	RSLT	SCORE	RECORD
1	10/6	@ WPG	W	5-4	1-0-0	41	1/8	CHI	W	4-1	21-11-9
2	10/8	DET	T	3-3	1-0-1	42	1/9	@ CHI	L	6-3	21-12-9
3	10/9	@ STL	W	6-3	2-0-1	43	1/12	@ PIT	W	7-0	22-12-9
4	10/14	TOR	W	6-2	3-0-1	44	1/13	TOR	W	2-1	23-12-9
5	10/16	CGY	W	8-4	4-0-1	45	1/15	EDM	L	10-4	23-13-9
6	10/18	STL	W	4-3	5-0-1	46	1/17	@ BOS	L	4-3	23-14-9
7	10/20	@ TOR	L	5-2	5-1-1	47	1/19	DET	W	3-2	24-14-9
8	10/23	@ WSH	W	3-1	6-1-1	48	1/22	HFD	W	7-2	25-14-9
9	10/24	@ NYR	L	4-2	6-2-1	49	1/25	@ STL	T	4-4	25-14-10
10	10/26	@ NJ	W	5-3	7-2-1	50	1/27	STL	T	3-3	25-14-11
11	10/28	DET	W	7-3	8-2-1	51	1/29	PHI	T	2-2	25-14-12
12	10/30	PHI	W	3-2	9-2-1	52	1/31	@ TOR	W	4-2	26-14-12
13	11/2	@ HFD	W	7-6	10-2-1	53	2/2	@ BUF	T	2-2	26-14-13
14	11/4	@ MTL	L	8-3	10-3-1	54	2/3	@ WSH	W	3-1	26-15-13
15	11/6	@ QUE	L	4-1	10-4-1	55	2/5	@ NYI	W	4-2	27-15-13
16	11/9	MTL	L	3-2	10-5-1	56	2/10	NYR	W	7-5	28-15-13
17	11/11	NYI	W	2-0	11-5-1	57	2/12	CHI	W	5-4	29-15-13
18	11/13	@ TOR	L	4-3	11-6-1	58	2/15	@ NJ	W	3-2	30-15-13
19	11/14	@ CHI	L	5-4	11-7-1	59	2/17	QUE	W	6-3	31-15-13
20	11/16	@ L.A.	W	8-3	12-7-1	60	2/19	BOS	L	6-2	31-16-13
21	11/18	BUF	W	2-1	13-7-1	61	2/22	@ DET	W	3-2	32-16-13
22	11/20	NJ	W	5-1	14-7-1	62	3/23	TOR	L	3-2	32-17-13
23	11/23	@ NYI	T	8-8	14-7-2	63	2/26	CHI	T	4-4	32-17-14
24	11/24	@ NYR	L	8-5	14-8-2	64	2/27	@ CHI	W	2-1	33-17-14
25	11/26	PIT	T	6-6	14-8-3	65	3/2	STL	T	4-4	33-17-15
26	11/29	CGY	T	3-3	14-8-4	66	3/5	@ DET	W	4-1	34-17-15
27	12/1	@ DET	W	4-1	15-8-4	67	3/6	L.A.	W	8-3	35-17-15
28	12/2	@ STL	W	6-3	16-8-4	68	3/8	BUF	W	5-1	36-17-15
29	12/4	WPG	W	4-1	17-8-4	69	3/10	@ PHI	L	6-3	36-18-15
30	12/9	VAN	W	9-6	18-8-4	70	3/12	@ QUE	L	6-3	36-19-15
31	12/11	EDM	W	5-4	19-8-4	71	3/14	VAN	W	6-3	37-19-15
32	12/14	HFD	T	3-3	19-8-5	72	3/16	PIT	W	3-2	38-19-15
33	12/16	WSH	T	4-4	19-8-6	73	3/19	@ STL	T	3-3	38-19-16
34	12/18	@ VAN	T	3-3	19-8-7	74	3/21	CHI	W	4-3	39-19-16
35	12/21	@ CGY	L	6-4	19-9-7	75	3/23	@ TOR	L	6-3	39-20-16
36	12/22	@ EDM	L	8-2	19-10-7	76	3/24	@ MTL	L	5-3	39-21-16
37	12/26	@ WPG	W	3-2	20-10-7	77	3/26	@ DET	W	7-5	40-21-16
38	12/29	DET	T	5-5	20-10-8	78	3/29	TOR	L	4-2	40-22-16
39	12/31	BOS	L	5-3	20-11-8	79	3/30	@ CHI	L	5-0	40-23-16
40	1/5	STL	T	3-3	20-11-9	80	4/2	@ L.A.	L	8-5	40-24-16

1983-84 GAME RESULTS

GM#	DATE	OPP'T	RSLT	SCORE	RECORD	GM#	DATE	OPP'T	RSLT	SCORE	RECORD
1	10/5	@ L.A.	T(OT)	3-3	0-0-1	41	1/7	VAN	W	2-0	20-17-4
2	10/7	@ VAN	L	10-9	0-1-1	42	1/10	HFD	L	6-3	20-18-4
3	10/9	@ EDM	L(OT)	4-3	0-2-1	43	1/12	TOR	W(OT)	5-4	21-18-4
4	10/12	CGY	W	7-5	1-2-1	44	1/14	@ STL	W	4-2	22-18-4
5	10/15	WPG	W	2-1	2-2-1	45	1/16	L.A.	W	9-3	23-18-4
6	10/16	@ CHI	L	4-3	2-3-1	46	1/18	@ TOR	L	9-4	23-19-4
7	10/20	MTL	L(OT)	5-4	2-4-1	47	1/20	@ DET	W	8-5	24-19-4
8	10/22	@ QUE	L	11-2	2-5-1	48	1/21	DET	W	5-1	25-19-4
9	10/25	@ MTL	W	4-3	3-5-1	49	1/25	@ CHI	W	5-3	26-19-4
10	10/27	BOS	L	8-1	3-6-1	50	1/27	@ STL	W	10-8	27-19-4
11	10/29	WSH	L	6-1	3-7-1	51	1/28	CHI	L	4-2	27-20-4
12	11/2	TOR	W	8-5	4-7-1	52	2/1	@ PIT	L	4-0	27-21-4
13	11/5	CHI	W	10-5	5-7-1	53	2/3	@ BUF	W	4-1	28-21-4
14	11/8	@ HFD	L	6-4	5-8-1	54	2/5	@ NJ	W	3-1	29-21-4
15	11/9	@ DET	W	5-3	6-8-1	55	2/9	NYR	T(OT)	4-4	29-21-5
16	11/12	STL	W	5-2	7-8-1	56	2/11	DET	L	6-4	29-22-5
17	11/15	NJ	W	6-0	8-8-1	57	2/13	WSH	L	4-0	29-23-5
18	11/17	@ PHI	T(OT)	5-5	8-8-2	58	2/15	@ TOR	W	3-1	30-23-5
19	11/19	WPG	W(OT)	8-7	9-8-2	59	2/17	@ BUF	L(OT)	5-4	30-24-5
20	11/20	@ CHI	W	4-3	10-8-2	60	2/18	QUE	L	7-2	30-25-5
21	11/23	TOR	L	6-4	10-9-2	61	2/20	L.A.	L	3-2	30-26-5
22	11/25	EDM	T(OT)	2-2	10-9-3	62	2/22	@ DET	L	5-2	30-27-5
23	11/26	@ TOR	W(OT)	7-6	11-9-3	63	2/23	@ PHI	T	3-3	30-27-6
24	11/29	PIT	W	6-4	12-9-3	64	2/25	BUF	W	5-1	31-27-6
25	12/1	@ PIT	W	6-4	13-9-3	65	2/28	@ STL	L	5-2	31-28-6
26	12/3	@ BOS	W	6-2	14-9-3	66	2/29	STL	L	7-5	31-29-6
27	12/4	@ NYR	L	6-4	14-10-3	67	3/3	CHI	W	6-3	32-29-6
28	12/7	DET	W	7-2	15-10-3	68	3/5	DET	W	5-1	33-29-6
29	12/10	NYI	W	4-2	15-11-3	69	3/7	NYR	W	6-3	34-29-6
30	12/14	STL	T(OT)	4-4	15-11-4	70	3/10	PHI	W	4-3	35-29-6
31	12/17	NJ	L	2-0	15-12-4	71	3/12	MTL	W(OT)	7-6	36-29-6
32	12/20	@ STL	W	5-2	16-12-4	72	3/14	@ TOR	T(OT)	3-3	36-29-7
33	12/22	@ BOS	W	4-2	17-12-4	73	3/17	@ DET	W	4-3	37-29-7
34	12/23	@ HFD	L	5-3	17-13-4	74	3/18	QUE	T(OT)	5-5	37-29-8
35	12/26	@ WPG	L	5-1	17-14-4	75	3/21	@ WSH	L	5-1	37-30-8
36	12/28	TOR	W	8-6	18-14-4	76	3/24	@ NYI	T(OT)	4-4	37-30-9
37	12/31	NYI	L	7-3	18-15-4	77	3/26	STL	W(OT)	4-3	38-30-9
38	1/2	CHI	W	6-5	19-15-4	78	3/28	@ CHI	W	6-3	39-30-9
39	1/4	@ EDM	L	12-8	19-16-4	79	3/30	@ VAN	T(OT)	3-3	39-30-10
40	1/5	@ CGY	L	5-4	19-17-4	80	3/31	@ CGY	L	10-3	39-31-10

1983-84

39-31-10 • 88 points • 1st Place, Norris Division

Goals: Brian Bellows 41
Assists: Neal Broten 61
Points: Neal Broten 89
Penalty Minutes: Willi Plett 316
Goalie Wins: Gilles Meloche 21

Playoffs: Beat Chicago, 3-2 • Beat St. Louis, 4-3 • Lost to Edmonton, 4-0

1984-85

25-43-12 • 62 points • 4th Place, Norris Division

Goals: Steve Payne 29
Assists: Dennis Maruk 41
Points: Brian Bellows 62
Penalty Minutes: Harold Snepsts 232
Goalie Wins: Don Beaupre and Gilles Meloche 10

Playoffs: Beat St. Louis, 3-0 • Lost to Chicago, 4-2

1984-85 GAME RESULTS

GM#	DATE	OPP'T	RSLT	SCORE	RECORD	GM#	DATE	OPP'T	RSLT	SCORE	RECORD
1	10/11	TOR	L(OT)	1-0	0-1-0	41	1/10	STL	L	5-3	13-21-7
2	10/13	NYR	W	3-1	1-1-0	42	1/12	HFD	W	5-4	14-21-7
3	10/14	@NYR	W	3-1	2-1-0	43	1/14	@WSH	L	6-3	14-22-7
4	10/18	EDM	L	7-5	2-2-0	44	1/16	STL	T(OT)	4-4	14-22-8
5	10/20	@MTL	L	4-2	2-3-0	45	1/19	PHI	L	4-1	14-23-8
6	10/21	@BUF	L	8-6	2-4-0	46	1/21	@CHI	L	7-2	14-24-8
7	10/23	PHI	L	7-2	2-5-0	47	1/23	PIT	W	4-3	15-24-8
8	10/27	HFD	L	5-3	2-6-0	48	1/26	DET	T(OT)	4-4	15-24-9
9	10/30	CHI	T(OT)	5-5	2-6-1	49	1/27	@NYR	L	3-2	15-25-9
10	11/2	@N.J.	T(OT)	2-2	2-6-2	50	1/29	@NYI	T(OT)	4-4	15-25-10
11	11/3	@PHI	L	5-1	2-7-2	51	2/2	@TOR	W	5-2	16-25-10
12	11/5	TOR	W	5-3	3-7-2	52	2/3	@QUE	L	5-1	16-26-10
13	11/7	BUF	L	9-6	3-8-2	53	2/6	BUF	L	3-1	16-27-10
14	11/10	VAN	T(OT)	5-5	3-8-3	54	2/8	EDM	L	5-3	16-28-10
15	11/11	@TOR	W	7-6	4-8-3	55	2/9	@STL	L	4-2	16-29-10
16	11/13	@WSH	T(OT)	3-3	4-8-4	56	2/14	@DET	T(OT)	5-5	16-29-11
17	11/15	@NYI	L	6-1	4-9-4	57	2/16	@STL	L	6-4	16-30-11
18	11/17	DET	T(OT)	3-3	4-9-5	58	2/17	QUE	L	4-3	16-31-11
19	11/21	TOR	W	7-1	5-9-5	59	2/20	BOS	L	3-2	16-32-11
20	11/23	N.J.	W(OT)	5-4	6-9-5	60	2/22	CHI	W	4-1	17-32-11
21	11/24	@TOR	W	4-2	7-9-5	61	2/23	PIT	L	3-1	17-33-11
22	11/27	@N.J.	L	3-2	7-10-5	62	2/25	@PIT	W	5-4	18-33-11
23	11/28	@HFD	W	4-2	8-10-5	63	2/27	@TOR	L	6-1	18-34-11
24	12/1	CGY	L	8-4	8-11-5	64	3/1	@DET	L	6-2	18-35-11
25	12/4	L.A.	T(OT)	2-2	8-11-6	65	3/2	DET	W	5-2	19-35-11
26	12/7	@EDM	L	6-3	8-12-6	66	3/4	MTL	W	4-3	20-35-11
27	12/9	@WPG	L	4-2	8-13-6	67	3/6	CHI	L	5-4	20-36-11
28	12/10	DET	L	4-3	8-14-6	68	3/9	STL	W	4-1	21-36-11
29	12/12	WSH	L	3-2	8-15-6	69	3/10	@CHI	W	3-2	22-36-11
30	12/15	CHI	L	5-3	8-16-6	70	3/13	@QUE	L	8-0	22-37-11
31	12/16	@CHI	W	5-3	9-16-6	71	3/16	@MTL	W	5-3	23-37-11
32	12/19	@STL	L	4-1	9-17-6	72	3/18	CGY	T(OT)	4-4	23-37-12
33	12/22	@DET	W(OT)	5-4	10-17-6	73	3/20	@WPG	L	5-2	23-38-12
34	12/23	@BOS	L	4-3	10-18-6	74	3/23	@STL	L	4-2	23-39-12
35	12/26	WPG	W	4-0	11-18-6	75	3/25	VAN	W	5-3	24-39-12
36	12/29	BOS	L	5-3	11-19-6	76	3/26	@DET	L	3-2	24-40-12
37	12/31	NYI	W	4-3	12-19-6	77	3/30	@L.A.	L	3-2	24-41-12
38	1/3	@L.A.	W	8-3	13-19-6	78	3/31	@VAN	L	9-7	24-42-12
39	1/5	@CGY	T(OT)	4-4	13-19-7	79	4/3	TOR	W	9-7	25-42-12
40	1/9	@CHI	L	4-3	13-20-7	80	4/6	STL	L	4-3	25-43-12

1985-86

1985-86 GAME RESULTS

GM#	DATE	OPP'T	RSLT	SCORE	RECORD	GM#	DATE	OPP'T	RSLT	SCORE	RECORD
1	10/10	@DET	T(OT)	6-6	0-0-1	41	1/11	WSH	W	5-3	16-18-7
2	10/12	BUF	L	6-2	0-1-1	42	1/14	CHI	T(OT)	3-3	16-18-8
3	10/15	@PIT	L	3-1	0-2-1	43	1/16	STL	W	4-3	17-18-8
4	10/17	DET	W	10-1	1-2-1	44	1/18	@TOR	W	5-2	18-18-8
5	10/19	@PHI	L	7-3	1-3-1	45	1/19	@PIT	L	3-2	18-19-8
6	10/22	STL	W	5-4	2-3-1	46	1/21	@WSH	L	7-5	18-20-8
7	10/23	@STL	T(OT)	4-4	2-3-2	47	1/23	MTL	L	5-2	18-21-8
8	10/26	@TOR	W	7-5	3-3-2	48	1/25	WSH	L	6-3	18-22-8
9	10/27	@BUF	L	3-2	3-4-2	49	1/27	N.J.	W	6-2	19-22-8
10	10/30	CHI	L	6-5	3-5-2	50	1/29	@L.A.	L	4-3	19-23-8
11	11/2	WPG	L	3-1	3-6-2	51	1/31	@VAN	L	10-5	19-24-8
12	11/6	MTL	T(OT)	3-3	3-6-3	52	2/6	TOR	W(OT)	8-7	20-24-8
13	11/9	NYR	W(OT)	4-3	4-6-3	53	2/8	@PHI	T(OT)	3-3	20-24-9
14	11/10	@BOS	L	2-1	4-7-3	54	2/10	@MTL	W(OT)	4-3	21-24-9
15	11/13	@HFD	L	5-2	4-8-3	55	2/11	@TOR	W	4-2	22-24-9
16	11/16	DET	L	4-2	4-9-3	56	2/13	@STL	L	5-3	22-25-9
17	11/17	@CHI	T(OT)	5-5	4-9-4	57	2/15	HFD	W	4-1	23-25-9
18	11/19	@CGY	T(OT)	3-3	4-9-5	58	2/16	BOS	L	5-3	23-26-9
19	11/21	STL	L	4-2	4-10-5	59	2/19	@CHI	W	6-5	24-26-9
20	11/23	L.A.	W	4-2	5-10-5	60	2/21	QUE	W	5-2	25-26-9
21	11/25	@BUF	W	4-3	6-10-5	61	2/23	TOR	W	4-3	26-26-9
22	11/27	NYI	T(OT)	4-4	6-10-6	62	2/24	@NYR	L	5-1	26-27-9
23	11/29	PHI	L	4-1	6-11-6	63	2/26	@HFD	W	5-2	27-27-9
24	11/30	@STL	L	4-3	6-12-6	64	3/1	NYI	W	5-4	28-27-9
25	12/3	CHI	W	9-2	7-12-6	65	3/3	@DET	W	8-5	29-27-9
26	12/7	@EDM.	L	8-4	7-13-6	66	3/5	TOR	W	4-3	30-27-9
27	12/9	N.J.	L	6-4	7-14-6	67	3/8	WPG	L	4-2	30-28-9
28	12/11	@DET	W	10-2	8-14-6	68	3/11	EDM	W	4-0	31-28-9
29	12/14	TOR	T(OT)	6-6	8-14-7	69	3/13	@STL	W	3-2	32-28-9
30	12/17	DET	W	6-3	9-14-7	70	3/15	@QUE	L	3-2	32-29-9
31	12/19	PIT	L(OT)	4-3	9-15-7	71	3/17	STL	W(OT)	6-5	33-29-9
32	12/21	@BOS	L	5-2	9-16-7	72	3/19	@CGY	W	6-5	34-29-9
33	12/22	@N.J.	W	8-3	10-16-7	73	3/21	@EDM	L(OT)	5-4	34-30-9
34	12/26	@WPG	W	6-5	11-16-7	74	3/22	@VAN	L	6-2	34-31-9
35	12/28	QUE	W	3-1	12-16-7	75	3/24	QUE	L	1-0	34-32-9
36	12/31	CGY	W	6-3	13-16-7	76	3/26	@TOR	W	6-1	35-32-9
37	1/2	VAN	W	3-2	14-16-7	77	3/29	@DET	W	5-4	36-32-9
38	1/5	@CHI	L	6-2	14-17-7	78	4/1	CHI	L	2-1	36-33-9
39	1/7	@NYI	W	3-2	15-17-7	79	4/2	@CHI	W	7-5	37-33-9
40	1/10	L.A.	L	4-3	15-18-7	80	4/5	DET	W	5-3	38-33-9

38-33-9 • 85 points • 2nd Place, Norris Divison

Goals: Dino Ciccarelli 44
Assists: Neal Broten 76*
Points: Neal Broten 105
Penalty Minutes: Willi Plett 231
Goalie Wins: Don Beaupre 25

Playoffs: Lost to St. Louis, 3-2

1986-87

30-40-10 • 70 points • 5th Place, Norris Division

Goals: Dino Ciccarelli 52
Assists: Dino Ciccarelli 51
Points: Dino Ciccarelli 103
Penalty Minutes: Willi Plett 263
Goalie Wins: Don Beaupre 17

No Playoffs

January 2, 1986: Lorne Henning gives orders to the North Star bench during a 3-2 win over Vancouver at the Met. (L to R) Dennis Maruk, Dirk Graham, Brian Lawton, Willi Plett.

1986-87 GAME RESULTS

GM#	DATE	OPP'T	RSLT	SCORE	RECORD	GM#	DATE	OPP'T	RSLT	SCORE	RECORD
1	10/11	@ QUE	T(OT)	4-4	0-0-1	41	1/8	BUF	W(OT)	5-4	17-20-4
2	10/13	@ MTL	L	6-4	0-1-1	42	1/10	HFD	W	6-4	18-20-4
3	10/16	BOS	L	5-3	0-2-1	43	1/12	STL	T(OT)	4-4	18-20-5
4	10/18	VAN	L	4-1	1-2-1	44	1/14	@ TOR	W	3-2	19-20-5
5	10/19	@ CHI	W	8-5	2-2-1	45	1/17	CHI	W	3-2	20-20-5
6	10/22	@ STL	W	8-3	3-2-1	46	1/18	@ WPG	L	5-3	20-21-5
7	10/24	@ WSH	L	8-2	3-3-1	47	1/20	BUF	W	5-0	21-21-5
8	10/26	@ PHI	L	4-1	3-4-1	48	1/23	@ L.A.	W	6-3	22-21-5
9	10/28	CGY	W	7-4	4-4-1	49	1/29	@ CGY	T(OT)	3-3	22-21-6
10	10/30	DET	L	3-1	4-5-1	50	1/30	@ EDM.	T(OT)	2-2	22-21-7
11	11/1	CHI	L	6-5	4-6-1	51	2/1	@ VAN	W	4-3	23-21-7
12	11/5	@ CHI	L	4-2	4-7-1	52	2/4	EDM	L(OT)	6-5	23-22-7
13	11/6	TOR	W	4-1	5-7-1	53	2/6	@ DET	L	6-4	23-23-7
14	11/8	PIT	L	4-2	5-8-1	54	2/7	DET	L	5-3	23-24-7
15	11/11	WSH	T(OT)	2-2	5-8-2	55	2/14	CGY	W	3-2	23-25-7
16	11/15	NYI	L	7-3	5-9-2	56	2/15	STL	W	3-2	24-25-7
17	11/18	STL	L	4-3	5-10-2	57	2/18	VAN	L	7-3	25-25-7
18	11/19	@ STL	L	7-5	5-11-2	58	2/19	@ STL	L	6-2	25-26-7
19	11/22	N.J.	W	6-2	6-11-2	59	2/21	BOS	L	1-0	25-27-7
20	11/26	CHI	W	5-2	7-11-2	60	2/23	@ MTL	W	4-3	26-27-7
21	11/28	TOR	W	6-3	8-11-2	61	2/24	@ QUE	L	5-4	26-28-7
22	11/29	@ TOR	W	7-2	9-11-2	62	2/28	L.A.	W	6-3	27-28-7
23	12/2	@ BUF	W	5-4	10-11-2	63	3/1	PHI	W	5-4	28-28-7
24	12/4	@ N.J.	W	5-3	11-11-2	64	3/3	@ L.A.	T(OT)	4-4	28-28-8
25	12/6	@ PIT	L	5-2	11-12-2	65	3/5	@ DET	L	9-3	28-29-8
26	12/9	EDM	L	3-2	11-13-2	66	3/7	PIT	L	7-3	28-30-8
27	12/11	@ DET	T(OT)	6-6	11-13-3	67	3/9	MTL	L	5-4	28-31-8
28	12/13	PHI	W	5-4	12-13-3	68	3/11	TOR	L	4-2	28-32-8
29	12/15	@ NYR	W	4-3	13-13-3	69	3/14	DET	L	4-3	28-33-8
30	12/16	@ NYI	L	4-2	13-14-3	70	3/15	@ CHI	W	4-2	29-33-8
31	12/18	@ TOR	W(OT)	6-5	14-14-3	71	3/17	CHI	T(OT)	3-3	29-33-9
32	12/20	QUE	L	4-1	14-15-3	72	3/19	@ BOS	L	6-2	29-34-9
33	12/23	TOR	L(OT)	4-3	14-16-3	73	3/21	HFD	L	5-1	29-35-9
34	12/26	WPG	W	4-2	15-16-3	74	3/23	STL	L	8-5	29-36-9
35	12/28	@ WPG	L	5-4	15-17-3	75	3/25	@ TOR	W	6-2	30-36-9
36	12/31	HFD	W	5-2	16-17-3	76	3/27	@ N.J.	L	5-2	30-37-9
37	1/2	@ DET	L	2-1	16-18-3	77	3/29	@ WSH	L	4-2	30-38-9
38	1/3	DET	L	3-2	16-19-3	78	3/30	NYR	L	6-5	30-39-9
39	1/5	@ NYR	T(OT)	3-3	16-19-4	79	4/1	@ CHI	T(OT)	4-4	30-39-10
40	1/6	NYI	L	5-3	16-20-4	80	4/5	STL	L	4-1	30-40-10

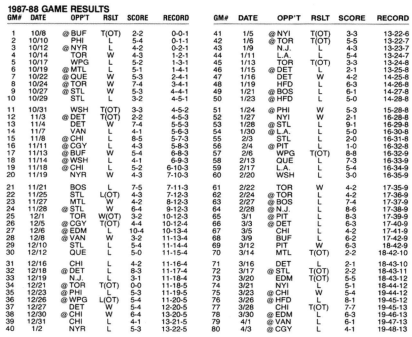

1987-88 GAME RESULTS

GM#	DATE	OPP'T	RSLT	SCORE	RECORD	GM#	DATE	OPP'T	RSLT	SCORE	RECORD
1	10/8	@ BUF	T(OT)	2-2	0-0-1	41	1/5	@ NYI	T(OT)	3-3	13-22-6
2	10/10	PHI	L	5-4	0-1-1	42	1/6	@ TOR	T(OT)	5-5	13-22-7
3	10/12	@ NYR	L	4-2	0-2-1	43	1/9	N.J.	L	4-3	13-23-7
4	10/14	TOR	W	4-3	1-2-1	44	1/11	L.A.	L	5-4	13-24-7
5	10/17	WPG	L	5-2	1-3-1	45	1/13	TOR	T(OT)	3-3	13-24-8
6	10/19	@ MTL	L	5-1	1-4-1	46	1/15	@ DET	L	2-1	13-25-8
7	10/22	@ QUE	W	5-3	2-4-1	47	1/16	DET	W	4-2	14-25-8
8	10/24	@ TOR	W	7-4	3-4-1	48	1/19	HFD	L	6-3	14-26-8
9	10/27	@ STL	W	5-3	4-4-1	49	1/21	@ BOS	L	6-1	14-27-8
10	10/29	STL	L	3-2	4-5-1	50	1/23	@ HFD	L	5-0	14-28-8
11	10/31	WSH	T(OT)	3-3	4-5-2	51	1/24	@ PHI	W	5-3	15-28-8
12	11/3	@ DET	T(OT)	2-2	4-5-3	52	1/27	NYI	W	2-1	16-28-8
13	11/4	DET	W	7-4	5-5-3	53	1/28	@ STL	L	9-1	16-29-8
14	11/7	VAN	L	4-1	5-6-3	54	1/30	@ L.A.	L	5-0	16-30-8
15	11/8	@ CHI	L	8-5	5-7-3	55	2/3	STL	L	2-0	16-31-8
16	11/11	@ CGY	L	4-3	5-8-3	56	2/4	@ PIT	L	1-0	16-32-8
17	11/13	@ BUF	W	5-4	6-8-3	57	2/6	WPG	T(OT)	8-8	16-32-9
18	11/14	@ WSH	L	4-1	6-9-3	58	2/13	QUE	L	7-3	16-33-9
19	11/18	@ CHI	L	5-2	6-10-3	59	2/17	L.A.	L	5-4	16-34-9
20	11/19	NYR	W	4-3	7-10-3	60	2/20	WSH	L	3-0	16-35-9
21	11/21	BOS	L	7-5	7-11-3	61	2/22	TOR	W	4-2	17-35-9
22	11/25	STL	L(OT)	4-3	7-12-3	62	2/24	@ TOR	L	4-2	17-36-9
23	11/27	MTL	W	4-2	8-12-3	63	2/27	@ BOS	L	7-4	17-37-9
24	11/28	@ STL	W	6-4	9-12-3	64	2/28	@ N.J.	L	8-6	17-38-9
25	12/1	TOR	W(OT)	3-2	10-12-3	65	3/1	@ PIT	L	8-3	17-39-9
26	12/5	@ CGY	T(OT)	4-4	10-12-4	66	3/3	@ DET	L	6-3	17-40-9
27	12/6	@ EDM	L	10-4	10-13-4	67	3/5	CHI	L	4-2	17-41-9
28	12/8	@ VAN	W	3-2	11-13-4	68	3/9	BUF	L	6-2	17-42-9
29	12/10	STL	L	5-4	11-14-4	69	3/12	PIT	W	6-3	18-42-9
30	12/12	QUE	L	5-0	11-15-4	70	3/14	MTL	T(OT)	2-2	18-42-10
31	12/16	CHI	L	4-2	11-16-4	71	3/16	DET	L	2-1	18-43-10
32	12/18	@ DET	L	8-3	11-17-4	72	3/17	@ STL	T(OT)	2-2	18-43-11
33	12/19	N.J.	L	3-1	11-18-4	73	3/20	EDM	T(OT)	5-5	18-43-12
34	12/21	@ TOR	T(OT)	0-0	11-18-5	74	3/21	NYI	L	5-1	18-44-12
35	12/23	@ PHI	L	5-3	11-19-5	75	3/23	@ CHI	W	5-4	19-44-12
36	12/26	@ WPG	L(OT)	5-4	11-20-5	76	3/26	@ HFD	L	8-1	19-45-12
37	12/27	DET	W	5-4	12-20-5	77	3/28	CHI	T(OT)	7-7	19-45-13
38	12/30	@ CHI	W	6-4	13-20-5	78	3/30	@ EDM	L	6-3	19-46-13
39	12/31	CHI	L	4-1	13-21-5	79	4/1	@ VAN	L	6-1	19-47-13
40	1/2	NYR	L	5-3	13-22-5	80	4/3	@ CGY	L	4-1	19-48-13

1987-88

19-48-13 • 51 points • 5th Place, Norris Division

Goals: Dino Ciccarelli 41
Assists: Dino Ciccarelli 45
Points: Dino Ciccarelli 86
Penalty Minutes: Basil McRae 382*
Goalie Wins: Don Beaupre 10

No Playoffs

March 23, 1987: *Mark Pavelich sends the Blues' Cliff Ronning into the net.*

Buzz Magnuson / St. Paul Pioneer Press

1988-89

27-37-16 • 70 points • 3rd Place, Norris Division

Goals: Dave Gagner 35
Assists: Dave Gagner 43
Points: Dave Gagner 78
Penalty Minutes: Basil McRae 365
Goalie Wins: Jon Casey 18

Playoffs: Lost to St. Louis, 4-1

1988-89 GAME RESULTS

GM#	DATE	OPP'T	RSLT	SCORE	RECORD	GM#	DATE	OPP'T	RSLT	SCORE	RECORD
1	10/6	STL	L	3-8	0-1-0	41	1/10	@ PHI	L	2-3	13-21-7
2	10/8	@ MTL	L	3-4	0-2-0	42	1/12	PIT	L	2-9	13-22-7
3	10/9	@ QUE	L	1-4	0-3-0	43	1/14	CGY	T(OT)	1-1	13-22-8
4	10/13	PHI	L	6-7	0-4-0	44	1/15	@ WPG	W	4-1	14-22-8
5	10/15	BOS	W	5-1	1-4-0	45	1/18	@ BUF	T(OT)	3-3	14-22-9
6	10/17	@ EDM	T(OT)	3-3	1-4-1	46	1/19	@ TOR	T(OT)	3-3	14-22-10
7	10/19	@ CGY	L	1-2	1-5-1	47	1/21	@ NYI	L	6-8	14-23-10
8	10/22	@ L.A.	L	2-8	1-6-1	48	1/23	@ N.J.	W	7-2	15-23-10
9	10/26	TOR	L	2-3	1-7-1	49	1/26	QUE	W	5-3	16-23-10
10	10/28	@ DET	L	1-4	1-8-1	50	1/28	N.J.	T(OT)	4-4	16-23-11
11	10/29	DET	W	3-2	2-8-1	51	1/30	WSH	T(OT)	4-4	16-23-12
12	11/3	@ CHI	L	1-4	2-9-1	52	2/1	BOS	T(OT)	4-4	16-23-13
13	11/5	CHI	T(OT)	5-5	2-9-2	53	2/4	@ QUE	L	3-6	16-24-13
14	11/9	DET	L	3-6	2-10-2	54	2/5	@ NYI	W	5-3	17-24-13
15	11/10	@ STL	T(OT)	5-5	2-10-3	55	2/9	VAN	W	3-2	18-24-13
16	11/12	HFD	L	1-4	2-11-3	56	2/11	DET	L	1-5	18-25-13
17	11/14	@ TOR	W	5-4	3-11-3	57	2/14	CHI	L	2-4	18-26-13
18	11/15	@ WSH	L	2-4	3-12-3	58	2/15	@ DET	L	2-4	18-27-13
19	11/17	VAN	W	7-6	4-12-3	59	2/18	HFD	L	3-4	18-28-13
20	11/19	NYR	L	1-4	4-13-3	60	2/21	@ PIT	W	2-1	19-28-13
21	11/23	EDM	T(OT)	3-3	4-13-4	61	2/22	@ CHI	T(OT)	5-5	19-28-14
22	11/25	TOR	W	5-3	5-13-4	62	2/25	TOR	L	2-4	19-29-14
23	11/26	@ TOR	W	6-3	6-13-4	63	2/28	@ WSH	W	4-3	20-29-14
24	11/29	CHI	W	5-2	7-13-4	64	3/1	@ CHI	L	1-5	20-30-14
25	12/1	@ BOS	W	4-1	8-13-4	65	3/4	NYI	W	4-3	21-30-14
26	12/3	@ HFD	W	4-2	9-13-4	66	3/5	@ N.J.	L	0-2	21-31-14
27	12/6	@ STL	L	0-3	9-14-4	67	3/7	DET	W	5-3	22-31-14
28	12/7	MTL	T(OT)	2-2	9-14-5	68	3/11	@ STL	T(OT)	2-2	22-31-15
29	12/10	STL	L	1-3	9-15-5	69	3/12	STL	W	5-3	23-31-15
30	12/13	@ DET	L	4-5	9-16-5	70	3/14	TOR	L	3-5	23-32-15
31	12/15	BUF	T(OT)	2-2	9-16-6	71	3/16	CHI	W	6-1	24-32-15
32	12/17	L.A.	W	3-2	10-16-6	72	3/18	BUF	W	3-0	25-32-15
33	12/19	@ VAN	L	1-5	10-17-6	73	3/20	PIT	W	7-2	26-32-15
34	12/21	@ L.A.	L	6-8	10-18-6	74	3/22	@ NYR	L	1-3	26-33-15
35	12/26	WPG	W	5-1	11-18-6	75	3/23	@ NYI	L	1-3	26-34-15
36	12/28	@ CHI	L	3-4	11-19-6	76	3/25	@ MTL	T(OT)	1-1	26-34-16
37	12/30	@ STL	T(OT)	5-5	11-19-7	77	3/27	CGY	L	2-3	26-35-16
38	12/31	STL	W	6-2	12-19-7	78	3/29	@ TOR	L	1-3	26-36-16
39	1/2	EDM	L(OT)	2-3	12-20-7	79	3/31	@ DET	W	5-1	27-36-16
40	1/5	PHI	W	5-3	13-20-7	80	4/2	@ WPG	L	2-3	27-37-16

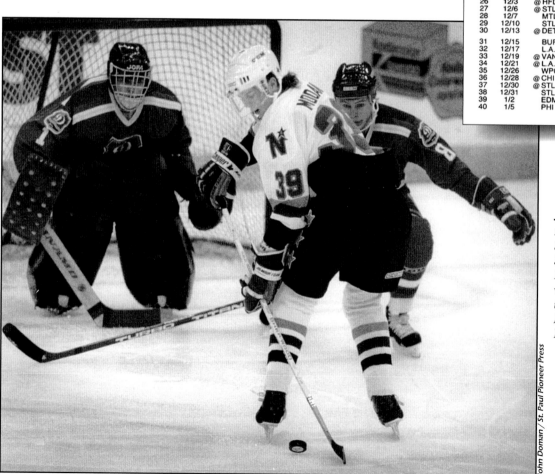

John Doman / St. Paul Pioneer Press

January 7, 1989: *Mike Modano makes his first appearance in a North Star uniform, playing in the North Stars' exhibition game against Dynamo Riga of the Soviet Union. Modano wears No. 39 because No. 9 belongs to Dennis Maruk. After the game, Modano rejoins his Junior team, the Prince Albert Raiders of the WHL.*

1989-90 GAME RESULTS

GM#	DATE	OPP'T	SCORE	RSLT	RECORD
1	10-5	NYI	6-5	W	1-0-0
2	10-7	@HFD	6-4	W	2-0-0
3	10-8	@BUF	2-2	T	2-0-1
4	10-12	STL	3-0	W	3-0-1
5	10-14	QUE	3-2	W	4-0-1
6	10-17	@NYI	6-3	W	5-0-1
7	10-18	@DET	4-3	L	5-1-1
8	10-21	@QUE	7-2	L	5-2-1
9	10-25	BUF	4-2	W	6-2-1
10	10-26	@STL	4-1	L	6-3-1
11	10-28	PHI	6-5	W	7-3-1
12	10-31	TOR	6-4	L	7-4-1
13	11-2	@CHI	4-3	L	7-5-1
14	11-4	CHI	3-0	W	8-5-1
15	11-6	@TOR	2-1	W	8-6-1
16	11-9	DET	5-1	W	9-6-1
17	11-11	CGY	3-2	W	10-6-1
18	11-12	TOR	6-3	W	11-6-1
19	11-15	@N.J	2-1	W	12-6-1
20	11-16	@PHI	6-3	L	12-7-1
21	11-18	STL	3-0	W	13-7-1
22	11-21	@STL	7-4	L	13-8-1
23	11-22	TOR	6-3	W	14-8-1
24	11-24	NJ	7-6	W	15-8-1
25	11-26	CHI	5-3	W	16-8-1
26	11-30	@CGY	5-2	L	16-9-1
27	12-2	@EDM	6-1	L	16-10-1
28	12-3	@VAN	6-5	L	16-11-1
29	12-6	MTL	4-1	L	16-12-1
30	12-8	@DET	2-1	L	16-13-1
31	12-9	DET	3-1	L	16-14-1
32	12-12	VAN	4-2	L	16-15-1
33	12-14	PIT	4-4	T	16-15-2
34	12-16	@TOR	4-3	W	17-15-2
35	12-19	EDM	5-0	L	17-16-2
36	12-21	@BOS	4-2	L	17-17-2
37	12-23	@HFD	4-3	L	17-18-2
38	12-26	@WPG	5-3	L	17-19-2
39	12-28	@CHI	1-1	T	17-19-3
40	12-30	@STL	3-2	L	17-20-3
41	12-31	STL	2-1	W	18-20-3
42	1-4	NYR	8-2	W	19-20-3
43	1-6	DET	4-3	W	20-20-3
44	1-9	@DET	9-0	L	20-21-3
45	1-11	NYI	8-4	L	20-22-3
46	1-13	DET	6-4	W	21-22-3
47	1-15	@MTL	4-3	L	21-23-3
48	1-17	@CHI	3-1	L	21-24-3
49	1-18	QUE	7-4	W	22-24-3
50	1-24	@TOR	7-3	L	22-25-3
51	1-26	@VAN	6-3	W	23-25-3
52	1-27	@CGY	3-1	L	23-26-3
53	1-29	WPG	4-2	W	24-26-3
54	1-31	WSH	4-3	L	24-27-3
55	2-3	@PHI	7-6	L	24-28-3
56	2-4	@NYR	4-3	L	24-29-3
57	2-7	HFD	5-3	L	24-30-3
58	2-10	CHI	6-4	W	25-30-3
59	2-11	@WSH	5-3	L	25-31-3
60	2-13	STL	2-1	L	25-32-3
61	2-15	L.A.	6-3	W	26-32-3
62	2-18	@EDM	3-2	L	26-33-3
63	2-21	@L.A.	4-2	L	26-34-3
64	2-24	BOS	3-2	L	26-35-3
65	2-27	WPG	8-3	W	27-35-3
66	3-3	MTL	3-2	W	28-35-3
67	3-4	@PIT	8-6	L	28-36-3
68	3-7	CHI	5-4	W	29-36-3
69	3-10	NYR	2-2	T	29-36-4
70	3-12	@TOR	4-1	W	30-36-4
71	3-13	N.J	3-1	L	30-37-4
72	3-17	@PIT	6-2	W	31-37-4
73	3-18	WSH	4-3	L	31-38-4
74	3-20	L.A	5-2	W	32-38-4
75	3-22	@DET	5-1	W	33-38-4
76	3-24	@BOS	7-6	W	34-38-4
77	3-26	TOR	5-4	W	35-38-4
78	3-29	@BUF	4-2	L	35-39-4
79	3-31	@STL	6-3	W	36-39-4
80	4-1	@CHI	4-1	L	36-40-4

1989-90

36-40-4 • 76 points • 4th Place, Norris Division

Goals: Brian Bellows 55*
Assists: Neal Broten 62
Points: Brian Bellows 99
Penalty Minutes: Basil McRae 351
Goalie Wins: Jon Casey 31*

Playoffs: Lost to Chicago, 4-3

October 5, 1989: *Brian Bellows is congratulated by Neal Broten and Mike Gartner after scoring his first goal of the season. The North Stars defeat the Islanders 6-5 in the home opener. Bellows will finish the season with 55 goals, tying the North Stars' record for most goals in a single season set by Dino Ciccarelli in 1981-82.*

John Doman / St. Paul Pioneer Press

MINNESOTA NORTH ST☆RS

1990-91

27-39-14 • 68 points • 4th Place, Norris Division

Goals: Dave Gagner 40
Assists: Neal Broten 56
Points: Dave Gagner 82
Penalty Minutes: Shane Churla 284
Goalie Wins: Jon Casey 21

Playoffs: Beat Chicago, 4-2 • Beat St. Louis, 4-2
        Beat Edmonton, 4-1
        Lost to Pittsburgh, 4-2 (Stanley Cup Finals)

1990-91 GAME RESULTS

GM#	DATE	OPP'T	SCORE	RESLT	RECORD
1	10-4	STL	2-3	L	0-1-0
2	10-6	NYI	4-2	W	1-1-0
3	10-8	@NYR	3-6	L	1-2-0
4	10-9	@NJ	2-5	L	1-3-0
5	10-11	BOS	3-3	T*	1-3-1
6	10-13	CHI	1-4	L	1-4-1
7	10-17	@LA	2-5	L	1-5-1
8	10-20	@STL	2-2	T*	1-5-2
9	10-21	@CHI	1-7	L	1-6-2
10	10-24	HFD	3-0	W	2-6-2
11	10-26	@DET	6-8	L	2-7-2
12	10-27	DET	2-2	T*	2-7-3
13	10-30	@TOR	4-5	L	2-8-3
14	11-1	@PHI	3-6	L	2-9-3
15	11-3	@QUE	2-0	W	3-9-3
16	11-4	@MTL	2-2	T*	3-9-4
17	11-8	QUE	3-2	W	4-9-4
18	11-10	HFD	2-3	L*	4-10-4
19	11-13	PIT	1-4	L	4-11-4
20	11-15	NYR	2-4	L	4-12-4
21	11-17	STL	2-3	L	4-13-4
22	11-19	@NYR	2-2	T*	4-13-5
23	11-21	@DET	3-4	L	4-14-5
24	11-23	VAN	6-4	W	5-14-5
25	11-24	NJ	3-5	L	5-15-5
26	11-27	@VAN	1-1	T*	5-15-6
27	11-30	@WPG	4-2	W	6-15-6
28	12-1	PIT	6-3	W	7-15-6
29	12-5	@TOR	3-2	W	8-15-6
30	12-6	TOR	1-2	L*	8-16-6
31	12-8	PHI	7-0	W	9-16-6
32	12-11	CGY	4-7	L	9-17-6
33	12-13	@STL	2-4	L	9-18-6
34	12-15	CHI	5-1	W	10-18-6
35	12-16	@CHI	2-5	L	10-19-6
36	12-20	@PIT	3-4	L	10-20-6
37	12-22	@BOS	2-6	L	10-21-6
38	12-23	@HFD	5-2	W	11-21-6
39	12-26	WPG	4-6	L	11-22-6
40	12-29	BOS	4-4	T*	11-22-7
41	12-31	LA	2-4	L	11-23-7
42	1-2	@DET	2-6	L	11-24-7
43	1-3	TOR	3-3	T*	11-24-8
44	1-5	VAN	5-6	L	11-25-8
45	1-8	@NYI	3-0	W	12-25-8
46	1-12	BUF	3-5	L	12-26-8
47	1-13	@CHI	3-5	L	12-27-8
48	1-15	MTL	1-5	L	12-28-8
49	1-17	WSH	5-2	W	13-28-8
50	1-21	@WPG	0-2	L	13-29-8
51	1-22	STL	7-3	W	14-29-8
52	1-25	@WSH	2-2	T*	14-29-9
53	1-26	@NJ	3-1	W	15-29-9
54	1-28	@TOR	0-4	L	15-30-9
55	1-30	DET	5-2	W	16-30-9
56	2-2	@QUE	6-4	W	17-30-9
57	2-4	@MTL	2-4	L	17-31-9
58	2-7	TOR	4-2	W	18-31-9
59	2-9	DET	6-5	W	19-31-9
60	2-12	@NYI	4-5	L	19-32-9
61	2-13	@BUF	6-6	T*	19-32-10
62	2-16	@DET	3-0	W	20-32-10
63	2-20	EDM	5-1	W	21-32-10
64	2-23	CHI	3-3	T*	21-32-11
65	2-26	PHI	2-2	T*	21-32-12
66	3-1	@EDM	1-1	T*	21-32-13
67	3-2	@CGY	1-5	L	21-33-13
68	3-6	EDM	5-1	W	22-33-13
69	3-9	DET	6-2	W	23-33-13
70	3-10	CGY	7-3	W	24-33-13
71	3-12	BUF	5-2	W	25-33-13
72	3-14	@STL	2-2	T*	25-33-14
73	3-16	@TOR	3-4	L*	25-34-14
74	3-17	TOR	4-3	W	26-34-14
75	3-22	@WSH	1-3	L	26-35-14
76	3-24	@CHI	4-5	L	26-36-14
77	3-25	STL	4-5	L	26-37-14
78	3-28	@LA	5-6	L	26-38-14
79	3-30	CHI	2-1	W	27-38-14
80	3-31	@STL	1-2	L	27-39-14

*OVERTIME

1991-92 GAME RESULTS

GM#	DATE	OPP'T	RSLT	SCORE	RECORD
1	10/5	CHI	W	4-2	1-0-0
2	10/10	QUE	W	3-2	2-0-0
3	10/12	DET	W	3-2	3-0-0
4	10/15	@CGY	L	3-6	3-1-0
5	10/17	@SJ	W	8-2	4-1-0
6	10/19	@LA	L	2-5	4-2-0
7	10/22	CGY	L	2-4	4-3-0
8	10/24	PHI	L	2-5	4-4-0
9	10/26	BOS	W	4-0	5-4-0
10	10/29	@NYR	L	2-3	5-5-0
11	10/31	@PIT	L	1-8	5-6-0
12	11/2	CHI	W	4-3	6-6-0
13	11/3	@CHI	T*	4-4	6-6-1
14	11/5	@DET	W	3-2	7-6-1
15	11/6	@TOR	L	3-4	7-7-1
16	11/9	PIT	L	2-3	7-8-1
17	11/12	TOR	W	7-0	8-8-1
18	11/16	@STL	L	3-5	8-9-1
19	11/19	NYI	L	4-7	8-10-1
20	11/22	@DET	L	3-4	8-11-1
21	11/23	DET	T*	2-2	8-11-2
22	11/29	TOR	L	2-3	8-12-2
23	11/30	@TOR	W	4-3	9-12-2
24	12/3	STL	T*	3-3	9-12-3
25	12/4	STL	W	5-2	10-12-3
26	12/7	WSH	L	2-4	10-13-3
27	12/8	@CHI	L	2-7	10-14-3
28	12/10	NJ	W	4-3	11-14-3
29	12/12	@VAN	L	5-7	11-15-3
30	12/14	@SJ	W	3-2	12-15-3
31	12/17	@LA	W	2-1	13-15-3
32	12/21	PHI	L	0-3	13-16-3
33	12/26	@WPG	W	3-2	14-16-3
34	12/28	STL	W	5-2	15-16-3
35	12/31	CHI	W	6-2	16-16-3
36	1/2	@STL	L	1-6	16-17-3
37	1/4	VAN	W	4-3	17-17-3
38	1/5	@CHI	L	2-5	17-18-3
39	1/7	@WSH	W	5-3	18-18-3
40	1/9	@DET	L	4-9	18-19-3
41	1/11	SJ	W	7-4	19-19-3
42	1/13	EDM	L	4-7	19-20-3
43	1/15	MTL	W	5-2	20-20-3
44	1/22	LA	T*	3-3	20-20-4
45	1/25	CHI	L	0-2	20-21-4
46	1/27	@BOS	L	2-3	20-22-4
47	1/28	@HFD	W	4-3	21-22-4
48	1/30	@PHI	L	3-5	21-23-4
49	2/1	NYR	L	1-2	21-24-4
50	2/3	TOR	W	4-2	22-24-4
51	2/5	@TOR	L*	2-3	22-25-4
52	2/7	@BUF	W	2-0	23-25-4
53	2/9	@HFD	T*	4-4	23-25-5
54	2/11	EDM	L	4-5	23-26-5
55	2/13	WPG	W	6-1	24-26-5
56	2/15	PIT	W	5-2	25-26-5
57	2/17	@MTL	L	0-8	25-27-5
58	2/18	@QUE	L	0-4	25-28-5
59	2/21	@NYR	L	4-5	25-29-5
60	2/22	@NYI	L	1-2	25-30-5
61	2/24	@NJ	W	3-1	26-30-5
62	2/26	MTL	L	1-4	26-31-5
63	2/29	HFD	L*	4-5	26-32-5
64	3/1	@TOR	L	2-6	26-33-5
65	3/3	@WSH	W	3-1	27-33-5
66	3/5	@DET	W	4-2	28-33-5
67	3/7	WPG	W	4-2	29-33-5
68	3/10	@STL	L	2-5	29-34-5
69	3/11	TOR	L	0-3	29-35-5
70	3/14	DET	W	4-1	30-35-5
71	3/17	BUF	W	3-1	31-35-5
72	3/19	@CHI	L	1-4	31-36-5
73	3/21	@QUE	L	2-4	31-37-5
74	3/24	VAN	L	2-4	31-38-5
75	3/27	@EDM	L	3-5	31-39-5
76	3/28	@CGY	L	3-4	31-40-5
77	3/31	BUF	W	5-3	32-40-5
78	4/12	STL	T*	1-1	32-40-6
79	4/14	DET	L	4-7	32-41-6
80	4/16	@STL	L	3-5	32-42-6

*OVERTIME

1991-92

32-42-6 • 70 points • 4th Place, Norris Division

Goals: Ulf Dahlen 36
Assists: Brian Bellows 45
Points: Mike Modano 77
Penalty Minutes: Shane Churla 278
Goalie Wins: Jon Casey 19

Playoffs: Lost to Detroit, 4-3

Cesare Maniago

Heinz Kluetmeier / Sports Illustrated

Rick Kolodziej

Dino Ciccarelli

Bobby Smith and Chicago's
Troy Murray

Rick Kolodziej

Heinz Kluetmeier / Sports Illustrated

Gump Worsley

Ulf Dahlen, Mike Modano
and Brian Bellows

Billy Robin McFarland

Jude Drouin

Billy Robin McFarland

Neal Broten and
Chicago's Dirk Graham

North Stars archives

Basil McRae

Billy Robin McFarland

MINNESOTA WELCOMES
1972 NATIONAL HOCKEY LEAGUE
ALL STAR GAME
TUESDAY EVENING
JANUARY 25, 1972

EAST
DIVISION
vs.
WEST
DIVISION

METROPOLITAN SPORTS CENTER

ALL STAR
GAME
METROPOLITAN
SPORTS
CENTER
TUESDAY
EVE.
JANUARY
25
1972

EST. PR. 7.08
CITY TAX .21
STATE TAX .21
TOTAL $7.50

1972 All Star Game ticket

Mike Modano

Billy Robin McFarland

Lou Nanne

North Stars archives

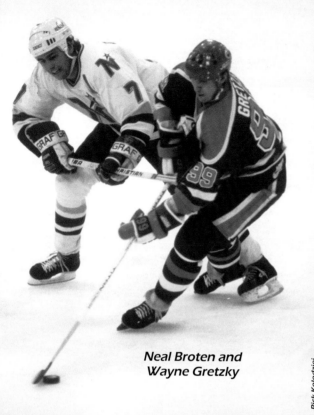

Neal Broten and
Wayne Gretzky

Gump Worsley

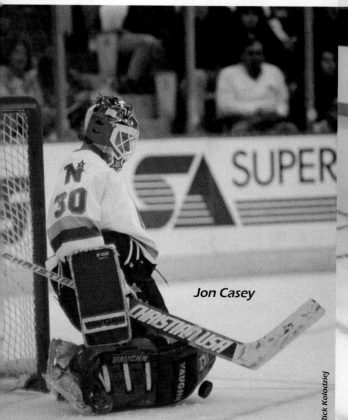

Jon Casey

Don Beaupre

J.P. Parise

Curt Giles

Rick Kolodziej

Craig Hartsburg
and goalie Kari Takko

Rick Kolodziej

Jon Casey

Larry Grace

Steve Payne

Rick Kolodziej

Jude Drouin takes the draw vs. the
California Golden Seals.

North Stars archives

Roland Eriksson

North Stars archives

Danny Grant

Rick Kolodziej

North Stars archives

On the bench with Glen Sonmor (L to R): Mark Napier, Steve Payne, Bo Berglund, Dennis Maruk, Paul Holmgren, Doc Rose, Curt Giles.

Jude Drouin and Lou Nanne

North Stars archives

Pete LoPresti and Gilles Meloche

North Stars archives

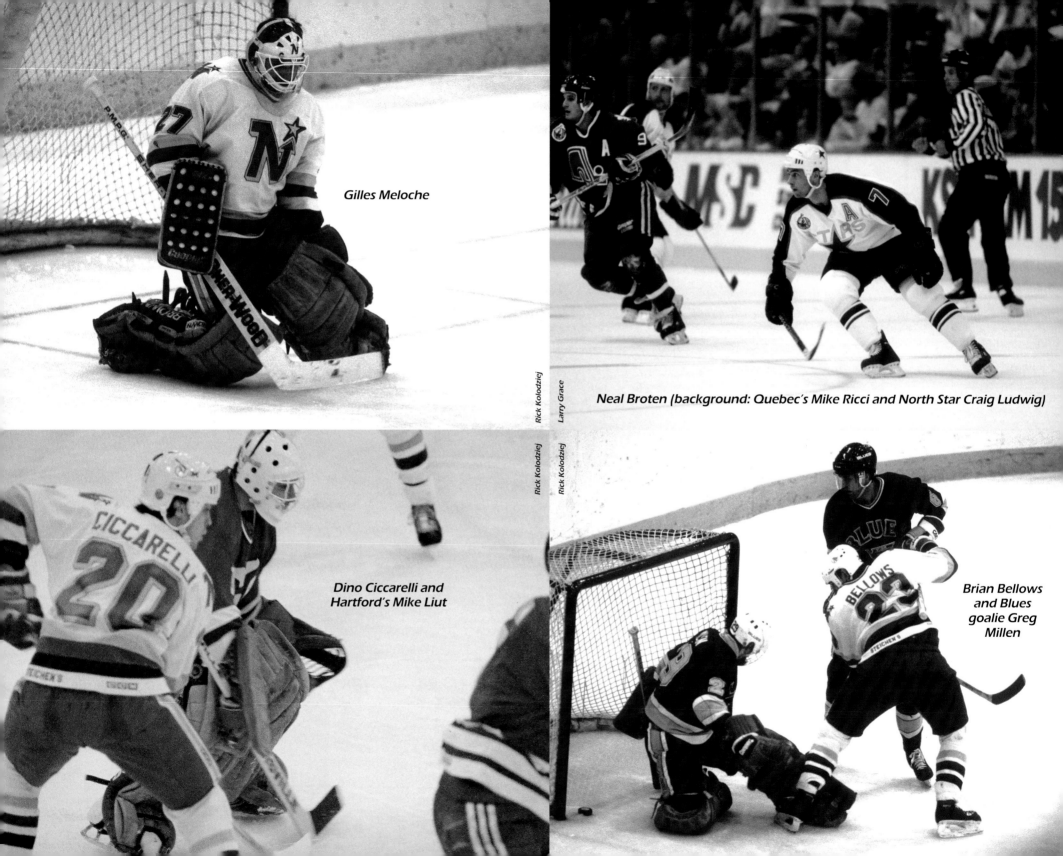

Gilles Meloche

Neal Broten (background: Quebec's Mike Ricci and North Star Craig Ludwig)

Dino Ciccarelli and Hartford's Mike Liut

Brian Bellows and Blues goalie Greg Millen

Pete LoPresti

LoPresti, O'Brien, Barrett and Talafous

North Stars' retired numbers:
Bill Goldsworthy 8
Bill Masterton 19

Larry Grace

October 5, 1991: *Brian Bellows and the North Stars open the season with a new uniform design and crest.*

April 13, 1993: In the final game at Met Center, Ulf Dahlen, Gaetan Duchesne and Neal Broten come down the stairs from the locker room and onto the ice.

1992-93 GAME RESULTS

#	Date	Opp	Score	Result	Record
1	10-6	@ St. Louis	4-6	L	0-1-0
2	10-8	ST. LOUIS	5-2	W	1-1-0
3	10-10	TAMPA BAY	2-1	W	2-1-0
4 *	10-13	CALGARY	3-4	L	2-2-0
5	10-15	@ St. Louis	5-4	W	3-2-0
6	10-17	@ Montreal	1-8	L	3-3-0
7	10-18	@ Toronto	5-1	W	4-3-0
8	10-22	QUEBEC	5-2	W	5-3-0
9	10-24	LOS ANGELES	5-5	T #	5-3-1
10	10-28	@ Edmonton	2-5	L	5-4-1
11	10-30	@ Vancouver	3-2	W	6-4-1
12	10-31	@ Calgary	3-5	L	6-5-1
13	11-5	NY ISLANDERS	3-0	W	7-5-1
14	11-7	EDMONTON	2-2	T #	7-5-2
15	11-10	PITTSBURGH	1-4	L	7-6-2
16	11-12	WINNIPEG	2-7	L	7-7-2
17	11-14	CHICAGO	3-0	W	8-7-2
18	11-15	@ Chicago	1-2	L	8-8-2
19	11-18	@ Washington	5-4	W	9-8-2
20	11-19	@ Tampa Bay	4-1	W	10-8-2
21	11-21	@ Buffalo	4-3	W	11-8-2
22	11-25	VANCOUVER	2-4	L	11-9-2
23	11-27	NY RANGERS	4-4	T #	11-9-3
24	11-28	SAN JOSE	10-3	W	12-9-3
25	11-30	@ NY Rangers	4-2	W	13-9-3
26	12-1	@ Ottawa	3-1	W	14-9-3
27	12-3	@ Detroit	4-2	W	15-9-3
28	12-5	@ Quebec	7-4	W	16-9-3
29	12-10	EDMONTON	2-3	L	16-10-3
30	12-12	CHICAGO	0-3	L	16-11-3
31	12-15	TORONTO	6-5	W	17-11-3
32	12-19	DETROIT	3-3	T#	17-11-4
33	12-20	@ Chicago	0-4	L	17-12-4
34	12-22	ST. LOUIS	2-2	T#	17-12-5
35	12-26	WINNIPEG	5-4	W	18-12-5
36	12-27	@ Winnipeg	4-7	L	18-13-5
37	12-31	BOSTON	5-3	W	19-13-5
38	1-2	@ NY Islanders	2-3	L	19-14-5
39	1-3	@ Hartford	6-6	T#	19-14-6
40	1-6	@ New Jersey	1-5	L	19-15-6
41	1-7	@ Pittsburgh	6-3	W	20-15-6
42	1-9	TAMPA BAY	6-4	W	21-15-6
43	1-12	CHICAGO	1-3	L	21-16-6
44	1-14	@ Chicago	1-3	L	21-17-6
45	1-16	CALGARY	4-3	W	22-17-6
46	1-19	@ Tampa Bay	4-2	W	23-17-6
47	1-21	OTTAWA	7-2	W	24-17-6
48	1-23	VANCOUVER	3-3	T #	24-17-7
49	1-24	@ Tampa Bay	2-2	T #	24-17-8
50	1-26	@ Toronto	2-1	W	25-17-8
51	1-28	NEW JERSEY	4-2	W	26-17-8
52	1-30	TAMPA BAY	3-4	L	26-18-8
53	2-1	@ Vancouver	5-4	W	27-18-8
54	2-3	@ San Jose	7-3	W	28-18-8
55	2-9	WASHINGTON	2-3	L	28-19-8
56	2-11	@ Tampa Bay	1-0	W	29-19-8
57	2-13	@ Toronto	1-6	L	29-20-8
58	2-14	TORONTO	5-6	L	29-21-8
59	2-17	LOS ANGELES	5-10	L	29-22-8
60	2-20	PHILADELPHIA	5-2	W	30-22-8
61	2-21	DETROIT	1-4	L	30-23-8
62	2-25	@ Boston	3-3	T #	30-23-9
63	2-27	@ St. Louis	2-3	L	30-24-9
64	2-28	@ Winnipeg	6-7	L	30-25-9
65	3-1	@ Toronto	1-3	L	30-26-9
66	3-6	MONTREAL	4-3	W	31-26-9
67	3-7	DETROIT	1-7	L	31-27-9
68	3-9	SAN JOSE	4-2	W	32-27-9
69 *	3-11	@ Vancouver	4-3	W	33-27-9
70	3-13	@ St. Louis	2-6	L	33-28-9
71	3-14	ST. LOUIS	1-3	L	33-29-9
72	3-16	@ Philadelphia	3-4	L	33-30-9
73	3-18	@ Detroit	1-5	L	33-31-9
74	3-21	DETROIT	2-6	L	33-32-9
75	3-25	TORONTO	3-3	T #	33-32-10
76	3-27	HARTFORD	1-2	L	33-33-10
77	3-31	@ Edmonton	2-5	L	33-34-10
78	4-1	@ Calgary	3-5	L	33-35-10
79	4-3	@ Los Angeles	3-0	W	34-35-10
80	4-6	BUFFALO	3-1	W	35-35-10
81	4-10	ST. LOUIS	4-3	W	36-35-10
82	4-11	@ St. Louis	1-5	L	36-36-10
83	4-13	CHICAGO	2-3	L	36-37-10
84	4-15	@ Detroit	3-5	L	36-38-10

* - Neutral-Site games in Saskatoon   # - Overtime   & - Sellout

1992-93

36-38-10 • 82 points • 5th Place, Norris Division

Goals: Russ Courtnall 36
Assists: Mike Modano 60
Points: Mike Modano 93
Penalty Minutes: Shane Churla 286
Goalie Wins: Jon Casey 26

No Playoffs

April 13, 1993:
Legendary anthem singer
Jim Bowers performs his
final Met Center rendition of
"The Star-Spangled Banner."

SNAPPING THE FLYERS STREAK

Lou Nanne:

In 1980, the Philadelphia Flyers were riding a 35-game unbeaten streak, the longest ever in professional sports, and they were coming into the Met Center. That's when our team was starting to become an excellent hockey club. Even though we were young, we were very talented.

The atmosphere was electric. The USA Network was covering the game, with Dan Kelly, who was a top broadcaster, brought in to do the announcing. Tickets were at a premium — people were going nuts to get into the building, and the place was jam-packed. Our team was really fired up.

Glen Sonmor, our coach, was so excited it was hard to contain him. Our club came out and played an unbelievable hockey game, and we were able to beat the Flyers 7-1.

Looking back, I'd have to say it was one of the key victories on the road to becoming the terrific hockey team that eventually played in the Stanley Cup Final.

January 7, 1980: The North Stars break the Philadelphia Flyers streak of 35 consecutive games without a loss, winning 7-1 at the Met. Flyers defenseman Jack McIlhargey slumps in disappointment as the North Stars celebrate a goal.

Steve Schluter / Minneapolis Star Tribune

Sonny John

TOM REID'S PENALTY SHOT

Al Shaver:

Let's not forget the shot that was heard around the world. Well, maybe just the hockey world. Allan Thomas Reid was not a prolific scorer among NHL defensemen. In a span of 10 shin-bruising seasons with the North Stars, Tall Tommy scored only 17 goals, but on the night of October 14, 1971, he performed a feat that put him in a class by himself and earned him a place in the team history book. On one of his rare good scoring opportunities, Reid was fouled by a Montreal player and the referee awarded him a penalty shot.

Coach Jack Gordon, showing supreme confidence in Reid's scoring prowess, asked the ref, "Does Reid have to take the shot?" To young Thomas that was the ultimate insult, but take the shot he did. Unleashing all of his anger over the coach's lack of confidence, Reid launched a blistering rocket that left Ken Dryden trembling in his skates. The twine behind Dryden bulged, the red light flashed, bells chimed, fireworks filled the air, brass bands started playing, and thousands of fans began chanting, "Tommy! Tommy! Tommy!" And so, a hero was born on that autumn evening, many years ago.

October 14, 1971: Tom Reid scores the first successful penalty shot in North Stars history, beating Montreal goalie Ken Dryden.

Tom Reid:

I came out of the penalty box and was heading toward the bench when a clearing pass hit my skate and careened toward the Montreal zone. Instead of going to the bench I went after the puck had a clear breakaway. Guy Lapointe tripped me from behind and I slid hard into the boards.

Referee Bruce Hood skated over and asked if I was okay. I said, "Yes," and then, "You're giving him a penalty, right?" He said, "You're getting a penalty shot." I said: "Bruce, go to hell. I don't want a penalty shot." "You got one," he replied.

When I got to the bench, coach Jack Gordon asked what was going on. Hood skated over and said, "Let's go." Jack said, "What do you mean?" and was then informed of the penalty shot. Jack said, "Does he have to take the shot?" and I informed Hood that I thought my leg was broken. Hood said, "Let's go or you'll get a delay of game."

Everyone on the bench was giving me advice about what to do with the shot, but J.P. Parise simply said, "Put the damn thing behind him."

I was so focused as I got ready to take the puck that I couldn't hear a thing. There were 15,000 people in the building, but I heard nothing. It was a warm October night so the ice was a bit wet, and I was worried about carrying the puck across the blue line. My main concern was just getting off a shot.

I skated in, got to the high slot, and shot the puck. Ken Dryden wasn't expecting a shot that quickly and he overreacted. I was aiming for the corner, but the puck went between his legs and into the net, my big claim to fame.

When I got back to the bench, I said to Jack, "Was there ever any doubt?"

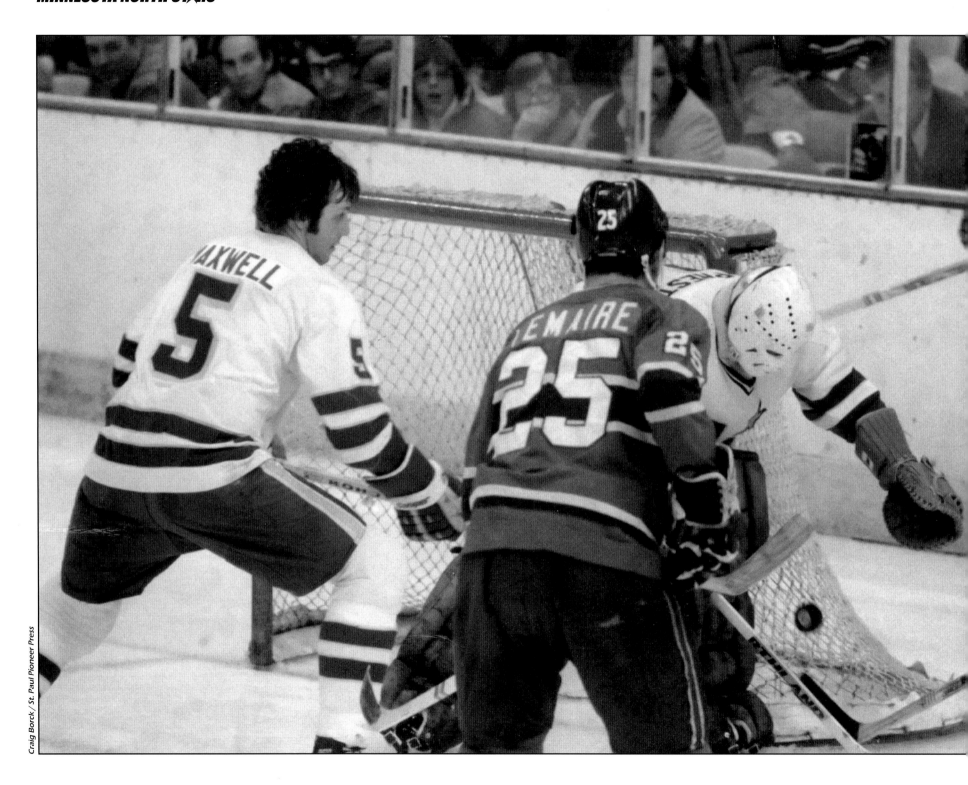

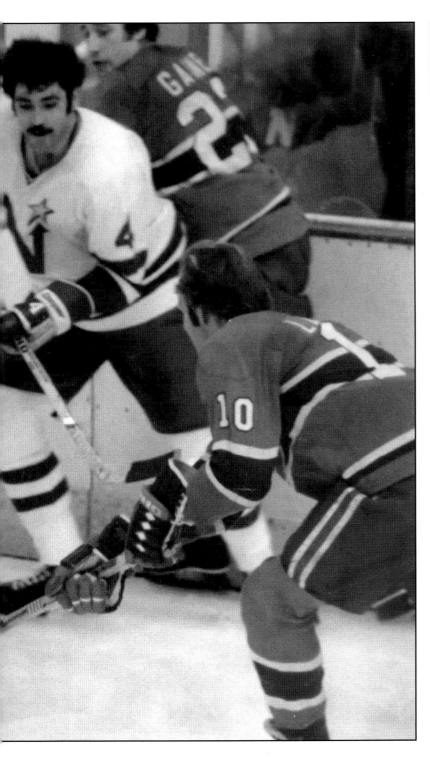

Lou's NHL Stories

Jean Beliveau

We were playing the Canadiens in Montreal the night Jean Beliveau scored his 500th NHL goal. It was February of 1971, the final season of Beliveau's great career. Gilles Gilbert had the distinction of being in net, and we lost 6-2.

That night while the game was being played, someone broke into Beliveau's house and robbed him of all his trophies and memorabilia, the whole works. Montreal people are such big hockey fans that everybody knows when a game is going on, so Beliveau was an easy target. He remembers that night not only for scoring his 500th goal, but for getting robbed at the same time.

Scotty Bowman

At the end of the 1978 season when I took over the North Stars, the playoffs began and "Hockey Night in Canada" asked me to do the color for them.

We got to the sixth game of the Stanley Cup Finals at Boston Garden between Boston and Montreal, and around 5 p.m. I went down to the Montreal locker room. When I walked in, Guy Lafleur, Serge Savard and Yvan Cournoyer were sitting there talking and having a cigarette.

Lafleur was one of those guys who chain-smoked like Gump Worsley and Bill Goldsworthy — they smoked before the game and in between periods. Scotty Bowman was Montreal's coach at the time. He was the preeminent coach, and also very strict and demanding with the players.

March 13, 1978: *Defensemen Brad Maxwell and Jerry Engele and goalie Pete LoPresti battle Montreal's Jacques Lemaire, Guy Lafluer and Bob Gainey. All three Canadiens become Hall of Famers under head coach Scotty Bowman.*

Lafleur saw me and piped up right away: "Hey Louie, we hear you're looking for a coach. Take Scotty. He's driving us nuts."

•

When you talk about great coaches in the NHL, you've got to talk about Scotty Bowman, Al Arbour, and Toe Blake as being the best, and Scotty was at the top. When he became general manager in Buffalo, we got to see another facet of his personality. Just watching his reactions to things was fun.

I used to talk with him quite a bit about making deals, but we never, ever made a trade. He calls me up one day and says, "Louie, would you like Jim Schoenfeld?'"

I said: "Yeah Scotty, I'd like Jim Schoenfeld. What do you want for him?"

He says, "No, I'm serious, do you want Schoenfeld?" I said, "I'm serious, what do you want for him?"

He says, "You don't want Schoenfeld, he can't help your team." I said: "Scotty, just tell me what you want for him. Schoenfeld can help my team."

On and on it went — me saying I wanted Schoenfeld, Scotty telling me why I didn't. He finally said, "Nah, he's overrated," and hung up.

Gerry Cheevers

The Boston Bruins of the '60s and '70s had more characters on their team than anybody else in the league, and goalie Gerry Cheevers was one of them. He was one of the wittiest guys who ever played the game. He would paint stitches on his mask where it was hit by a puck.

One night, Cheevers was in net for the Bruins when they were trounced 10-2 by the Canadiens. After the game, Bruins' GM Hap Emms stormed into the locker room and said, "Cheevers, what the hell happened out there?" Cheevers looked up and said, "Hap, it's like this: Roses are red, violets are blue, they got 10, and we got two."

•

Early in his career, Cheesy, as we liked to call him, was coached by Bruins legend Milt Schmidt. Milt was one of the truly great players in the NHL during the '40s and '50s. He formed the famous "Kraut Line" with Bobby Bauer and Woody Dumont. John Mariucci always said that Milt Schmidt was as tough as any player he'd ever seen.

Well, Cheevers was in net one night and gave up five goals, the last of which was very soft. After the game, Milt Schmidt came into the locker room and said, "Cheevers, I can't understand how you missed that last goal." Cheevers said, "I guess I should've kept my legs closed." Milt replied, "No, maybe your mother should have."

February 23, 1977: *Steve Jensen streaks past Boston defenseman Brad Park and beats goalie Gerry Cheevers. Assisting on the play is No. 10 Alex Pirus.*

Mike Zerby / Minneapolis Star Tribune

Joe Crozier

One of my favorite J.P. Parise stories happened before he came to the North Stars. He was playing for Rochester in the American Hockey League and his coach was Joe Crozier, who was a different kind of guy and a different kind of coach.

Joe was giving one of his classic pep talks before a game when he turned to J.P. and said, "Parise, we know you're going to score a goal this year. Would you mind just telling us when it will be so we can quit counting on you night after night?"

Joe went on to coach the Buffalo Sabres and considered himself to be a master motivator. One night he addressed his team by saying: "I went to church today and asked God what we need to do to win, and God said, 'Joe, you've brought them this far, tonight they have to do it on their own.' So I'm telling you guys to do it on your own. I can't do anything more. God told me it's up to you."

Don Cherry

When we faced Montreal in the 1980 playoffs, Glen Sonmor was coaching us and Claude Ruel was coaching the Canadiens.

Don Cherry was doing the television coverage, and I'll never forget the remark he made one night. As the game went on, it got more heated, and Glen started yelling across the ice at Claude, and Claude started yelling back.

Now you've got to remember Glen Sonmor's got just one eye, and Claude Ruel's only got one eye. Both lost an eye in hockey accidents. Don Cherry is watching as a camera focuses on the coaches yelling at each other, and he says, "I guess they don't see eye to eye."

Don Cherry

Staff Photo / St. Paul Pioneer Press

At the time I became general manager in '78, the North Stars had never beaten the Bruins in Boston. I asked Boston coach Don Cherry to come to Minnesota and shoot a TV commercial for our upcoming season, because we were in the same division as the Bruins. He accepted and did a terrific job. He talked about how tough a time the North Stars would have against his team and how the Bruins were looking forward to pounding us. It really got our fans excited when Boston came to town.

Many years ago, Don Cherry and I were involved in a sports celebrity banquet in St. Louis. Legendary Cardinals baseball broadcaster Jack Buck was the emcee.

When it was time for Cherry to speak, Buck introduced him by saying, "Here is a fellow so well known in Canada he can't walk the streets without being recognized, but I've never heard of him." Cherry stepped to the podium and said, "Well, Mr. Buck, I've never heard of you, either."

Jack Buck then grabbed the microphone and said: "Cherry, you're from Canada, so maybe you don't understand the English language. You don't end a sentence with a preposition." To which Cherry responded, "Then let me correct myself, Mr. Buck. I've never heard of you either, asshole."

Phil Esposito

Phil Esposito and I grew up together from about the age of 5. We played together in the schoolyard — baseball, softball, football and hockey.

At the start of his pro career, Phil was in the Central League playing for St. Louis, and I was still working and arguing about a contract with Chicago. Whenever he came to the Twin Cities to play a Central League game, we would have dinner.

Then, he was called up to the Chicago Blackhawks. After his initial year with Chicago, the first thing he did was buy a cabin right around the bend from our family's cabin at Pointe aux Pins on Lake Superior.

We all had signs on our cabins — ours was Casper the Ghost — and Phil needed an identifying sign out front on his, so he put up a big Indianhead, the crest of the Chicago Blackhawks.

We were there one day during the summer of '67 when a call comes to Phil from Tommy Ivan of the Blackhawks. He said to Phil, "You've just been traded to the Boston Bruins."

Phil hangs up the phone, and the first thing he says is not, "Geez, why is this happening?" It is, "What am I going to do with my Indianhead sign?"

We are playing the Bruins at Met Center, Phil has two goals so far, and it is now the third period. The puck comes into our zone, but I don't go anywhere — I just stand beside Phil and grab his stick.

In those days, defensemen used to have the palms of their gloves cut out so they could hold onto an opponent's stick. I grab Phil's stick and he says, "What are you doing?"

I said, "You're not scoring, not while I'm on the ice." He says: "Leave me alone. I need a hat trick." I said: "You're not scoring a goal while I'm on the ice. I don't care if anybody else scores, you're not going anywhere."

The whole shift I'm holding his stick and he's yelling at the referee, "He's got my stick!" When he'd do that, I'd let go. He never did get the hat trick.

Through Phil I got to know Bobby Orr really well. Bobby was an unbelievable player, but he was also a good practical joker. In fact, the whole group of Bruins — Orr, Cheevers, John McKenzie, Wayne Cashman, etc. — was probably the most fun-loving group that hockey has ever seen.

February 28, 1979: The Rangers' Phil Esposito and Don Maloney are confronted by defenseman Gary Sargent and goalie Gilles Meloche.

Pete Hohn / Minneapolis Star Tribune

On the day after the end of one season, the Bruins were having their team break-up party, and Phil wasn't there because he was in the hospital recovering from knee surgery. So a group of players left the Branding Iron bar, went to the hospital, got Phil and his hospital bed, put him in the elevator, wheeled him out to the street and took him to the bar.

One night a Bruins player ended up in jail. The police gave him one phone call, and he called a Chinese restaurant and had food delivered. When Phil went to pick him up, he and two policemen were eating his takeout meal.

Tony Esposito

When Tony Esposito was goalie for the Blackhawks, I was certain his leg pads were too wide and illegal. It drove me crazy because I would complain to the officials but they would say they measured them and they were the proper size. I knew I wasn't just seeing things and that those pads were bigger than they should be.

In the 1981 Canada Cup, Tony was not a member of Team Canada, so I had him get United States citizenship and put him on Team USA. The rules for the Canada Cup were the same as those for the NHL, and the officials told us that they would measure goalie pads in the afternoon before every game. I was in the locker room when the officials came in and measured Tony's pads. They were perfect.

Well, as soon as the officials left, Tony went to the back room, cut the side laces to his pads, and began stuffing in huge wads of cotton. After the pads were about two inches wider, Tony sewed them back up.

The mystery was solved. I said to him, "Now I know what you've been doing all these years."

When I took over as general manager, league president John Ziegler called and asked me to be part of management's negotiating committee with the players' association.

Two years later, Tony Esposito was president of the players association and we were involved in collective bargaining for a new agreement. I came up with an idea of how to structure compensation if we lost a player.

A copy of the plan (without my name on it) was given to the players' bargaining committee. Ziegler said to me: "Louie, when we go in the meeting I don't want you to talk. I don't want the players to know you had anything to do with this, because that won't help us."

John passed out copies to the players' side of the table and asked everyone to take a look at the proposal and respond to it. Tony Esposito read it and said: "Who wrote this thing? I can't understand it."

Then he looks at me and says: "Louie, I know you wrote this damned thing. How could you do that? You were on our side a couple of years ago, and you would never have agreed to this." I said, "Tony, I didn't realize what a parasite I was until I got on this side of the table."

Glenn Frey

Prior to a game at the Met against the Detroit Red Wings, I was sitting in the press box. Just before the game started our Promotions Director Dick Meredith asked if I minded having someone sit with me and I said it would be fine.

A young guy sits down and says: "Thanks, Lou. I'm a big hockey fan and watched Detroit a lot when I was growing up, and I'll really enjoy sitting beside you during the game."

So we watched the game and I talked to him a little bit about hockey. At the end of the first period I said, "If you want to get a Coke or a beer or something, just go down to the end of the press box and down the steps to the press room."

When he left I asked an intern from the P.R. department, "Who's this guy sitting beside me?" He says, "Glenn Frey."

I said, "Who's that?" He says, "He's with the Eagles." I said, "The Philadelphia Eagles?"

It became a running joke that I didn't know who the Eagles were. Frey himself told the story for years. Two decades later, Frey went on a golf trip with my son Marty and told him the story.

Bill Gadbsy

One of the funniest things I ever saw took place when we were playing at Detroit in 1969. I was on the ice beside the Red Wings bench, waiting for a faceoff.

A phone on their bench started ringing, and apparently it was Bruce Norris, who owned the team. Detroit coach Bill Gadsby answered the call, then hung up and ripped the phone out of the bench. He obviously wasn't too happy with the orders he had just been given.

Norm Green

When Norm Green first arrived in Minnesota, I took him around town and introduced him to CEOs, hoping to get support from their companies.

We had finished a meeting in downtown St. Paul with Doug Leatherdale of St. Paul Travelers and were getting into my car. Across the street two women noticed me, waved and said hello, and I waved back as I got in my car. Norm got in on the other side and didn't notice us waving at one another.

As I drove down the street, I passed the two ladies. They waved at me again. Norm then turned to me and said: "I can't believe this town. I've only been here two weeks and they already know me. This really is a true hockey town."

Wayne Gretzky

During Wayne Gretzky's first year in the league, the All-Star game was in Detroit. At three o'clock that afternoon, the phone rang in my hotel room and it was Glen Sather, the Edmonton general manager and a former teammate.

Glen says: "Louie, you gotta help me out. I need two tickets for the game for Wayne Gretzky's parents. They decided to come at the last minute, and we've distributed all our tickets."

I said: "You're lucky. I have two extras. I'll leave them at the box office." He said: "No, Wayne is standing right here. He'll come up and get them right now."

So Gretzky came up to my room, I gave him the tickets, and his mom and dad sat with me at the game. From then on, whenever I saw Wayne's dad Walter, he would tell those around us that he sat with me at Wayne's first All-Star game. He is a real gentleman.

●

We were playing an exhibition game against Edmonton five years later in Kitchener, and it was our "home" game. At 5 p.m., I went to the arena and checked on ticket sales. The person at the box office said, "We only have 2,500 sold." I said, "You have 6,000 seats, and Edmonton's coming in."

He said, "Yes, but they made an announcement a couple days ago that Gretzky wasn't going to play." I said, "You have to be kidding," and went down to Edmonton's dressing room to find Sather.

I said, "Glen, you've got to dress Gretzky." He said, "I promised him the night off."

I said: "I've only got 2,500 tickets sold — I can't afford this. I'll tell you what. Just use him on the power plays. By the time the league finds out you dressed 21 guys, no one's going to say anything."

Sather said: "He's right there. Go ask Wayne."

I said, "Wayne, I need a favor." He said, "Whatever I can do to help."

I said, "I need you to play tonight, even if it's just for the power plays. I've only got 2,500 tickets sold, and if I can get you in the lineup I know we can sell a lot more tickets."

He said, "If you really want me to, I will."

I went back upstairs and said: "Call the TV and radio stations right now. Gretzky's playing."

They sold out the rink in an hour and a half.

Max McNab

We held many of our NHL winter meetings at The Breakers resort in Palm Beach, and each one included a dinner and dance in its schedule. Since it was always mid-season and games were being played, guys were constantly leaving the dance to get updates.

One particular year, I asked all of the general managers at our meeting not to check on scores so we could relax with our wives and enjoy the evening. Everyone agreed, and we had a very nice dinner in the ballroom.

Right before the dance started, I noticed Max McNab wasn't at his table. Max was the GM for New Jersey, and the North Stars were playing the Devils that night, so I kept an eye on his table.

Ten minutes later Max comes back into the ballroom, almost running because he's so excited. He grabs his wife June and they start dancing. Max is spinning and twirling his wife, so I walk out on the dance floor and say: "Damn it, Max, I know you checked on the game and we must be losing. What's the score?" He says, "Yeah, you're losing 3 to1."

Harry Neale

Harry Neale, who coached Vancouver as well as the Minnesota Fighting Saints, became the lead broadcaster for "Hockey Night in Canada" and probably has as quick a wit as ever came down the pike. He's the originator of that great line, referring to the National Anthem, "Every time I hear that song I have a bad game."

One night I was listening to Harry during the Stanley Cup Finals when he came up with another memorable quip: "You know you're having a good year when you look at the scoreboard during the playoffs and there are no out-of-town games."

Brian O'Neill

Brian O'Neill, the league's executive vice president, was a wonderful guy all the way through my career. He was one of the real treasures of the National Hockey League. However, he used to get upset with me every now and then at some of the things I did.

For example, Bill Torrey and Cliff Fletcher were among my closest friends in the league, and we were trying to keep the Central League alive, so we wanted to put a franchise in Birmingham, Alabama.

Torrey and Fletcher said: "Louie, why don't you go there? You don't have any ties where you are, and maybe we can develop that market." I said: "That's fine, that's not a problem. So I'll go to Birmingham."

At the end of that season, Frank Beaton was playing for the Islanders' farm team in Indianapolis. Frank's nickname, by the way, was Frank "Never Beaten" Beaton, because he could really fight.

So I called him up in May and said, "Frank, I want to sign you to go to Birmingham." He says: "OK, I'd like that. You know, it's my wife's hometown." So I signed him to a minor league contract.

Then Bill Torrey calls me and says, "Hey, you just signed my player

before June 1st." I said, "That's right." He says, "Well, the rules say no signings before June 1st." I said, "You want me to go to Birmingham, I'm going, and I need Beaton as a draw." He says, "Well, you've got to give me something for him." I said, "OK, I'll buy you dinner at The Palm."

He says, "OK."

So when we sent in the form for the trade, it said, "Frank Beaton traded to the North Stars for dinner at The Palm." Brian O'Neill calls me up

Lou with fellow GMs (from left) Bill Torrey, Harry Sinden and Cliff Fletcher.

Lou Nanne archives

and says: "Louie, do you think you can make a mockery of the league? You can't trade somebody for dinner at The Palm." I said, "Brian, that will cost more than waivers, which are only $100."

He says, "You guys have got to change this." We sent the form back in amended to, "Frank Beaton traded for future considerations." So that winter when I went to New York, I called up Bill and we went to dinner at The Palm. I got the receipt for $157 and sent it in with a note that said, "See Brian, I told you it was worth more than waivers."

Bobby Orr

I was GM in November of '78 when the North Stars were scheduled to play the Canucks in Vancouver. My wife and I went to Vancouver a few days ahead of the team to visit family that lived in the area. While we were there, we attended a game between the Canucks and Blackhawks. I wanted to say hello to my old friends Tony Esposito and Bobby Orr following the game, but they had to leave immediately for the airport.

An hour or so later, Francine and I are having dinner at The Four Seasons when suddenly Bobby Orr appears. I ask, "What are you doing back here?" and he says: "The Chicago airport is closed so we had to return. Do you mind if I join you?"

Orr sits down, calls for the waiter and says, "Bring us your best bottle of champagne." I asked what the occasion was, and he says: "I want to toast my career. My knees are really bothering me and I can't play. I've decided to retire. I'll make the announcement tomorrow in Chicago." Sure enough, the next day, November 8, 1978, Bobby Orr retired.

ELEVENTH
WILLIE KIDD INVITATIONAL
INTERLACHEN COUNTRY CLUB - 1978

Lou with Bobby Orr.

Bud Poile and the 1980 Olympic Team

After the 1980 Olympic team had its camp in Colorado Springs, Herbie felt that playing games against college teams wouldn't provide enough competition. I told him I could talk to a couple NHL teams that might be willing to play exhibition games, but he wanted more than that. I suggested we visit Bud Poile. At the time, I was chairman of the board of the Central Hockey League and Bud Poile was league president.

Herb and I flew to Dallas and asked Bud if he could incorporate the U.S. Olympic team into the Central League schedule. Bud was terrific and had great foresight. He realized it would be a boon for the Central League having the Olympic team visit each city a couple of times. The Olympic team used the Twin Cities as their home base.

The games counted in the CHL standings, and were very competitive. When Herb looked back after winning the Gold Medal, he said a key part of their training was playing in the Central League. And Bud Poile made it happen.

Sammy Pollock

When I was vice president of the players' association and playing with the North Stars, we had a Board of Governors meeting in Montreal. One of the questions we were concerned with was attendance in some of the cities, including Minnesota — the kind of gate receipts we had.

We were discussing ways that we could improve revenues, and I said: "The North Stars are not drawing very much in the exhibition season with the teams we are playing. I think we could do a lot more at the gate if we had the opportunity to play teams from the other conference, most notably Montreal and Toronto — teams that we only see twice during the year. Our exhibition schedule should include the other conference, and we'd have much more attractive games."

Montreal's Sammy Pollock, who was the dean of general managers, says, "Louie, I'm willing to help with our teams in a lot of ways, but when you bring up exhibition games, you ain't gettin' any." The Canadiens would sell out all their exhibition games against their rivals, and they were getting big dollars.

●

Sammy Pollock was respected by everybody. When I was thinking of quitting during the 1987-88 season, he happened to be at the All-Star game, so I walked up to him and said, "Sammy, could I ask you a question?" He says, "What is it?" I said, "When did you know that you wanted to retire?"

And I remember he said, "You'll know." That struck a chord with me when Bobby Clarke retired last year. The first time he retired, he called at 7 in the morning and asked, "Louie, when did you know you wanted to retire?"

I said, "I'm going to tell you what Sammy Pollock told me: 'You'll know.'"

Bob Pulford

Whenever we played golf during a general managers meeting, we were always cautious around Bob Pulford. He had a knack for swiping golf balls.

One time I happened to walk around the corner of the clubhouse in time to see him reaching into Harry Sinden's golf bag, pulling out all the golf balls, and putting them in his own bag. Bob was noted for getting golf balls anywhere he could, and he joked about putting his son through college with money saved after retrieving balls from the lake at Medinah Country Club.

I always enjoyed playing golf with Pully, even though I'd end up a few golf balls short. Our rivalry with the Blackhawks was fierce, and the golf course was a place where we could relax. It was almost inconceivable how supportive Bob Pulford and Bill Wirtz were towards the North Stars and the Gunds when the situation didn't involve direct competition between the two teams. They loved Minnesota and truly treasured the rivalry.

Gene Ubriaco

I grew up with a fellow named Gene Ubriaco. Gene went to St. Mike's at an early age to play Junior hockey, and one of his teammates there was Cesare Maniago.

Gene wound up with Oakland. The three of us would see each other whenever Oakland and Minnesota played. This time, we were ending the season in Oakland.

Before the game, Cesare and I were walking to the rink. Ubriaco saw me, waved me over and said: "Louie, I got 19 goals. I need one more for a $2,000 bonus."

Well, $2,000 was substantial, especially when you were making around $21,000. He says, "You've got to tell Cesare to help me out." I said, "OK, I'll help you, and I'll get Cesare to help you, because the game means nothing."

I told Cesare, "Ubie needs a goal," and he said, "Tell him to put it on the net."

The game starts, Ubriaco comes down the left wing on me, and I'm saying, "Go inside, go inside," as I move to the outside. He goes outside, and I knock him down.

The next shift he comes out, he's down in front of the net, and I'm saying to him, "Get behind me, get behind me, I'll let a rebound go." So he goes behind me, and the puck hits him.

The next period he's coming down, and I'm saying, "Shoot it through my legs." Instead, he tries to go around me and falls down.

In the third period, we're in front of the net, and I'm telling him, "Shoot the puck, shoot the puck." He tries to stick-handle it and I knock him down.

Then, he looks at me and says, "Play your own game — I've got a better chance." He never did get the goal; never even got a shot on net.

Gene Ubriaco

North Stars archives

Bill Wirtz

Bill Wirtz probably has done more for the National Hockey League than any owner in the history of the game, and I believe he should be honored with one of the league's trophies. The league has not recognized all of this man's accomplishments.

During the '80s we were trying to speed up the game, which was going a little too long, even for television, and particularly for cable and the satellite network. One idea that came up at the Board of Governors meeting was shortening the intermissions from 20 minutes to 15. That got Bill, who was chairman of the board, really excited. He said, "There's no way I'm giving up five minutes of drinking time. That's where we make our revenues." The night in Chicago when they sold out of beer is a good example of how important this was to Bill.

The other guys prevailed upon him, and Wirtz, being the way he was, bit the bullet and agreed to go down from 20 to 15 minutes. Now, in the last few years, I see they've gone back up from 15 minutes to 18.

When you think of the success of the National Hockey League, you have to think of Bill Wirtz. He was very adamant that the success of the league was dependent on division rivalries, on people really getting to know the opposition and getting to despise the opposition. And he fought for it long and hard.

Wirtz would wear you out to get your vote. If he needed your vote, he'd stay up all night long at a Board of Governors meeting and work on you. A lot of times he and his GM, Bob Pulford, worked on a group of us that hung around together — Harry Sinden, Cliff Fletcher, Bill Torrey, John Ferguson and myself — because more often than not we agreed on things. He knew that we would then help work on other board members.

Deep Sea Fishing

We had a free afternoon during one of our Board of Governors meetings in Florida, so a group of us including John Ferguson and Harry Sinden took the opportunity to go deep sea fishing. After an hour of fishing on big swells, Jim Gregory starts getting seasick and throws up. Upon seeing this, I get sick myself. Right then, I also catch a fish.

I'm reeling in the fish while throwing up. It gets so bad I have the dry heaves. I quit reeling and tell the boat captain to take us in. He says no. So I turn to Fergie and Sinden and say, "I'll give each of you a first-round pick if you get me in to shore."

The captain says, "We're not going in yet." I say, "Either we're going in to shore or you're going in the ocean." He finally took us in, and the floor beneath me didn't stop spinning all night.

The Top NHL PLayer

We had a GM meeting in January 1988, and one of the things we discussed was Gretzky being so great.

We had 12 general managers sitting around, and one says: "OK, we're starting a team today, let's have a vote. Who would we pick? Which all-time player would you take?"

Six picked Gretzky and six picked Orr.

If you expand that to the four greatest, you think of Gretzky, Orr, Gordie Howe — and let's not forget Mario Lemieux. When Lemieux came into the draft in 1984, I offered all 12 of the North Stars' picks to Pittsburgh's Eddie Johnston for the No. 1 overall so I could take

Lemieux. Johnston gave me the correct reply: "No way, Louie, he will be a franchise player."

We played Detroit one night and Gordie Howe came through for the Red Wings in a big way, even though he was an older player by then. After the game a few of us were sitting around discussing Howe and somebody said, "Howe's got to be the greatest player that ever lived." And Danny Grant says, "No, it's got to be Bobby Hull."

And Claude Larose says: "Howe is better than Hull, and I'll tell you why: The best checker in the game today is Claude Provost from the Montreal Canadiens. If he checks Howe or if he checks Hull, who do you think has the better night?"

Grant says, "I think Hull would."

Larose says: "No way. Howe would have a much easier night, because after the first period Provost wouldn't be playing anymore. Howe would knock him out of the game."

Still, I believe the argument comes down to Orr and Gretzky. Orr changed the game and was a terrific teammate, an unbelievable player, and the most dominant defenseman of all time. Gretzky elevated the offense to a new level in the sport, and the only challenges he had were to beat his own records. And the main thing about Gretzky and Orr: Both of them were the classiest people off the ice that you could ever find.

1981: At the Met, Lou presents Gordie Howe with the Outstanding Achievement Award from the Greater Minneapolis Chamber of Commerce.

Lou Nanne archives

The Cup

Both the North Stars and the New York Islanders qualified for the 1979-80 playoffs. Prior to the Islanders' first game, I wrote a poem about the Islanders and sent it to my friend Bill Torrey, their GM. The Islanders won, so Bill returned the favor by writing a poem about the North Stars and sending it to me. We won, so the writing and exchanging of poems continued. Both teams kept winning, and the number of poems kept growing. We were eventually knocked out in the semifinals by Philadelphia, but the Islanders eliminated Buffalo to earn their first-ever trip to the Stanley Cup Finals.

The Islanders defeated the Flyers four games to two to win their first Stanley Cup. I was at the game at Nassau Coliseum when the Islanders won the series and was invited to a post-game party at Bill Torrey's home. They had a wonderful celebration with the Cup, and it made quite an impression on me. On the flight back to Minnesota the next morning, I wrote a final poem to Bill.

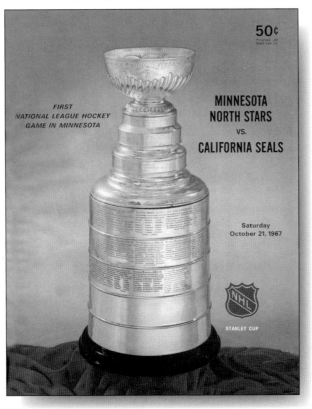

FIRST NATIONAL LEAGUE HOCKEY GAME IN MINNESOTA

50¢

MINNESOTA NORTH STARS VS. CALIFORNIA SEALS

Saturday October 21, 1967

STANLEY CUP

"THE CUP"

I

You start with it, maybe it's a dream.
Who cares if it's only in your mind.
Then, as in all projects, successful or not,
Backwards you go…
Telling yourself one must take 2 steps back to go 3 forward,
Struggle, frustrate, toil, anger,
Emotions come and they go, but a single thought persists,
The Cup!

II

Many times you've quit—albeit only in mind.
And surely just to test your resolve.
First things come second, knowing second understands.
Hopefully, you sleep although sleep is just an extension of the dream.
Looking all the while for signs of progress and a
faint glimmer of that moment.
Yet, all the while a glance askew at other fields,
Wondering if the goal of each could ever equal
The Cup!

III

A loss, a win, a tie, a trade, a draft;
Despair, exhilaration, uncertainty, a change, a chance;
Exhaustion, debate, struggle and agonization;
Is there time enough, patience and understanding?
Asking is checking and that in turn keeps one's sanity,
Because very few will have the privilege of reaching, then receiving,
The Cup!

IV

Tell a story or start a rumor, having it spread,
Hoping it again will weave its web around the fly.
With a big smile, pat on the back and kindness that shrouds
The aim, the obsession, the need—yes, even the desperation.
Feeling the result of it will be the achievement of Camelot,
Vivid pictures in your head become a constant companion,
And, as you concentrate on them,
you hear past sounds along the pavement, heading to
The Cup!

V

Family, friends, employers, employees, all the ingredients of a shelf,
But, did they know how heavy it would be to hold?
Now you ask yourself while sitting drained with the frenzy,
Wanting to shout the answer for all of them to hear,
Yet, fearful, though only slightly,
that they may not feel the way you dreamed
While first seeing it only in mind's eye.
God, yes they know, and you know, that the shelf loves holding
The Cup!

VI

How fast the thoughts travel now — back over all the years.
People thinking fun and games are only that.
The price a tag too rich, because of the rules, even for
Millionaires to manipulate and control at their whim,
Hopefully thinking, praying, guarding that this will remain
So the fortunate few in years to come can appreciate
It takes other things than money alone to own
The Cup!

VII

Allow congratulations from competitors to be your assurance,
What it may in past times seemed too much to pay.
Let those sacrifices be but the champagne that you drink,
Savoring the feelings of a moment I so much long to experience.
Because, should you ever decide and then tell the cost was too high,
Those of us on the chase would be quickly
disillusioned and disheartened,
The dream changing immediately to a nightmare known as
The Cup!

VIII

For you, please heed this view from a longing to be peer,
One with genuine respect and admiration for your superiority,
While observing the state that seemed to encompass you and the shelf.
There became no doubt that the road was graveled in many stretches,
But, suddenly the track narrowed and became paved,
With little images resembling the silver bowl.
And now, I for one, would surely bet that the journey was worth
THE CUP!

THEY PLAYED THE MET CENTER

In addition to being the home of the North Stars, the Met Center played host to the top acts in music and entertainment. The following is a chronological listing of concerts that took place at the Met, along with the number of tickets sold for each show. (List courtesy of Jack Larson, former Executive Director of Met Center.)

CONCERT	DATE	TICKETS SOLD
Sergio Mendez	12/16/67	3,154
Lassie	5/11/68	4,751
Frank Sinatra	7/26/68	12,044
Lawrence Welk	9/3/68	6,281
Tiny Tim	10/18/68	4,639
Eddie Arnold	11/3/68	6,931
Andy Williams	12/6/68	15,844
Grand Ole Opry	12/28/68	1,758
Vanilla Fudge	4/11/69	2,900
Johnny Carson	4/26/69	12,203
Eddie Peabody	7/26/69	10,500
Herb Alpert	11/21/69	12,003
Glen Campbell	12/6/69	12,917
The Four Tops	2/6/70	3,716
Led Zeppelin	4/12/70	10,720
Bob Hope	5/8/70	6,282
Crosby, Stills, and Nash	7/9/70	9,214
Tom Jones	7/19/70	9,825

CONCERT	DATE	TICKETS SOLD
Iron Butterfly	11/13/70	6,120
Grand Funk Railroad	11/22/70	8,734
Three Dog Night	1/8/71	11,717
Savoy Brown & Grease Band & Small Faces	2/20/71	6,939
The Guess Who	3/18/71	4,590
Grass Roots	4/23/71	3,755
Tom Jones	6/3/71	6,445
The Who	8/15/71	15,313
Jackson Five	9/8/71	4,795
The Bee Gees	9/24/71	2,178
Three Dog Night	10/15/71	11,726
Jesus Christ Superstar	10/19/71	12,587
Grand Funk Railroad	10/27/71	10,282
Johnny Cash	10/29/71	8,186
Elvis Presley	11/5/71	17,084
Deep Purple	1/21/72	14,354
Sly and the Family Stone	2/4/72	9,520

CONCERT	DATE	TICKETS SOLD	CONCERT	DATE	TICKETS SOLD
Henry Mancini & Roger Williams	3/3/72	13,348	The Guess Who & Poco	12/7/73	3,012
Rock 'n Roll Revival	3/4/72	6,085	Yes	3/5/74	13,338
Joe Cocker	4/3/72	8,099	Seals and Crofts	3/20/74	7,545
Ten Years After	4/19/72	9,863	Bachman Turner Overdrive	5/11/74	8,673
James Brown	4/28/72	1,503	Ten Years After	5/31/74	12,766
Credence Clearwater Revival	5/5/72	15,000	Cat Stevens	7/6/74	10,719
Jethro Tull	6/5/72	11,187	Uriah Heep	7/28/74	9,150
Rolling Stones	6/18/72	17,385	Mac Davis (afternoon)	8/4/74	9,250
Three Dog Night	7/15/72	13,545	Mac Davis (evening)	8/4/74	9,250
Osmond Brothers	8/19/72	8,866	Steppenwolf	9/29/74	2,804
Grand Funk Railroad	10/13/72	8,517	Deep Purple	12/9/74	6,710
Moody Blues	10/29/72	16,673	Led Zeppelin	1/18/75	16,772
Chicago	11/17/72	16,494	Johnny Winter	2/14/75	6,296
Deep Purple	12/3/72	15,936	Jethro Tull	2/17/75	12,435
Neil Young	1/7/73	12,617	ZZ Top	4/26/75	7,607
Sha Na Na	2/3/73	10,823	Alice Cooper	6/28/75	8,559
The Guess Who	2/16/73	7,105	War	7/3/75	2,596
Santana	3/19/73	13,356	Eric Clapton	7/7/75	10,429
Ten Years After	4/30/73	10,972	Eagles	8/11/75	12,532
Alice Cooper	5/30/73	9,293	Ten Years After	8/16/75	10,390
Sonny and Cher	6/8/73	9,659	Up With People	9/13/75	7,579
Jethro Tull	7/3/73	15,713	Doobie Brothers	9/25/75	10,817
Roberta Flack	7/27/73	6,116	Chicago	10/22/75	9,432
B.B. King			Charlie Rich	11/30/75	2,963
& Quicksilver Messenger Service	8/12/73	4,214	Sha Na Na	3/5/76	7,134
Elton John	8/23/73	12,946	Roy Clark	3/18/76	5,650
Three Dog Night	9/2/73	10,296	Robin Trower	3/20/76	11,507
Sha Na Na	10/7/73	6,358	Loretta Lynn & Conway Twitty	4/10/76	7,642
Grateful Dead	10/23/73	8,410	Bad Company	5/28/76	5,074
Allman Brothers Band	11/11/73	14,147	Seals and Crofts	8/8/76	8,757
Loggins and Messina	11/16/73	5,285	ZZ Top	9/11/76	12,956
Doobie Brothers	11/28/73	4,327	Charlie Daniels Band	9/25/76	12,111
Emerson, Lake, and Palmer	12/1/73	6,612	Earth, Wind, and Fire	10/7/76	13,351

CONCERT	DATE	TICKETS SOLD	CONCERT	DATE	TICKETS SOLD
Elvis Presley	10/17/76	15,701	Alice Cooper	2/23/79	9,689
Eagles	11/18/76	15,938	Boston	3/17/79	16,763
Waylon Jennings	12/2/76	8,322	The Tubes	4/12/79	1,659
KISS	2/6/77	16,739	Jethro Tull	4/17/79	11,220
Loretta Lynn & Conway Twitty	3/11/77	9,195	Statler Brothers	4/20/79	12,194
Led Zeppelin	4/12/77	14,831	Diana Ross	4/24/79	9,549
Engelbert Humperdink	4/16/77	7,062	Yes	4/28/79	16,132
Up With People	5/12/77	5,449	UFO & Judas Priest	5/3/79	1,742
Tom Jones	5/14/77	5,792	Parliament Funkadelic	5/4/79	7,613
Tammy Wynette			Journey	5/15/79	2,881
& The Statler Brothers	5/21/77	5,635	Charlie Daniels Band	5/19/79	12,078
Disco Dance Concert	5/28/77	1,797	Nazareth	5/25/79	4,733
Waylon Jennings	7/15/77	10,799	Supertramp	6/14/79	12,017
Frankie Valli	8/17/77	7,144	Village People	6/20/79	6,459
Frank Zappa	9/25/77	5,683	Allman Brothers Band	6/24/79	8,432
Commodores & The Emotions	9/28/77	9,573	Kansas	7/8/79	7,892
Hall and Oates	11/22/77	7,993	Cheap Trick	7/21/79	12,107
Rush	1/27/78	7,691	REO Speedwagon	8/2/79	12,762
Willie Nelson	1/29/78	12,039	Sha Na Na	8/10/79	9,875
Merle Haggard	2/5/78	3,591	KISS	9/28/79	11,453
Maynard Ferguson	2/9/78	1,933	Engelbert Humperdink	10/17/79	7,324
Eric Clapton	2/18/78	12,914	Blue Oyster Cult	10/26/79	6,584
Loretta Lynn & Conway Twitty	3/11/78	8,865	The Outlaws	10/30/79	11,259
Bob Seger	4/22/78	9,068	Merle Haggard & Marty Robbins	11/30/79	5,561
The Statler Brothers	4/29/78	10,774	Kenny Rogers	3/13/80	16,783
Bruce Springsteen	6/10/78	6,384	Con Funk Shun	4/25/80	2,598
Oak Ridge Boys	8/10/78	2,164	Fleetwood Mac	5/9/80	13,812
Willie Nelson	10/27/78	7,832	Fleetwood Mac	5/10/80	13,592
Commodores	10/29/78	9,158	Bob Seger	5/16/80	12,818
David Gates & Bread	11/2/78	4,956	Bob Seger	5/17/80	13,236
Chicago	11/19/78	8,362	Mahogany Rush	5/29/80	3,117
Heart	11/27/78	7,725	Grateful Dead	5/31/80	9,643
J. Geils Band	1/25/79	6,201	Waylon Jennings	6/7/80	12,143

CONCERT	DATE	TICKETS SOLD
Alice Cooper	7/3/80	4,677
Foghat	7/18/80	11,002
Heart	7/26/80	11,384
Beach Boys	7/28/80	9,765
Journey	7/30/80	14,279
Sha Na Na	8/8/80	8,208
Black Sabbath & Blue Oyster Cult	8/19/80	12,783
AC/DC	9/11/80	11,578
Merle Haggard & Ronnie Milsap & Johnny Paycheck	10/28/80	3,879
Molly Hatchet	11/30/80	9,173
Allman Brothers Band & The Outlaws	12/9/80	7,142
Head East	12/26/80	3,112
REO Speedwagon	2/21/81	16,901
REO Speedwagon	2/22/81	16,877
Kansas	3/14/81	13,640
Sweet Comfort	5/2/81	1,445
Judas Priest	5/14/81	3,221
Joe Walsh	6/10/81	6,867
Rush	7/2/81	12,170
Rush	7/3/81	11,713
Marshall Tucker Band	7/4/81	6,159
Kenny Rogers	7/8/81	17,029
Styx	7/20/81	13,501
Styx	7/21/81	13,971
Ronnie Milsap	8/13/81	2,047
Tom Petty	8/14/81	10,416
Waylon Jennings	9/12/81	7,083
The Kinks	9/13/81	4,450
Devo	10/13/81	5,260
Blackfoot	10/14/81	3,619
Foghat & Blue Oyster Cult	10/29/81	12,660

CONCERT	DATE	TICKETS SOLD
Nazareth	11/15/81	1,954
AC/DC	11/22/81	12,458
AC/DC	11/23/81	14,156
Foreigner	11/29/81	16,072
Grand Funk Railroad	12/8/81	2,611
Rossington Collins Band	12/13/81	5,531
Rod Stewart	1/10/82	13,993
Ozzy Osbourne	1/15/82	11,568
J. Geils Band	1/31/82	11,513
The Police	2/2/82	16,920
Molly Hatchet	2/12/82	6,717
The Cars	2/18/82	13,334
Prince	3/7/82	5,850
Black Sabbath	3/13/82	12,023
Rock 'n Roll Revival	3/21/82	3,067
Willie Nelson	4/17/82	12,063
Kenny Rogers	6/1/82	17,181
Rainbow	6/2/82	5,629
Eric Clapton	6/7/82	14,935
Cheap Trick	6/20/82	2,599
.38 Special	6/23/82	9,358
Charlie Daniels Band	7/2/82	9,731
Santana	7/10/82	4,443
Joan Jett	7/17/82	3,456
Scorpions	7/30/82	4,866
Kansas	7/31/82	9,761
Alabama	8/13/82	11,908
Imperials	8/14/82	4,059
Todd Rundgren	8/21/82	2,303
Heart	9/8/82	13,181
REO Speedwagon	9/14/82	14,217
Judas Priest	9/17/82	7,005
Fleetwood Mac	9/23/82	15,456

CONCERT	DATE	TICKETS SOLD	CONCERT	DATE	TICKETS SOLD
April Wine	9/26/82	7,424	Neil Diamond	8/4/84	16,794
Go Go's	10/5/82	10,348	Neil Diamond	8/5/84	16,778
B.J. Thomas	10/15/82	3,027	Neil Diamond	8/6/84	16,819
Aerosmith	1/28/83	14,823	Night Ranger	8/7/84	4,242
KISS	2/18/83	5,370	The Cars	8/14/84	14,628
Tom Petty	3/11/83	10,388	Barry Manilow	10/10/84	10,652
Prince	3/15/83	13,729	Quiet Riot	11/6/84	3,778
Billy Squier	4/8/83	16,767	Imperials	11/30/84	6,048
Kenny Rogers	4/13/83	17,020	Iron Maiden	12/20/84	9,965
The Kinks	4/16/83	8,825	REO Speedwagon	1/13/85	13,040
Sammy Hagar & Molly Hatchet	4/30/83	3,775	Dio	1/27/85	5,256
Bob Seger	5/24/83	14,246	Deep Purple	2/15/85	12,409
Bob Seger	5/25/83	14,558	Kenny Rogers	4/26/85	13,288
English Beat	6/3/83	4,070	Kenny Rogers	4/27/85	13,468
Neil Young	7/7/83	13,481	Petra	5/11/85	4,703
ZZ Top	7/8/83	12,676	Foreigner	9/17/85	12,559
The Police	8/25/83	14,709	AC/DC	9/29/85	12,078
Supertramp	8/29/83	8,610	Dio	10/16/85	6,921
Iron Maiden	9/14/83	4,555	Marlboro Country Music Tour	10/26/85	9,015
Imperials	9/23/83	5,861	Ratt	11/12/85	8,653
Alabama	11/4/83	15,470	Thompson Twins	11/24/85	3,375
Black Sabbath	11/20/83	13,029	Anne Murray	12/2/85	5,514
KISS	2/12/84	4,784	Twisted Sister	2/3/86	4,386
Ozzy Osbourne	3/9/84	13,685	Heart	4/11/86	13,826
Kenny Rogers	4/11/84	16,960	Amy Grant	4/19/86	14,379
Bob Barker	4/14/84	16,518	Kenny Rogers & Dolly Parton	4/25/86	17,922
Ted Nugent	5/4/84	7,219	The Firm	5/5/86	8,082
Dan Fogelberg	5/5/84	10,972	Aerosmith	5/9/86	16,566
Ronnie Milsap & Merle Haggard	6/8/84	9,265	Eddie Murphy	6/29/86	13,507
Blue Oyster Cult	6/15/84	2,714	Dio	7/2/86	3,955
Rush	6/26/84	10,993	Ozzy Osbourne	7/9/86	7,554
Rush	6/27/84	8,155	Pointer Sisters	8/3/86	6,547
Neil Diamond	8/3/84	16,666	AC/DC	8/29/86	13,247

CONCERT	DATE	TICKETS SOLD	CONCERT	DATE	TICKETS SOLD
David Lee Roth	9/2/86	6,842	David Lee Roth	4/26/88	10,073
Hank Williams, Jr.	9/7/86	7,157	Michael Jackson	5/4/88	17,170
Sandi Patti	9/18/86	11,833	Michael Jackson	5/5/88	17,402
Journey	9/25/86	14,022	Michael Jackson	5/6/88	17,405
Bill Cosby	10/11/86	18,143	Bruce Springsteen	5/9/88	17,396
.38 Special	10/12/86	11,849	Bruce Springsteen	5/10/88	17,399
Triumph	10/15/86	3,728	Bill Cosby	5/14/88	15,082
Neil Young	10/17/86	10,970	Oak Ridge Boys	5/20/88	5,588
Steve Winwood	11/5/86	6,927	Robert Plant	5/31/88	8,103
Cyndi Lauper	12/8/86	5,987	AC/DC	6/4/88	13,716
Bob Seger	12/15/86	11,711	AC/DC	6/5/88	13,765
Bob Seger	12/16/86	12,574	Lynyrd Skynryd	6/15/88	7,275
Ratt	12/28/86	8,862	INXS	6/16/88	14,492
Iron Maiden	4/17/87	10,043	Grateful Dead	6/17/88	14,869
Kenny Rogers	4/22/87	11,514	Hank Williams, Jr.	6/18/88	8,366
Luciano Pavarotti	4/28/87	14,433	Iron Maiden	6/21/88	10,990
Bon Jovi	6/6/87	16,825	Whitesnake	7/6/88	10,341
Bon Jovi	6/7/87	16,894	George Strait	7/7/88	4,389
Stevie Ray Vaughan	6/9/87	4,248	Def Leppard	7/8/88	17,383
Tom Petty	6/16/87	7,048	Def Leppard	7/9/88	17,385
Neil Diamond (4 concerts, 4 days)	7/11/87	70,133	Def Leppard	7/10/88	17,387
Motley Crue	7/14/87	13,307	Judas Priest	8/27/88	18,026
Motley Crue	7/15/87	13,670	Prince	9/14/88	14,682
REO Speedwagon	7/21/87	6,019	Prince	9/15/88	16,221
The Cure	7/27/87	6,901	Sandi Patti	9/17/88	10,446
Huey Lewis & The News	8/7/87	14,158	Scorpions	10/2/88	6,397
Roger Waters	9/10/87	7,141	Eric Clapton	10/4/88	13,459
Boston	10/11/87	16,190	Jimmy Page	10/16/88	4,715
Conway Twitty & Loretta Lynn	11/15/87	6,047	Rod Stewart	10/27/88	8,823
John Cougar Mellencamp	2/12/88	15,201	Amy Grant	10/28/88	12,896
Dio	2/25/88	6,443	Poison	11/4/88	12,523
Frank Sinatra & Sammy Davis, Jr.	3/22/88	13,406	Kenny Rogers & Dolly Parton	11/6/88	12,301
Rush	4/4/88	9,008	Living Legends	11/10/88	5,218

CONCERT	DATE	TICKETS SOLD
Jackie Mason	12/12/88	2,457
Ratt	2/10/89	8,439
The New Edition	2/17/89	15,296
REM	3/8/89	12,621
Bon Jovi	4/4/89	16,450
Chicago	4/7/89	10,470
Grateful Dead	4/17/89	15,405
Salt-N-Pepa	4/19/89	2,895
Metallica	4/21/89	13,889
Bobby Brown	5/14/89	11,247
Poison	5/23/89	12,878
Metallica	6/10/89	13,478
Doobie Brothers	6/14/89	6,936
Cinderella	7/11/89	7,414
Neil Diamond	7/15/89	17,262
Neil Diamond	7/16/89	17,265
Neil Diamond	7/17/89	17,361
Eazy-E	7/23/89	4,083
Bon Jovi	8/1/89	16,604
LL Cool J	8/9/89	4,249
Hank Williams, Jr.	8/11/89	6,969
Country Explosion '89	11/19/89	3,546
New Kids on the Block	1/16/90	16,727
New Kids on the Block	1/30/90	16,757
Tom Petty	2/20/90	12,757
Motley Crue	3/6/90	14,651
Motley Crue	3/8/90	14,023
The Highwaymen on Tour	3/9/90	10,724
Janet Jackson	4/5/90	16,331
Janet Jackson	4/6/90	14,465
Whitesnake	4/27/90	10,451
Steve Miller Band	6/1/90	12,653
Cher	6/4/90	9,653

CONCERT	DATE	TICKETS SOLD
Rush	6/19/90	10,725
B-52's	7/15/90	6,987
Milli Vanilli	7/19/90	8,390
Don Henley	7/22/90	8,390
Billy Idol	9/2/90	7,384
M.C. Hammer	9/23/90	12,390
James Taylor	9/25/90	8,303
Robert Plant	9/29/90	6,170
AC/DC	11/30/90	15,187
INXS	3/19/91	8,528
Scorpions	4/3/91	7,062
AC/DC	6/27/91	13,111
Tom Petty	9/4/91	8,158
Kenny Rogers	10/1/91	5,230
Frank Sinatra	1/24/92	13,352

Photo courtesy of Walter Bush, Jr.

MEMORABLE PERFORMANCES

FRANK JIRIK was the original Building Supervisor of Met Center in 1967, and ultimately became Executive Vice President for the North Stars and Met Center. He left Minnesota in 1990 to become Executive Vice President for the San Jose Sharks and San Jose Arena. During his 23-year career at Met Center, Frank was in charge of booking concerts and dealing with performers. The following are some of Frank's favorite memories:

LASSIE

One of our first events was the dog Lassie. A small stage was set up in the middle of the arena, so it was Lassie-in-the-round. After a few opening animal acts, Lassie came out and walked around the stage. She would occasionally sit and bark, but that was it. She wasn't allowed to be petted, and the show didn't last much longer than an hour.

TINY TIM

After Tiny Tim did his sound check, he wanted to go to the North Stars dressing room, put on goalie equipment, and have pucks shot at him, which we did.

THE WHO

Our first and worst gate-crashing incident took place during The Who concert in '71. People without tickets were trying to force their way through every entrance. There was a huge mob trying to crash the doors on the north side, so the Bloomington Police started using tear gas. It was the first time the Bloomington Police Department had ever used tear gas, and instead of rolling the canisters they threw them like grenades. The wind was out of the north that night and the tear gas blew back into the faces of the policemen. We had more Bloomington police officers in our first aid room than we did inebriated Who fans.

ELVIS

Prior to the first Elvis show at the Met in '71, I was a bit nervous. While the opening act was on stage, I went to one of the vacant dressing rooms to calm down and change clothes. When I walked in, there was Elvis, all alone, ready and waiting for his show to begin. He apologized because he thought he was in my way. I told him no apology was necessary, and then we had a nice down-to-earth conversation that lasted 20 minutes or so. He complimented me on what a nice building the Met Center was.

NEIL DIAMOND

Neil Diamond had always performed at the St. Paul Civic Center, and I wanted him at the Met. I found out that he loved to eat fish, so I shipped him an assortment of fresh Minnesota fish along with recipes from some top local chefs. From that point on, Neil Diamond performed at the Met.

FRANK SINATRA

Frank Sinatra loved the colors orange and white, so before he played the Met we had to completely re-do his dressing room in those colors. The walls were painted orange, the carpet was orange, fixtures were white, the phone was white, and we even brought in a white piano. When he arrived at the Met, his limo drove straight inside the building on the west end. He walked down the corridor where the dressing rooms were, opened the door to his room and looked inside without entering. He then kept walking and went to the backstage area. When his performance was finished, he walked back down the corridor, looked inside the orange and white dressing room again, and said, "Nice." He got back into the limo and left the building. We spent $4,000 on his dressing room, and he never set foot inside.

"THE CROWD WAS CRAZY. THEY TRIED CLIMBING OVER THE GLASS AND ANYTHING ELSE THEY COULD DO TO GET TO THE STAGE. THE ATTENDANCE WAS ONLY 6,000 BUT THEY WERE 6,000 ROWDIES."

JACK LARSON *began his Met Center career in 1970 at the age of 16. He started as a member of the operations crew and worked his way up to the position of Met Center's Executive Director. He left the Met in 1991 to become Director of Operations for the new San Jose Arena, home of the Sharks. In 2001, Jack was named Vice President and General Manager of the Xcel Energy Center in St. Paul. During his time at Met Center, Jack was involved in every aspect of arena management and day-to-day operations. The following are some of Jack's favorite memories:*

THE ROLLING STONES

The Rolling Stones came to the Met in 1972. In the lower level of the building, we had a catering room set up for members of the production crew and our operations staff. When the Stones were finished with their sound check, they didn't go to their dressing room and get wild, they came to the catering room. They waited in line for food, filled their plates, and sat down to eat along with the rest of us. Things were extremely low key. That night during the show, we had big problems with gate crashers and needed to use tear gas, but we never had a problem with the Stones.

BLUE OYSTER CULT

In the late '70s, crowds at the rock concerts became more and more wild. We were having problems with people coming onto the main floor and rushing the stage. There was a stretch of shows — Heart, J. Geils, Alice Cooper and Boston — where the crowds were so bad that we put up the hockey plexiglass surrounding the floor to hold people back. Things reached their peak with the Blue Oyster Cult concert in '79. The crowd was crazy. They tried climbing over the glass and anything else they could do to get to the stage. The attendance was only 6,000 but they were 6,000 rowdies.

KISS

KISS made their first appearance at the Met early in '77. This was during their heyday when they supposedly were never seen without their makeup, and all kinds of wild stories were flying around. When they arrived at the Met they weren't wearing any makeup and were very cordial. I spent some time with them in their dressing room. They still didn't have their faces painted, and were talkative and easygoing.

NEIL YOUNG

We had a sellout for Neil Young in the early '80s. The arena was packed 15 minutes before the show when Neil got sick in his dressing room. After a short delay, he decided not to perform. A member of his management staff took the stage and announced that the show had been cancelled. Surprisingly, the crowd took the news in mellow fashion. Instead of anger, people left in a very controlled manner.

REO SPEEDWAGON & THE HARLEM GLOBETROTTERS

The most hectic time for our operations crew occurred in '81. We had an REO Speedwagon show on Saturday night with almost 17,000 people in the building, followed by a Harlem Globetrotters game on Sunday afternoon with a crowd of 13,000, then a second REO Speedwagon concert Sunday night with another 17,000 fans. In just over 24 hours, we prepared the Met for a concert, then tore down the stage, cleared the main floor and installed the basketball court, then removed the court and quickly rebuilt the concert stage. At the same time, we were constantly cleaning the arena from the previous big crowd. To top things off, we had to get the Met ready for a North Stars game on Monday night. By then, things seemed back to normal.

Ernie Hicke

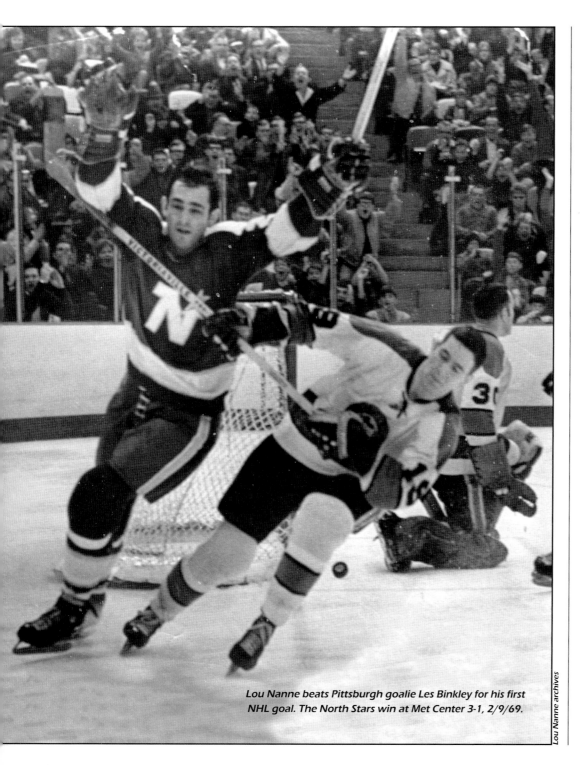

Lou Nanne beats Pittsburgh goalie Les Binkley for his first NHL goal. The North Stars win at Met Center 3-1, 2/9/69.

Lou Nanne archives

"HE SHOOTS— HE SCORES!"

Lou Nanne:

One night at the Met, we were trailing Chicago 2-1. I got the puck behind our net and took it the length of the ice. I came in alone on the goalie and got off a shot that he saved and held for a faceoff. The crowd gave me a nice ovation.

When the whistle blew, Wren Blair pulled me off the ice and said, "What do you think you're doing trying to score a goal?" I said, "I thought it would be a good idea since we're losing 2-1." And he said: "Let somebody else score. You just want to hear the crowd cheer."

Neal Broten

Rick Kolodziej

Steve Christoff

North Stars archives

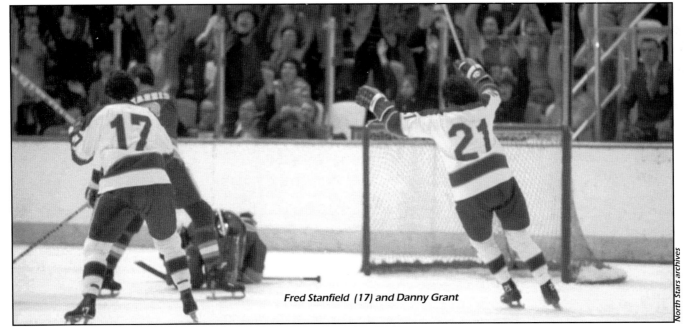

Fred Stanfield (17) and Danny Grant

North Stars archives

Bill Hogaboam

North Stars archives

Bill Fairbairn

North Stars archives

Steve Payne congratulates Dennis Maruk amidst much rejoicing.

Rick Kolodziej

Murray Oliver (10) and Charlie Burns

North Stars archives

Gary Sargent and
Bobby Smith

Pete Hohn / Minneapolis Star Tribune

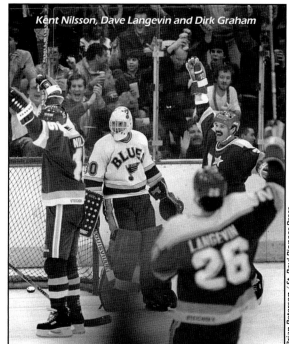

Kent Nilsson, Dave Langevin and Dirk Graham

Brian Peterson / St. Paul Pioneer Press

Jack Carlson

North Stars archives

Jimmy Roberts (at net) and Nick Beverley

Pete Hohn / Minneapolis Star Tribune